# COUNTRY BOUND!™

*Trade Your Business Suit Blues
For Blue Jean Dreams*™

# COUNTRY BOUND!™

*Trade Your Business Suit Blues
For Blue Jean Dreams*™

by

Marilyn and Tom Ross

**Communication Creativity**

P.O. Box 909 ★ 425 Cedar Street
Buena Vista, CO 81211
(719) 395-8659

Copyright © 1992 Marilyn & Tom Ross. Printed and bound in the United States of America. All rights reserved. No part of this book may be reproduced or transmitted in any form or by any means, electronic or mechanical, including photocopying, recording, or by an information storage and retrieval system—except by a reviewer who may quote brief passages in a review to be printed in a magazine or newspaper—without permission in writing from the publisher. For information, please contact Communication Creativity, P.O. Box 909, Buena Vista, CO 81211.

The following trademarks appear throughout this book: Allied Van Lines, Baskin-Robbins, Blue Cross, Blue Shield, BMW, Cadillac, Campbell's Soup, Citibank, Coldwell Banker, Colgate-Palmolive, Country Bound!, Domino's, Federal Express, Gaines, General Motors, Gucci, MasterCard, Mercedes-Benz, Nike, OshKosh, Pacific Bell, Pan Am, Post-it Notes, Pringle's, Realtor, Reebok, Rolodex, Trade Your Business Suit Blues for Blue Jean Dreams, VISA, Weed Eater, Yellow Pages, ZIP Code. The following service mark appears: Personalized Ring.

This book contains information gathered from many sources. It is published for general reference and not as a substitute for independent verification by users when circumstances warrant. Any recommendations of companies or careers we make is our own opinion based on the data available to us. The reader must do further research on his or her own to determine if a career or a company is the right choice. It is sold with the understanding that the publisher is not engaged in rendering legal, psychological, or accounting services. If legal, tax or other expert advice is required, the services of a competent professional should be sought. The publisher and authors disclaim any personal liability, either directly or indirectly, for advice or information presented within. Although the authors and publisher have used care and diligence in the preparation, and made every effort to ensure the accuracy and completeness of information contained in this book, we assume no responsibility for errors, inaccuracies, omissions, or any inconsistency herein. Any slights of people, places, or organizations are unintentional.

---

Library of Congress Cataloging-in-Publication Data

Ross, Marilyn Heimberg.
    Country bound! : trade your business suit blues for blue jean dreams / by Marilyn and Tom Ross.
       p. cm.
    Includes bibliographical references and index.
    ISBN 0-918880-30-0
       1. Urban-rural migration--United States. 2. Career changes--United States. 3. United States--Rural conditions. 4. New business enterprises--United States   I. Ross, Tom, 1933-   . II. Title.
HB1965.R59  1992
307.2'612'0973--dc20                                                      92-3259
                                                                                CIP

---

**ATTENTION: GOVERNMENT AGENCIES, CORPORATIONS, EDUCATIONAL INSTITUTIONS, AND PROFESSIONAL ORGANIZATIONS:** Quantity discounts are available on bulk purchases of this book for educational purposes, gifts, or fund raising. Special books or book excerpts can also be created to fit specific needs. For information, please contact our Special Sales Department, Communication Creativity, P.O. Box 909, Buena Vista, CO 81211, or call (719) 395-8659.

# Dedication

Although not the usual . . . this book is dedicated by one of the authors to a very special lady. Without her readiness to abandon the familiar—her comfort zone—for a pilgrimage far outside the arena of her experience, there would be no foundation for *Country Bound!* Her willingness to eagerly accompany me through a sojourn of extreme highs . . . to total disasters has been the motivation, nay the cornerstone, of this book. During the recapture of our adventures and tremendous additional research, she was paramount in fleshing out this work into useful, factual data—a monument and guide to fellow country bound folks. It has been a joy and honor to participate in this whole adventure with a lady extraordinaire—my wife and lead author, Marilyn Ross. Thank you, partner!

# Acknowledgments

We are indebted to many competent people who helped bring this book to fruition. Suzanne Miller orchestrated a multitude of tasks—coordinating, researching, getting permissions, and applying her "eagle eye" to catch mistakes before they become embarrassments. Larkin Wiegert took a rough manuscript and turned it into a pleasing, easy-to-use, and attractive book.

Sarah Hemingway, Hugh Goding, Teresa Boyer, and Michelle Worthey edited with a deft touch. They read and re-worked pages, honing them to a fine edge. Dick Foss took an idea and catapulted it into a dynamic cover. Phyllis Bruun, Aron Campbell, and Ginger Eby also contributed to this project. Thank you *all* for your caring and capabilities.

We also want to gratefully acknowledge several people who gave so generously of their time and expertise to read the manuscript. Those who shared their insights and feedback include Kathy Black, Alley DeVore, Ken Waddell, Jack Lessinger, and Pegi Brown.

A book of this nature can only come about as a result of intensive research. Countless people answered our pleas for help. Certainly we've overlooked some, and for that we apologize. Among those who contributed greatly were: Dewitt John, Marci Levin, Judy Krueger, Lou Francis, Bill Seavey, Patricia John, Louise Reynnells, Scott McKearney, Cindy Murphy, Jim Henderson, Calvin Beale, David Savageau, Mary Pekas, Dan Gibb, Peggy Counce, Jeff Ollinger, Lew Lowe, Patricia Mokhtarian, Cheryl Chepeus, Bill Obermeier, Gil Gordon, and Jack Niles.

Help was also extended by Donna Watkins, Tim Karlinger, Kary Smith, Jeanne Foster, Elaine Long, Eleanor Perry-Harrington, Claryce Burt, Suzanne MacDonald, Margery Dorfmeister, Bob Bone, Bill Horvath, Mark Lackey, Marlys Whitley, Toni Murray, and Amy Mascillino.

Thank you each and every one for your energy, enthusiasm, and encouragement!

# Table of Contents

Introduction . . . . . . . . . . . . . . . . . . . . . . . . . . . . . . . . . . 1

PART I . . . PERSONAL CONSIDERATIONS

1 **Contemplating the Great Adventure** . . . . . . . . . . . . . . . . . . . 14
   Exploring the Pleasures and Pitfalls of Rural Life ▪ Sharpening Your Focus on What's Involved

2 **Seven Criteria to Measure Your Move** . . . . . . . . . . . . . . . . . 34
   Deciphering the Cost of Living ▪ Coping with Crime Risks ▪ Wending Your Way Around the Weather ▪ Health at the Crossroads ▪ Investigating Environmental Concerns ▪ Putting Leisure in Your Life ▪ Evaluating an Area's Infrastructure

3 **Turning the Dream into Reality** . . . . . . . . . . . . . . . . . . . . . . 91
   Cashing Out with Your Urban Equity ▪ Four Walls and a Small Fortune ▪ Quit Work and Live Off My Proceeds? ▪ Places, Patterns, and People ▪ Narrowing the Field ▪ Hitting the Research Trail ▪ Planning Your Visit

4 **Checking Out Rural Edens** . . . . . . . . . . . . . . . . . . . . . . . . 108
   Finding More Resources ▪ Tactics for Testing the Waters ▪ Choosing Your Specific Dream Home or Land ▪ Working Through a Broker ▪ What to Look for in a Country Home ▪ Pointers for Picking Parcels of Unimproved Property ▪ Living on the Land

5 **Making the Move—Without Making Yourself Crazy** . . . . . 132
   Contract It Out or Do It Yourself? ▪ List It–File It . . . but Don't Forget It ▪ The ABC's of School Transfers ▪ Moving With Fido and Kitty ▪ Saying Goodbye ▪ Taking the Panic Out of Packing ▪ Mastering Moving Week ▪ A Calendar for Moving

6  **Letting the Small Town Viewpoint Work for You** ........ 149
    Developing a Mind-Set for Change ▪ Attitudes: Yours and Theirs
    ▪ Sorting It Out and Settling In ▪ Overcoming Negative Feelings
    Towards Outsiders ▪ Losing Your Anonymity ▪ Playing the Big
    City/Small Town Trade-Off Game ▪ Child Care in the Boonies
    ▪ More Differences ▪ Being a Big Fish in a Little Pond

 7  **Cultivating a Satisfying Social Life** ................... 159
    What's Your F.Q. (Fun Quotient)? ▪ Recreation and Entertainment Tips ▪ Dealing with the Family Issue ▪ Making New Friends ▪ The Virtues of Volunteering ▪ Ingenious Ways to Enrich Your Life

 **PART II ... BUSINESS ASPECTS**

 8  **Evaluating Your Entrepreneurial Options** ............. 178
    Determining if You Have Self-Employment Potential ▪ Exploring the Alternatives ▪ Brainstorming to Break Your Barriers ▪ Occupational Variety to Add Spice to Your Life ▪ Turning Avocational Pastimes into Regular Paydays ▪ What's Your Passion? ▪ 900 Phone Numbers Open New Doors ▪ Making the Most of Your Money ▪ Diversify to Multiply

 9  **Researching for the Right Opportunity** ................ 214
    Taking the First Easy Step ▪ Tracking the Trends ▪ Sleuthing As You Schmooze ▪ Detection Methods Worth a Fine Ransom ▪ Flushing Out Sophisticated Facts

10  **Buying an Existing Business or Professional Practice** ..... 229
    Finding a Suitable Business ▪ Evaluating Prospective Ventures ▪ A Warning to the Wise is Sufficient ... ▪ What's a Body to Pay?

11  **Investigating the Franchise Alternative** ................ 237
    Fertile Fields ▪ Separating the Wheat from the Chaff ▪ If Home Is Where Your Heart Is ▪ Matchmaker, Matchmaker ▪ Finding Specific Help ▪ Putting Franchisors Under the Microscope

12  **Working from Home: "The Information Age" Option** ..... 247
    Who's Doing It and Why? ▪ Achieving the Three "F's" ▪ Making It Work for You ▪ Using Equipment as Your Staff ▪ Designing Your Perfect Office and Getting Organized ▪ Cottage Industry Coexistence: Melding Business and Personal ▪ All That Glitters Isn't Gold ▪ Zapping the Zoning Ordeal

13  **Finding a Rural Job:**
    **Gutsy Strategies Mother Never Told You** .............. 261
    Getting Off on the Right Foot ▪ Molding Your Career Focus
    ▪ Resources to Ease Your Quest ▪ Planning Your Job Search
    ▪ Some Random Thoughts . . . ▪ 23 More Tips to Enhance
    Your Chances ▪ Choosing a Company That's Right for You

14  **Telecommuting: A Growing Solution for Urban Blues** .... 275
    Understanding What It Is ▪ How Telecommuting Answers
    Personal Needs ▪ From the Corporate Perspective ▪ Communities
    Also Benefit

15  **Generating Capital to Launch Your Venture** ........... 284
    Tapping into Personal Resources ▪ Reaching Beyond Yourself
    ▪ Money from Heaven ▪ Securing Conventional Bank Financing
    ▪ Franchise Financing: Using the Team Approach ▪ Getting the
    Government on Your Side ▪ Enterprise Zones: Waiting Bonanzas
    ▪ Developing a Business Plan ▪ More Funding Ideas

16  **Pivotal Start-Up Considerations** ..................... 300
    Business Structure Options ▪ Name Registration Requirements
    ▪ Licensing and Regulatory Procedures ▪ The Telephone: Lifeline
    to Opportunity ▪ Location, Location, Location ▪ Miscellaneous
    Details ▪ Business Incubators as Early Guardians ▪ Locating
    Reliable Suppliers ▪ Prospecting for Qualified Employees

17  **Creating Attention Getters and Revenue Reapers** ........ 317
    Establishing Your Image ▪ Deciding on a Seemly—or Sensa-
    tional—Name ▪ Creating a Winning Slogan ▪ Generating Logos,
    Letterhead, and Business Cards ▪ Evaluating Signage Needs

18  **Persuasive Marketing Strategies to Boost Your Bottom Line** 326
    "Positioning" Yourself for Greater Profits ▪ 21 Ways to Separate
    Yourself from the Herd ▪ Developing an Effective Marketing
    Plan ▪ Budgeting: How to be an Astute Spender ▪ Secrets for
    Capturing Free PR ▪ Devising Dynamic Promotional Events
    ▪ Advertising's Exciting Options ▪ More Innovative Sales Tech-
    niques

19  **Tactics for *Staying* Prosperous and Happy** .............. 344
    Community Involvement: Reaching Out—Getting In ▪ Mingle
    Management: The Art of Networking ▪ Growing Your Business
    to Its Zenith ▪ Outsmarting the Isolation Factor ▪ Remaining
    Mentally Stimulated ▪ Staying Abreast of Your Industry

20  **Big Business Bolts: Large Companies Find Small Towns** . . . 354
Household Name Companies with Country Adresses ▪ What Prompts Urban Flight? ▪ An Abundant Resource of Conscientious Employees ▪ More Corporate Success Stories

**Afterword** . . . . . . . . . . . . . . . . . . . . . . . . . . . . . . . . . . . . 363

**PART III . . . RESOURCES TO EASE YOUR RELOCATION PROCESS AND STRENGTHEN YOUR BUSINESS**

**State Tourism Offices and Chambers of Commerce** . . . . . . . . . 366
A list for all 50 state tourism offices and chambers of commerce.

**Government Sources** . . . . . . . . . . . . . . . . . . . . . . . . . . . . 373
Business and commerce connection points, Small Business Administration contacts, money lending and real estate property sources, federal grants and loans, miscellaneous government information.

**Private Sector Help** . . . . . . . . . . . . . . . . . . . . . . . . . . . . . 383
Resources on home-based businesses, telecommuting, education, telephones, lending sources, associations, and selected suppliers. Also includes a unique list of manufacturers' representative contacts.

**Maps, Tables, Charts** . . . . . . . . . . . . . . . . . . . . . . . . . . . . 393
Data on where to find every conceivable kind of map, plus tables and charts about population counts, financing, capital investment.

**Bibliography/Recommended Reading** . . . . . . . . . . . . . . . . . . 401

**Index** . . . . . . . . . . . . . . . . . . . . . . . . . . . . . . . . . . . . . . 411

**Authors' Biography** . . . . . . . . . . . . . . . . . . . . . . . . . . . . . 433

# Introduction

Do you dream of getting away from it all? Or maybe of *having* it all? You're not alone. Three out of four Americans say they would prefer *not* living in a metropolitan area. After all, don't thousands of people take to the road each weekend to escape the city? A Gallup Poll reveals that given their druthers, 29 percent would live in a city of 10,000 to 100,000 residents, and 52 percent prefer a rural area or small town. While trading the fast lane for a country road is the dream of countless millions, until recently most were thwarted by lack of job opportunities. They simply couldn't earn a living outside the city.

Now *Country Bound!* comes to the rescue with practical, thought-provoking ideas you can use to prosper in paradise. Picking up where back-to-the-land books left off several years ago, it proposes viable strategies to help you trade Wall Street for Main Street—strategies everyone contemplating leaving the big city scene and taking charge of their destiny in the countryside can use. Now you can follow your dream . . . without tripping over a nightmare!

David Birch, the head of Cognetics, Inc. and a guru on small business, recently told *Inc.* magazine: "With modern telecommunications facilities, far-reaching parcel delivery service, (the national) interstate highway system, and a U.S. Post Office, the possibilities for growing a successful company in the boondocks are quite real."

Combine that fact with a career poll reported by the *Wall Street Journal*, which showed the majority of people asked to describe their dream job responded overwhelmingly: "Head my own business." After buying a comparable house in a rural area, most folks have enough money left over to do just that. They become "Countrypreneurs." This book is for them.

It not only shows how to *get started* in a small town business, but how to *stay in business and be successful.* Big city types must learn how to deal with less cosmopolitan folks, fit into a rural community, and prospect for business in new ways. *Country Bound!* covers this and much more.

Of course, whether urban transplants find what they're looking for depends on how realistic their expectations are. We're the first to say small town life isn't for everyone. Our mission is not only to point the way for those who want slower paces and friendlier faces, but also to caution others who aren't suited for this transition.

Frankly, some people would feel stifled in rural America. For them, saying *sayonara* to sophisticated civilization makes about as much sense as mice getting together to chase a cat. We'd like to spare these individuals the heartache, frustration, and possible financial ruin such a relocation could entail. They, however, are the minority.

## Why This Book at This Time?

Faith Popcorn, founder of BrainReserve—a forward-thinking marketing consulting firm—addresses the primary reason in her recently-released book, *The Popcorn Report.* She identifies "Cashing Out" as one of the 10 top trends for this decade. This is when men and women leave the corporate rat race in search of quality of life. "It's not copping out or dropping out or selling out," explains the nationally acclaimed trend-spotter. "It's cashing in the career chips you've been stacking up all these years and going somewhere else to work at something you want to do, the way you want to do it." Popcorn feels the Cashing Out movement will signal no less than the economic decentralization of America—for the better. People are anxious to get away from the masses of strangers in the city. "More than the romance of the country, it's a promise of safety, of comfort, and of old-fashioned values . . . and the living costs are lower," she observes.

The editors of Research Alert, whose new book is titled *The Lifestyle Odyssey: 2,001 Ways Americans' Lives Are Changing,* also feel career-obsessiveness is on the wane. They expect less emphasis on "things" and increased pleasure in the simple aspects of life. "While this scaling back of the traditional American Dream may feel frightening or depressing, I see it as an entrance into another kind of Dream," says author Eric Miller. "This new ethic will open the door to another kind of optimism and activism—the era of quality of life."

There is no question materialism was the mantra of the acquiring '80s. It was the decade of overconsumption. The successful drove Mercedes' with vanity license plates, had cosmetic surgery, and shopped at expensive clothing boutiques. But today people are beginning to realize their joy isn't dependent on status symbols. They are questioning their values, reprioritizing their lives. They strive to *be* the best . . . and are not satisfied just to *have* the best. The greed weed has been composted into beautiful blossoms. Greater self-reliance, a wish to take control, a slower pace, more time with one's family, a closeness with nature: These are shaping up as the preferences for this decade. Quality of life has become more important than quantity in life.

Dr. Jack Lessinger, a frequently quoted real estate and urban development expert, has been studying America's migration cycles all his adult life. "The 20th century gave us suburbia," he says. "The 21st will shift the nation's center of gravity in a massive swerve . . . from suburbia to penturbia." Penturbia is an emerging region of growth and opportunity consisting of small cities and towns interspersed with farms, forests, lakes, and rivers.

Lessinger's excellent new book, *Penturbia* (a term he coined), tells where real estate will boom after the crash of suburbia. Inhabitants of this new utopia will "yield their hearts to the surrounding territory, with its ample meadows and mountains, as much as to the town," he forecasts. "People are penturbia's leading resource," observes Lessinger: "hard-working, dedicated, know-what-they-want kind of people.

"The present migration is no flash in the pan . . . the decision to leave suburbia is part of a long trend that will continue for decades," he says. Lessinger predicted in his earlier book that suburbia was in trouble. His theory is that we're well along on the fifth great migration since the beginning of industrialization. This forecast is being borne out daily.

The authors of *The Lifestyle Odyssey* also predict, "There will be dramatic growth for penturbia—formerly non-commutable small towns that will gain urban refugees and urban unconventionals." Twenty years ago this was considered the sticks. Now it is precisely where more and more people want to live. Country living allows you to gain more control over your life, rather than suffering alienation and feeling like a victim of destiny.

The work force is in tremendous transition. Massive layoffs—the October 2, 1991, issue of *USA Today* put them at 2,200 *a day*—are hitting middle managers and professionals the hardest. With the new philosophy of decision making coming from the bottom up, companies contend they don't need as many managers. Additional people are sacrificed as corporations change direction, priorities, and ownership. The once secure "corporate career" is in tatters.

Layoff announcements have for years been keeping workers shaking in their boots. Union Carbide, Pan Am, DuPont, Pacific Telesis, First Union Corp., Southwestern Bell, Frito Lay Inc., American Express, Colgate-Palmolive, IBM, and General Motors lead the pack in trimming personnel. Record numbers of jobs are eliminated as U.S. corporations struggle for profits.

## Something for Almost Everyone

Using *Country Bound!* as a road map, disenchanted baby boomers, squeezed out by downsizing, may well discover a better lifestyle and the bonus of more rewarding work. Middle- and upper-level managers trapped by layoffs, career plateauing, or early retirement can create meaningful new careers. Many are formulating their own survival kits, preparing for a different future, redefining priorities, bringing their loyalty back to self and family.

And what of individuals who voluntarily unshackle themselves from the mighty achiever's ball and chain? Frequently these are men going through the male menopause. Tired of what they've been doing for 20 or so years, they want to relieve their boredom and find new zest in what they do. They're discovering less stressful ways to earn a living with fresh pizazz. Management guru Peter Drucker says we're likely to form a new breed of older, more sophisticated entrepreneurs who bring skills and competitive expertise to start-ups. (Not to mention existing enterprises.)

Owners of many home-based businesses and cottage industries located in congested metropolitan areas are ideal candidates for small town life. If they specialize in information management, their slogan might be: "Five Acres and a Modem." Not being location-specific, they can conduct business from virtually anywhere with a personal computer, phone, fax, overnight delivery service—and *foresight*.

Another burgeoning group fleeing the city includes employees of large companies who work in information management fields. They "telecommute" via a satellite home-based office complete with computer, modem, and telephone—plus an occasional trip into corporate headquarters. Today workers from such companies as Travelers' Insurance, AT&T, Citibank, Pacific Bell, J.C. Penney, New York Life, and Blue Cross/Blue Shield telecommute.

This innovative approach to the workplace is growing at 7-10 percent a year as employees cut deals with their bosses to perform tasks ranging from collection to marketing, billing to inventory control. And it's a win-

win arrangement which offers the parent company savings in office rent and other benefits. *The Futurist* magazine, in their May-June 1991 issue, reported, "Work will move to unconventional sites and arrangements. Employers are becoming willing to consider almost any work arrangement that will get work done at less cost. Businesses are seeking to contain costs and are responding to the need for flexibility."

Retirees represent an additional group who can benefit from the message in this guide. They are more physically fit and energetic than ever before. A satisfying later life may mean leaving a crime-ridden, congested metropolitan area for a personal oasis in some recreational wonderland. Adventuresome mature people welcome a change of scene as much as their younger counterparts. Some seek the challenge of entrepreneurship and have money to invest in their own businesses. For folks in their golden years who seek to augment social security, income supplementing ideas abound.

Parents dreaming of raising their children in a safe, healthy environment will find they can do so—and even afford to own a comfortable home without a crippling mortgage. What was a convenient location before you had kids becomes congested and confining after they come along. More important, mothers and fathers worry about busing, violence, and drugs. Or classrooms that are overcrowded, overspecialized, and undersupervised.

Children of the corporate ladder grow up with a whole different set of experiences. While they can regale you with tales of the nearest fast food restaurants, they don't experience the excitement of harvesting wild asparagus, feeling the rough pebbly tongue of a calf as it learns to drink milk from a bucket, or eating fresh radish snacks from seeds they personally planted and watched peek from the ground.

People considering purchasing a vacation or second home will also find useful information here. Weekend farmers grow everything from Christmas trees to goats on their spare-time spreads. For some, their country place is a simple farmhouse or cabin, a few acres of pasture or woods, perhaps a pond or creek. Others buy undeveloped land and visit it frequently in their campers, trailers, or RVs. Recreational property ownership will rise dramatically over the next 20 years. Fully a third of current owners of such property say they see it as an investment or a source of income. The expanding affluent sector that stays in metropolitan areas will be all the more anxious to have a country hideaway as cities and suburbs further deteriorate. The theme song for many may be Visit Now, Retire Later.

"Death sucking lemons," someone once said in describing the face of a person caught out during a smog alert. Swollen, teary eyes. Furrowed brow. Turned down mouth. (And this says nothing about the sore throat and rasping breath.) Yes, health is another major reason prompting many to flee the metropolitan madness. Where you live affects more than your sense of beauty and your wallet. It can also determine how long you will live. The two top killers are cardiovascular disease (including strokes) and cancer. Carcinogens proliferate in big cities. So do stress causing situations. How can people feel laid back when they're fighting to maintain their place on a clogged freeway, clawing their way up the corporate ladder, or making ends meet in a "keep up with the Joneses" neighborhood? Good health is our greatest blessing. Do we dare continue to jeopardize it?

Environmentalists will also welcome the option *Country Bound!* provides. They recognize we don't inherit our land from our parents—we borrow it from our children. Countless urban nests have been soiled beyond repair. Those concerned about ecology and the environment may want to disperse to unspoiled places.

Country life affords special opportunities for grass-roots environmental activism. Your voice is heard; your actions felt. Issues surrounding clear-cutting, dams, road building, endangered species, mining, waste disposal, soil erosion, overgrazing, pesticides in the water supply, and many other causes can be lobbied effectively. It's easier to be a master of your own fate in the country, to truly practice stewardship of the land. Clearly, one individual *can* make a difference.

Decision makers at all levels of government will benefit from this breakthrough book. Rural economic development is one of this nation's most critical problems. It is being addressed at all levels: by the towns themselves, counties, states, and the federal government. But it is viewed from the *inside out*. Towns ask how they can help existing farms and businesses, keep their young people from leaving, and establish a more reliable tax base. Conferences are held. Pilot projects launched. Bulky reports written.

Yet no one is looking at this issue from the *outside in*. The out-migration from major cities is a trickle now. Forecasters predict it will be a steady stream by the mid '90s. At the turn of the century, it may be a torrent. Smart towns and counties should be addressing how they can capitalize on this trend to attract more than their share of the new residents.

The people looking at rural America as a lifestyle option are exactly the kind of folks small towns need: well-educated, affluent, talented individuals and families who will bring to the community new ideas, enterprises, and energy. These people will start new businesses and infuse the community with jobs. We believe a major component of the solution to rural revitalization lies in looking at it from a fresh perspective! Why don't rural areas help people recognize country living is an opportunity they can't afford to pass up, then create a welcoming climate in which all can prosper? As Ann Cole, director of federal affairs for the National Association of Towns and Townships, so aptly observed in *Governing* magazine, "The question is not whether it will happen, but whether elected officials can take the lead in a parade that has already begun."

In fact, anyone who wants to escape to the hinterland will find this book a useful tool for locating their special Eden. Do greener pastures beckon you? Do you want to unplug from the system to avoid being victimized by it? Are you ready to liberate yourself from your limitations? Then read on. Our vision is to connect people with their futures.

One caution however: make sure you're not running *away* from anything, but rather running *to* something. Changing location to solve one's problems is like sitting on a cheap waterbed—the problem, like the water, still pops up somewhere else. James Joseph says it eloquently, "They (urban expatriates) are not fleeing the good life but seeking the far better. They are not dropouts from society but rather drop-ins to an environment from which all society sprang. They are the uprooted putting down roots in the soil of their heritage."

## New Trend: Starting Over in Country Settings

The covers of magazines sport lead stories detailing this trend. *USA Weekend* ran "So Long, Big City" in September of 1990; *Home Office Computing's* cover read "Living Your Dream: Setting Up Business in Shangri-La" in February 1991; "The Simple Life" was splashed across the April 8, 1991, issue of *Time*. And "Kissing the Big City Goodbye" headlined a recent issue of *Changing Times*. The list goes on and on. *American Demographics* carried a story titled "A Place in the Country" while *Entrepreneur* did a feature on "Trading Places." And a popular recent book is G. Scott Thomas' *The Rating Guide to Life in America's Small Cities*, which reports on 219 *micro*politan alternatives to metropolitan hassles.

Yes, Americans are flinging open the doors and revolting against the big city mind-set. Tired of trendiness and materialism, they are rediscovering the joys of home life, basic values, and things that last. They abhor the megalopolises that stretch from Boston to Washington, DC and San Diego to Los Angeles. They want to get out of corporate cultures that know them only as a number and ignore the dignity of the individual. They're tired of perpetual, meaningless memos, rigid dress codes, and endless meetings. They understand that when the work is done, real satisfaction is not in what you end up with, but in how much of yourself you've left behind. These Renaissance souls are founding a silent revolution.

In their newest book, *Megatrends 2000*, John Naisbitt and Patricia Aburdene explain that more people are expected to abandon big cities. They predict a massive rush to places that offer the best quality of life. In fact, the dash to these mostly rural areas has already begun. This migration is one of our great untold stories.

What spawns this trend? The confluence of new technological, social, and economic forces.

Information management is emerging as the engine of our economy, fueling job creation and making possible exciting new choices. Affordable high-tech equipment has released people from traditional ways of working. Many now run technologically sophisticated and highly profitable rural businesses. Others, while still employed by Fortune 1,000 companies, telecommute from their homes—going into the office perhaps once a week. Naisbitt and Aburdene say, "Technology has evolved to a point that workers are no longer location bound. This will contribute to the decline of the cities. There'll be a new electronic heartland."

There's another way of looking at this migration, say Paul and Sarah Edwards, authors of *Working From Home* and *Making It on Your Own*. "People who make major moves are not motivated by what they don't like. They are searching for a better life." Circumstances such as a safer setting for raising their children, lower living costs, and environmentally safe surroundings attract these folks. The Edwards have found that many who ditch the city are couples in their 40s and 50s. They've had their fill of the fast lane and are ready to sell their California holdings, move to Montana, and start a business of their own. Those who own pricey real estate can sell their expensive urban residences and move where their property dollars stretch much further. (We'll explain how later.)

For the first time in 200 years, more people are moving to rural areas than urban. According to *American Demographics* magazine, Los Angeles County has as many people moving out as moving in. They crave roots: a place to feel at home, a sense of security and community. These people are abandoning cities for quality of life, reports the March 1990 issue of *Success* magazine. They're trading the boardroom for the backyard.

This migration is not proceeding unnoticed. Foote, Cone & Belding, a large national advertising agency, placed undercover researchers in a midwest community of 12,000 people. The mission of this unusual social laboratory? To learn what makes the townspeople tick. The information they gleaned is being used to develop future consumer ad campaigns for their clients. Even home decorating reflects our penchant for a simpler lifestyle. The design of the decade is Country Chic: classic, comfy furnishings rather than futuristic decors. Another indicator is Hearst Magazine's recently launched *Countryside*, a publication devoted to young professionals seeking a simpler, unspoiled lifestyle closer to nature. "We feel that one of the great movements in America today is the return to the land," says editor Carol Sheehan.

This movement is pervasive, believes sociologist Stephen Warner of the University of Illinois in Chicago. "This is not something simply happening to the burnouts from Wall Street. There is an American phenomenon going on that crosses all social lines." Displaced and disenchanted Americans have fallen out of love with their lifestyles.

We're in the early throes of a migratory flux. People are trading demanding careers for more rewarding lifestyles. Executive dropouts are deciding their kids went to bed one too many times before dad or mom got home.

People are leaving the executive suite to become fishing guides, school teachers, shopkeepers, or to run bed and breakfast inns. Most of us are eager to leave behind smog—noise pollution—congestion—crack houses—youth gangs—terrorism—school busing—street people— corporate politics—and endless gridlock.

## Defining The Rural Renaissance

When we talk of a rural renaissance we don't mean agriculture. Sadly, our nation's small farms have largely been gobbled up in foreclosure sales. Farmers and ranchers trying to hang on to homesteads that have been in their families for generations experience ever-growing frustration.

The Rural Renaissance to which we refer is the out-migration from urban centers. In the 13th century, cities were vibrant but sparsely populated. They served primarily as trading headquarters and cultural centers. Most of the work was done elsewhere. Before the turn of the century we may see this pattern occur again. In their book, *American Renaissance: Our Life at the Turn of the 21st Century*, Marvin Cetron and Owen Davis predict that 88 percent of the labor force will be employed in the information industry. Twenty two percent of these people will be working at home. Estimates put these numbers at more than 24 million. This opens enormous new options.

Here's a breakdown to define sizes of places this book addresses:

| | |
|---|---|
| Small cities | 25,001 to 50,000 population |
| Big towns | 5,001 to 25,000 population |
| Small towns | 5,000 or fewer people |
| Rural locales | hamlets, farms, ranches, remote retreats located 60+ miles from a metropolitan hub |

## Them Who Do . . . and Them Who Try

Untried theories here? Never! We know of what we speak; we've lived this book. In the process, we've made virtually every known mistake anyone can under similar circumstances—and probably invented some new ones! Learning from these blunders, however, we've become successful countrypreneurs. Our route was speckled with hardship, humor, and hard work.

First the mistakes. In 1980 we left a suite of offices overlooking the Pacific Ocean in La Jolla, California, to buy a 320-acre ranch in Colorado. We had a thriving consulting business in San Diego. But, while it is indeed America's finest big city, we'd arrived at a point in our lives where more bucolic surroundings beckoned. A vacation in a mountain log cabin at Big Bear Lake—surrounded by God's natural wonders, blessed silence, friendly squirrels playing on the roof, and deer grazing by the front door—made us realize our values had shifted. Since our writing, book publishing, and marketing clients were all over the country—and we worked with them primarily by phone and correspondence—it became obvious our business was portable. But, oh, the things that weren't so obvious . . .

We bought raw land: lush meadows with two creeks bubbling through them, surrounded by craggy mountains. There were aspen groves, blue spruce, and pine trees galore. Deer and antelope cavorted in our meadows. What we didn't have, however, was a house, telephone lines, a well, or a power source. Never ones to back away from a challenge, we figured we'd be self-sufficient: build our home, develop our own potable water source, and generate our own power. Mistake number one.

Lunching in the historic hotel dining room in the nearby town of 500 people—which we will call "First Try" throughout the book to avoid offending the folks who find it to their liking—our real estate agent mentioned the hotel had recently fallen out of escrow. You can't run a consulting business from a tent on bare land . . . Marilyn looked around and the wheels started whirling. *Gee, this would give us a place to live, plenty of office space, and phone lines. Besides we're entrepreneurial souls. Certainly a 16-room hotel and restaurant can't be that hard to run. And the price is a steal compared to California real estate!* You know what comes next. We bought the place. Mistake number two.

We don't, however, want to overwhelm you with all our foibles at one time. Stupidity, like castor oil, is best tolerated in small doses. So we've sprinkled what we've gleaned throughout these pages—with the hope our lapses in logic will serve as your bridges to country savvy.

A few words of redemption: We later made a second move to Buena Vista, Colorado. It's a town of 2,000 people nestled in a beautiful valley surrounded by 14,000-foot mountain peaks. This relocation has proven both soul satisfying and financially rewarding. We'll tell you about that too, including how to strategize and organize a successful move.

## What's Included Here and How to Squeeze the Most from It

By now you're probably starting to realize this hands-on guide is loaded with practical advice to help you triumphantly cope with change. In it we challenge you to ask, and answer, the hard questions. And we encourage you to take a *realistic* look at your skills, capabilities, expectations, and values. In addition to our experiences, we've interviewed dozens of countrypreneurs to develop a source book of practical information and friendly advice. The subject is explored in depth—warts and all.

Part I explores personal considerations: cashing in on your urban equity and picking the ideal location. You will be shown how to understand small town attitudes, cultivate a social life, and become involved in your new community.

Part II deals with rural business aspects. You'll learn how to turn avocational interests into vocational pursuits, create a new career focus, or purchase an existing establishment in a small town. Business start-up considerations are addressed, as are tactics for successful ongoing operation. Scores of proven profit-making ideas are offered.

Part III encompasses a resource section worth its weight in bullion. It's full of useful governmental and private sector sources. This unique collection overflows with data to help you make informed decisions, have a more pleasant experience, and live a more fulfilled life. You'll also find a list of hard-to-locate books we've tracked down and now offer for sale.

This is a compendium of hundreds of facts found nowhere else. We've tried to eliminate for you the frustration of locating all this information yourself. Far from the typical "how-to" book, it's more like a cross between a friendly chat of homespun wisdom and a unique reference book.

Here you'll discover checklists, exercises, surveys, quizzes, examples, and case histories to help you determine if you want to swap yesterday's boondocks for today's "boomdocks." Let your own needs and experiences fill in the answers.

This is the most timely and complete resource available for moving to the country—easily—happily—prosperously. Our statistics are the latest available as of the writing. It's amazing how long it takes various government agencies and private research firms to collect final results . . . sometimes as much as three years. So when you see something from 1989, for instance, it isn't that our data is old—it's just that it took a long time for the source to collect and disseminate the information.

The ideal approach is to read *Country Bound!* from start to finish. That will give you a complete overview, plus creative options you probably never thought of. Next go back and review those chapters that pertain specifically to you. Really apply what's here; you can't make scrambled eggs without breaking the yolks. *Use* the various checklists and research aids provided. Get started. Get thinking. Get involved. You just may be embarking on the most exciting, rewarding adventure of your life!

# Part I
## Personal Considerations

# 1

# Contemplating the Great Adventure

Americans are searching. We're looking for answers. Our senses are assaulted, our energy invaded, our peace of mind threatened. The culprit? Big City Stress. (You know you're pushing too hard when you drop your bank deposit in the mailbox instead of the bank . . . and put raw potatoes on the table as you microwave the salad.) If you feel unsettled, exploited, stifled—journey with us in exploring a new option. It may not be the right path for you. On the other hand, it may offer a pilgrimage to freedom. Freedom is, after all, a matter of choice.

## *Exploring the Pleasures and Pitfalls of Rural Life*

Should you choose to live out in the country, in a small town, or in a smaller city—where the pace is slower and the costs are lower? Or will this make you feel like a salmon constantly hurling herself against the current? Let's evaluate the tradeoffs, examine what *you* really want from life. This chapter will titillate any desire you have to move to a more bucolic environment. We'll investigate the pros and cons of living and working in the boonies. Keep an open mind. What you initially perceive as a limitation may actually be an advantage. This will help you get clear about your intentions; to focus on what you want from life.

What's causing this new migration? Why are people in their prime turning their backs on bright lights, big cities, and hefty salaries? While the reasons are diverse, they center around certain issues. *Values* are becoming more important than things. We're starting to demand quality time with our children and emotional relief for ourselves. "The search for community, safety, and meaning will preoccupy boomers in the 1990s," predicts David Meer, a senior vice-president at Daniel Yankelovich Group, Inc., a market research firm.

Baby boomers are discovering, after the extravagance of the '80s, that time with family is priceless. They're finding the long hours at work required to maintain the standard of living they thought was necessary just aren't worth it. As these people reach middle age, their children are growing up. Precious moments are being lost. According to the Gallup Poll, 43 percent of women ages 26 to 45 will reduce their job commitments in the next five years. And 23 percent expect to quit altogether. As for the men, 33 percent also want to reduce time spent at work and 64 percent want to take more long weekends.

## Rediscovering Our Roots

Rootlessness is one of the most pervasive, and least publicized, problems of modern life. Today many people feel lost, cut off, powerless. In the old days, generations lived together or families stayed near each other. They had a tightly woven psychological and emotional safety net. Now we've become a restless, migratory society. Twenty percent of us move every year. Yet many of us crave a place to call home and a community to feel a part of.

While pining for one place and living in another is a typical American state of mind, today's urbanites are missing something. We don't have the sense of community and permanence our ancestors had. Qualities once taken for granted—trust and honesty, regional and ethnic heritage, clean air and friendly neighbors—are special treasures. As the news highlights the emerging global economy, many of us simply hunger for a supportive local network. We need to feel *connected*.

Community is the *soul* of a place. It grows out of discovering and nurturing the things you share with your neighbors. It doesn't happen overnight. Most good things don't. It's often an accumulation of little, almost insignificant details—learning the history and ambiance of a town, knowing who to go to when you need something, joining a group that works for civic betterment.

In rural areas you can become personally involved in the government, get acquainted with local and regional legislators, and take an active role in area affairs. Roots require commitment. Nurturing and getting nurtured. Being willing to give of yourself. It speaks of personal pride when the downtown area blooms with flower boxes overflowing with colorful blossoms, and inviting redwood benches welcome shoppers to rest a spell.

Big is not always better. Some of us are loneliest in the busiest of places. We cling to talk radio, seeking human interaction with complete strangers. What a poor substitute when we could put down roots and cultivate a true celebration of life!

After we were settled in First Try, a prospective client hunted us down without remembering our names or the title of the book he had read (our *Complete Guide to Self-Publishing*) which introduced him to us. How did he do it? He luckily remembered where we were, so he traveled to our little village, went to the post office, and inquired as to whether the postmaster knew anyone who did this sort of work. The postmaster did, so he drew the man a map.

In 1981 Peter Moyer and his wife made a life-changing decision. They completely restructured their priorities and opted to live in a place that was smaller, simpler, and less expensive. That's not surprising . . . until you realize Moyer was an attorney with the venerable Wall Street law firm of David, Polk & Wardwell. Not only that, had he stayed he would be earning $1.2 million a year and would have achieved partner status. Is he sorry he pulled the plug on such a promising career? Absolutely not. Moyer figures that money "would probably be spent on alimony, taxes, and private schools."

Today he, his wife, and their three children live in Jackson, Wyoming—a trendy town of about 5,000 people. Despite a drastic drop in earnings and an initial verbal thrashing from the local judge, he soon had enough clients to hang out his own shingle. All kinds of entities now turn to him for legal counsel: banks, the local hospital, corporations, even some big resorts in the valley.

## Feeling Safe and Secure

We would all agree our personal safety, and that of our families, is a paramount concern. Gang wars and drive-by shootings are foreign concepts in Small Town America. You don't find skinheads, crack houses, or high rape and homicide rates in Muskogee. In our village, the law enforcement officers' biggest challenge is teenage mischief and occasional vandalism or petty theft.

Yet *Public Opinion* magazine recently reported that 59% of U.S. citizens feel it's risky to go for a walk in their own neighborhood after dark. So much for moonlight strolls unless you live in the country, where you can wander aimlessly after a late dinner and admire the stars. (Since there's no smog, you can actually *see* them.)

Are vicious felonies an overriding concern for you? Then listen up. According to figures from the Department of Justice, to avoid violent crimes, stick to the upper Midwest and shun coastal cities. The top five safest areas they've identified include Grand Forks and Bismarck, North Dakota; Eau Claire, Wisconsin; Parkersburg-Marietta, West Virginia; and Saint Cloud, Minnesota. We'd bet most small towns fit in the elite group. The violence hot spots are New York City; Miami-Hialeah; Los Angeles-Long Beach; Jacksonville, Florida; and Flint, Michigan.

James Kennedy escaped all that. He publishes two highly respected newsletters for consultants and executive recruiters. You'd think such canny advice would emanate from New York City, Los Angeles, Chicago, or maybe Boston. Rather it comes out of tiny Fitzwilliam, New Hampshire (population 1,795). The Kennedy family moved to their New England vacation home full time because they "liked the country and conservative values . . . It was the height of drug times in suburbia," Kennedy explains.

Today he sounds like a man in heaven. He and his wife live in a red colonial house across from his office, which overlooks a panorama of woods and hills. Classical music wafts on the breeze. Upstairs is a whirlpool bath, downstairs a fully appointed kitchen. The $1.5 million he rakes in annually from his newsletters and directory publishing allows him to indulge in his fancy of traveling. Recent jaunts included Brazil, Switzerland, Canada, Austria, Germany, and Italy. Not bad for a country boy!

## Enjoying True Quality of Life

"Quality of life" is a catch-all phrase that has different connotations for different people.

The current reawakening of environmental concerns is drawing many out of metropolitan hibernation. They are tired of polluted air, tainted water, dangerous landfills, littered streets, and blaring ghetto blasters. They want natural, quiet, unsullied surroundings to walk a gentle path. To reach that goal many are heading for a rural setting.

Along with those who want to heal the environment by consuming fewer natural resources, are people highly motivated to live long, healthy lives. There is a proven link between country living and greater longevity. "Living in a large city shortens life expectancy," states Norman Shealy, M.D., Ph.D.—founder and director of the Shealy Institute for Comprehensive Care and Pain Management in Springfield, Missouri. Cancer incidence is *six percent higher* in urban areas such as Los Angeles and

Houston, where petroleum refineries emit carcinogens into the atmosphere says the *Atlas of Cancer Mortality*.

The three places in America with the cleanest, driest air are Sedona, Arizona; Boulder City, Nevada; and Greeley, Colorado. And the healthiest states? According to the Northwest National Life Insurance Company, they are predominantly rural: Utah, North Dakota, Idaho, Vermont, Nebraska, Colorado, Wyoming, and Montana.

Healthy bodies also need healthy minds and spirits. Those of a rural persuasion enjoy a serenity seldom found in the city. When you get away from the metropolis you get to quietude. While it may not be hundreds of miles in distance, this quest for reverie is a galaxy apart in emotional terms.

In the country you can find a quiet spot—away from the shrill disorder of modern ambition and the urgency of ongoing power struggles. Solitude is the well into which you dip for refreshment of the soul—a laboratory in which you distill the pure essence from the raw materials of your experiences.

Well perhaps your refuge isn't totally quiet. Crows may caw their opinions or woodpeckers tap out their messages. Quaking aspen trees may whisper a secret known only to them and God, as a gurgling creek reveals its confidences to those who listen. If you're exceptionally lucky, you may hear the mating bugle of a bull elk. This is the silence of nature, awash with the sound of living things. To be alone, yet part of it, is awesome.

Along with quietude comes a simpler lifestyle. Wearing apparel is more functional, less glitzy. Escargot and oysters on the half shell give way to meat loaf and mashed potatoes. Pickup trucks outnumber snazzy sports cars. Entertainment centers around people rather than places. Religious ties are stronger and the church often plays a social as well as spiritual role. Parades, band concerts, and school events replace ballet, opera, and gallery openings.

That's not to say you must give up the social amenities of a big city. Seldom will you locate more than a couple of hours from a major metropolitan hub. We're two and a half hours from Denver. We frequently go in for the weekend, sometimes catching a play Saturday night, then meeting friends for a gourmet Sunday brunch. Museums, art galleries, and festivals are never more than a short trip away.

Before you start feeling deprived, be truthful with yourself: Just how many cultural events do you attend now? In many country environments the most beautiful works of art are right outside your door. Mother nature puts on a touching and constantly changing show. Take a good look at yourself and your family. What's your bliss?

## Trade Your Business Suit Blues for Blue Jean Dreams™

Let's try a little experiment. Think about activities you particularly relish. Are you an avid golfer? Do you get absorbed in the *Times* crossword puzzle? Do Moonlight Madness sales at the mall get your heart pumping or would you prefer an easy chair, a fireplace, and a good book? What are the specific joys in your life? Do they lie in the realm of "city happenings" or can they just as easily be enjoyed in the country? As the days go by, keep a running agenda and see which column fills up faster. What must you have to feel complete and what can be transformed to its rural counterpart? Don't try to evaluate these pros and cons in a day . . . take time to step back and ponder.

One alternative is to locate in a college town where a vibrant cultural climate exists. Here you can see plays and film festivals, hear guest lecturers or chamber music concerts, and spectate at collegiate sporting events. A college brings a continual supply of new blood and intellectual stimulation to its locale. (Additionally, the students it attracts provide an eager work force.) And if you mingle, many cultures can be observed.

Of course with today's technology you can keep informed, entertained, and educated as long as you have a satellite receiving dish. Old movies, operas, and sporting events abound. Plus PBS and some of the other channels offer a potpourri of fun and learning. And there's always the VCR.

Even in tiny towns entertainment thrives. Here in Buena Vista we have an eclectic and artsy mix of people. Our little theater group, the Pick and Shovel Players, puts on a melodrama and olio each summer. It's a wonderful evening of boos, aaahs, and laughs. And what makes it especially fun is you know most of the cast. The woman who wrote the play selected for last year is a friend. So we got to share her opening night glory.

Furthermore, your social diversions may change drastically! Being a couch potato could give way to hikes, bird watching, photography, hunting, snowmobiling, skiing, fishing, picnics, or whitewater rafting. And these are just some of the natural attractions awaiting rural recruits.

Another advantage of a small town is *living* the country life instead of merely emulating it. The "Country Look" is now a chic way to decorate and dress. Country cooking is in. Perhaps this is part of the move back to a more basic, sensual, tactile existence. What many of us want is to go back to dinner at Grandma's. There's a lot to be said for functional wood fireplaces on chilly winter evenings and the goodness of a "from scratch" cake just plucked from the oven.

Rural rhythms are definitely slower. Time is *not* of the essence. While a more laid-back lifestyle is one of the attributes that draws people to the country, old habits die hard. We had a difficult time realizing rural folks are less governed by appointments and time constraints than their urban counterparts. This may take some adjustment on your part as well.

Quality of life dramatically impacts those of us with children. We want to raise them in a more wholesome atmosphere. We want them to grow up valuing themselves and others more than material possessions. In countrified settings families are more likely to do inexpensive, family-oriented activities together—rather than hiring a babysitter while Mom and Dad go out with other couples. Parents are more involved with their kids.

The Loughlin family lives in a town of 17,000. Says Paulette, "Anytime my children do anything—win an award in school, score the most points in a basketball game—they're in the daily newspaper." That fosters pride and self-esteem. So does participation in such organizations as the 4-H club. Nothing outshines the smile of a kid whose heifer or lamb has just captured a blue ribbon at the county fair. Youngsters raised on farms and in small towns seem to have more self-reliance. They gain an education from *doing*, not just book learning. If you want to influence the quality of education personally, chances are you can—by getting elected to the school board, helping coach a sport, or doing informal tutoring.

Here's another plus for city-weary parents: no more playing chauffeur! In rural USA you don't have to car pool the youngsters half way across town for lessons or sports. The kids can hop on their bikes (or horses) and take themselves.

## A Natural Stress Buster

One of the biggest reasons for escaping the city is burnout. It takes enormous energy to live in a place like Los Angeles, Chicago, New York, Detroit, or Houston. Unfortunately just *surviving* takes a lot of effort. Yet such energy is the lifeblood of the cosmopolitan connoisseur of urbane living. The only outdoors Mr. and Mrs. Sophisticate want to experience is what they pass through to get from their condo to a taxi.

For most of us, however, such a lifestyle translates into tension. Too many people too close together. Too much corporate politicking. We'd as soon *not* cope with hailing a cab in Manhattan, navigating LA freeways, or flying out of O'Hare Airport. We'd rather see a country sunrise than a downtown high rise.

That's what Christian and Lea Andrade finally decided. They traded engrossing jobs in San Francisco for a new life on San Juan Island off the northwest coast of Washington. They are now the proprietors of Olympic Lights, a bed and breakfast that overlooks the sea. "It was as though we were obsessed," recalls Christian. "Wound up." The husband of the other couple, who also left San Francisco to run the B&B with them, gave his brother-in-law a parting gift: his prized collection of 150 neckties. "Take them," he urged. "I'll never use them again."

"Our guests bring us all the company and outside stimulation we need," remarks Lea. Not that they didn't like San Francisco. "But it was the pace, the pressure, that finally got to us," she says. "That and the freeways and fast-food chains and all the craziness about making as much money as possible."

Hours of commuting to and from work each day take a toll on our health. Raymond Novaco, Ph.D., of the University of California at Irvine has been studying the stressful effects of commuting on a group of Southern California drivers. Novaco has shown that traffic congestion is a threat to physical and psychological well-being. He has further confirmed that traffic induces antagonistic behavior. On the other hand, in a rural community you can often walk or bike to work or enjoy a brief scenic car ride. Instead of concentrating on avoiding a wreck and traffic jams, you can mentally prepare yourself for the day ahead. Furthermore, many people start cottage industries right in their own homes. We address this in depth in Part II's chapter, "Working from Home."

In big cities, gridlock is creating wall-to-wall cars. In some metropolitan areas there are no longer rush hours; freeways are constantly clogged. And this is not just happening in Los Angeles, Atlanta, and Dallas. One reporter observed the only way to change lanes on the LBJ is to "trade cars." Workers in San Francisco, Washington, DC, Portland, and even Charlotte, North Carolina, suffer varying degrees of frustration and terror as they creep from the far reaches of suburbia. For them, being stuck in traffic has become a way of life . . . and a dangerous one at that.

"Due to congestion," reports the November-December 1989 issue of *The Futurist*, "the average travel speed on roads in Southern California is expected to drop to 15 mph by the year 2000." Author and futurist Alvin Toffler says, "Commuting is the single most anti-productive thing we do."

Other work-bound urban dwellers must cope with this dilemma in a different way. They descend into the bowels of the city to grapple with thousands of other bodies crushed into a subway. What a way to begin and end each day. Wouldn't you rather have a more *stretch-ful* life than such a *stressful* one?

## Slashing the Cost of Living

If you enjoy a six-figure income that you consider "barely making a living," in all likelihood countrypreneuring isn't for you. In a non-urban environment people typically earn less. Other factors, however, balance this lower income. People also spend less. The gap in real estate prices could span the Grand Canyon. According to the August 1990 issue of *Changing Times* magazine, while a four-bedroom family home might cost $421,000 in Los Angeles, a comparable house in Carson City, Nevada, would sell for $135,300. In Charlottesville, Virginia, an equivalent residence goes for $144,500. And what you'd pay $334,100 for in New York City, can be had for $165,200 in Laconia, New Hampshire. With today's interest rates and taxes, this alone changes earning requirements drastically.

If you're looking for a starter house, or want to retire to something less spacious, the price drops dramatically. Bargains in the $20,000 to $40,000 range are not unusual in some small communities.

Other financial considerations include groceries, gasoline, and miscellaneous goods. Usually these cost a bit more. That's because they are trucked in to the more out-of-the-way locations, plus local merchants lack the volume buying power their big city counterparts enjoy. Also look at state and local taxes. Some places have none—while in Milwaukee, for instance, they're as high as a Halloween cat's back. Many areas offer inviting tax inducements for new businesses as well. (More about that in a future chapter.)

Your clothes budget will definitely shrink. There is little call for a fancy wardrobe, and clothes stay in style longer. The pressure to sport designer jeans, Gucci loafers, or Oscar De La Renta suits diminishes in direct proportion to the population. Unless you're a professional (and even then, perhaps not) you usually won't need a coat and tie—nor dress and heels—unless you're going to church, a funeral, or a special event. On the other hand, if you enjoy dressing fit to kill, do it—but prepare for some stares and whispers. What we do is save our more cosmopolitan attire for recreational trips into Denver and for business trips when we travel to lecture or consult with clients around the nation.

## Deciphering the Drawbacks

Are there disadvantages to less citified ways? You bet. Practiced though we are in the feint and parry of debate, we won't dance away from this issue. Some people would feel as though they'd been exiled to Siberia. Living—and making a living—in rural America isn't a magic talisman that banishes all cares. It can feel as uncomfortable as walking around in someone else's shoes. So study this guide carefully. Hindsight is a painful and exacting science.

Unless you originally hail from a small town, you'll suffer some culture shock. In the country you can't go to the grocery store looking your worst without running into friends or neighbors. Nor can you check trashy novels out of the library without people being privy to your reading taste. And it's virtually impossible to carry on an undetected affair. (On the other hand, you're unlikely to be stranded on the side of the road while stoic-faced passerbys look the other way and ignore your plight. Nor are you likely to go a day without your neighbors waving a friendly hello.)

On a more practical level, transportation may be a problem. If you frequently travel by plane, you'll find some inconvenience in not having a major airport handy. When taking a commuter flight to connect with an airline servicing a metropolitan area, prepare yourself for skyway robbery. Many tiny towns don't have taxi or bus service, so those without a car could feel stranded. Of course, you may be within walking distance of where you need to go anyway.

Something people generally don't think to check out in this information age is whether radio and television reception is available. And if it isn't, can you get cable? Some people walk around this by setting up their own satellite dishes. But with scramblers now in place, you may not be able to get all the channels you want. In other words, don't count on HBO. Here in Buena Vista cable is accessible, and it's a good thing—without it our valley would be very isolated.

When shopping, you won't always find what you want. Some things are like a slippery bar of soap: you can't get a handle on them. There are not as many retail stores, personal services, or repair facilities. In smaller towns you have to shop through the *mails* instead of the *malls*, or travel to bigger cities where shopping becomes an adventure instead of an ordeal. This does subdue impulse buying, however, which can be a real plus if you're on a tight budget. Some recreational facilities are scarce. If you are into a specific sport—racquetball, for instance—be sure your new locale has a court.

A sudden shift in their personal support system is difficult for many people at first. Letters and phone calls just aren't the same as a warm hug. While any move interrupts relations with friends and loved ones, changing from an urban to a rural environment can provide those you left behind with an occasional escape to "The Good Life." We had more company from San Diego the first year we moved to Colorado than we had the previous five years when San Diego was our hometown! Sure, change tends to cause discomfort; but should we stay miserable in an environment that no longer personally serves us just for the proximity to friends and relatives? (More about that, plus how and where to meet new prospective friends, later.) Another countrified drawback is that reaching sophisticated medical facilities usually requires extra driving. On the other hand, rural areas frequently have terrific volunteer systems. Because emergency rooms are not always close by, you'll often find well-trained local EMT crews ready to respond at a moment's notice.

For the person setting up a business, having an adequate labor pool is another major consideration. Some small towns don't have a lot of highly skilled potential employees. Computer specialists may also be hard to come by. We found this in the village of 500 we lived in before moving to Buena Vista. Many of the residents were either retired or on welfare. Others frequently worked high paying seasonal jobs . . . then relied on unemployment the rest of the year. After generations of partaking at the public trough, they had little concept of a true work ethic. Consequently we had to import employees from other cities to staff our small historic hotel and restaurant. This proved to be about as practical as a mud fence in a rainstorm. (We share this in a future chapter.)

Our attempt at total self-sufficiency also left much to be desired. While this book is not aimed primarily at people who want to be back-to-the-landers—those who generate their own power and pioneer in the purest sense—this can certainly be one facet of doing business in the boonies. We'll share those trials, tribulations, and elations shortly.

Oh, one other point. Small towns don't boast of Marriotts, Hiltons, or Four Seasons hotels. Clean, relatively comfortable motels, yes. Maybe a Holiday Inn if you're lucky. If you require urbane conference facilities or need to impress clients or customers by putting them up in luxury accommodations, you'll need to be more creative—or settle for a mid-sized city. On the other hand, a rustic log cabin or historic bed & breakfast might be a refreshing change of pace for the travel-jaded. And certainly less expensive for you.

For those of you who feel the pleasures outweigh the pitfalls, or who remain undecided, let's move on to the next chapter. There we'll explore in detail what it's like to trade concrete for country.

## *Sharpening Your Focus on What's Involved*

"The difference between the city and the country is that there are far more people around you in the city," says Patrick Anderson in *The Washingtonian.* "This means more congestion and chaos, but it also means that you have the luxury of choosing your friends and the option of ignoring your neighbors."

Small Town USA is stripped of glitz. It's a place where less is more—where life's frills are streamlined while values are telescoped. A place where little joys abound: the smell of freshly cut hay, the majesty of a fiery sun setting over rolling hills, the nicker of a friendly horse. A place where things can still happen on a handshake.

Some say time will be to the 1990s what money was to the '80s, that leisure will replace the treadmill. Slow is the cultural backdrop of this decade; a balanced life the new currency. The previous money-making binge left us with spiritual hangovers. Many of us got drunk on greed one too many times. Now we want to return to God, country, and family.

## Pinpointing Priorities

Take a hard look at your priorities. Getting clear on what you value is fundamental to deciding if country life is for you.

When psychologist Abraham Maslow developed his need hierarchy, he put survival on the bottom. Next came security, then belonging. Above that is self-esteem. Most people reading this book are either entering—or comfortably established at—this level. Upon reflection, however, those who are comfortable may find their self-image tied to what they *own*. Some people feel it is paramount to live in the right part of town, belong to the right country club, drive the right car, tour Europe in the right way, and wear only the right designer clothes. And many are miserable; especially if they measure their personal worth by material possessions. Keeping up with the Joneses is a vicious trap. Superficial paraphernalia may appear glamorous, but it often makes a wasteland of the soul.

Earning the money to support such habits becomes another trap. Children grow up while their parents are at work 12 to 14 hours a day. Workaholics find peace and personal serenity unfamiliar turf, so entangled are they in earning a living.

On the other hand, those who approach self-esteem in a more healthy manner may be ready to step up to the top of the pyramid, to move on to self-actualization. If you are in this group, you're inclined to follow your bliss. You know what excites you, what it is that makes you feel vibrantly alive. Having this kind of handle on your individual needs gives you an immense advantage. It allows you to fulfill your life's purpose and express your full potential . . . instead of teetering on the brink of overload. The wise know quality living is more a result of attitude than of affluence.

Of course, fresh beginnings can have identical endings unless we refuse to carry the corpse of yesterday's mistakes. We can move from one side of the globe to the other, find a new life partner, create another career—and be in the same rut. Why? Because we take ourselves with us. Unless we handle problems as we meet them, we'll likely find ourselves looking at the same scenario—simply played by a new cast of characters in a different setting.

## The Small Town Viewpoint

Marilyn discovered there is a world of difference in *how things work* and *how folks treat one another* in the country. First off, in tiny towns and farm areas you get in the habit of waving at every vehicle that passes. Chances are you know the occupant, or at least their kin. And speaking of being cordial, don't be surprised if you're saying "hello" to the same person in the market, then the video store, and finally at the hairdresser's. This universe is much more finite.

People go out of their way to be helpful. We had a new employee who was moving from one mobile home to another. Though she had only been in the area a couple of months, men from her church turned out in a snowstorm to haul the heavy objects for her. Another employee had an emergency and couldn't reach her sister by phone. So a co-worker drove to the adjacent town where the sister lives (a round trip of more than 70 miles) to convey the message. Local grocers sometimes extend credit if they know you're in a bind. When a family is struck by tragedy, residents rally immediately to raise funds through auctions, bake sales, collection jars at area merchants, etc. Only in small towns does such caring flourish.

Barter is also big in the boonies. We had extra frozen homemade butter left over from when we were milking a cow. Our neighbor had a robust garden. Soon she was spreading our butter and we were crunching her veggies. And recently we did an advertising flier and news release to announce a grand opening for a local merchant . . . in exchange for credit to purchase merchandise at her shop. Those who have a pond stocked with fish might swap fishing rights for firewood.

Another person, who owns high mountain property, has a handy agreement with the power company—who has to keep trees cut under the power lines that cross her land. The property owner is responsible for tree removal. As Christmas approaches each year, she invites people up to cut their trees and serves hot chocolate with peppermint schnapps, or hot cider. In another case a motel proprietor gives a generous discount when family members of local residents come into town for weddings or family reunions. A friend told of doing a small glasswork job for an elderly lady in town. When the job was completed, the woman asked what she owed. He said she could pay him in Christmas cookies. She did.

Here in Buena Vista, the local bakery is a popular gathering spot as fresh donuts telegraph their tempting aroma around town each morning. And the owners are great about accommodating last minute requests. When we overlooked a birthday, they had a personally decorated cake for us in less than three hours. This old-fashioned bakery's quaint charm is enhanced by an antique bread slicer that was bought secondhand in 1936—and still works today.

The country can also humble you. If you think individuals must have initials like Ph.D.—M.B.A.—M.D.—B.A.—or B.S. behind their names before they're worth much, you're in for a big surprise. Ranchers with barely a grade school education have held us spellbound with their knowledge about animals, weather patterns, and the land. Rural life offers a wonderful mixture of folk wisdom found nowhere else. Additionally, many country people can fix virtually anything with almost nothing. (What a priceless gift this resourceful, "can-do" attitude would be for city kids whose self-esteem is shattered!)

Rural is also a lot more trusting. Roadside stands are sometimes left untended. Money boxes perch on the counters waiting for customers to pay for the produce or flowers they take. It's the honor system at work. People usually don't lock their cars . . . and many leave their houses unlocked at night.

There is also a special sense of *coming home* we experience here in Colorado that never touched us in California. When returning from out of town, we find ourselves eagerly straining to catch that first glimpse of the majestic mountains and feel a peace encircle us as we head into our lovely little valley. Previously, we were too busy coping with the freeway traffic that held our lives hostage to even think of our natural surroundings.

## Allowing Kids to be Kids

Children of industry, sophistication, and science (the city) are often strangers to the world of other living things. Does this deny them their birthright? Urban life has a tendency to make kids conceited, self-centered, and exploitive. Many demand expensive techie toys, rebel against doing chores and being responsible, and insist on hanging out with friends who give their parents the creeps.

Country kids have a different lifestyle. Rather than staring glued to the television, they're more likely to be outdoors doing something adventuresome. They enjoy roaming in wide open spaces—discovering a fox's lair, a bird nest, or a beaver dam. A day's outing might include admiring the delicate work of a cobweb or finding a berry patch and overdosing on sweet, ripe raspberries. These youngsters create special hideouts, hike, swim, fish, or skate on a winter pond.

If they are truly rural, they'll learn to drive a tractor and pilot the family pickup far before the legal age. These kids don't need field trips and expensive summer camps to understand what life is all about. Nature is their friend and their teacher. They become worldly in a different way:

hearing gunshots ringing from the woods during hunting season, seeing wildlife alongside the highway, observing a newborn calf and orphaned lambs raised on a bottle. Thus, they take for granted a whole range of experiences from caring for livestock to killing an animal cleanly when it comes time for butchering. This gives them a sense of perspective; it reminds them of what matters and what doesn't. In most cases it makes them stouthearted, resilient, compassionate adults with lots of self-reliance.

Metropolitan life, on the other hand, teaches kids to be streetwise—savvy in negative ways. Country kids have fewer limitations imposed on them—which, in a way, makes their world larger. They are less protected, less fussed over. Adults in sophisticated suburbia are more like security guards, while in small towns folks look out for each other's children.

Another bonus of country life for kids is the consistency of long-term friendships. Michelle Worthey, one of our past employees, grew up in a town of 5,000. She says one of her most treasured memories is going to school with the same people from kindergarten through twelfth grade. It gave her a sense of extended family and belonging. Now when she goes back to Texas for holidays and vacations she returns full of stories of old friends, families, and new babies.

In a rural environment you also have more control over your child's education. You can talk to the principal and teachers personally before your youngster ever enters school. And probably you already know several of those serving on the school board. Want to give them direct feedback? (Or run for that position yourself?) Go for it!

In higher grades, kids get very specialized in large metropolitan schools. Competition is fierce. If a youth goes out for football, the pressures are such he won't have time for band. And he'd better be an outstanding athlete, or he'll spend most of playing time warming the bench. Interests like drama, music, art, and athletics collide. If you do one, there's no time to accommodate another. Why must children suffer this stress and conflict at such an early age? Don't they deserve a lifestyle free of unnecessary anxiety and tension as much as we adults?

In rural school systems, teams and casts need every able-bodied student. Each person has a chance to contribute and shine. The environment for developing leadership in young people flourishes. Because there are fewer students to carry the load, each person can make a significant contribution to the whole. Students, by necessity, learn to wear many hats. In turn, these feats are publicized and applauded by local newspapers and service clubs.

## Criteria For Making a Decision

Realism, backed by knowledge of self, is the key to happily picking a country home. Carefully evaluating what you want will allow you to glide from pressure to pleasure.

Kathy, with close family ties to Atlanta, didn't want to be far removed from those she loved. So she got a map and drew a radius of 200 miles around the city core. This gave her freedom, yet placed reasonable boundaries. Kathy located a charming smaller town about 170 miles away and can easily get home for weekends.

Another man, Leonard, was concerned he would become mentally stifled in a small town. When he talked with a local merchant, he discovered that social life and business life are interwoven. The merchant told him that customers, who have also become his friends, provide him with stimulating conversation, as well as a livelihood.

The Jamison family was worried about the overall cost of living. While they knew real estate prices were typically much lower in rural areas, they wondered about other items. According to the Bureau of Labor Statistics' 1989 Consumer Expenditures Survey, the average annual spending in the country is $23,106 versus $28,584 in the city. (We address this issue in more depth later, as well as providing information on crime, pollution, leisure, and entertainment, etc.)

What this says is you can live on approximately 80 percent of what it now takes when you move to the country. And even that may be an inflated figure. Say, for instance, you start raising your own food or create an office in the home and no longer have to pay for child care. Such actions dramatically slash what it takes to live.

Cynthia was used to shopping in malls. She wondered how she could get along without stores to browse. Then she discovered catalog shopping. About half of both men and women regularly buy products via direct mail. Catalog consumers are typically upscale, well-educated, married, middle-aged professionals. And it is forecast that electronic shopping will grow dramatically as consumers become impatient with checkout lines and inattentive sales clerks. This new shopping mecca will take the form of both televised home shopping networks and computer shopping via your home PC.

How do you pinpoint your own fears and concerns? One of the best ways is by taking a personal inventory. Grab a large pad. Title your list MY PERSONAL INVENTORY. Now number from 1 to 15 on the left side. Think about the activities or pastimes you enjoy that you have done within the last year. (Only list those things you've actually *done*. While you may love sailing, if you live far from a body of water and haven't indulged during the last 12 months, it doesn't count—for now.) Next note the frequency of times you've done each thing. Then assign a value to each item. It may be easiest to just rewrite your inventory in priority order. Save this sheet.

Now we're going to start your JOY LIST. Again number from 1 to 15. (Sailing might be the first entry on this one.) Here you'll put down everything you love to do, whether or not you've had the time or opportunity recently to actually do it. Again, give each entry a value so you get a clear picture of your personal priorities.

Naturally you should do this in conjunction with your partner if you're in a committed relationship. Consider both parties' needs. School-aged children should also become a part of this planning process. From about eight years up, a child can create inventories and joy lists of his or her own.

Compare your two sheets, plus any feedback from your children. Are you living your bliss? Let's say you're an opera buff. But if you only go once or twice a year, does it really make sense to stay in the city for that reason? Does that offset the rush hour traffic jams? The crime? The turf battles at the office? If you're candid, you may discover what limited use you actually make of metropolitan facilities. This isn't a graded test, so only you can discern what your priorities are. But it's worth taking a look and making some evaluations.

Let's do another exercise. Pretend you're trying to negotiate a beautiful stream in a canoe—but there are several large boulders in your way. Do a rough sketch of water and scatter four or five large rocks in the way. These represent the things that scare you about moving to the country. Think about your apprehensions. Now name the boulders. One might be "leaving my family," another could be "boredom." You might label other rocks "fear of change" or "missing my friends." If you need more boulders, add them.

Now get a fresh piece of paper and draw another stream. Add the boulders. This time we want you to label the rocks with the things that bug you about the city. Your stream may be strewn with such comments as "crime," "drugs," "traffic congestion," "street people," "noise," "unfriendly people," "my boss," "this neighborhood," "smog," etc. Add more boulders as needed. Compare your two streams. Interesting, eh?

Using this method for clarifying our reservations and concerns helps us face our fears. Then we can deal with them effectively. We can look for healthy ways to cope, recognize there is little holding us back, or decide the risk is too great and we want to stay where we are.

Another way to tune in to what you really want out of life is to pay attention to your daydreams. Not necessarily aimless mind wanderings, daydreams are small windows that allow us to get fleeting glimpses of our inner selves. They can help us plan for the future.

## Thinking Through Your Work Alternatives

With our longer life span, people are likely to have more multiple careers than ever before. During the 1990s, this country's 70 million baby boomers will enter mid-life—a time when, according to popular mythology, many people make the break and go for a career change. While we later devote an entire part of this book to business aspects and "Evaluating the Options," let's touch briefly on this topic now. (If you're retired and have no interest in working, simply skip to the next heading.)

Do you seek a job, a career, to have your own business, to homestead, or to become a farmer or rancher? Each of these groups has its place.

Those who just want a job are looking strictly at the bucks. They are more concerned with the wage than with performing mentally stimulating tasks or anticipating long-term advancement. Temporary, part-time, or seasonal work often falls in this category. We have a friend who just retired. To flesh out his meager social security and monthly income from a little business he just sold, he drives a potato truck for two months during the summer.

Career seekers, on the other hand, want to affiliate with a company that offers growth and personal fulfillment. They are much more selective. And if they bring well-honed skills and strong managerial ability, they are likely to be welcomed in the country. Life in a big business, however, doesn't fully prepare you for life in a small one. Part of our later mission is to help you see why not—and to help you correct for that.

More and more career people will remain with their companies, yet operate from countrified settings. Telecommuting is the wave of the future. In seconds personal computers can link us with headquarters offices anywhere on the globe. All that's required to merge office and home is a PC, printer, modem, photocopier, fax machine, and a telephone. The home office will soar to new zeniths as workers operate from their houses, clad in comfy running suits and gazing out at restful, pastoral country scenes. There's a whole chapter on telecommuting coming up.

Entrepreneurial types who want to call their own shots—either by purchasing an existing business or creating one of their own—are prime candidates for out-migration. The primary **thrust** of *Country Bound!* aims at those who want to do their own **thing.** Twenty percent of all discharged managers today start their own businesses. (That figure is almost triple the number 10 years ago.)

This is possible today in ways that didn't exist a decade ago. Many of the new opportunities hinge on the electronic marketplace. Computers and fiber optics, faxes and phone lines . . . these are the currencies of the '90s. Professionals can operate at a distance from their clients. Businesses can learn new ways to court prospects and service their customers.

Telephones will take on new business roles as 900 and 1,000 numbers become more responsive. For a fee, these numbers will put consumers in touch with everything from an expert who can coach them through fixing an overflowing washing machine to a therapist offering instant family counseling. We address this issue in the chapter on "Evaluating Your Entrepreneurial Options."

## Looking at Homesteading

Homesteading, farming, and ranching can be a wonderfully rewarding lifestyle . . . or it can drive you bananas! Unplugging from the system takes courage. It also takes a huge measure of hard work. Frontier fantasy sounds romantic. In reality, there is little romance when you collapse into bed dead tired after 14 to 18 hours of physical labor.

Farm routine is unlike office and factory work. As you do the daily chores, there are no ringing telephones or clattering machines. Usually you're alone. You'll actually have time to think—to ponder—to speculate! Yet there is an unending parade of things that need fixing: the water pump, the generator, the tractor, the fence, etc. It's also different in another way: if you have animals, many require care every day—365 days a year. Cows can't wait to be milked.

On the plus side, there's nothing like plucking your own veggies from the garden for the noon meal, or making peach pies with your own fruit. Then there's the pride you feel when you open your root cellar and show off scores of canning jars filled with the bounty you grew. Many would say, "This is the country God has made. Rejoice and be glad in it."

But let us also take a practical look at farming. Why do you want to do it? 1) Does it represent some form of escape for you? 2) Do you see it as an investment? 3) Perhaps your dad or granddad did it and you're following family tradition. 4) The lifestyle appeals to you. 5) Do issues like your family's health and welfare play an important role? 6) Do you feel called to do this work? 7) Do you see it as a long-term investment? 8) Are you going into farming because you feel forced to? 9) Or because you should be able to survive if you grow all your own food? Once you've thought through your motivation, then you can analyze just how logical the step would really be.

Don't set out to buy a farm or ranch until you know what you mean to get into. Will you grow corn? Raise poultry? Grow truck farm vegetables? Herbs? Exotic fruit? Have an orchard? Raise horses? Beef? Hogs? Breed earthworms? Sheep? Llamas? Catfish? Actually, it's a good idea to combine two or more of these. Mixed crop and livestock operations spread the risk, and they benefit from interrelationships.

Have you researched thoroughly to learn about your chosen animals or crops? Do you know how long it will take to get a cash crop? Is there a market handy for your product? Can it be shipped or sold through mail order? Have you talked to other growers? Also consider whether you have experience at farming or are educated—either through schooling or being self-taught—in farm matters. If not, get informed—or team up with someone who is—before taking the plunge!

No matter which way you go, it takes guts to leave your ruts. But the rewards can be delicious. With this in mind, let's proceed by using seven standards to measure your "move quotient."

# 2

# Seven Criteria to Measure Your Move

What walks in four directions at the same time and speaks Spanish while chanting in Latin? You guessed it: statistics. They say everything—and nothing. Statistics can be extremely misleading indicators. Statewide averages, for instance, hide local realities. Nonetheless, having various facts at your disposal is useful. Just realize they must be weighed with caution when applied to your individual needs. And what precisely are your needs?

Measuring quality of life is an inexact science, to say the least. What is significant to one person is trivial to another. Characteristics refuse to line up neatly like a can of Pringle's potato chips. Don't let all this overwhelm you—or if it does, skip it and come back later. It's all down hill from here.

In this chapter we will examine seven yardsticks for measuring an area's quality of life. They include: cost of living, crime, weather (climate), health care, environment (pollution), leisure (culture, arts, recreation, attitude, and entertainment), and infrastructure (education, transportation). To aid you in this appraisal, several tables and maps are included: everything from the location of nuclear power plants to hate-group strongholds, earthquake fault areas to hurricane prone locations. And you'll find even more maps in Part

III. We hope with these you'll get the whole story. Thoroughness is an important trait, as the following story proves:

If you've ever lived on a ranch or farm, you may remember that when a horse is infested with larvae of the botfly—has "bots," as they say—you have a serious problem. Several years ago a farmer in west Texas came to his neighbor's house and asked him, "Joe, didn't you have a horse come down sick with the bots one time?"

"Yep," replied Joe.

"Well, what did you do for it?"

"Fed him turpentine," came the answer.

"Hmmmm, thanks," the farmer said and went back home shaking his head in wonder.

A few weeks later the farmer returned and asked, "Joe, what did you say you gave your horse for the bots?"

"Turpentine," Joe replied.

"Hmmmm," said the farmer, "that's what I thought you said. Well, by golly, I fed mine some turpentine—and it killed him!"

"Yep," Joe said dryly, "killed mine, too."

We hope the following information gives you the *whole story*. And that these seven gauges supply remedies for your urban blues.

## *Deciphering the Cost of Living*

Most of us are trying to do more with less—and slipping a little further behind each year. Economists come up with elaborate formulas and detailed explanations for what things cost in different locales. There is no question that it's cheaper overall to live away from metropolitan centers. How much cheaper, and in what ways, we'll examine here.

### Analyzing Expenses

In a recent study, Runzheimer International, a relocation consulting firm, analyzed a family's expenses in four areas. Their typical family had a couple and two children, an annual income of $50,000, and a four-bedroom house. The segments analyzed encompassed housing (including the mortgage, insurance, utilities, maintenance, and real estate tax); transportation (maintenance and insurance for two relatively late model vehicles); goods and services (which includes food, clothing, medical care, and recreational expenses); and miscellaneous (such things as savings and life insurance.)

They found huge disparities. In Los Angeles, for instance, it costs $60,507 to buy what $50,000 buys in Small Town USA! And in 1989 a

Bureau of Labor Statistics' Consumer Expenditure Survey showed that average urban annual spending amounted to $28,584—compared to $23,106 in rural areas. Could you find ways to use that extra $5,478?

If you want to do serious comparisons, cost of living consultants can be hired for current information and guidance. While these companies usually serve large corporations in analyzing proposed relocations, some will also work with individuals. BTA Economic Research Institute was especially gracious in talking with us. They provide comparisons for over 3,000 destinations, charge an $89 fee for a one-page comparison (see the following Relocation Assessment), and can be reached at 800-627-3697.

Right Choice, Inc. also does comparative analysis and specializes in working with individuals. They even include commuting costs in their site evaluations. Additionally, they can customize an analysis to include such expenses as day care. "Most people don't consider all the financial ramifications of relocation," says Right Choice CFO, James Angelini. Their one-time fee is $150. Reach them at 800-872-2294 (603-626-6374 in New Hampshire).

Another source of information is the American Chamber of Commerce Researchers Association (ACCRA). Every three months they survey costs of housing, food, services, transportation, and health care at 250 sites around the country. For $100 you can order an annual subscription, or just the last quarter for $50. If you belong to a larger chamber of commerce, which probably holds membership in ACCRA, chamber personnel can probably get information on two or three destination points free of charge for you. These are likely to be larger cities, however.

## Housing Costs

Curious about what your house would cost elsewhere? You can hire an appraiser to check in the *Residential Cost Handbook* by Marshall and Swift. Using multipliers, the appraiser can compute values in some 500 locations around the nation.

The adjacent Home Affordability Index ranks 219 markets as to affordability as a percentage of the average household's gross monthly income. It is also a useful guide for comparing home prices across North America. While much of the information contained in both targets heavily populated areas, they can still serve as guides to getting a sense of prices. Generally, the most affordable homes are in the Midwest and the South. In September of 1991 the National Association of Home Builders reported that regionally, the most reasonable housing markets were in the Saginaw area in the Midwest; Amarillo, Texas in the South; Nashua, New Hampshire in the Northwest; and Greeley, Colorado in the West. Of course your home isn't the only consideration.

## Relocation Assessment

Information based on a family of four, owning their own home, with estimated earnings of $56,000.

| Areas Compared | Denver, Colorado | Durango, Colorado | Difference |
|---|---|---|---|
| **Consumables:** Other | $11,984 | $10,111 | ($1,873) |
| **Housing:** Utilities/Property Taxes/Other | $20,048 | $16,820 | ($3,228) |
| **Services:** Medical/School/Other | $10,416 | $8,882 | ($1,534) |
| **Taxes:** Federal/State/Local/Other | $8,904 | $7,653 | ($1,251) |
| **Transportation:** Public/Automobiles/Other | $4,648 | $3,780 | ($868) |
| **TOTALS** | $56,000 | $47,246 | ($8,754) |
| Compared to U.S. National | 98.70% | 83.24% | -15.46% |
| **Original Data:** | | | |
| # of Autos: Used Auto Value | 2 $3,985 | $7,290 | |
| Estimated Value 3 Bedroom House | $116,826 | $99,898 | ($16,928) |

Source: *BTA Economic Research Institute, Box 7655, Newport Beach, CA 92660, 800-627-3697.*

Seven Criteria to Measure Your Move

# Home Affordability Index-Ranks 219 Markets

★ The Index measures affordability as a percentage of the average household's gross monthly income needed to cover a 30-year, fixed mortgage payment on an average-priced home in the area, after a 20% down payment.

| RANK | DESCRIPTION | STATE | PRICE | INCOME | INDEX |
|---|---|---|---|---|---|
| 1 | Galveston-Texas City | TX | $56,858 | $34,594 | 13.563% |
| 2 | Brazoria | TX | $62,177 | $37,769 | 13.567% |
| 3 | Wheeling | WV | $44,500 | $26,906 | 13.648% |
| 4 | Appleton-Oshkosh | WI | $59,389 | $35,690 | 13.718% |
| 5 | Flint | MI | $60,368 | $35,476 | 14.038% |
| 6 | Peoria | IL | $57,500 | $32,785 | 14.458% |
| 7 | Davenport-Rock Island | IA | $57,652 | $32,809 | 14.484% |
| 8 | Johnstown | PA | $46,453 | $26,330 | 14.539% |
| 9 | Cedar Rapids | IA | $62,769 | $35,239 | 14.677% |
| 10 | Amarillo | TX | $59,968 | $32,824 | 15.062% |
| 11 | Duluth | MN | $50,570 | $27,617 | 15.121% |
| 12 | Houston | TX | $66,028 | $36,005 | 15.131% |
| 13 | Des Moines | IA | $66,100 | $35,823 | 15.208% |
| 14 | Kalmazoo | MI | $66,925 | $36,285 | 15.213% |
| 15 | Green Bay | WI | $66,267 | $35,441 | 15.406% |
| 16 | South Bend-Mishawaka | IN | $65,239 | $34,578 | 15.547% |
| 17 | St. Cloud | MN | $64,356 | $33,830 | 15.638% |
| 18 | Youngstown-Warren | OH | $57,938 | $34,417 | 15.702% |
| 19 | Houma-Thibodaux | LA | $50,285 | $26,296 | 15.789% |
| 20 | Racine | WI | $68,835 | $35,442 | 16.015% |
| 21 | Wichita | KS | $69,600 | $35,719 | 16.059% |
| 22 | Oklahoma City | OK | $61,900 | $31,525 | 16.178% |
| 23 | Lansing-E. Lansing | MI | $69,800 | $35,580 | 16.189% |
| 24 | Omaha | NE | $71,400 | $36,322 | 16.222% |
| 25 | Fort Smith | AR | $56,128 | $28,424 | 16.296% |
| 26 | Lincoln | NE | $66,213 | $33,492 | 16.302% |
| 27 | Fort Pierce | FL | $71,500 | $36,040 | 16.349% |
| 28 | Grand Rapids | MI | $71,900 | $36,173 | 16.388% |
| 29 | Detroit | MI | $81,675 | $40,986 | 16.425% |

*Trade Your Business Suit Blues for Blue Jean Dreams™*

| RANK | DESCRIPTION | STATE | PRICE | INCOME | INDEX |
|---|---|---|---|---|---|
| 30 | Yakima | WA | $58,352 | $29,285 | 16.432% |
| 31 | Spokane | WA | $60,600 | $30,108 | 16.620% |
| 32 | Saginaw-Bay City | MI | $68,720 | $34,017 | 16.650% |
| 33 | Gary-Hammond | IN | $67,260 | $33,252 | 16.673% |
| 34 | Biloxi-Gulfport | MS | $55,142 | $27,042 | 16.818% |
| 35 | Fort Wayne | IN | $72,861 | $35,612 | 16.882% |
| 36 | Hamilton-Middletown | OH | $72,682 | $35,526 | 16.889% |
| 37 | Lorain-Elyria | OH | $68,803 | $33,500 | 16.943% |
| 38 | Macon-Warner Robins | GA | $71,892 | $34,890 | 16.991% |
| 39 | Springfield | MO | $62,610 | $30,188 | 17.093% |
| 40 | Lake Charles | LA | $61,507 | $29,621 | 17.136% |
| 41 | Erie | PA | $66,000 | $31,720 | 17.175% |
| 42 | Roanoke | VA | $78,995 | $37,879 | 17.202% |
| 43 | Ocala | FL | $58,011 | $27,821 | 17.210% |
| 44 | Rockford | IL | $71,292 | $34,026 | 17.281% |
| 45 | Beaver County | PA | $62,180 | $29,439 | 17.405% |
| 46 | Springfield | IL | $70,785 | $33,479 | 17.456% |
| 47 | Huntsville | AL | $87,705 | $41,450 | 17.457% |
| 48 | Salem | OR | $62,968 | $29,608 | 17.549% |
| 49 | Beaumont-Port Arthur | TX | $64,294 | $30,223 | 17.550% |
| 50 | Shreveport | LA | $64,428 | $30,279 | 17.557% |
| 51 | Evansville | IN | $70,200 | $32,849 | 17.644% |
| 52 | Vancouver | WA | $71,739 | $33,174 | 17.833% |
| 53 | Lafayette | LA | $65,004 | $30,034 | 17.860% |
| 54 | Kansas City | MO | $81,739 | $37,585 | 17.943% |
| 55 | Little Rock | AR | $72,000 | $33,045 | 17.975% |
| 56 | Johnson City-Kingsport | TN | $66,007 | $30,307 | 17.976% |
| 57 | Canton | OH | $68,587 | $31,266 | 18.077% |
| 58 | Hickory | NC | $73,701 | $33,624 | 18.094% |
| 59 | Lubbock | TX | $68,325 | $31,074 | 18.150% |
| 60 | Indianapolis | IN | $80,392 | $36,530 | 18.166% |
| 61 | Salt Lake City | UT | $76,777 | $34,875 | 18.168% |

Seven Criteria to Measure Your Move

| RANK | DESCRIPTION | STATE | PRICE | INCOME | INDEX |
|---|---|---|---|---|---|
| 62 | Louisville | KY | $73,300 | $32,935 | 18.363% |
| 63 | Longview-Marshall | TX | $65,792 | $29,536 | 18.364% |
| 64 | Boise City | ID | $74,297 | $33,376 | 18.372% |
| 65 | Gainesville | FL | $74,487 | $33,394 | 18.399% |
| 66 | Toledo | OH | $76,400 | $34,208 | 18.417% |
| 67 | Huntington-Ashland | WV | $60,597 | $27,169 | 18.418% |
| 68 | Jackson | MS | $71,020 | $31,674 | 18.488% |
| 69 | Milwaukee | WI | $85,046 | $37,882 | 18.531% |
| 70 | Fayetteville | NC | $70,539 | $31,202 | 18.653% |
| 71 | Pensacola | FL | $74,000 | $32,516 | 18.785% |
| 72 | Rochester | NY | $86,600 | $37,776 | 18.901% |
| 73 | Joliet | IL | $87,437 | $38,125 | 18.917% |
| 74 | St. Louis | MO | $88,991 | $38,807 | 18.924% |
| 75 | Jacksonville | FL | $82,400 | $35,835 | 18.954% |
| 76 | Utica-Rome | NY | $71,700 | $31,161 | 18.985% |
| 77 | Akron | OH | $80,700 | $35,067 | 18.992% |
| 78 | Augusta | GA | $82,832 | $35,944 | 18.996% |
| 79 | Greenville-Spartanburg | SC | $79,400 | $34,485 | 19.000% |
| 80 | Dayton-Springfield | OH | $80,100 | $34,630 | 19.093% |
| 81 | Eugene-Springfield | OR | $67,053 | $28,899 | 19.143% |
| 82 | Champaign-Urbana | IL | $73,396 | $31,504 | 19.198% |
| 83 | Tallahassee | FL | $79,707 | $34,207 | 19.224% |
| 84 | Tulsa | OK | $74,500 | $31,855 | 19.287% |
| 85 | Killeen-Temple | TX | $63,779 | $27,206 | 19.319% |
| 86 | Montgomery | AL | $77,900 | $33,022 | 19.442% |
| 87 | Fort Myers-Cape Coral | FL | $84,313 | $35,686 | 19.470% |
| 88 | Melbourne-Titusville | FL | $88,650 | $37,472 | 19.503% |
| 89 | Provo-Orem | UT | $66,871 | $28,261 | 19.532% |
| 90 | Waco | TX | $65,656 | $27,654 | 19.570% |
| 91 | Columbia | SC | $85,900 | $36,164 | 19.577% |
| 92 | Mobile | AL | $68,800 | $28,991 | 19.578% |
| 93 | Madison | WI | $85,900 | $36,156 | 19.582% |

*Trade Your Business Suit Blues for Blue Jean Dreams™*

| RANK | DESCRIPTION | STATE | PRICE | INCOME | INDEX |
|---|---|---|---|---|---|
| 94 | San Antonio | TX | $75,447 | $31,791 | 19.590% |
| 95 | Daytona Beach | FL | $74,600 | $31,389 | 19.612% |
| 96 | Chattanooga | TN | $78,900 | $33,064 | 19.671% |
| 97 | Denver | CO | $92,936 | $38,930 | 19.697% |
| 98 | Minneapolis-St. Paul | MN | $101,600 | $42,304 | 19.800% |
| 99 | Harrisburg-Lebanon | PA | $86,591 | $36,014 | 19.826% |
| 100 | York | PA | $86,551 | $35,836 | 19.924% |
| 101 | Baton Rouge | LA | $75,300 | $31,086 | 19.996% |
| 102 | Columbus | GA | $73,980 | $30,343 | 20.090% |
| 103 | Pittsburgh | PA | $83,605 | $34,273 | 20.132% |
| 104 | McAllen-Edinburg | TX | $51,885 | $21,257 | 20.153% |
| 105 | Scranton-Wilkes Barre | PA | $75,018 | $30,614 | 20.226% |
| 106 | New Orleans | LA | $73,218 | $29,724 | 20.307% |
| 107 | Brownsville-Harlingen | TX | $55,007 | $22,225 | 20.409% |
| 108 | Phoenix | AZ | $94,158 | $37,994 | 20.435% |
| 109 | Orlando | FL | $97,200 | $39,221 | 20.438% |
| 110 | Buffalo | NY | $82,900 | $33,379 | 20.492% |
| 111 | Lakeland-Winter Park | FL | $76,300 | $30,563 | 20.574% |
| 112 | Charleston | WV | $74,521 | $29,832 | 20.595% |
| 113 | Visalia-Tulare | CA | $74,347 | $29,693 | 20.651% |
| 114 | Corpus Christi | TX | $73,900 | 29,350 | 20.770% |
| 115 | Cleveland | OH | $90,708 | $35,930 | 20.807% |
| 116 | Binghamton | NY | $88,852 | $35,214 | 20.821% |
| 117 | Asheville | NC | $79,500 | $31,410 | 20.860% |
| 118 | Richmond-Petersburg | VA | $108,700 | $42,687 | 20.999% |
| 119 | Aurora-Elgin | IL | $104,341 | $40,926 | 21.023% |
| 120 | Reading | PA | $91,945 | $35,821 | 21.172% |
| 121 | Cincinnati | OH | $92,860 | $36,145 | 21.181% |
| 122 | Syracuse | NY | $92,600 | $35,923 | 21.245% |
| 123 | Austin | TX | $91,673 | $35,528 | 21.279% |
| 124 | Columbus | OH | $90,215 | $34,963 | 21.280% |
| 125 | Fort Collins-Loveland | CO | $85,658 | $33,047 | 21.388% |

| RANK | DESCRIPTION | STATE | PRICE | INCOME | INDEX |
|---|---|---|---|---|---|
| 126 | Portland | OR | $85,652 | $33,018 | 21.407% |
| 127 | Norfolk-Virginia Beach | VA | $97,861 | $37,676 | 21.435% |
| 128 | Ann Arbor | MI | $109,064 | $41,670 | 21.598% |
| 129 | Bradenton | FL | $87,750 | $33,376 | 21.680% |
| 130 | Nashville | TN | $98,400 | $37,244 | 21.781% |
| 131 | Lancaster | PA | $99,120 | $36,993 | 22.091% |
| 132 | El Paso | TX | $74,800 | $27,920 | 22.092% |
| 133 | Knoxville | TN | $86,100 | $31,889 | 22.277% |
| 134 | Charleston | SC | $91,000 | $33,539 | 22.362% |
| 135 | Pawtucket-Woonsocket | RI | $103,277 | $38,051 | 22.391% |
| 136 | Greensboro Winston-Salem | NC | $100,733 | $36,915 | 22.495% |
| 137 | Las Vegas | NV | $97,800 | $35,842 | 22.499% |
| 138 | Anchorage | AK | $123,493 | $45,127 | 22.576% |
| 139 | Memphis | TN | $92,000 | $33,433 | 22.684% |
| 140 | Colorado Springs | CO | $93,579 | $33,944 | 22.732% |
| 141 | Lexington-Fayette | KY | $91,400 | $32,940 | 22.878% |
| 142 | Ft. Lauderdale | FL | $112,617 | $40,462 | 22.955% |
| 143 | Lawrence-Haverhill | MA | $131,701 | $46,937 | 23.137% |
| 144 | Tucson | AZ | $92,042 | $32,458 | 23.403% |
| 145 | Albuquerque | NM | $95,500 | $33,617 | 23.417% |
| 146 | Merced | CA | $89,999 | $31,682 | 23.445% |
| 147 | Savannah | GA | $98,000 | $34,448 | 23.479% |
| 148 | Baltimore | MD | $123,827 | $43,397 | 23.532% |
| 149 | Bremerton | WA | $97,800 | $34,191 | 23.585% |
| 150 | Fresno | CA | $95,611 | $33,339 | 23.648% |
| 151 | Ft. Worth-Arlington | TX | $108,295 | $37,655 | 23.710% |
| 152 | Bakersfield | CA | $94,498 | $32,877 | 23.725% |
| 153 | West Palm Beach/Boca Raton | FL | $127,700 | $44,123 | 23.879% |
| 154 | Charlotte-Gastonia | NC | $110,486 | $38,105 | 23.902% |
| 155 | Dallas | TX | $116,483 | $40,206 | 23.907% |
| 156 | Boulder-Longmont | CO | $120,200 | $41,322 | 23.987% |
| 157 | Nassau-Suffolk | NY | $170,413 | $58,463 | 24.036% |

*Trade Your Business Suit Blues for Blue Jean Dreams™*

| RANK | DESCRIPTION | STATE | PRICE | INCOME | INDEX |
|---|---|---|---|---|---|
| 158 | Birmingham | AL | $95,100 | $32,433 | 24.198% |
| 159 | Lake County | IL | $167,260 | $56,841 | 24.278% |
| 160 | Wilmington | DE | $125,430 | $42,401 | 24.396% |
| 161 | Raleigh-Durham | NC | $122,300 | $40,688 | 24.803% |
| 162 | Washington | DC | $167,342 | $55,356 | 24.930% |
| 163 | Nashua | NH | $169,724 | $55,980 | 25.016% |
| 164 | Tacoma | WA | $96,050 | $31,594 | 25.068% |
| 165 | Miami-Hialeah | FL | $114,200 | $37,200 | 25.323% |
| 166 | Atlantic City | NJ | $119,150 | $38,457 | 25.556% |
| 167 | Allentown-Bethlehem | PA | $112,990 | $36,443 | 25.585% |
| 168 | Trenton | NJ | $147,330 | $47,494 | 25.597% |
| 169 | Waterbury | CT | $130,130 | $41,908 | 25.599% |
| 170 | Tampa-St. Petersburg | FL | $106,291 | $33,800 | 25.953% |
| 171 | Atlanta | GA | $137,700 | $43,566 | 26.057% |
| 172 | Seattle | WA | $126,218 | $39,290 | 26.511% |
| 173 | Albany-Schenectady | NY | $118,600 | $36,883 | 26.516% |
| 174 | Modesto | CA | $108,425 | $33,476 | 26.706% |
| 175 | Philadelphia | PA | $134,705 | $41,126 | 27.019% |
| 176 | Poughkeepsie | NY | $149,225 | $45,489 | 27.066% |
| 177 | Chicago | IL | $131,048 | $39,771 | 27.186% |
| 178 | Lowell | MA | $165,107 | $49,910 | 27.289% |
| 179 | Reno | NV | $120,383 | $36,153 | 27.450% |
| 180 | Riverside/San Bernardino | CA | $118,283 | $35,391 | 27.566% |
| 181 | Monmouth-Ocean | NJ | $157,965 | $47,146 | 27.642% |
| 182 | Stamford | CT | $308,000 | $91,547 | 27.750% |
| 183 | Middlesex-Somerset | NJ | $192,369 | $57,101 | 27.782% |
| 184 | Orange County | NY | $140,875 | $41,690 | 27.863% |
| 185 | Boston | MA | $175,973 | $50,924 | 20.513% |
| 186 | New London-Norwich | CT | $146,061 | $42,239 | 28.523% |
| 187 | Portland | ME | $137,258 | $38,791 | 29.172% |
| 188 | Vallejo-Fairfield-Napa | CA | $137,421 | $38,821 | 29.211% |
| 189 | Brockton | MA | $149,085 | $41,922 | 29.340% |

# COUNTRY BOUND!™

| RANK | DESRIPTION | STATE | PRICE | INCOME | INDEX |
|---|---|---|---|---|---|
| 190 | Hartford | CT | $181,400 | $50,961 | 29.364% |
| 191 | Sarasota | FL | $137,425 | $38,409 | 29.524% |
| 192 | Springfield | MA | $140,000 | $39,058 | 29.556% |
| 193 | Stockton | CA | $119,936 | $33,021 | 29.945% |
| 194 | Worcester | MA | $157,000 | $42,894 | 30.186% |
| 195 | Danbury | CT | $225,769 | $61,063 | 30.500% |
| 196 | Santa Cruz | CA | $140,485 | $37,771 | 30.690% |
| 197 | Providence | RI | $146,100 | $39,212 | 30.725% |
| 198 | New Haven-Meriden | CT | $176,200 | $47,045 | 30.890% |
| 199 | Newark | NJ | $196,718 | $51,680 | 31.393% |
| 200 | Sacramento | CA | $139,497 | $36,339 | 31.668% |
| 201 | Honolulu | HI | $177,244 | $43,756 | 33.403% |
| 202 | Salem-Gloucester | MA | $208,400 | $50,976 | 33.710% |
| 203 | Bridgeport-Milford | CT | $198,163 | $48,409 | 33.762% |
| 204 | Portsmouth-Dover | NH | $174,854 | $42,047 | 34.304% |
| 205 | New Bedford | MA | $142,948 | $33,563 | 35.146% |
| 206 | Anaheim-Santa Ana | CA | $218,724 | $50,836 | 35.479% |
| 207 | Santa Rosa-Petaluma | CA | $161,206 | $37,108 | 35.831% |
| 208 | Jersey City | NJ | $158,864 | $34,182 | 35.844% |
| 209 | San Jose | CA | $247,204 | $52,359 | 38.939% |
| 210 | Salinas-Seaside | CA | $171,898 | $36,074 | 39.286% |
| 211 | Bergen-Passaic | NJ | $263,578 | $54,704 | 39.748% |
| 212 | Los Angeles | CA | $207,868 | $43,128 | 39.761% |
| 213 | Santa Barbara | CA | $208,038 | $41,990 | 40.867% |
| 214 | New York | NY | $198,100 | $39,908 | 40.954% |
| 215 | Oxnard-Ventura | CA | $231,146 | $45,596 | 41.819% |
| 216 | San Diego | CA | $199,171 | $38,188 | 43.019% |
| 217 | Oakland | CA | $239,763 | $43,209 | 45.768% |
| 218 | Chico | CA | $154,115 | $27,623 | 46.005% |
| 219 | San Francisco | CA | $281,993 | $45,598 | 51.002% |

Source: *Prudential Real Estate Affiliates, Published in the National Relocation and Real Estate Directory.*

## Power and Other Expenses

Power bills vary considerably, especially if you're moving into an area that requires air conditioning or is colder than you're used to. Electric bills may zoom. (Or a wood stove may cut them to almost nil.) Publicly owned electric power companies, those that are municipal, typically have much lower rates than their privately owned cousins. For instance, to purchase 750 kilowatt hours of monthly service in Cowlitz, Washington, costs $160. With San Diego Gas & Electric, however, the same hours go for a whopping $1,144. See the adjacent maps which show comparative energy prices by state. Telephone bills are often higher in the country because most calls are billed as long distance.

There are other less obvious variables. While you're saving on commuting expenses, your gasoline mileage may plummet. Why? Because the terrain is uneven and the top speed might be 35 mph. Auto insurance, however, is typically much cheaper in rural areas. But fire insurance may be higher if you're served by a volunteer fire department with an engine headquartered several miles away. Groceries may also cost more. You pay 13 percent more for them in Medford, Oregon, for instance, than you do in Los Angeles. On the plus side, you'll spend less on clothing and entertainment. Much of what country people do for fun carries no price tag.

If you're retired military, locating near a base or post where your military ID card gives you exchange or commissary shopping privileges could be a major consideration. Ditto on health considerations. Being near a veterans' hospital can pay big dividends. College tuition and expenses can also be dramatically affected by where you relocate. Moving to a college town where there is an appropriate institute of higher education may allow your son or daughter to live at home while attending classes.

## Taxes as Taskmasters

Most people are about as fond of taxes as American car manufacturers are of foreign-made vehicles. Taxes take a big bite out of everyone's income. According to the Tax Foundation, the average worker spends two hours and 48 minutes of every eight-hour work day earning enough money to pay all federal, state, county, and local taxes. Social security taxes and federal personal income taxes are constants no matter where you live. Others, like gasoline taxes, differ immensely.

Let's take property taxes first. According to the National Association of Realtors, property taxes paid per $1,000 range from a low of $12 in Alabama to a high of $92 in Wyoming. The U.S. average is $35.

# Average Price of Natural Gas Delivered to Residential Consumers, 1989
(Dollars per Thousand Cubic Feet)
U.S. Average $5.64

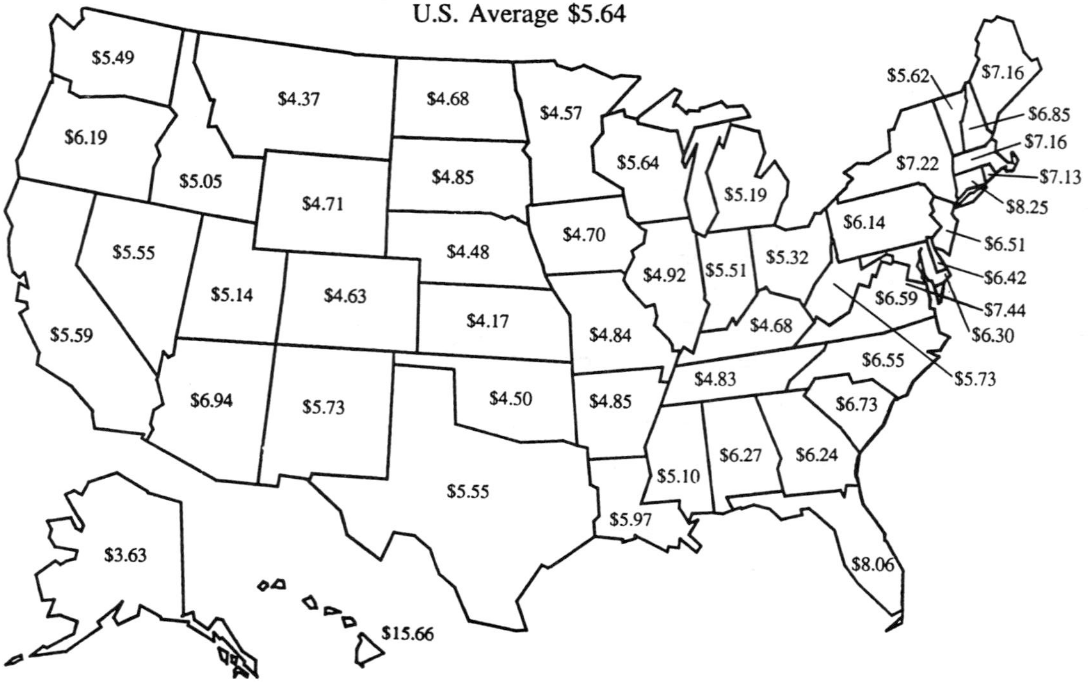

Source: *Energy Information Administration, Form EIA-176, "Annual Report of Natural and Supplemental Gas Supply and Disposition."*

# Average Revenue per Kilowatt Hour for the Residential Sector by State, 1989
(Residential Average Revenue per kwh is 7.6 Cents)

Note: The average revenue per kilowatt hour of electricity sold is calculated by dividing revenue by sales.
Source: *Energy Information Administration, Form EIA-861, "Annual Electric Utility Report."*

## Property Tax Rankings on a $104,000 House by State*

| # | State | Property Tax | # | State | Property Tax |
|---|---|---|---|---|---|
| 33 | Alabama | $852.80 | 16 | Montana | $1,372.80 |
| 33 | Alaska | $852.80 | 7 | Nebraska | $2,298.40 |
| 37 | Arizona | $707.20 | 38 | Nevada | $634.40 |
| 22 | Arkansas | $1,133.60 | 10 | New Hampshire | $1,612.00 |
| 24 | California | $1,102.40 | 2 | New Jersey | $2,423.20 |
| 22 | Colorado | $1,133.60 | 27 | New Mexico | $1,050.40 |
| 12 | Connecticut | $1,518.40 | 6 | New York | $2,308.80 |
| 35 | Delaware | $759.20 | 27 | North Carolina | $1,050.40 |
| 20 | Dist./Columbia | $1,216.80 | 15 | North Dakota | $1,424.80 |
| 31 | Florida | $925.60 | 23 | Ohio | $1,123.20 |
| 30 | Georgia | $936.00 | 30 | Oklahoma | $936.00 |
| 40 | Hawaii | $530.40 | 5 | Oregon | $2,350.40 |
| 29 | Idaho | $946.40 | 15 | Pennsylvania | $1,424.80 |
| 9 | Illinois | $1,653.60 | 11 | Rhode Island | $1,549.60 |
| 19 | Indiana | $1,331.20 | 36 | South Carolina | $728.00 |
| 8 | Iowa | $2,038.40 | 3 | South Dakota | $2,402.40 |
| 24 | Kansas | $1,102.40 | 25 | Tennessee | $1,081.60 |
| 21 | Kentucky | $1,144.00 | 13 | Texas | $1,497.60 |
| 41 | Louisiana | $260.00 | 28 | Utah | $967.20 |
| 18 | Maine | $1,258.40 | 1 | Vermont | $2,631.20 |
| 17 | Maryland | $1,352.00 | 14 | Virginia | $1,476.80 |
| 23 | Massachusetts | $1,123.20 | 21 | Washington | $1,144.00 |
| 5 | Michigan | $2,350.40 | 32 | West Virginia | $915.20 |
| 26 | Minnesota | $1,071.20 | 4 | Wisconsin | $2,360.80 |
| 34 | Mississippi | $800.80 | 39 | Wyoming | $592.80 |
| 31 | Missouri | $925.60 | | | |

* Property tax estimates from 1986 State average property tax rate and home value of $104,000.
Source: *Prepared by Price Waterhouse for the National Association of Realtors.*

For retired people there are other incentives. In Alaska, for instance, once you reach 65, you escape property taxes completely. And eight other states allow special exemptions or credits to older homeowners, no matter what their incomes are. These include: Hawaii, Illinois, Kentucky, Mississippi, New Jersey, South Carolina, Texas, and West Virginia. Furthermore, 17 states permit the elderly to legally postpone paying some or all of their property taxes. Under these programs, the state puts a lien on the property. The money becomes due when the home is sold, given away, or when the owner dies.

The Tax Foundation also rates state and local tax burdens by state. Their recap shows Alaska being a culprit in this category with the highest ratio: $129.20 per $1,000 of personal income. New Hampshire holds the honor of having the lowest taxes at $25.82 per $1,000. As we go to press, seven states have no sales tax. But this may soon change as states scurry to generate new revenue sources to cope with budget shortages.

If you anticipate incorporating in your new locale, also consider state annual fees and corporate income taxes. This is often less in states trying to attract new industry.

For additional information on the cost of living, plus greater detail on the next six criteria, we recommend you get a copy of *Places Rated Almanac* by Richard Boyer and David Savageau.

Savageau's *Retirement Places Rated* may also be useful. Try your local library or get it directly from us by seeing ordering information under "Bibliography/Recommended Reading." (All books listed there in bold print can be ordered through us.) The bottom line? You'll make less money—and live better—in the country.

## *Coping with Crime Risks*

For the first time in the history of humankind, it's safer to live in the wilderness than in civilization.

Violent crimes, which involve bodily injury or the threat of injury, are the most feared by everyone. They include murder, rape, robbery, and assault—and make up 10 percent of all crimes committed in the U.S. In some cities your chance of being the target of one of these terrifying acts is more than one in 100. In Miami and New York City this drops to one in 61! Grand Forks, North Dakota, on the other hand, is 30 times as safe as New York. *Public Opinion* magazine reports that 59 percent of the population feel it's risky to go for a walk in their own neighborhoods after dark. This fear inhibits our freedom as surely as does a barbed wire fence.

## State and Local Tax Burden* by State

| State | Taxes per $1,000 Income | State Tax Burden Ranking | State | Taxes Per $1,000 Income | State Tax Burden Ranking |
|---|---|---|---|---|---|
| AL | $63.76 | 44 | NE | $55.66 | 43 |
| AK | $129.20 | 1 | NV | $67.85 | 15 |
| AZ | $73.27 | 20 | NH | $25.82 | 50 |
| AR | $67.65 | 42 | NJ | $54.06 | 10 |
| CA | $70.16 | 9 | NM | $93.43 | 14 |
| CO | $49.57 | 45 | NY | $72.38 | 5 |
| CT | $63.20 | 4 | NC | $73.23 | 22 |
| DE | $84.62 | 3 | ND | $69.48 | 35 |
| FL | $55.27 | 37 | OH | $60.34 | 36 |
| GA | $64.49 | 31 | OK | $71.57 | 29 |
| HI | $104.02 | 2 | OR | $57.13 | 39 |
| ID | $74.61 | 25 | PA | $59.59 | 28 |
| IL | $55.55 | 27 | RI | $65.23 | 18 |
| IN | $65.26 | 30 | SC | $74.73 | 26 |
| IA | $69.17 | 21 | SD | $45.27 | 49 |
| KS | $59.89 | 32 | TN | $55.09 | 47 |
| KY | $77.44 | 24 | TX | $51.70 | 48 |
| LA | $67.29 | 40 | UT | $72.87 | 38 |
| ME | $73.90 | 16 | VT | $67.85 | 23 |
| MD | $61.70 | 11 | VA | $54.02 | 34 |
| MA | $68.78 | 7 | WA | $80.88 | 8 |
| MI | $66.52 | 19 | WV | $90.44 | 17 |
| MN | $83.21 | 6 | WI | $76.59 | 13 |
| MS | $73.11 | 46 | WY | $82.23 | 12 |
| MO | $55.16 | 41 | DC | $157.43 | Exhibit |
| MT | $71.04 | 33 | * (the higher the number the lower the taxes) | | |

Population as of 1990. Source: *U.S. Department of Commerce, Bureau of the Census, Bureau of Economic Analysis, and Tax Foundation computations.*

## The Threat of Gangs

Street gangs have grown into a major menace, especially with the proliferation of crack cocaine. While they vary in size and power, a 1990 University of Chicago study of 45 cities reports 1,439 gangs. They are no longer isolated in major crime-ridden cities. Youth gangs—with a tragic average member age of only 13½—are also proliferating in Seattle, Cleveland, Denver, Phoenix, Milwaukee, and Cleveland.

Another expanding threat is hate groups. Recruitment has swung into high gear and racially motivated crimes are on the rise. Skinheads, Neo-Nazi groups, and the Ku Klux Klan are mushrooming in certain parts of the country. (See the adjacent map.) Experts see the flood of hate crimes rising in proportion to economic difficulties.

Afraid for their safety, some Americans are becoming prisoners in their own homes. According to *The New England Journal of Medicine*, this is affecting their health. An increase in obesity, hypertension, and diabetes is the result of people missing needed exercise.

City size has a direct bearing on crime. So does a transient population and even the climate. Perhaps this is why the Miami-Hialeah, Florida, area leads even Los Angeles in violent crimes. Cops and crooks are busier in warmer parts of the nation. And areas where there is high immigrant relocation and racial strife are hotbeds of illegal activities.

## Property Crimes

Property crime is defined as something directed against a person's possessions. It includes burglary, grand larceny, auto theft, and vandalism. Property crimes, while not life-threatening, are expensive and unsettling. When your home is broken into, your privacy is invaded and your sense of security destroyed. Auto theft, traditionally considered a non-violent act, has taken a vicious turn.

"Carjacking" has given new meaning to Detroit as the Motor City. Over a six-week period, nearly 300 drivers there were forced to abandon their cars at gunpoint. Instead of heisting *empty* vehicles, thieves are walking up to motorists at stoplights and shopping malls, demanding cars—and killing those who hesitate. While there is no set pattern, carjackers are also at work in Atlanta, San Francisco, Los Angeles, and Houston.

A recent TV special reported that some New York teenagers are better armed than the police force! The kids tote deadly 9 millimeter semi-automatics. Searches before school are becoming commonplace in big cities. But junior high school students in Indianapolis were shocked recently

# White Supremacist Groups In the United States—1991

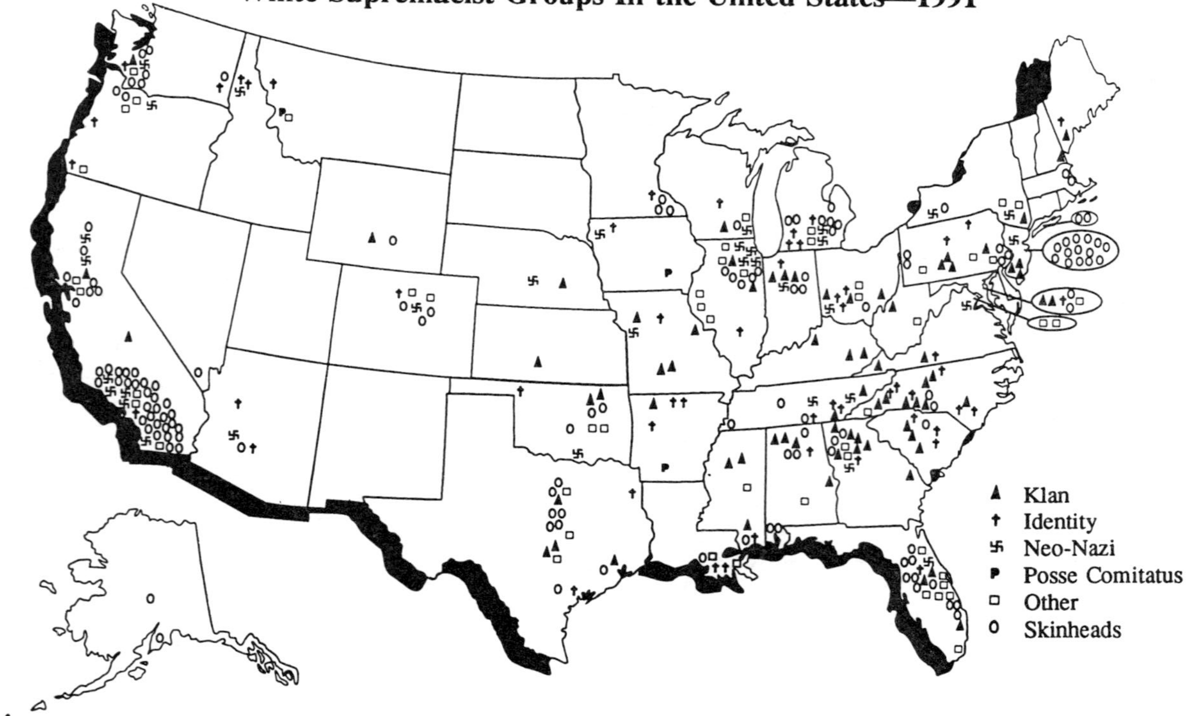

Klan ◀
Identity †
Neo-Nazi 卐
Posse Comitatus ♠
Other □
Skinheads ○

These Symbols indicate the types of groups and their approximate location in a particular state.

Source: *Provided by The Southern Poverty Law Center; Klanwatch Project.*

when they climbed off the school bus—and were confronted with security guards and metal detectors before being permitted to attend classes. A 1990 Centers for Disease Control study revealed that within the prior 30 days, more than one in three high school boys admitted to carrying a gun, knife, or club.

Even Washington, DC VIPs are not immune to the upward spiraling crime rate. One senator's wife was attacked as she opened the door of their townhouse. She felt a gun at her head, was knocked to the ground, and was dragged away to a busy intersection. The gunman fled with her purse leaving the woman and her husband to wonder how anyone can ever be safe. Their conclusion? "We're moving."

The impact of crime in our lives is becoming outrageous. According to the Bureau of Crime Stats, roughly one in 10 people is a victim every year!

The solution? There's no simple answer. But removing yourself and your family from potential everyday contact with the criminal element is one obvious remedy. Metropolitan areas average 28 percent more offenses than do small cities. Want to be safer? Go rural, young man, go rural. In small towns people look out for each other.

## Ferreting Out the Figures

The FBI publishes a detailed report that shows figures for some 16,000 law enforcement jurisdictions. This computer printout, called *Crime by County*, can be ordered for $18 from: Uniform Crime Reporting Section, FBI Headquarters/GRB, 10th & Pennsylvania, Washington, DC 20535, (202)-324-3000. Suppose you're interested in locations within a particular state—or want figures for crimes like narcotics sale and possession, gambling, prostitution, commercial vice, fraud, or driving under the influence? County and city arrest figures for these offenses are published by 41 states. You can find these in the FBI's *Crime in the United States*. It's a reference book carried by most libraries.

Another way to determine the scene of crime in towns you're considering as relocation sites is to check out the rate of reported criminal offenses. What's the total crime rate? How much of it is violent crime? How strong is the police presence in the community? Are they adequately staffed? Does the town provide enough financial commitment so the police force can do its job?

The above statistics dramatize the tendency of people to resort to violent behavior. Fortunately such occurences are far less frequent in the country. So making good choices about where you live and watching out for your own personal safety become more and more important.

# *Wending Your Way Around the Weather*

Don't knock the weather. Many people couldn't start a conversation if it weren't for the weather. True, sometimes it's so hot there's nothing left to do but take off your flesh and sit in your bones. And other times it's so cold when you open your closet, your spring coat is wearing your overcoat. If you suffer from either of these extremes, maybe it's time to consider making a move.

## What Determines Climate

When speaking of weather, we use the word "climate" interchangeably. Climate is determined by five geographic factors: water, latitude, elevation, prevailing winds, and mountain ranges. Towns near large bodies of water tend to be cooler in the summer and warmer in the winter. The higher (more northerly) the latitude, the more severe the weather is likely to be. As to elevation, you can figure the temperature lowers by 3.3 degrees for each 1,000 feet of elevation. Thus if you were considering locating in Arizona, there would be a substantial difference in temperature between small towns near Flagstaff and those in the vicinity of Tucson.

Prevailing winds in this country blow from west to east. Towns along the West Coast get the benefits of the Pacific winds. (For wind speeds look under "Meteorology" in the almanac.) Mountains also play a role in various climes. They serve as barriers to divert nasty weather or channel winds. The climate on one side of a mountain range can be quite different from that of the other side. To find your ideal climate you probably want to consider the following Weather Watch Questionnaire.

## WEATHER WATCH QUESTIONNAIRE

How many days does it fall below freezing (32 degrees F)?

How many days does it fall below 0 degrees?

How many days does it get over 90 degrees?

What is the average annual rainfall?

What is the average annual snowfall?

What is the average January temperature?

How about the average July temperature?

How long is the growing season?

How many days during the year does the sun shine?

What is the average summer humidity percentage?

What is the altitude?

What is the average mph of wind velocity?

Are there thunderstorms and lightning strikes?

Earthquakes?

Tornadoes?

Hurricanes?

Cyclones?

Floods?

Droughts?

Volcanoes that are not extinct?

Most people, if they were considering only climate, would prefer to live in mild, sunny locations . . . especially as they age. Such locales are abundant on the Pacific Coast, along the South Atlantic, in Florida, and along the Gulf Coast Shore. But settling for such moderate climes also has disadvantages. Those who love the blaze of autumn color when the leaves change—and the miracle of a distinct spring—will miss experiencing the four seasons. And people who love winter sports will also feel cheated. Additionally, real estate is expensive in these highly desirable locations.

Many folks opt for other parts of the country. The following table of Climatic Data for Leading American Cities gives valuable indicators to help in your search for the ideal place.

## Hiding From Humidity

Do consider what the humidity will be like. When there's a lot of moisture in the air, you feel like you're in a steam bath. Humidity saps your energy and leaves you perpetually damp and sticky. Creature comfort is hard to come by in the summer in places like Galveston, Texas; New Orleans, Louisiana; or Biloxi, Mississippi. At the other extreme are Las Vegas, Nevada, and Phoenix, Arizona—two of the driest places in the U.S. While dry climates are healthful for some people, they too can have aggravating side effects. Dry, flaky skin is almost guaranteed for new migrants. (When we first moved to Colorado, we went through gallons of body lotion.) Some people also suffer from tickling sore throats and nosebleeds in areas with very low humidity.

# Climatic Data for Leading American Cities

| State and City | Average Temp., °F Winter | Average Temp., °F Summer | Sunny Days | Humidity % | Precipitation Rain (in.) | Precipitation Snow | Average Wind (mph) | Elevation (Feet) |
|---|---|---|---|---|---|---|---|---|
| Alabama (Montgomery) | 55.1 | 76.0 | 233 | 71.80 | 47.10 | 0 | 1.5 | 183 |
| Alaska (Juneau) | 25.8 | 49.1 | 100 | 77.20 | 53.70 | 150.2 | 8.2 | 114 |
| Arizona (Phoenix) | 60.5 | 96.4 | 289 | 33.50 | 10.87 | 0 | 7.3 | 1,117 |
| Arkansas (Little Rock) | 41.3 | 82.1 | 212 | 69.30 | 43.08 | 4.0 | 6.0 | 257 |
| California (Los Angeles) | 60.6 | 72.5 | 293 | 63.30 | 6.54 | 0 | 7.8 | 270 |
| California (San Francisco) | 52.7 | 59.6 | 211 | 76.00 | 20.79 | trace | 9.3 | 52 |
| Colorado (Denver) | 36.3 | 63.5 | 210 | 55.00 | 16.87 | 83.2 | 8.7 | 5,280 |
| Connecticut (Hartford) | 33.7 | 64.0 | 165 | 71.00 | 64.55 | 58.2 | 8.5 | 169 |
| Delaware (Wilmington) | 41.1 | 76.1 | 181 | 69.50 | 48.13 | 9.5 | 9.1 | 74 |
| Florida (Tampa) | 66.5 | 79.8 | 233 | 75.25 | 42.18 | 0 | 8.7 | 19 |
| Florida (Miami) | 72.1 | 79.7 | 252 | 76.25 | 63.11 | 0 | 8.3 | 7 |
| Florida (Orlando) | 67.9 | 80.7 | 231 | 72.00 | 51.35 | 0 | 8.5 | 108 |
| Georgia (Atlanta) | 50.2 | 71.5 | 206 | 70.80 | 50.61 | trace | 9.2 | 1,010 |
| Hawaii (Honolulu) | 72.9 | 79.6 | 244 | 68.80 | 26.90 | 0 | 13.2 | 7 |

| State and City | Average Temp., °F Winter | Average Temp., °F Summer | Sunny Days | Humidity % | Precipitation Rain (in.) | Precipitation Snow | Average Wind (mph) | Elevation (Feet) |
|---|---|---|---|---|---|---|---|---|
| Idaho (Boise) | 34.5 | 62.3 | 216 | 57.50 | 11.43 | 21.4 | 9.1 | 2,838 |
| Illinois (Springfield) | 35.3 | 67.8 | 176 | 74.30 | 32.03 | 26.2 | 11.2 | 588 |
| Indiana (Indianapolis) | 36.4 | 66.9 | 159 | 72.30 | 40.27 | 18.1 | 9.7 | 792 |
| Iowa (Des Moines) | 29.1 | 62.3 | 176 | 73.50 | 36.02 | 36.7 | 10.4 | 938 |
| Kansas (Topeka) | 37.7 | 68.4 | 180 | 69.80 | 31.21 | 26.1 | 9.9 | 877 |
| Kentucky (Louisville) | 42.4 | 69.5 | 177 | 69.00 | 49.38 | 10.4 | 9.0 | 477 |
| Louisiana (New Orleans) | 59.7 | 77.5 | 234 | 78.80 | 63.98 | 0 | 8.5 | 4 |
| Maine (Portland) | 28.6 | 58.1 | 178 | 74.80 | 48.62 | 123.7 | 9.6 | 43 |
| Maryland (Baltimore) | 41.8 | 67.7 | 186 | 69.00 | 52.33 | 13.0 | 8.8 | 148 |
| Massachusetts (Boston) | 36.5 | 64.3 | 175 | 68.30 | 53.11 | 40.7 | 11.4 | 15 |
| Michigan (Detroit) | 25.6 | 63.8 | 188 | 66.50 | 29.96 | 30.6 | 10.6 | 619 |
| Minnesota (Duluth) | 15.2 | 53.9 | 165 | 74.00 | 39.61 | 110.2 | 9.8 | 1,428 |
| Mississippi (Jackson) | 55.0 | 77.4 | 226 | 76.00 | 50.03 | trace | 7.4 | 310 |
| Missouri (Kansas City) | 38.7 | 70.6 | 194 | 66.80 | 27.75 | 15.9 | 10.3 | 1,014 |
| Montana (Helena) | 27.1 | 55.1 | 169 | 57.00 | 8.22 | 40.0 | 8.3 | 3,828 |

| State and City | Average Temp., °F Winter | Average Temp., °F Summer | Sunny Days | Humidity % | Precipitation Rain (in.) | Precipitation Snow | Average Wind (mph) | Elevation (Feet) |
|---|---|---|---|---|---|---|---|---|
| Nebraska (Omaha) | 32.6 | 66.3 | 185 | 71.80 | 35.56 | 27.1 | 9.8 | 977 |
| Nevada (Reno) | 37.0 | 60.8 | 245 | 48.30 | 5.52 | trace | 8.4 | 4,404 |
| Nevada (Las Vegas) | 52.4 | 80.1 | 297 | 28.80 | 4.85 | 0.4 | 9.5 | 2,162 |
| New Hampshire (Concord) | 27.7 | 58.8 | 167 | 77.00 | 42.07 | 100.3 | 7.2 | 342 |
| New Jersey (Trenton) | 40.2 | 66.8 | 193 | 70.60 | 47.13 | 17.2 | 6.4 | 56 |
| New Mexico (Albuquerque) | 44.0 | 69.4 | 271 | 42.30 | 10.11 | 6.4 | 9.7 | 5,311 |
| New York (New York) | 39.9 | 67.8 | 232 | 67.80 | 67.03 | 22.9 | 8.8 | 132 |
| North Carolina (Raleigh) | 47.8 | 69.1 | 201 | 70.50 | 51.74 | 4.0 | 8.6 | 434 |
| North Dakota (Bismark) | 19.9 | 58.8 | 171 | 67.00 | 15.16 | 45.6 | 9.6 | 1,647 |
| Ohio (Columbus) | 36.4 | 63.4 | 151 | 69.80 | 45.60 | 27.1 | 9.7 | 812 |
| Oklahoma (Oklahoma City) | 45.2 | 74.0 | 226 | 65.50 | 27.63 | 14.6 | 12.8 | 1,285 |
| Oregon (Portland) | 44.4 | 63.6 | 156 | 61.00 | 38.82 | 6.5 | 8.1 | 21 |
| Pennsylvania (Harrisburg) | 38.8 | 66.8 | 191 | 68.00 | 59.27 | 33.4 | 7.5 | 338 |
| Rhode Island (Providence) | 35.8 | 63.4 | 179 | 71.00 | 65.06 | 30.4 | 10.5 | 51 |
| South Carolina (Charleston) | 56.2 | 74.7 | 226 | 75.50 | 42.86 | 0 | 9.2 | 40 |

| State and City | Average Temp., °F Winter | Average Temp., °F Summer | Sunny Days | Humidity % | Precipitation Rain (in.) | Precipitation Snow | Average Wind (mph) | Elevation (Feet) |
|---|---|---|---|---|---|---|---|---|
| South Dakota (Rapid City) | 28.5 | 59.6 | 202 | 64.30 | 17.19 | 23.1 | 11.1 | 3,162 |
| Tennessee (Nashville) | 47.4 | 71.8 | 198 | 71.80 | 54.41 | 2.5 | 9.1 | 590 |
| Texas (Austin) | 57.9 | 79.0 | 221 | 67.50 | 26.07 | trace | 9.0 | 597 |
| Utah (Salt Lake City) | 37.5 | 67.2 | 211 | 51.30 | 15.74 | 76.8 | 9.5 | 4,220 |
| Vermont (Burlington) | 25.5 | 59.2 | 151 | 73.00 | 38.10 | 121.6 | 8.0 | 332 |
| Virginia (Richmond) | 45.9 | 66.8 | 188 | 73.50 | 59.34 | 14.3 | 7.4 | 164 |
| Washington (Seattle) | 42.9 | 69.4 | 151 | 72.50 | 48.36 | 22.2 | 8.6 | 400 |
| West Virginia (Charleston) | 42.9 | 66.1 | 128 | 71.30 | 51.15 | 26.5 | 6.1 | 939 |
| Wisconsin (Madison) | 25.2 | 60.8 | 163 | 75.50 | 30.96 | 50.2 | 10.0 | 858 |
| Wyoming (Cheyenne) | 31.8 | 57.6 | 204 | 53.30 | 12.04 | 48.6 | 13.5 | 6,126 |

Source: *U.S. Department of Commerce, National Oceanic and Atmospheric Administration.*
Based on standard 30-year period.

## Cantankerous Considerations

Listening to the old sultry song, "Stormy Weather," is fun. Experiencing storms isn't. Blizzards are familiar visitors in snowy regions and put a damper on anyone's spirits. The majority of severe storms happen in the southern half of the nation. Thunder and lightning can provide a majestic spectacle . . . as long as they keep their distance. In many places they don't. Hurricanes, with their immense power, can last for days and cut a swath across hundreds of miles. Tornadoes concentrate their destruction and killing potential.

Volcanoes, though not officially storms, cause incredible destruction and death when they erupt—as those living near Mount St. Helens on May 18, 1980, can testify. Sixty people died before that catastrophe ended. The nearby community was devastated, and countless trees were flattened like matchsticks.

Earthquake-prone areas can be like a serial killer waiting to go on a rampage. A quake is the result of slippage or fractures of the earth's crust far below ground level. It occurs because of extreme stress. While California has the dubious distinction of being the earthquake capital, another part of the country may be even more volatile. We refer to the New Madrid Fault that runs along the eastern border of Tennessee.

In fact, an earthquake in the Mississippi Valley in 1812 measured even *more* on the Richter scale than the devastating San Francisco earthquake. Scientists fear a recurrence before the year 2000. Experts say it could register as high as 7.5 and affect states from Kansas east to Pennsylvania and from Illinois south to Louisiana. At the end of this discussion we include maps to help you avoid these natural disasters if one or more of them holds special terror for you.

## Comparative Data

The National Climatic Data Center publishes statistics for thousands of locations in this country. Their *Comparative Climatic Data for the United States* surveys 300 primary weather stations for both month-by-month and annual summaries. They include such particulars as: normal daily maximum and minimum temperatures, average and maximum wind speed, percent of possible sunshine, rainfall, snowfall, plus morning and afternoon humidity readings. You can purchase it for $3 from National Climatic Data Center, Federal Building, Asheville, NC 28801, 704-259-0682. They accept credit card orders. There is, however, a $13 minimum so you may want to get some additional information.

# Tornado and Hurricane Risk Areas

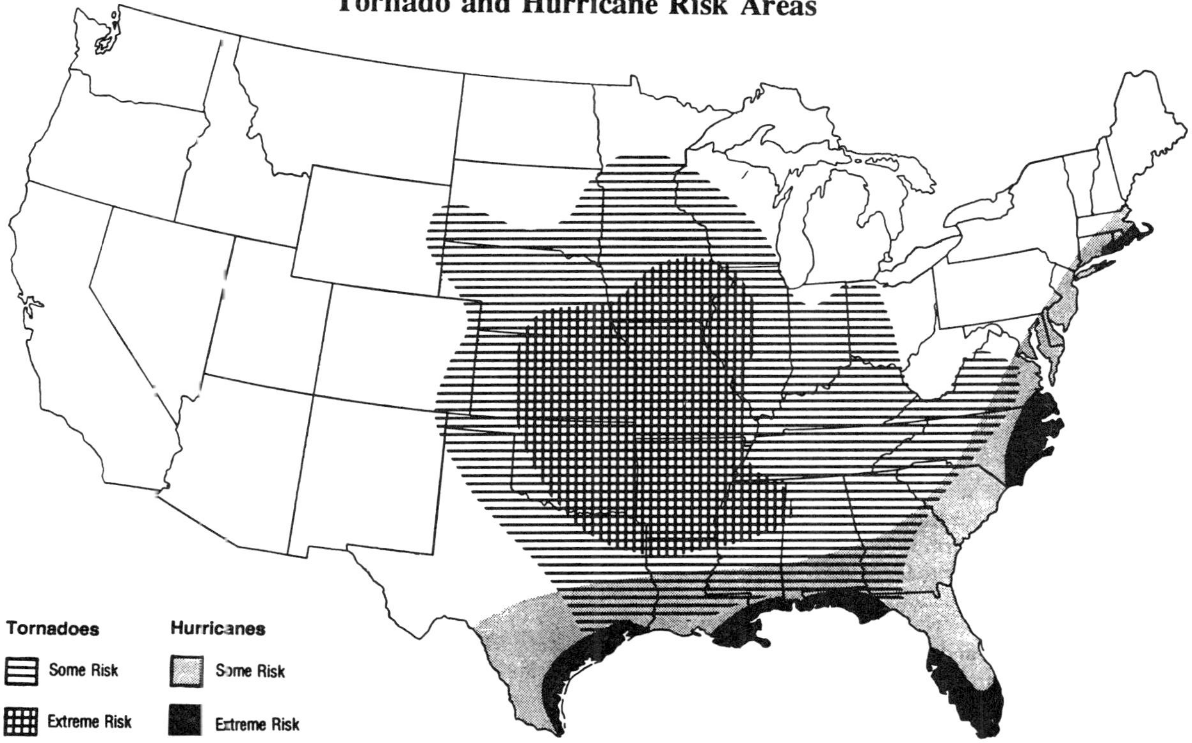

**Tornadoes**
- Some Risk
- Extreme Risk

**Hurricanes**
- Some Risk
- Extreme Risk

Source: *U.S. Geological Survey Open-File Report 76-416, 1976.*

## Earthquake Hazard Zones

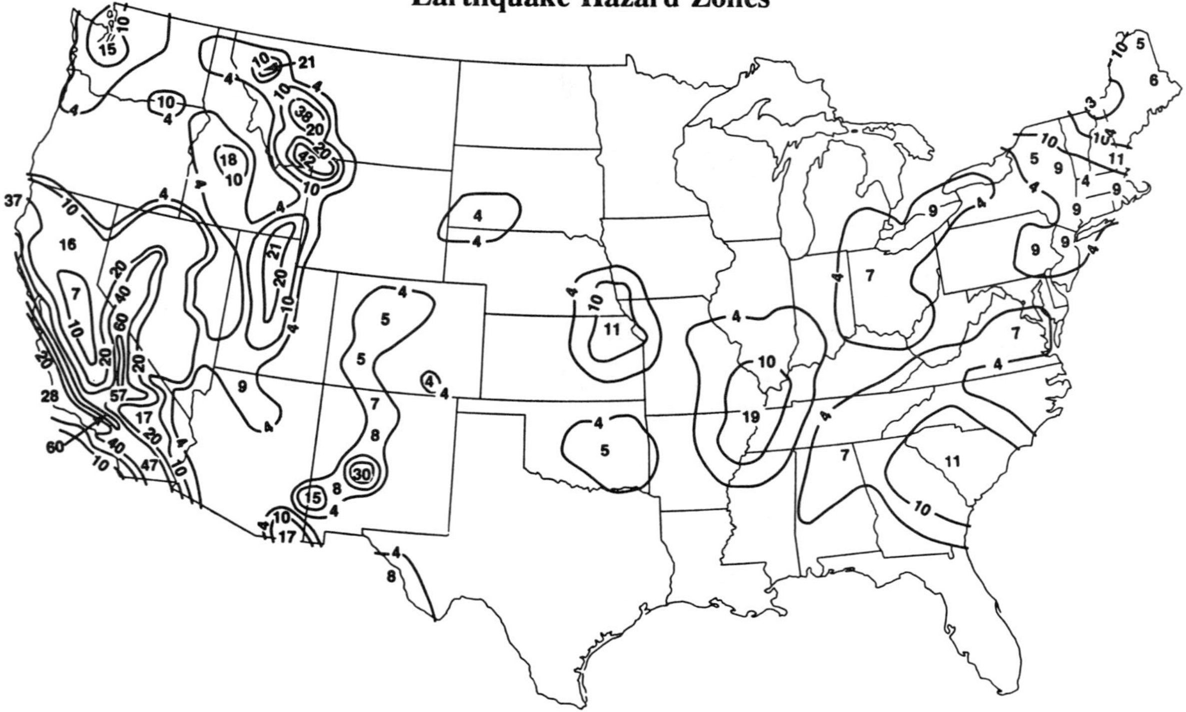

The higher the number, the greater the possibility of an earthquake, and the more severe it will be.

Source: *U.S. Geological Survey Open-File Report 76-416, 1976.*

If the places you're considering don't have first order weather stations, they may be one of the 1,063 locations with a cooperative station. That data is contained in *Climatography of the United States, Series 20*. It provides two-page publications for each location and can be ordered for $1 per location, plus a $5 shipping and handling charge from the address above.

## Health at the Crossroads

Tension and anxiety are proven killers. An overwhelming three-quarters of Americans say they live with a notable amount of stress in their lives. Few would disagree the stress level of people residing in a rural setting is lower than individuals trying to cope with today's urban madness. This is an enormous consideration when looking at overall health issues. Where you live affects more than just your sense of beauty and your wallet. It can also affect how long you live.

*Psychology Today* magazine did a study to determine cities with the lowest stress. Not surprisingly, they're smaller towns. They are: 1) State College, Pennsylvania; 2) Grand Forks, North Dakota; 3) St. Cloud, Minnesota; 4) Rochester, Minnesota; 5) McAllen/Pharr, Texas; 6) Altoona, Pennsylvania; 7) Bloomington, Indiana; and 8) Provo/Orem, Utah.

Americans will take their health more into their own hands in the '90s. We will see more emphasis on *wellness*, a lifestyle that reflects people striving for a balanced and preventive state of physical being. Middle-aged Americans will be doing fitness walking, biking, swimming, gentle exercise, and enjoying nature as they hike, camp, and bird watch. The bottom-line motivation will be maintaining weight, keeping fit, holding stress down, and preserving healthy organs—rather than weight loss.

### Evaluating Health Care

To evaluate health care in small towns you'll want to look at the ratio of doctors per capita. In some rural areas they are as low as 53 per 100,000—compared to 163 per 100,000 in urban areas. How far is the hospital? Does it have 24-hour a day emergency coverage? If sickness has been a frequent visitor, you may want to investigate if a teaching hospital, medical school, or VA hospital is within reasonable commuting distance. What are health care costs compared to what you're used to paying? How far is the dentist and optometrist? If you use chiropractic adjustment, be sure there's a chiropractor handy. And for some, a massage therapist or physical therapist is an important person. In other family situations, having a convalescent hospital, nursing home, or hospice nearby will be a consideration.

**Mildest and Wildest Metro Areas**

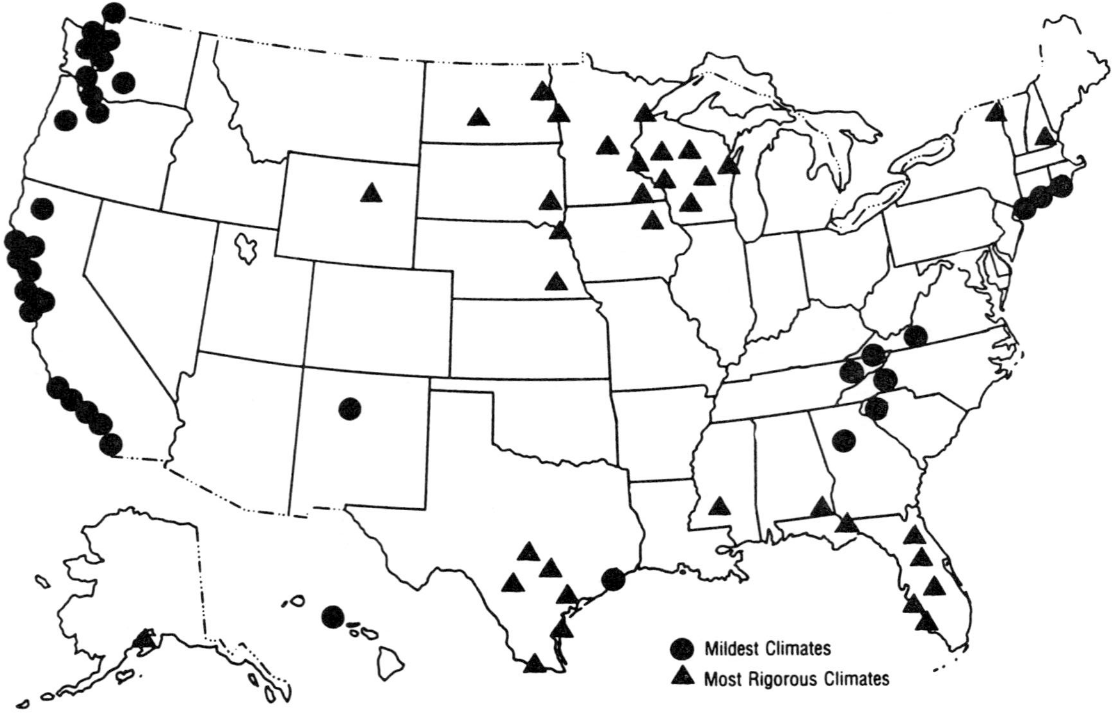

Source: PLACES RATED ALMANAC, Richard Boyer and David Savageau, 1989. Reprinted by permission of Prentice Hall Travel.

# Climatic Regions of the United States

Source: *PLACES RATED ALMANAC*, Richard Boyer and David Savageau, 1989. Reprinted by permission of Prentice Hall Travel.

Health care is one area where most small towns take a back seat to big cities. Physicians cluster in metropolitan areas where they will be well paid for their services. State-of-the-art medical facilities, high-tech equipment, personnel trained to use them, plus fascinating new procedures are all more abundant in larger metropolitan areas. Right now the statistics are still bleak: Nationwide there are 176 counties with no primary care doctor. And 13 percent of current country doctors are 65 or older.

The dwindling number of rural hospitals aggravates the problem. Doctors are reluctant to launch practices where they can't be associated with a local hospital. But as the demand mushrooms in rural America, and people with the means to care well for themselves increase, we see this as the cure for what ails both sides.

## Small Towns Court Creative Solutions

Already some small towns are taking innovative steps to attract quality medical care. Ashland, Maine, (population 3,000) made a deal to get a doctor. One of their residents, Roger Pelli, was very involved with the community—serving on the volunteer ambulance, in church, and with youth groups. He wanted to become a doctor but couldn't afford to support his family and go to medical school. The town needed a physician, as the closest doctor was 20 miles away. So Roger and the surrounding town councils developed a creative partnership. The townsfolk voluntarily raised their own taxes to send him to medical school and make him their doctor. He signed a contract to come back and practice medicine for a minimum of eight years. That was in August of 1982. Today he knows hundreds of his patients by name and even makes house calls around Ashland.

The little town of Weiser, Idaho, launched a mighty campaign to woo a physician to their community of 4,700 people. "It was a real grassroots effort," reports Phil Lowe, chairman of the Doctor Recruitment Committee and administrator of Memorial Hospital. "The whole community got involved. A wide spectrum of different professionals met regularly. People felt real ownership. We persisted until we were successful," he elaborates. To raise money to entice a doctor, the townsfolk held bake sales, auctions, and garage sales. They collected donations from private citizens, corporations and businesses, plus civic clubs.

With the help of Merritt Hawkins & Associates, a physician recruitment firm which did a pro bono search for them, they located Dr. Deland Barr in Kansas. They lured him with an all-expense paid trip and courted him like Romeo courted Juliet. He was greeted with a banner declaring "Welcome Dr. Barr," given a plane tour of the area, and afforded opportunities to visit with key people. Since it was homecoming week, he also attended the parade and game. (Indicative of the community's spirit, the home team won in overtime.) Impressed, Dr. Barr made a second trip, then signed a contract to come to Weiser to practice medicine.

"This was a textbook example of what a small town can do," explains Phil Miller of Merritt Hawkins & Associates. Weiser had realistic expectations of what they would have to pay a doctor and they emphasized the strength of a rural practice. They promoted the "high touch" caring opportunity and how a physician plays a pivotal role in a small town. They also did an economic impact study and discovered that their hospital was the area's second largest employer. Without a good doctor and a hospital they would be unable to attract new industry and would lose young families needing medical care.

Some states are also taking aggressive action to hike the waning number of rural doctors. Louisiana recently set aside $271,000 for grants to pay off the medical school debts of up to 20 doctors and eight nurses willing to practice in areas with shortages. And Arkansas provides tax incentives to doctors agreeable to setting up practices in its rural areas.

## Federal Government Targets More Answers

Federal health officials recently unveiled plans for a long overdue national Medicare physician fee schedule designed to pay family and general practice doctors more, and specialists less. The goal of the fee schedule revisions is to correct imbalances in Medicare payments to rural physicians. It will also correct inequities between primary-care doctors, those most needed in small towns, and specialists such as surgeons. By raising Medicare fees for rural and primary physicians, the government hopes to encourage doctors to practice in these areas.

The current system leads physicians away from rural areas and into higher-paying metropolitan locations. It also encourages doctors to specialize instead of opening family and general practices. A general practitioner treats diseases and injuries, provides preventive care, and gives routine checkups. They also perform some surgery, prescribe drugs, and refer patients to appropriate specialists when necessary. The following maps show the number of physicians per residents by state, plus the number of hospitals.

Unfair government programs, such as Medicare, that fail to account for rural-urban differences, have contributed to the closure of many country hospitals. Medicare pays 35 to 40 percent less for a service in a rural hospital than it does for the same service in an urban hospital. While the cost of living is lower in country settings, the cost of medical supplies is exactly the same. Consequently rural hospitals and physicians are not fully

# Comparison of Total Number of Urban and Rural Community Hospitals

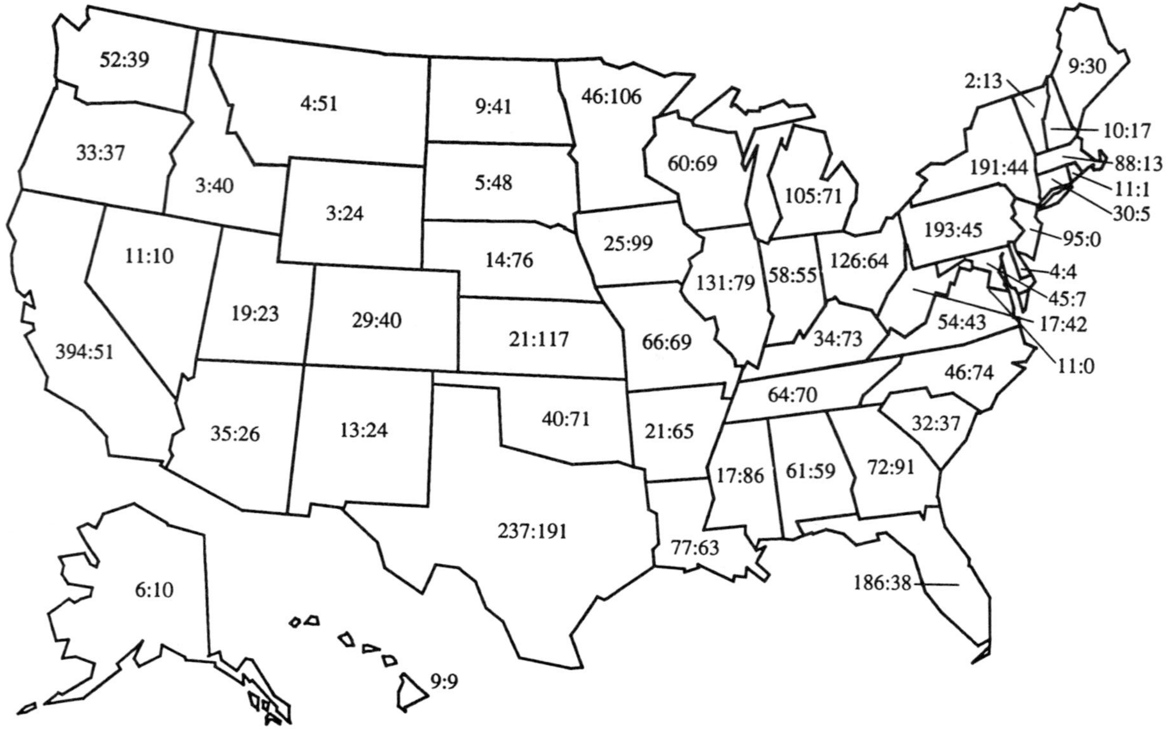

Source: *American Hospital Association Hospital Statistics, 1990 data.*

**Number of Physicians per 1,000 Residents by State**

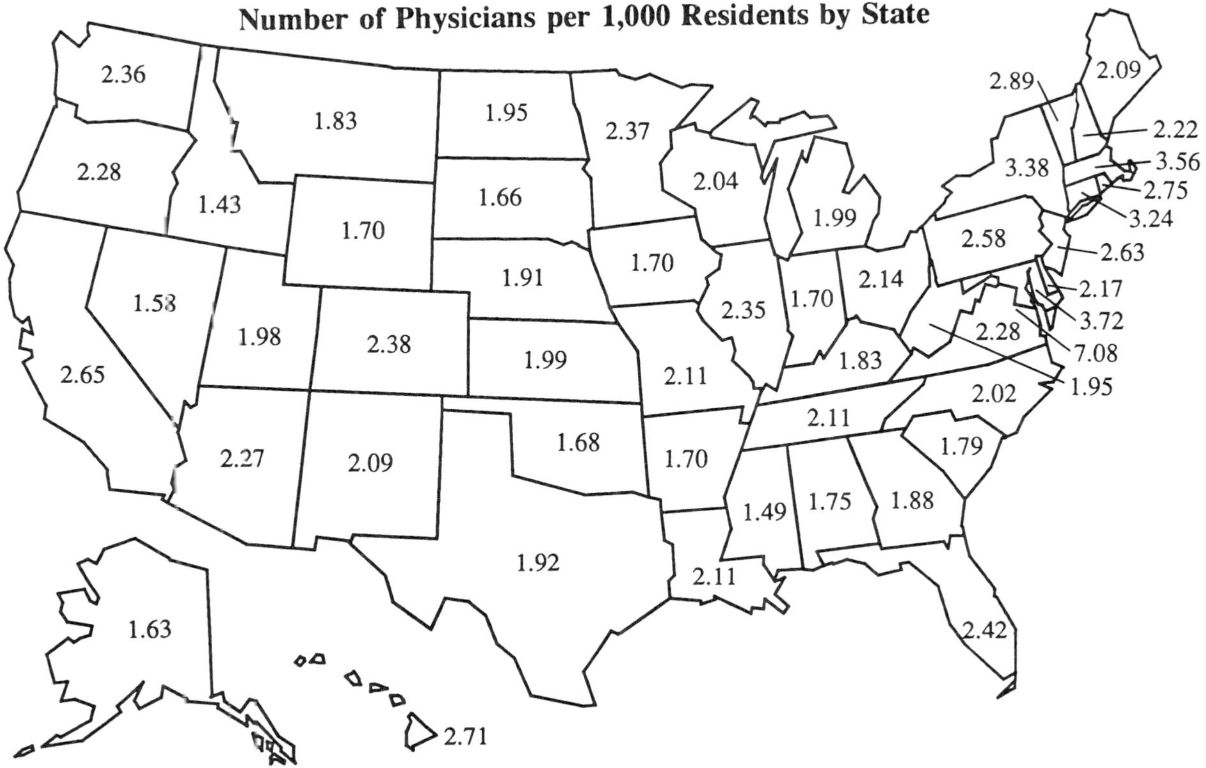

Source: *Calculated from U.S. Census Bureau 1990 figures and The American Medical Association 1989 data.*

reimbursed for treating Medicare patients. One physician computed his overhead per Medicare patient was $27 for a routine office visit. Yet Medicare paid him only $9.98. This is further compounded by the fact that the elderly comprise 12 percent of the total U.S. population, but account for 25.4 percent of the population in rural communities.

This, plus lower reimbursements from insurance companies and a high rate of patient nonpayment, makes it difficult to maintain essential services. Some full-scale hospitals have been downgraded to emergency centers, health clinics, or nursing facilities. Others have closed their doors.

Regional collaboration helps overcome some of the limitations of small size and limited scale. But it must be implemented in tandem with solving transportation needs. Other visionary planning ideas include scholarships to get doctors interested in the "outback," dispersing of residency programs into rural areas, and programs to help family physicians cover the cost of malpractice insurance. Many refuse to perform OB-GYN functions because their liability is enormous.

Another option is Physician's Assistants (PAs). We had two very capable PAs in First Try. While they were required to work under a doctor's supervision, the full M.D. was there just one day a week. There are over 22,000 PAs practicing medicine today in the United States.

As telecommunications and computer technology become more and more sophisticated, rural patients will also benefit. For instance, by the turn of the century it is expected rural hospitals can let big-city medical experts examine CAT scans and other sophisticated tests via video hookups.

Congress has finally become cognizant of the dire need for improved rural health care. A National Health Service Corps Revitalization bill, designed to encourage doctors to practice in rural areas, was recently passed.

## Answers for Environmental Illness and Allergies

Thousands of people suffer from Multiple Chemical Sensitivities or Environmental Illness (EI). They seek pristine surroundings free of toxic substances such as smog, molds, pollen, electromagnetic rays, industrial and agricultural poisons, and toxic waste dumps. The search is not easy. Many EI victims have relocated to Arizona, Idaho, and Washington to escape allergens. There are two rays of hope for people afflicted with Environmental Illness. One is Dr. Gunnar Heuser, a clinical ecologist with UCLA. Dr. Heuser can be reached at 805-497-3518. There is also a newsletter called *The Wary Canary* that addresses environmental health concerns. (See issues 6 and 7 for relocation tips). For subscription information, contact P.O. Box 2204, Ft. Collins, CO 80522, 303-224-0083.

Many more people endure troublesome allergies. Hay fever afflicts 18 million Americans. It's an allergic reaction to airborne particles. It is brought on by pollen from seed-bearing trees, grasses, and weeds (especially ragweed), plus spores from certain molds. These proliferate in the middle regions where grasses and flowerless trees dominate. Yes, hay fever hunkers down and waits for victims in America's heartland. The Southwest deserts used to attract asthmatics and hay fever sufferers. But as they become more populated, landscaping—and its accompanying problems—multiply. You can contact the American Academy of Allergy & Immunology at 611 E. Wells Street, Milwaukee, Wisconsin 53202-3349 or call their Physicians' Referral and Information Line, 800-822-2762. Alaska and the southern half of Florida are still havens for hay fever sufferers.

Some parts of the country are breeding grounds for unpopular creepy crawlers and flying fugitives. If certain insects cause you grief, inquire about such culprits as black widows, brown recluse spiders, scorpions, chiggers, mosquitoes, etc. For instance, our dog was close to resembling a Mexican hairless when we left San Diego. The flea problem was so severe she had practically scratched herself bald. Six months after we arrived in Colorado, Brindle had a full, glossy coat again.

Just where are the healthiest states? A Northwest National Life Insurance study ranks them according to lifestyle, access to health care, disability, disease, and mortality. Note the following State Health Rankings.

A final point before we leave this subject: let's discuss health insurance for a moment. If you don't qualify for public assistance and have a health problem with large potential financial exposure, where you live can be extremely important.

> Tom: *I have a chronic disease that insurance companies typically insist on excluding from coverage. Their excuse is the good old "pre-existing condition" ploy. Insurance coverage was going to cost about $600 a month! That is until Marilyn discovered the Colorado Uninsurable Health Insurance Plan. Now I pay $270 a month for a policy with Blue Cross.*

Not every state has such a benefit. Many state high-risk insurance pools have long waiting lists and don't offer economical coverage.

It's impossible to talk about health and not look at environmental problems. Many times our health deteriorates as a direct result of self-created dangers—insidious substances too tiny for the eye to see, yet capable of rendering humankind extinct unless they are controlled.

## The NWNL State Health Rankings

The Northwestern National Life Insurance study ranked healthiest states by criteria in five areas (* indicates a tie):

- **Lifestyle:** Smoking, motor vehicle deaths, violent crime, risk of heart disease, high school graduation.
- **Access to health care:** Unemployment, prenatal and primary care, public health care.
- **Disability:** Activity limitations, acute illnesses.
- **Disease:** Heart disease, cancer, infectious disease.
- **Mortality:** Total and infant; premature deaths.

| | | | |
|---|---|---|---|
| 1 | Hawaii | * | Wyoming |
| 2 | Minnesota | 27 | Oklahoma |
| 3 | Utah | 28 | Delaware |
| * | New Hampshire | * | Michigan |
| 5 | Nebraska | 30 | North Carolina |
| * | Wisconsin | * | Texas |
| 7 | Connecticut | 32 | Illinois |
| 8 | Iowa | * | Missouri |
| * | Kansas | * | New York |
| 10 | Colorado | 35 | Idaho |
| 11 | Maine | 36 | Georgia |
| * | Massachusetts | * | Kentucky |
| * | Virginia | * | Tennessee |
| 14 | Vermont | 39 | Oregon |
| 15 | New Jersey | 40 | Arizona |
| * | Rhode Island | * | Arkansas |
| 17 | North Dakota | 42 | Alabama |
| 18 | Indiana | * | Florida |
| 19 | Montana | 44 | Nevada |
| * | Ohio | * | South Carolina |
| * | Pennsylvania | 46 | Louisiana |

| 22 | California    | 47 | Mississippi   |
|----|---------------|----|---------------|
| 23 | Maryland      | *  | New Mexico    |
| *  | Washington    | 49 | Alaska        |
| 25 | South Dakota  | 50 | West Virginia |

Source: © *1991, The NWNL State Health Rankings, NWNL Insurance Co.. Reprinted with permission.*

## *Investigating Environmental Concerns*

About 20 years ago we started hearing a lot about pollution, contaminants, additives, acid rain, asbestos, chemical spills, nuclear meltdowns, ecology, rain forests, ecosystems, and environmental hazards. Before that few of us realized what was happening. We had no idea our world was being systematically raped. Until then we didn't know that unusually high rates of certain cancers had been linked directly to hazardous waste dumps, chemical spills, insecticides, industrial wastes, and other contaminants. That multinational business interests were lobbying the government to keep needed, but restrictive, legislation at bay. That as concerned individuals we could have an impact.

We ignored the clues like signs along the freeway warning of radar monitored speed checks; it wasn't until we saw the flashing red lights in our rear view mirrors that we realized the consequences of our apathy. Now the judge is in his chambers, and the ticket must be paid. We're now paying for molesting the balance God provided. Our children and grandchildren will pay an even greater price. Our great-grandchildren? Hopefully our belated actions will allow them to fare better. Air, earth, and water is the triangle upon which civilization rests. Without them, nothing else matters.

### 20th Century Tampering

While no part of the country is completely free of 20th century tampering, some have fared better than others. In its Green Index Report, the Institute for Southern Studies assesses the environmental health of all 50 states. They use 35 indicators in four general categories to draw conclusions. The results? New England, especially Vermont, is the most environmentally healthy part of the U.S. The South, led by Alabama, has the worst score—seizing nine of the 10 bottom spots.

If you want to really educate yourself, we'd suggest you get a copy of the *1991-1992 Green Index* by Bob Hall and Mary Lee Kerr. (You can order it from our "Bibliography/Recommended Reading.") It's a state-by-state guide to the nation's environmental health and is brimming with tables, maps, and little known facts. Our focus must be on saving our species on the planet earth.

Fortunately people are awakening. A Special Consumer Survey Report, conducted by The Conference Board in October of 1990, revealed that while only 65 percent felt pollution was a serious concern in 1989, the number had risen to 80 percent by 1990. Watery eyes, a runny nose, shortness of breath, mild chest pain—not to mention feeling like your throat and lungs are being seared—are earmarks of a heavy pollution day. They're as prevalent in big cities as ethnic restaurants. The top five violators of clean air standards are Los Angeles, Houston, New York, San Diego, and Atlanta.

As the decade matures, more and more of us will be *eco-settling*: giving it all up to go to a cleaner, healthier, safer place. For good. And for the good of our children. Being more conscious about the choices we make, we're destined to become more ecologically responsible in both our personal lives and our business dealings.

California, the ozone capital of the country, has announced a concept called the "LA Plan." It calls for over 120 measures affecting everything from barbecues to buses. By 2009 all autos would have to be electric or burn clean fuel.

The Environmental Protection Agency (EPA) sometimes finds its hands tied. Since the amendments, in 1990, to the Clean Air Act of 1970—there are now more regulations on air emissions, incinerators, and landfills. Industry still often sues, however, when the EPA strives to clean up our environment. The EPA's goal is healthy air throughout the country by the end of 2010. Possible fixes include tougher vehicle emission inspections, development of alternative fuels, and greater reliance on car pooling. In other areas, pollution standards are being discussed for wood stoves, which dirty the air in winter. Cuts in industrial hydrocarbon emissions is another area under investigation. Meanwhile . . . breathing may be hazardous to your health.

Of course, industry is a large contributor to pollution. Businesses that emit sulfur dioxide, carbon monoxide, nitrogen dioxide, smog, and lead are among the worst offenders, according to the EPA. For information on air-quality standards and any polluting source in areas you're considering, look in that locale's phone book for a local or state air pollution agency. Or call your regional branch of the EPA. They maintain an Emergency Planning and Community Right-To-Know Hotline at 800-535-0202. They report on polluted lakes and beaches, toxic waste sites, and contaminated landfills. And they're a referral service for information on local pollution rates, the major chemical culprits, and other resources. This is an excellent information source for urban opt-outs.

## The Twin Villains: Acid Rain and Odor

Acid rain was first thought harmful only to buildings. In the late 1960s it ate away details on stone and marble monuments around the world. Today it is known to pose grave danger to living creatures as well. The major cause of acid rain is the pollutant sulfur dioxide, a principal emission of coal burning. The effects of acid rain are seen predominantly in the Appalachian Mountains and along the eastern seaboard. Here trees are growing deformed limbs, producing inferior wood, and failing to ward off insects and disease. The effects of this sinister plague are widespread. Fishing and forests alike are threatened. Fishermen in the Atlantic noticed a rapid decline of striped bass. It seems water in their breeding and feeding grounds is now so acidic the larvae and eggs die most of the time. Other kinds of fish are also dwindling.

People with breathing or heart problems are also at greater risk. The almanac lists acid rain trouble areas (and hazardous waste site information) in the "Environment" section.

Another aspect of air pollution is odor. In some parts of the country taking a deep breath borders on being a masochistic act. Several towns vie for stench capital of the USA. So be sure *sniffing* is part of your relocation research! Clinton, Iowa, city administrator George Langmack explains, "Once you've experienced it, you can always refer to it as the dead animal odor from the rendering plant. When it's hot and humid and you get a direct shot, it will cause you to catch your breath in order to keep your supper."

Berlin, New Hampshire, has a nickname: "The city that paper built." The foul fumes from the paper plant used to be so bad the paint would actually peel from the houses. Today getting a whiff makes your eyes water and your lungs ache. Devils Lake, North Dakota, also has the diSTINKtion of reeking like a sewer. Says city commission President Berta Soper of the fiberglass manufacturing plant, "It's an industrial odor." Residents of Chillicothe, Ohio, think their town has a stench like decomposed bodies. Not so, contends city personnel manager Robert Wakefield. He says it "smells like money." And little Red Bay, Alabama, stinks like putrid dog food. The reason for the pungent smell is just that: dog food cooking. The factory works a lot of people in that town.

Let's face it: in some places the nose doesn't want to know! In others, the lure of sagebrush and eucalyptus are a welcome reprieve from big city garbage aroma.

## The Life Blood of Water

Water, water everywhere . . . and not a safe drop to drink. That could be our lament if things continue like they are. Almost 17 percent of the population drinks water with excessive amounts of lead, a heavy metal that impairs children's IQ and attention span and can cause high blood pressure and other health problems in adults. To get your questions answered about lead, call the EPA's safe drinking water hotline at 800-426-4791.

In the early summer, half the rivers and streams in America's Corn Belt are laced with unhealthy levels of pesticides. It's no secret that inept regulation, reckless land use, and irresponsible handling of chemicals are compromising the quality of the nation's drinking water.

Four out of five of the most hazardous waste dumps are leaking toxins into the groundwater. People living in New Jersey, New England, and the western mountain states face an additional threat. Radon, a radioactive gas that permeates groundwater, is found in these regions. The EPA estimates that in 38 states pesticides have already fouled the ground water used by half of all Americans as their main source of drinking water.

When checking out a water supply, look for groundwater that runs deep so it isn't likely to be contaminated by fertilizers, pesticides, mine tailings or microorganisms. Or there's another alternative. For several years we took our water from a high mountain stream. It was pure snow melt. There were no people nor mining operations above us. But even using such natural water has risks. A few people have been known to ingest a microorganism called giardia, which causes diarrhea and headaches and can linger for months. Of course, filters offer more pure water and bottled water is an option.

Some people contend that pesticide residues on produce are even more dangerous than hazardous waste dumps or air pollution! The lean chicken may be poisoned with salmonella. And the fish we've opted for in place of a steak may have spent its life swimming in an alphabet soup of toxic nightmares. An evaluation of sport fish taken from the Great Lakes found that nine out of 10 fish were tainted with levels of toxic chemicals. One in four contained levels regarded as harmful to humans.

Noise and big cities go together like salt and pepper. And noise pollution can also be unnerving and stressful. People in large cities learn to cope with ever-present clamor. But first time visitors to Manhattan are amazed by the constant honking of taxi horns, blaring of sirens, and clattering of garbage trucks.

In the country, serenity is precious. Noise pollution isn't a factor. To be honest, when we go into major cities to speak, or meet with clients or the media, we have to steel ourselves to cope with the pandemonium. At busy restaurants, large social functions, or conventions, we end up feeling flogged by the noise—physically buffeted by an invisible negative vibration. Noise can make you feel weary in a hurry.

Before we leave the environment, there is one further point to address: nuclear power. Think about how you'd feel living near a nuclear power plant. (See the following map showing their locations.) While Three Mile Island and Chernobyl are isolated cases, a catastrophic meltdown or low-level environmental contamination are legitimate concerns. At the end of 1988 the U.S. had 110 nuclear electric plants licensed to operate. New England, as a region, has the most reactors, although Illinois has more than any other state. As electric energy needs soar, this power source may again become popular to meet the pending power crisis.

If you're interested in receiving the most up-to-date information possible, consider subscribing to our *The Country Bound!*™ *Connection.* This is a newsletter detailing country trends, employment ideas, relocation and real estate tips. You can order it for an annual subscription rate of $89 from Communication Creativity, P.O. Box 909, Buena Vista, CO 81211.

# *Putting Leisure in Your Life*

Leisure, like the happy and sad masks of the theater, runs a wide gamut. There are the more sophisticated cultural pursuits, the arts. And there are recreational activities, entertainment, and nature's bounty. What's interesting is that the new breed of urban to rural migrants are as inclined to show up at a country fiddling contest or a community event as they are to attend the ballet or a chamber music performance.

## A Dollop of Culture, My Dear?

Nowhere but New York City will you find 49 art museums, 34 professional theaters, 26 orchestras, 14 professional opera companies . . . and a partridge in a pear tree (say what?). But frankly, who needs it? How many times do you partake of each? Many of us find stimulation and enjoyment at the other end of the spectrum.

All across America the lively arts are struggling to survive. Because of increased competition and a severe drop in government funding, they are becoming endangered species just like the spotted owl and the Florida panther. Symphonies are filing for bankruptcy or cancelling their seasons. Most professional theaters are operating in the red. Major ballet companies are merging in an effort to endure. Museums are cutting back on their hours.

# Commercial Nuclear Power Reactors in the United States
## (31 December 1990)

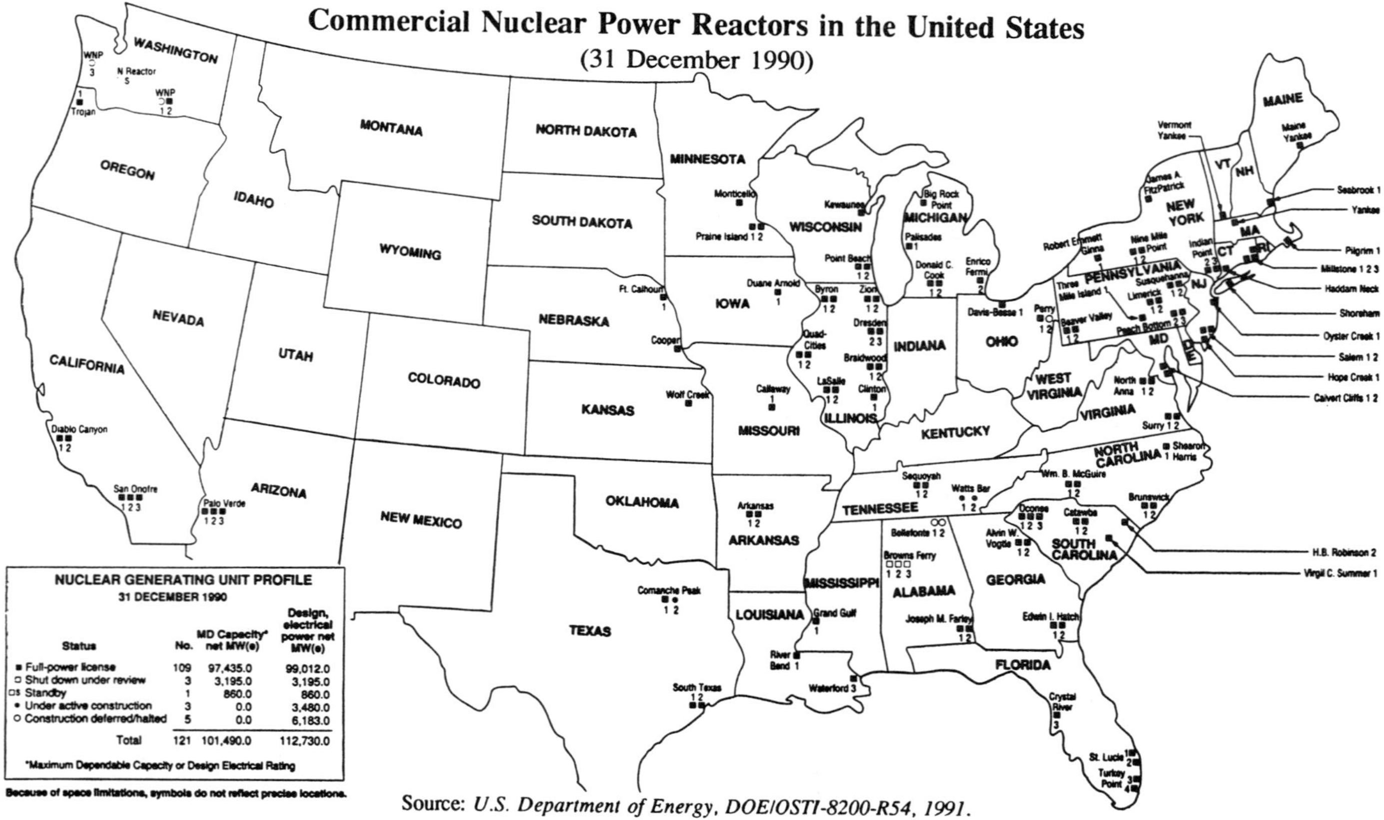

| NUCLEAR GENERATING UNIT PROFILE 31 DECEMBER 1990 |||||
|---|---|---|---|---|
| Status | | No. | MD Capacity* net MW(e) | Design, electrical power net MW(e) |
| ■ Full-power license | | 109 | 97,435.0 | 99,012.0 |
| □ Shut down under review | | 3 | 3,195.0 | 3,195.0 |
| ☐ Standby | | 1 | 860.0 | 860.0 |
| ● Under active construction | | 3 | 0.0 | 3,480.0 |
| ○ Construction deferred/halted | | 5 | 0.0 | 6,183.0 |
| Total | | 121 | 101,490.0 | 112,730.0 |

*Maximum Dependable Capacity or Design Electrical Rating

Because of space limitations, symbols do not reflect precise locations.

Source: *U.S. Department of Energy, DOE/OSTI-8200-R54, 1991.*

Small town museums house works of considerably less value, but the docents are intimately familiar with the displays and infinitely more cordial. Art galleries? They're likely to be the walls of restaurants. (Sometimes the "finds" are astonishing.) Here in Buena Vista we have several art shows during the year. They feature all sorts of media and many works I'd be proud to have in my home. Last summer the grassy lawn of a local restaurant was the setting of a Sunday brunch and outdoor jazz concert. There's a lively square dance every other Saturday night, and the area pubs don't need much of an excuse to bring in a band. As we write this, a touring ballet company is performing The Nutcracker in the nearby town of Salida. Local churches bring in musicians and speakers. In fact one of our churches recently brought in noted actor Anthony Zerbe to speak and perform a reading. We were thrilled!

In the summertime, festivals sprout like mushrooms in rural America. They celebrate everything from ethnic holidays and customs to harvest time and religious events. Here we have the annual Burro Festival, complete with amateur and professional burro races. And our Folklife Festival features wonderful entertainment, booths, food, and fun. Small town summer diversions also often center around bandboxes, gazebos, or pavilions where local musical groups perform.

In case you're wondering what else there is to do in a small town, we just received the chamber of commerce event schedule for next year. Here are some highlights: Optimists Club Talent Show, Moonlight Ski Tours, Gun Club Gun Show, Snowmobile Rally, and the Trout Creek Pass Marathon Run. Then there's the opening of the Court House Art Gallery, performances of the Annual Melodrama, Collegiate Peaks Enduro Dirt Bike Race, and the Quilt Show—which overflows with exquisite handmade items each year. Next comes an Old Fashioned Fourth of July Celebration, Mountain Mania Annual Car Show, Collegiate Peaks Stampede Rodeo, and the Rock and Gem Show. In September the Autumn Color 5 and 20 K Walk/Run beckons fitness buffs to enjoy the changing leaves. And this is all happening in a town of only 2,000 residents!

In our headlong rush to abandon the big city must we also forsake artistic and intellectual fare? Not really. The Public Broadcasting Service is available in most areas. PBS can typically be accessed by way of cable. A flick of a switch brings The Bard, opera, symphony, programs on science and the universe, even engrossing children's shows. Programming has artistic, educational, and cultural merit. And we wake up to National Public Radio (NPR) each morning. The news is global and thorough, the interviews enlightening, the music delightful.

Another wonderful resource is the public library. Many loan everything from videos to CDs, books on tape to the latest best-sellers. Virtually all participate in interlibrary loan programs so they can usually get whatever you want. If you have youngsters, investigate the children's story hours. And if there isn't a great books or best-seller discussion group, perhaps you could start one.

## The Sporting Life

Entertainment, of course, needn't be highbrow. More people like sports than cultural activities. (Though by the turn of the century futurists predict this will change.) While you won't be in the stands rooting for the Washington Redskins, the Chicago Bulls, or the Los Angeles Dodgers from your rural eden—there are other alternatives.

If you settle in a college town, some darn good football and basketball spectating may be in the offing. Collegiate sports are big crowd pleasers. And it needn't be just the most touted sports. You can watch tennis tournaments, swim meets, wrestling matches, and gymnastic competitions—not to mention track and field events.

Rooting for the home team can also be fun at the high school level.

> Marilyn: *I always thought wrestling was like the grunting, gaudy baboons on TV . . . until we went to a high school wresting meet. Then I discovered it as a true sport and got caught up cheering for our neighbor's son, right along with Tom.*

Other possibilities are that a minor league or semipro team may play in or near your new town. They're like margarine is to butter: Not the real thing, but a good imitation . . . and a lot cheaper.

If you're a big baseball fan, consider relocating to Arizona or Florida. That's where the spring training camps are located for the major league baseball teams. The Cactus League rendezvous in Arizona and the Grapefruit League, in Florida. Imagine watching as Nolan Ryan develops his pitching style, Tony Gwynn hones his batting ability, or Cecil Fielder whips his first base skills into shape.

Many of us want to actively participate in sports. While in the country, you're not likely to find a posh private country club with a valet to park your car—there's lots of good golf available though. It isn't miles and miles away and you don't have to make reservations weeks in advance to get a good tee time. With 23 million golfers, the demand for courses dictates that even most tiny towns have facilities.

Tennis, anyone? You bet! Not all courts are lit at night, however, and there may not be indoor facilities. You could also find yourself playing at the local high school during off hours when the students don't need the courts. Racquetball may also be a possibility. For instance, here in Buena Vista, we're currently considering building a recreation complex that will house tennis and racketball courts.

Softball is big in many rural areas. Teams are sponsored by local merchants, and games are lively. This is a good way to get acquainted quickly with the other jocks in the community. Tournament competition can be fierce and the winning team revered in the community. Of course, there are the usual teams for youngsters.

Bowling is another rural pastime. Towns from about 5,000 up usually have a tenpin bowling center. This is not only good family fun, but many adults join teams (another good way to get acquainted) and participate in tournaments. Once considered strictly a blue-collar, indoor sport, today doctors are prescribing it for older adults and as therapy for many ailments.

Sporting enthusiasts will appreciate a survey conducted by *Outside Magazine*. Out of the Top 10 Sporting Towns they picked, six are small U.S. communities. Here they are in no particular order: Moab, Utah; Bend, Oregon; Talkeetna, Arkansas; Bozeman, Montana; Bishop, California; and Leavenworth, Washington.

## Recreation and the Pursuit of Nature

There's lots to do besides sports. Going to the movies is as American as apple pie. If it is an amusement you expect to do a lot, be sure your proposed community has at least one movie theater. Many tiny towns don't. It isn't economical. When we lived in First Try (population 500) a family moonlighted from their day jobs and opened the movie each Friday and Saturday night. Here there is no movie and the population is about 2,000. However, we have two video stores and a roller skating rink the kids love.

Maybe you're among the one in 10 people who enjoys going out to dinner at least once a week. Check out the cuisine scene. In rural areas it isn't easy to find restaurants that combine the three ideals: quality food, good service, and a pleasant atmosphere. That isn't easy anywhere these days unless you're in a five star eatery. Before you decide it's impossible, however, visit our "Talk of the Town Cafe" and nearby, "The Prospector" in Leadville or the "Country Bounty" in Salida. You can find diners where the cook makes food as tasty as grandma does and serves portions fit for a lumberjack. And you can find menus with imagination: like "Jan's Restaurant's" chuck wagon soup and fuzzy navel pie . . . a combination of peaches and orange juice. You could be as lucky as we are and find a waitress so conscientious she calls you when the daily special is your favorite.

Country recreation offers a wondrous kaleidoscope of options.

A body of water—and all the pleasures it can deliver—is usually close at hand. Water sports abound. In the summertime that may be swimming, fishing, water skiing, jet skiing, wind sailing, or various kinds of boating. Winter in cold climates turns a pond into an ice skating rink. And some folks love ice fishing. Of course, if there's snow that means both downhill and cross-country skiing, sledding, snowmobiling, sleigh rides, and rambunctious snowball fights.

The great outdoors has something for everyone. It ranges from the less strenuous (pleasure drives, sightseeing, photography, nature walks, picnicking, bird-watching, camping, and fishing) to the more active (hiking, backpacking, running, biking, mountain climbing, and white water rafting).

The U.S. is graced with an abundance of national forests, parks, and wildlife refuges. Over a quarter of a million miles of paved roads crisscross national forests. They lead to such destinations as marinas, ski lodges, privately operated resorts, plus great fishing, camping, and hiking. The purpose of the parks is to protect the natural beauty from an onslaught of thoughtless chain saw users and capitalists wanting to take advantage of the splendor. In the process, the forest service grows and harvests wood.

We have the oldest national park system in the world. Its mission is to preserve irreplaceable geographic and historic treasures for public recreation. (See the adjacent map of National Parks and Recreation Areas if you want to locate near one.) State areas range from small day-use parks in wooded areas to beaches to large rugged parks with hiking trails and developed campsites. Most state recreation areas offer older visitors reduced entrance fees.

If you want to view flora and fauna up close, head for a national wildlife refuge. There are 477 of them sprinkled around the country. This is a perfect place to observe and photograph birds, animals, and plants. And many of the refuges have visitor centers with fascinating displays about the inhabitants.

But you needn't depend on designated outdoors spots. In the country, the world is your oyster.

Spending time with nature—from backyard gardening to wilderness trekking—helps us feel less stressed. Dr. Roger Ulrich, a professor of urban and regional planning at Texas A&M, conducted a study in which he showed students slides of trees, plants, water, and city scenes. The students reported the nature scenes, especially those containing water, made them feel more elated and relaxed. In contrast, the urban scenes tended to elicit

# National Parks and Recreation Areas

Source: *National Park Service*.

sadness and fear. Further evidence was presented when electroencephalograph readings of the students' brain-wave activity showed significantly stronger alpha waves when viewing nature scenes.

Why is the earth's bounty so soothing? It gives us a feeling of connectedness. There is an invitation to care for something other than yourself. Exposure to other living things is deeply satisfying and pleasurable. And many of us associate nature with good times. Maybe we found a wild orchard and enjoyed the tasty pleasure of a harvest for which we had neither planned nor worked. Or we visited a grandparent's or aunt and uncle's farm when we were kids. Memories of gathering eggs, riding a friendly old horse, shelling peas on the back porch, and perhaps trying to milk a cow, still warm our hearts.

We can give such memories to our children on a daily basis. For a small-town child, little things seem larger, more magnificent. The sun glistening on early morning dew that has been caught in a well-engineered spider web is a unique delight. So is a nest containing robin's eggs—and the antics of the ensuing tiny birds. Crops planted—tended—harvested are lessons in life. There are no bag ladies and no racial tension. Excitement comes in different doses: making a dam in the stream and cooling soda pops or watermelon for a summer snack; building a jump trail for dirt bikes; having deer look in your windows while you're eating dinner. These replace (or augment) excursions to zoos, aquariums, and expensive theme parks.

Think of your leisure as a block of marble waiting to be shaped and yourself as a sculptor. Will you mold it with culture and the arts? Recreation? Sports? Entertainment? Nature? We hope the country will enrich your life with new experiences and expectations, that it will allow you to shape a more satisfying destiny.

## *Evaluating an Area's Infrastructure*

This represents the underlying foundation or basic framework of a community. It embraces the demeanor of a town: whether it welcomes newcomers, is formal or laid back, conservative or liberal. Small towns can be either proud or decaying. Some are *Mayberry RFDs*, others more like *Peyton Places*. As you evaluate them, tune in to their attitudes towards planning and growth. In this discussion of infrastructure we will also help you address the topics of education and transportation.

## Population Trends and Planning Approaches

Few places remain the same for long. Either they progress or regress. Some grow fast, some slowly, some not at all. Others lose ground. Young people leave, businesses fail, storefronts are boarded up.

Especially if you intend to operate a business dependent on the area economy, you need to know a county's policy toward growth. Talk with the planning commissioners. Ask to review recent meeting minutes. Request a copy of any master plan. Do the planning kingpins demonstrate a willingness to support a high level of activity? Is this an area on the grow? Will its primary characteristics remain constant? (Or is it being re-positioned, for instance, as a retirement haven?)

What's the work ethic like? Is this a thriving community with an eager work force? Is local business and government leadership open to change? Is there an adequate phone system? Without up-to-date switching equipment, you may encounter complications operating a fax machine, punching in extension numbers on long distance phone calls, and using a modem.

In our nation, telephone service is, for the most part, a given. It tends to be one of the last concerns of a relocating countrypreneur.

> Tom: *Sure, we noticed our pristine ranch land didn't have phone lines. No problem. We set up a meeting with the then Mountain Bell to discuss our phone requirements. After an hour or so of adding machines clicking and computers humming we were informed Mountain Bell could install lines to meet our requirements for $60,000. Well it's a gross understatement to say Marilyn nearly fainted and I contracted severe heartburn!*
>
> *But, being an engineer as well as an entrepreneurial spirit, I resolved to come up with something more feasible. A couple of weeks later, after a short recovery period, I devised an alternative to Ma Bell's scheme. And we decided to go ahead with our plans to buy the land, knowing that if my ideas didn't work out, we could always pull lines from town for 60K.*
>
> *After months of engineering analysis, trial, and error, we determined we could use the Motorola Pulsar 4 mobile telephone—given to us by a good samaritan—in conjunction with a high gain antenna perched atop a 100-foot tower.*
>
> *In theory it worked. In practice, it worked 50 percent of the time—not good for a consulting service completely dependent on mail and telephone service. However, we got by. As adaptable beings we tend to accept things after awhile. We were doing okay*

*and we maintained a telephone in town for long conversations, conference calls, and critical communications.*

*Except for the fact that I was now spending approximately 50 percent of my time re-engineering—and repairing—our systems, life settled down to normal in unbelievably beautiful surroundings. From our window we could look up Bear Creek nearly to the Continental Divide. It seemed you could see forever. The eagles swooped, soared, and played in a sky so blue it seemed the creation of an artist's mind. Well, it was—the greatest artistic Mind of all!*

*For months we went about our routine in a semi-orderly manner—until one day a Mountain Bell truck arrived at our front door. After asking us about how our service was performing and saying how much they appreciated our business—probably the largest monthly mobile telephone bills in recorded history!—the representative nonchalantly mentioned they were going to move the base antenna. "We don't really feel it will affect your reception much, but we'll keep in touch. We certainly want to make sure we maintain your service," he assured us.*

*A few days later we got a call from another Ma Bell rep checking signal quality and clarity. After recording these he said, "Now we are going to switch antennas." That's the last word we ever heard over our mobile telephone link. And because our system was beyond the specified reception range to begin with, we had no recourse with the phone company. Silence fell. By this time our aforementioned folly of the historic hotel and restaurant had siphoned off the $60,000 needed to install lines. Now what? . . .*

*As we strolled down our country lane, like we had hundreds of times before, Marilyn confided concerns about continuing our present remote lifestyle. With what could have been a tear in the corner of my eye—or maybe it was due to the brisk breeze we were walking into—I murmured, "Honey, I guess it's time to leave."*

So don't take things for granted. Check them out. We were so happy with real phone lines when we moved to Buena Vista that we overlooked the fact the lines were going through a complex conversion system to make them work on the pulse-modulated lines of today. This made fax use tricky and was very aggravating when trying to interface with the multitudes of current voice mail.

Fortunately this story has a happy ending. In December of 1991, U S West Communications (formerly Mountain Bell) threw the switch to activate the new switching system. Now we're just like downtown Los Angeles—except for no smog, no traffic, and we have a clear view of the 14,000-foot peaks to the west. Oh well, we can't have everything. Thank God.

## The ABCs of Education

If you have children, the quality of their education is probably a major concern. There's a lot to be said for small town schools. The teacher-pupil ratio is usually smaller. Teachers get to really know their students and take into consideration personal situations. In a metropolitan setting educators typically aren't aware if parents are divorcing, or there is a grave illness in the family that might be affecting how Janie or Johnny is performing.

Computers and cable TV are also coming to the rescue of country schools that couldn't offer advanced, sophisticated training. Thanks to cable hookups, students can now take advanced courses in calculus, astronomy, and English, for instance.

Rural doesn't have to mean rinky-dink. Take Harrison, Arkansas: With a population of 9,567 this mountain town is one of the lowest-spending school districts in the country. Yet their test scores are in the top 10 percent nationally and high school graduates go off to prestigious places like Harvard, Princeton, Georgetown, and MIT. Furthermore their band is so good it has been invited to Washington for presidential inaugurals. What's the secret? High expectations. Parent involvement. Teacher empowerment. Site-based management. Community support.

Parents volunteer in their kids' classrooms. Honor Cards, good for discounts or free services at 52 local businesses, are presented for good grades. Parents and teachers collaborate to determine goals, then publish them via ads in the *Harrison Times*. Beginning in junior high, kids are encouraged to become comfortable taking college admission exams. By the time they're seniors, the SAT and ACT are old friends. This is a town where everyone works together to educate kids!

Another small town success story revolves around the schoolhouse itself. It is the heart of the community in tiny Milford, New York. Besides the 40 classrooms used daily for students, it also houses the Boy Scouts, Girl Scouts, dance lessons, alumni basketball, the Rotary Club, the theater group . . . but it almost didn't exist. The children were almost bussed two hours a day to another school. A bond issue to pay for a new school failed miserably in 1984. That's understandable in a town where the typical household earns $14,780 annually and only about 30 percent of the homes have kids.

But school administrators and concerned citizens finally convinced voters the town needed a school. The community pulled together and grew together . . . then when the new school opened in September of 1988 morale skyrocketed. The new school has advanced science labs and a theater that rivals off-Broadway facilities (pitched floors, upholstered seats, and a huge stage). Each classroom is wired for computers and cabled for video. Determination and cooperation won out. Today Milford students go off proudly to exclusive colleges like Yale and Cornell.

Are you looking for the ideal school? An Ohio company called SchoolMatch (800-992-5323) will use their database of nearly 16,000 school districts to ferret out 15 school systems that come closest to meeting your needs. You pay them $97.50, complete a questionnaire citing your priorities, and the computer spits out customized suggestions. Company President William Bainbridge says the most important measure of a school district's success comes as a surprise to most people. Rather than the tax base or property values, it's the educational level of parents and the amount of money spent on library and media services.

The training of our youth is perhaps our greatest challenge. Nationally only three-fourths of ninth graders eventually graduate from high school. Because many public school districts are failing to educate their charges, private schools are a thriving alternative.

One out of nine school-aged children attends a private school. Private school applications have risen almost 33 percent from 1990. The vast majority of these schools are run by various religious groups. They dispense spiritual training along with rigorous education and are known for smaller classes and pupils scoring higher on SATs. Surprisingly enough, many small towns have good private schools. While tuitions' national average is $6,400 a year, rural offerings charge quite a bit less. In our town a small private church school charges $1,340 per year for grades 1-12.

Education is in the midst of a revolution. "Increasingly independent and assertive teachers, striving for empowerment, are in the forefront of the simmering upheaval," reports the November 21, 1991, issue of *John Naisbitt's Trend Letter*. Naisbitt predicts a wave of the future is that a handful of teachers will become private practitioners. This is already happening in Milwaukee where 50 such pioneers work with public and parochial schools to deliver entire instruction programs in such areas as foreign languages and remedial education. This may be a viable alternative for small rural school districts that have problems attracting qualified instructors for specific programs.

Another alternative is home schooling. Some parents are taking the education of their children into their own hands and turning out knowledgeable and self-reliant young people. If this appeals to you, the following magazines are excellent: *The Teaching Home*, *Home Education Magazine*, and *Growing Without Schooling*.

## Transportation Tradeoffs

Getting to and from work is one of the greatest deterrents to living in the city. Commuting—which runs from approximately 7:00 to 9:00 in the mornings and 4:30 to 7:00 in the evenings—is a fact of life for millions of Americans. Commuting time increases with city size. Those needing to reach New York City spend an average of an hour and 21 minutes getting to and from work. That equals almost 39 eight-hour days each year!

Ribbons of interlacing freeways await others who wage a daily battle with gridlock. According to the Federal Highway Commission, congestion on the nation's freeways will be four times worse in twenty years. In Houston, where the Southwest Freeway is known to be one of the most grueling, they are proposing building a 24-lane freeway. It would make the west section of Loop 610 the widest in the world. Those who drive in larger cities have their lives further complicated by parking tabs that are as high as $390 per month in Manhattan.

Millions of others climb aboard grimy cars to join the legions of subway straphangers. Big city travel options include driving or taking a bus, subway, or railroad. We have a client who even catches a ferryboat to work.

Contrast this to country meanderings. The tension of competing with hundreds of thousands of other commuters is a thing of the past. Here human legs are often the preferred means of travel. (This is a much more ecologically sound solution: pedestrians rely on food for fuel.) Some bicycle to work. A few even ride horses. And if you do drive, it typically takes less than five minutes from your doorstep to the portals of work.

A disadvantage of small towns is that some do not have any means of public transportation. Whereas buses and taxis are taken for granted in the city, they are not a given in Small Town USA. Especially for those who don't drive, it is important to determine that a shuttle service or some reliable method of local transportation exists. (For those seeking to establish a rural business, a void in this category may be an opportunity begging to be filled.)

Getting *in* and *out* of your rural paradise may be less than perfect. Most small towns are a distance from major airports. While many are served by feeder airlines, it can cost almost as much to get from your locale to the principal airport, as it does to fly across country. If business travel plays an important part in your everyday life, bear this in mind when relocating.

Speaking of business concerns, proximity to interstate highways and airline facilities may also influence the cost of delivery of goods. Furthermore, with the merger of Greyhound and Trailways, bus service to remote places has been curtailed. The inescapable conclusion? Maximum mobility is diminished in rural locations. Many people feel the benefits outweigh this inconvenience.

Now that you've had an opportunity to gauge your move quotient by these seven criteria, let's move on to practical advice on how to turn the dream into reality.

# 3

# Turning the Dream into Reality

Some people plan meticulously for a two-week vacation . . . yet don't thoroughly educate themselves for making lifestyle decisions that affect their whole future. In this and the following chapters, you'll find hundreds of information nuggets to help you successfully turn your dream into reality. To make that job easier, we share many strategies and tips to simplify your investigation into rural relocation. Knowing too much is far better than not knowing enough.

"Most people's planning process lasts from six months to six years," reports William L. Seavey, director of the Greener Pastures Institute, a quality of life consulting organization. Seavey, who also publishes a newsletter dedicated to the search for countryside edens called the *Greener Pastures Gazette*, has noticed a growth trend over the last five years. "There's no mass exodus," he observes, "but a continued migration of retirees. And young professional types now see it as possible. There are definitely more interstate moves going on today."

His *Greener Pastures Gazette* is packed with useful tips. So is *Small Town Observer,* edited and published by Tom Evons. This meaty quarterly magazine helps those who want to flee big cities and rediscover America's heartlands. It profiles inviting individual small towns and includes personal stories from people who moved there. With special emphasis on the

Northwest, it also includes relocation hints, ads, listings of special events, etc. (For subscription information on both of these publications, see the newsletters and magazines part of the "Bibliography/Recommended Reading" section.)

As you fashion a new future remember each of us wears a set of psychologically ground eyeglasses. The prescription includes our likes and dislikes, fears and joys, good and bad experiences—plus some truly distorted information. Being fair to yourself requires that you recognize your biases and correct any misinformation you've acquired.

## *Cashing Out with Your Urban Equity*

You need capital to make your dream come true. There are as many ways to generate cash as there are flavors of Baskin-Robbins ice cream. But for the person seeking to move to the booming backwaters and purchase or set up a rural business, some are more viable than others. We'll explore and exploit all those methods in a future chapter, "Generating Capital to Launch Your Venture." Here we address the most natural avenue for funding your move: your urban real estate.

## *Four Walls and a Small Fortune*

Assuming you're a homeowner, the most obvious money source is to cash in on your home equity. If you own valuable real estate, you can apply 20th century fiscal savvy by selling your expensive urban property and setting up shop in the country. Many of the people reading this book bought their homes several years ago. This real estate has appreciated at a mind-boggling rate. These windfall profits can be huge for property owners in most bigger cities.

The best way to turn paper profit into actual earnings is to sell and leave the city. If you stay in your present area and maintain your standard of living, you'll be spending about the same amount you gained. (Perhaps *more* by the time you consider paying middleman fees for mortgages, lawyers, surveys, closing costs, and real estate commissions.)

By moving further afield, however, the money you'll gain from your city property sales will be more substantial. Let's look at some figures from the Home Price Comparison Index by Coldwell Banker Residential. (See the following table.) The typical home profiled has approximately 2,200 square feet, 4 bedrooms, 2 ½ baths, a family room (or equivalent), and a 2-car garage. The home and neighborhood are typical for a corporate middle manager.

*Trade Your Business Suit Blues for Blue Jean Dreams™*

Going from Bergen County, New Jersey, ($320,625) to Ft. Smith, Arkansas, ($95,590) means you'd have an excess of $225,035. Take out what's owed on the old mortgage and chances are you'll still have a respectable nest egg for going into business. The contrast between a Chicago area house and one in Evansville, Indiana, is even more extreme: $491,667 versus $89,575. That leaves a whopping $402,092 to play around with! Who ever said "be it ever so *humble*, there's no place like home?"

## COMPARABLE HOME PRICE INFORMATION SHOWN IN EACH COMMUNITY

| STATE | MARKET | 1990 PRICE | DAYS ON MARKET** | INDEX*** |
|---|---|---|---|---|
| ALABAMA | Birmingham | $121,000 | B | 61 |
| | Mobile | 116,833 | A | 58 |
| | Montgomery | 107,250 | B | 54 |
| ALASKA | Anchorage | 152,625 | A | 77 |
| | Fairbanks | 120,807 | A | 61 |
| | Juneau | 150,167 | A | 75 |
| ARIZONA | Mesa | 114,500 | A | 58 |
| | Phoenix | 120,750 | A | 61 |
| | Scottsdale | 160,083 | C | 80 |
| | Tempe | 139,905 | B | 70 |
| | Tucson | 145,875 | A | 73 |
| ARKANSAS | Fort Smith | 95,775 | A | 48 |
| | Little Rock | 112,875 | B | 57 |
| CALIFORNIA | Fremont | 390,000 | A | 196 |
| | Fresno | 143,850 | A | 72 |
| | Modesto | 225,094 | A | 113 |
| | Monterey Peninsula | 390,500 | B | 196 |
| | Oakland/Montclair | 383,500 | A | 193 |
| Northern California | Pleasanton | 349,700 | A | 176 |
| | Sacramento | 278,488 | A | 140 |
| | San Francisco | 615,000 | A | 309 |
| | San Jose | 383,625 | A | 193 |
| | San Mateo | 567,500 | B | 285 |
| | San Rafael | 370,000 | B | 186 |
| | Walnut Creek | 329,875 | A | 166 |
| | Beverly Hills | 1,491,667 | C | 749 |
| | Encinitas | 300,250 | A | 151 |
| | La Jolla | 686,625 | B | 345 |
| | Long Beach | 436,250 | A | 219 |
| Southern California | Mission Viejo | 291,833 | B | 147 |
| | Newport Beach | 606,667 | A | 305 |
| | Palos Verdes | 533,333 | B | 268 |
| | Riverside | 200,750 | B | 102 |
| | San Marino | 639,000 | A | 321 |
| | San Diego | 242,750 | B | 122 |
| | Temecula | 194,667 | B | 98 |
| COLORADO | Colorado Springs | 125,450 | A | 63 |
| | Denver | 120,025 | A | 60 |
| | Fort Collins | 120,460 | B | 61 |
| CONNECTICUT | Danbury | 244,100 | A | 123 |
| | Greenwich | 585,000 | B | 294 |
| | Greater Hartford | 249,667 | B | 125 |
| | New Haven | $222,733 | C | 112 |
| | New London | 174,750 | A | 88 |
| | Stamford | 362,663 | B | 182 |
| | Watertown | 223,500 | B | 112 |
| DELAWARE | Dover | 140,750 | B | 71 |

| STATE | MARKET | 1990 PRICE | DAYS ON MARKET** | INDEX*** |
|---|---|---|---|---|
| D.C. Washington | Inside Beltway | 357,250 | A | 179 |
| | Outside Beltway | 170,500 | A | 86 |
| FLORIDA | Clearwater | 149,250 | B | 75 |
| | Ft. Lauderdale | 153,975 | A | 77 |
| | Jacksonville | 112,125 | C | 56 |
| | Miami | 141,725 | A | 71 |
| | Naples | 162,875 | A | 82 |
| | Orlando | 138,375 | A | 70 |
| | Tallahassee | 127,475 | C | 64 |
| | Tampa | 127,725 | B | 64 |
| | West Palm Beach | 141,667 | B | 71 |
| GEORGIA | Athens | 114,167 | B | 57 |
| | Atlanta | 139,350 | B | 70 |
| | Augusta | 110,800 | B | 56 |
| | Savannah | 108,767 | B | 55 |
| HAWAII | Honolulu | 506,250 | B | 254 |
| IDAHO | Boise | 105,375 | B | 53 |
| | Coeur d'Alene | 136,633 | A | 69 |
| ILLINOIS | Barrington | 280,667 | C | 141 |
| | Bloomington | 113,133 | B | 57 |
| | Chicago — Lincoln Park | 491,667 | B | 247 |
| | Libertyville | 258,875 | A | 130 |
| | Naperville | 170,100 | A | 85 |
| | Palos Heights | 182,000 | A | 91 |
| | Peoria | 135,163 | A | 68 |
| | Rockford | 142,649 | B | 72 |
| | Schaumburg | 196,167 | A | 99 |
| | Wilmette | 322,667 | A | 162 |
| INDIANA | Evansville | 89,933 | A | 45 |
| | Fort Wayne | 116,800 | A | 59 |
| | Indianapolis | 115,450 | B | 58 |
| | South Bend | 106,625 | A | 54 |
| IOWA | Des Moines | 128,900 | A | 65 |
| KANSAS Kansas City | Johnson County | 122,938 | A | 62 |
| | Wyandotte County | 93,303 | B | 47 |
| | Topeka | 132,113 | C | 66 |
| | Wichita | 118,725 | A | 60 |
| KENTUCKY | Lexington | 124,433 | A | 63 |
| | Louisville | 139,833 | A | 70 |
| LOUISIANA | Baton Rouge | 109,167 | A | 55 |
| | Shreveport | 123,494 | B | 62 |
| MAINE | Bangor | $160,600 | B | 81 |
| | Brunswick | 177,000 | B | 89 |
| | Portland | 181,500 | B | 91 |
| MARYLAND | Baltimore | 205,833 | A | 103 |
| | Easton | 168,500 | C | 85 |
| MASSACHUSETTS | Acton | 249,333 | A | 125 |
| Boston Area | Framingham | 253,783 | A | 128 |
| | Wellesley | 380,750 | C | 191 |
| | Barnstable/Cape Cod | 182,000 | B | 91 |
| | Beverly | 248,167 | B | 125 |
| | Lexington | 336,667 | A | 169 |

Turning the Dream into Reality

# COUNTRY BOUND!™

| STATE | MARKET | 1990 PRICE | DAYS ON MARKET** | INDEX*** | STATE | MARKET | 1990 PRICE | DAYS ON MARKET** | INDEX*** |
|---|---|---|---|---|---|---|---|---|---|
| | Reading | 253,480 | B | 127 | | Dayton | 124,875 | A | 63 |
| | Springfield | 202,500 | C | 102 | | Toledo | 103,938 | A | 52 |
| | Worcester | 178,650 | C | 90 | OKLAHOMA | Oklahoma City | 85,200 | A | 43 |
| MICHIGAN | Ann Arbor | 194,313 | A | 98 | | Tulsa | 92,443 | A | 46 |
| Detroit | Macomb County | 123,725 | A | 62 | OREGON | Eugene | 115,475 | A | 58 |
| Area | Oakland County | 143,725 | A | 72 | | Portland | 104,225 | A | 52 |
| | Wayne County | 152,000 | A | 76 | PENNSYLVANIA | Allentown | 177,564 | B | 89 |
| | Grand Rapids | 136,250 | A | 68 | | Harrisburg | 163,300 | A | 82 |
| | Jackson | 92,253 | C | 46 | | Phil. Mainline/Sub E. | 332,500 | B | 167 |
| | East Lansing | 147,625 | A | 74 | | Phil. Mainline/Sub W. | 212,333 | A | 107 |
| | Traverse City | 121,750 | A | 61 | | Pittsburgh | 134,725 | A | 68 |
| MINNESOTA | Minneapolis | 171,300 | B | 86 | | York | 146,350 | B | 74 |
| | Rochester | 112,375 | A | 56 | RHODE ISLAND | Providence | 244,900 | B | 123 |
| | St. Paul | 145,667 | B | 73 | SOUTH CAROLINA | Charleston | 120,625 | A | 61 |
| MISSISSIPPI | Jackson | 115,375 | B | 58 | | Columbia | 135,475 | A | 68 |
| MISSOURI | Kansas City | 120,850 | A | 61 | | Greenville | 112,600 | B | 57 |
| | St. Louis | 111,625 | A | 56 | SOUTH DAKOTA | Rapid City | 126,125 | A | 63 |
| MONTANA | Billings | 106,375 | A | 53 | | Sioux Falls | 120,375 | A | 60 |
| | Great Falls | 134,625 | B | 68 | TENNESSEE | Knoxville | $112,725 | B | 57 |
| NEBRASKA | Omaha | 99,846 | A | 50 | | Memphis | 97,293 | A | 49 |
| NEVADA | Las Vegas | 133,572 | A | 67 | | Nashville | 128,975 | C | 65 |
| | Reno | 131,976 | A | 66 | TEXAS | Austin | 115,000 | A | 58 |
| NEW HAMPSHIRE | Manchester | 201,000 | B | 101 | | Corpus Christi | 82,338 | B | 41 |
| | Nashua | 178,000 | B | 89 | | Dallas | 124,350 | A | 62 |
| | Portsmouth | 174,000 | C | 87 | | El Paso | 130,083 | B | 65 |
| NEW JERSEY | Bergen County | 320,625 | B | 161 | | Ft. Worth | 109,667 | A | 55 |
| | Camden County | 157,725 | B | 79 | | Houston | 122,375 | B | 61 |
| | Essex County | 139,750 | B | 70 | | Plano | 132,333 | A | 66 |
| | Hunterdon County | 216,625 | B | 109 | | San Antonio | 94,000 | B | 47 |
| | Mercer | 247,167 | A | 124 | UTAH | Salt Lake City | 122,800 | B | 62 |
| | Middlesex | 221,250 | B | 111 | VERMONT | Burlington | 205,625 | A | 103 |
| | Monmouth | 248,225 | C | 125 | VIRGINIA | Norfolk | 114,731 | B | 58 |
| | Morris County | 278,750 | B | 140 | | Northern Virginia | 233,333 | A | 117 |
| | Passaic | 256,500 | B | 129 | | Richmond | 203,250 | A | 102 |
| | Somerset County | 284,000 | B | 143 | | Roanoke | 133,983 | A | 67 |
| | Union | 288,333 | B | 145 | WASHINGTON | Bellevue | 222,125 | A | 112 |
| NEW MEXICO | Albuquerque | 140,986 | A | 71 | | Seattle | 172,333 | A | 87 |
| | Santa Fe | 145,975 | A | 73 | | Spokane | 146,302 | A | 74 |
| NEW YORK | Albany | $197,333 | B | 99 | | Tacoma | 149,150 | A | 75 |
| | Binghampton | 152,338 | A | 77 | | Vancouver | 145,350 | A | 73 |
| | Buffalo | 143,725 | A | 72 | WEST VIRGINIA | Charleston | 134,167 | C | 67 |
| | Syracuse | 160,606 | A | 81 | WISCONSIN | Appleton | 115,063 | A | 58 |
| | Rochester/Penfield | 153,100 | A | 77 | | Green Bay | 116,875 | A | 59 |
| | Long Island | | | | | Madison | 131,388 | A | 66 |
| | Nassau, N. Shore | 288,333 | C | 145 | | Milwaukee | 171,875 | A | 86 |
| New York | Nassau, S. Shore | 220,167 | B | 111 | WYOMING | Cheyenne | 136,000 | A | 68 |
| City | Suffolk, N. Shore | 265,000 | B | 133 | COUNTRY | | | | |
| Area | Suffolk, S. Shore | 168,500 | B | 85 | CANADA | Calgary | 180,342 | A | 91 |
| | Rockland County | 231,250 | B | 116 | (In U.S. Dollars) | London | 186,004 | B | 93 |
| | Westchester County | 319,475 | B | 161 | | Montreal | 187,393 | A | 94 |
| NORTH CAROLINA | Asheville | 123,470 | B | 62 | | Newmarket | 188,034 | A | 94 |
| | Charlotte | 129,833 | B | 65 | | Niagara Falls | 180,342 | B | 91 |
| | Greensboro | 136,963 | B | 69 | | Toronto | | | |
| | Raleigh | 153,967 | B | 77 | | Central | 283,761 | A | 143 |
| | Wilmington | 147,133 | B | 74 | | East | 179,487 | A | 90 |
| | Winston-Salem | 130,875 | B | 66 | | West | 172,650 | A | 87 |
| NORTH DAKOTA | Fargo | 137,717 | B | 69 | | Vancouver B.C. | 504,701 | A | 254 |
| OHIO | Akron | 122,233 | A | 61 | | Windsor | 172,934 | A | 87 |
| | Canton | 120,250 | B | 60 | | Winnipeg | 154,701 | A | 78 |
| | Cincinnati | 149,500 | A | 75 | PUERTO RICO | San Juan | 237,833 | A | 119 |
| | Cleveland | 138,000 | A | 69 | | | | | |
| | Columbus | 141,833 | A | 71 | | | | | |

* These figures are based on existing market conditions in the fourth quarter of 1990.
** A market time of less than 90 days is rated "A", 91-180 days is rated "B", 181 days and up is rated "C."

This index shows the sale price and days on the market of a similar home in 219 markets in the last quarter of 1990. Data reflects the average of three recently sold homes in each market. © 1991 Coldwell Banker Residential Real Estate

Source: *Coldwell Banker Residential Group*

## *Quit Work and Live Off My Proceeds?*

In such high profit cases, the individuals involved could have a mortgage-free home, invest their proceeds, stop working, and comfortably live off the interest. City-dwellers who sell their homes for big bucks sometimes try to get around the capital gains tax by sinking everything into what amounts to a palace in a smaller town. Instead it might be smarter to buy a comparable home, take the capital gains tax hit, and finance your future with the rest.

One family we know of sold their urban home for $475,000. Then they bought a house they liked even better in Eugene, Oregon, for $150,000. They paid the capital gains tax, then plunked the rest in government bonds. They have no mortgage payments and their treasury bonds provide them a secure income of more than $20,000 a year. (Do be aware, however, your tax bill could actually go up slightly because you won't have as much to deduct on property taxes.)

While younger Americans who trade down to a cheaper house must pay tax on the profits, those over 55 may take up to $125,000 of home-sale profits tax-free. Of course, property tax bills and insurance bills ride like leeches on soaring real estate values. Trading down also shakes off many of these parasites.

If you're not 55 yet, consider an installment sale for your home—which postpones or reduces the capital gains tax. A wrap-around mortgage could also offer advantages in certain tax situations. Pick the brain of your accountant or tax attorney for guidance here.

Should selling your home be too drastic an initial step for you, consider using it for a line of credit. Home-equity loans go up to about 75 percent of the appraised value of the house—less the balance due on the mortgage, of course. Your house secures the debt. Interest rates are typically 1½ points over the prime rate and interest is fully deductible up to $100,000 of debt, no matter how you use the money. Some lending institutions charge up-front fees of around $300. About a fifth of all banks and credit unions, however, offers lines of credit with no closing costs. It pays to shop around. Once you've secured your funding, you can rent your home and head for the hinterland for some trial fun, renting there as well.

Or with interest rates the lowest in 18 years—a pleasing 8.5 percent on 30-year mortgages with fixed rates—you may want to totally refinance if you don't plan on selling right away.

So you've discovered a windfall. Now keep reading to figure out how to spend it wisely.

The Index number is provided to help you determine how much your current home would cost in another market. For instance, if you live in Sacramento, California, how much will it cost to replace your house if you move to Billings, Montana? Multiply the market value of your current home by the index number of the destination city where you plan to move, then divide that number by the index number of the market where your current home is located. Here's an example: A Sacramento home is $278,488, multiplied by 53, equals $14,759,864. Now divide by 140; that number equals a comparable replacement cost in Montana of $105,428.

## *Places, Patterns, and People*

We were some of the early urban opt-outs. According to the California Department of Motor Vehicles, 15,700 California drivers relinquished their licenses for Colorado ones in 1990, up from 9,900 in 1986. Two factors drive this exodus: the astounding appreciation of California real estate and discontent over the stress of living among ever accelerating numbers. People are swapping housing equity for lifestyle amenities. In southwest Colorado, for instance, homes priced at $200,000 are comparable to those carrying price tags of $1 million in southern California. Other top states attracting cash-rich Californians include: Arizona, Oregon, Texas, Nevada, and Florida.

People are spreading out in random patterns that have no single focus. There are more dimensions to this out-migration than have been seen before. It's not a movement in the traditional sense. It has no center, no leaders, and no clear direction—other than one that leads *away* from the cities. John Herbers of *The New York Times* dubs it "the new heartland."

Based on the 1990 census, the Northeast is packed with people. Nearly 51 million individuals live in this most densely populated region. (Yet even here there are pockets of openness. Most of Maine is less populated, as is upper New York state and upper Pennsylvania.) Today 78 percent of residents are jammed into metropolitan areas that claim only 17 percent of the land. The 10 largest metropolitan areas in 1988 began with New York (at a population of 18,120,000), Los Angeles, Chicago, San Francisco, Philadelphia, Detroit, Boston, Dallas/Fort Worth, Washington, then Houston.

Surprisingly, one-quarter of the area of the United States still meets the Census Bureau's definition of "frontier territory": two persons per square mile. Millions of us dream of mounting a horse, donning a cowboy hat, and riding into the western sunset. Louis L'Amour books offer readers a way to get back to their most cherished dreams and desires. And the rugged Marlboro Man appeals to our sense of adventure, romance, and freedom. Today many are turning this fantasy into reality.

One hundred fifty U.S. counties continue to qualify for the Census Bureau's definition of frontier land. All of them are west of the 98th meridian—which is bounded by the east side of Texas, Oklahoma, Kansas, Nebraska, plus South and North Dakota. According to *American Demographics* magazine most of the frontier lies in three regions: the Great Basin in Nevada and Utah, the Great Plains from Montana to Texas, and the Owyhee-Bitterroot valleys of the Northwest. And Alaska offers untold opportunities, even allowing homesteading on state-owned land.

The rural Midwest is also trying homesteading with the hope that free land will attract hardworking young people to reverse the aging population and economic decline. Koochiching County, on the Minnesota-Canada border, began a program in 1988 dubbed "Bidstead." It offered 40 acres of county-owned land to anyone agreeing to build a house and live on the land for 10 years.

Many smaller towns in the midwest are blossoming. People are fleeing cities on the east and west coasts and seeking sturdier soils in which to sink roots. They want traditional values, family ties, parks and blue skies, the smell of home baked apple pie, uncrowded golf courses a few minutes from home, time for fathers to go shooting with their sons or snowmobiling with their daughters. There is a longing for the basics and living close to nature. *In* things now include: religion, sewing, the work ethic, nostalgia, home cooking, regular people; even the demolition derby is making a comeback. It's not geography, but rather a state of mind.

Ethnic diversity will also shape our future. Many major cities now have a "minority-majority." According to the September 17, 1991, issue of *USA Today*, 57 percent of New Yorkers are minorities—due to the rapid growth of Black, Asian, and Hispanic communities. Houston tips the scales at 59 percent minorities, Memphis 56 percent, San Francisco 53 percent, Cleveland and Dallas are at 52 percent each. This increase in urban minorities is a result of the largest wave of immigrants since the early 1900s. The influx is mostly from Mexico, Central America, South America, Asia, and now Eastern Europe. Zooming Hispanic and Black birth rates further contribute. Demographers predict the state of California will have a minority-majority in about 20 years.

Other states with large Spanish-speaking populations include Florida, New York, New Jersey, Illinois, New Mexico, and Texas. Blacks are still overrepresented in southern states relative to their percentage in the national average. There are fewer Black people, however, in northern New England, the Rocky Mountains, and the upper Great Plains states. Here Blacks make up less than one percent of the population . . . a terrific opportunity for a person of color wanting to capitalize on EEO-based hiring quotas.

Be aware that many small towns and rural areas are predominantly Caucasian. If you have youngsters, perhaps you don't want your children growing up in a clone-like society where everyone is of one race and ethnic background. Exposure to diverse languages, traditions, and thoughts can be enriching. Consider this when evaluating your relocation plans.

If you're a single person who hopes to find a mate, some states may be better than others. Ladies, you'll be interested to know Hawaii, Alaska, Nevada, and Wyoming have higher male populations. And for you gents, New York, Rhode Island, Massachusetts, and Florida offer greater pickin's. A lot of people feel it's harder to find a fun date or a life mate in small towns. This isn't necessarily true. You're a big fish in a little pond. While there are fewer potentials to choose from, it's easier to get acquainted. One of our employees met her honey while browsing at the local rock shop. Three of the four single women we've hired from out of the area were in committed relationships a few months after arriving.

Because people are friendlier in small towns, it's just natural to strike up a conversation with someone who interests you. What may be perceived as "coming on" in swinging suburbia is accepted as being congenial in rural USA. Sure it's lonely sometimes. But you can be even lonelier in a city of one million. Tom contends before he became a teetotaler, his loneliest times were in some of the "swingingest" bars in the country. Everything and everyone was artificial. If you hope to find a country life partner, when selecting your new hometown consider the age make-up of the residents. If you're in your twenties or thirties, a retiree's haven would be a poor community to choose.

Country bound singles might want to contact the Rural Network at 6236 Borden Road, Boscobel, WI 53805. They help country-oriented singles provide support to each other. Their *Advocate* newsletter carries news, letters, pictures, and ads sent by people wanting to introduce themselves and share the adventure in their lives. While marriage is on the minds of some, others simply want to visit with like-minded individuals of either sex—and even sometimes open their homes to traveling singles.

There are other aspects to consider when selecting potential hometowns—whether you're a solo, couple, or family. Tempers flare more easily when people of different backgrounds, religions, and viewpoints get together. Some places are extremely difficult to break into. They have distinct biases. For instance, there are communities in the west that are almost exclusively Mormon. Unless you follow that faith, you'd probably be an outsider.

And many small towns are extremely intolerant. If you aren't second or third generation townsfolk, you have a difficult time being accepted. In Pottsville, Pennsylvania, for instance, 94 percent of the residents are natives of the state. On the other hand, Bullhead City-Lake Havasu City, Arizona, is extremely heterogenous. Only 16 percent of its population originally hails from Arizona. There are even strong pockets of political persuasion. Beware if you're a donkey lover and 90 percent of the area are elephants.

There is another important point to consider when selecting your utopia, one many people overlook. If you're moving to get away from the hustle and bustle—and you don't want to end up with the same thing again—avoid picking one of the most desirable places on the planet. If you don't, chances are you'll soon have lots of company. Bend, Oregon, is a classic example. Once a sleepy little town of about 8,000, it's been discovered. The population is now on its way to tripling. When you've narrowed your list of possible towns, investigate the area's population trends. If they're on the grow, realize things will change. In fast growing towns septic tanks give way to sewer systems, fancier water treatment techniques are mandated, taxes for schools go up. And there will be more people. If you're seeking a no-growth situation, don't pick a garden spot.

## *Narrowing the Field*

Now it's time to think through what you want. Are you looking to purchase a house in town? A farm or ranch? Perhaps a mobile home on a small parcel of land is more within your budget. Do you want to buy an existing business? Unimproved acreage? A second or vacation home? A subdivision lot as a future building site? Or maybe you're toying with the idea of joining a commune.

One growing trend is that of young families moving back to parental households. Advantages are numerous, but among the greatest are the reduced expenses. Imagine trading an expensive, small New York apartment for a spacious house in a small town with a real *Leave It to Beaver* neighborhood. Plus, as parents age, they are provided the attention they need, and are spared suffering the loneliness most of that generation are doomed to endure. Yes, there are drawbacks, but the advantages for many outweigh who gets the master bedroom.

Some people are finding that a home in intentional communities is a sanctuary of security and spiritual growth. Living is more affordable and there is a built-in support system for people as they age. The communes of this decade, however, are not the turf of freewheeling hippies intent on doing drugs and having sex. They attract more professional, mainstream people. The October 15, 1991 issue of *USA Today* ran a cover story about communes, saying the weak economy may fuel their popularity. Should you want more information on the subject of cooperative living, get a copy of the *Directory of Intentional Communities* and *Builders of the Dawn: Community Lifestyles in a Changing World.*

Now that you've decided the type of property you want, how do you pare down the multitude of possibilities to three or four actual towns or counties to investigate? Think about areas that impressed you while vacationing or traveling on business. Has a colleague relocated to an area that he or she keeps telling you is nirvana? Do you have friends or relatives in a charming little town? Has a certain state captured your heart?

There are several helpful books that provide area report cards. Get a copy of G. Scott Thomas' *The Rating Guide to Life in America's Small Cities.* (See easy ordering information for this and many other books mentioned within these pages in the "Bibliography/Recommended Reading.") Coining them "*Micro*politan" areas, Thomas profiles 219 towns between metropolitan areas and country crossroads. To qualify, however, his cities must have a population of 15,000 . . . not "small" by some people's standards. He uses a statistical system to grade the quality of life in each place.

While not at all rural, another useful resource is *Places Rated Almanac* by Richard Boyer and David Savageau. It looks at the best places to live in America. Perhaps it could serve as a compass to guide you to a favorable area, then you could locate a small town within proximity of the larger place it recommends. And for mature people seeking a change there is *Retirement Places Rated.*

Another treasure trove is *The World Almanac and Book of Facts.* Here you'll discover information on cost of living, the environment, geographical data, record temperatures, humidity, altitude, the latitude and longitude of cities, even climatological statistics. Refer to your previous list to refresh your memory about personal priorities.

## *Hitting the Research Trail*

With three or four possible destinations in mind, it's time to visit your largest area library. Enlist the aid of a friendly reference librarian. Don't rely just on printed material. Computer databases offer a wealth of up-to-the-minute facts and figures.

One of the best ways to get a *feel* for a place is to read back issues of the local newspaper. Look in Editor & Publisher's *International Yearbook* to identify the daily newspaper. Write for subscription information, plus details on how to order a month's back issues. If the town is tiny, it may only have a weekly paper. If so, the nation's 6,890 semi-weekly and weekly newspapers are listed in *Gale's Directory of Publications*.

By carefully reading an area's papers you can mine tremendous knowledge. What are the lead stories? Do they reflect issues that are positive or negative? Read the letters to the editor to find out about area controversies. Are there stories about town spruce-up projects? An inordinate amount of crime? Special recreational or cultural activities? Planned tax increases? Peruse the ads too. They help you get a sense of what retail outlets are available and the price levels. Don't overlook the classifieds. By studying real estate ads you quickly get a sense of availability and the range of property values.

Next track down the addresses and phone numbers for the chambers of commerce and the state tourism offices. (You can find out local ones from the U.S. Chamber of Commerce at 1615 H Street NW, Washington, DC 20062, 301-468-5128.) You'll want to write the areas you're considering to request their Newcomers Packet or Relocation Kit. Identify yourself as a prospective new resident (and business owner, if applicable).

Also study the current year's *Statistical Abstract of the United States* and the most current *City and County Data Book*. Be sure and look at the dates on all charts, figures, graphs, and lists. Though it appears in a current reference work, much of this information may be three to five years old. You may also want to look at the *Digest of Education Statistics* and the *Occupational Outlook Handbook*.

Back at home, additional research waits.

Talk to people. Use your network to try and find *anyone* who has moved to an area that interests you. Contact these individuals and solicit their help and feedback.

To make your job simple, there is a real estate company that specializes in rural property. United National Real Estate has more than 300 affiliated offices in 40 states. They publish two catalogs a year. Talk about a dream book! Their one-of-a-kind catalogs are jam-packed with tempting photographs and descriptions of rural hideaways: ranches, farms, country estates, homes in small towns, business opportunities, commercial properties, land, you name it. To get a copy call 800-999-1020, fax 816-753-0257, or write United National Real Estate, 4700 Belleview, Kansas City, MO 64112. Be sure to tell them the areas you're considering so regional offices can send you updates on any recent area listings that have come in since the catalog was printed.

Also get applicable copies of regional magazines—such as *Sunset*, *Yankee*, or *Southern Living*—and sift through the classified section for real estate ads. Ask local chambers of commerce for a list of area brokers to help you size up the market too.

Although your chances of finding an ideal place are slim, there are less conventional ways of locating property. One is by writing to the Consumer Information Center, Pueblo, CO 81009, and asking for their *U.S. Real Property Sales List*. This is real estate no longer needed by the federal government. It varies widely in value and type and is acquired either by auction or sealed bid. While most properties are commercial or industrial, their most recent sales list included a Victorian home in Dorchester, Massachusetts; a U.S. Postal Service facility in Rochester, New Hampshire; two working avocado farms in Miami, Florida; and a concrete building on 29 acres in Butler County, Ohio.

We located the church that now houses our offices through the Federal Deposit Insurance Corporation (FDIC), which has properties from failed banks. It took incredible tenacity. Each long distance phone call led to another in a widening circle of confusion. But the result was worth it as we succeeded in purchasing the property for about half its market value. FDIC regional liquidation offices are listed in Part III under "Government Sources."

The Resolution Trust Corporation (RTC) is the FDIC's counterpart. It was created by Congress in 1989 to dispose of the assets of failed savings and loans. Almost two-thirds of the $27.3 billion worth of property, mostly single-family houses, that the RTC inherited is still on the market. Texas leads the pack with 5,685 homes available, Louisiana is a distant second with 2,193. While most RTC properties are in larger cities, it still may be worth your while to investigate the offerings. For an up-to-date listing for any particular area, call 800-782-3006. Part III contains more particulars.

For a small fee, you can order any phone directory published in this country by calling Pacific Bell directories at 800-848-8000. The mother lode you'll likely find will be well worth it. Sift through the yellow pages from cover to cover. You're looking to see if the health care providers you need are there, what kind of restaurant fare is available, what entertainment is offered, who your competition might be if you plan to open a business, what kind of educational facilities are available, etc. Another good resource is *Lesko's Info-Power* by Matthew Lesko. It's a compendium of over 30,000 free and low cost sources of information.

It might also be informative to call your local Coldwell Banker real estate agent and request a current copy of their Home Price Comparison Index. This is a free recap of what houses are selling for in over 200 communities. Although it covers mostly metropolitan areas, you might use the nearest big city as a gauge.

Map reconnaissance is definitely in order. Trying to plan a move without maps is like attempting to repair an 18-wheeler with jeweler's tools. Several types will be helpful. Start with an atlas if you have one. It will help explain the physical geography and climatological zones. DeLorme Mapping (P.O. Box 298-6565, Freeport, ME 04032) publishes atlases that cover individual states. They are ideal for backcountry exploring. So is a good odometer to measure distances on rural byways that aren't well marked. And don't overlook the everyday variety of maps you use when traveling. If you belong to an auto club, call and get appropriate state and city maps.

Remember as you begin looking at different kinds of maps to refer to the legend or key. It will explain the symbols and colors used to specify areas of importance or interest. Also, the scale of miles will be different on various maps, so be sure you're using relevant information versus details from other sources.

Topographic maps, which show the elevation and terrain, can save a lot of time. Look in your yellow pages to find a local map store. Depending on how sophisticated you want to get, there are also soil, mining, hydrology (ground water), flood plain, and census maps—not to mention city master plans and zoning maps. Aerial photos can also be helpful in certain situations.

Always read the legend of a map first. It usually appears in the lower right or bottom margin. By using a piece of string, you can measure the scale on the legend and quickly interpret distances. More information on where to get maps is contained in Part III.

Also ask your auto club for tour guide books of the area, pre-trip packets of information, and routing details. (Request back roads routing . . . you learn much more.) Additionally check with your travel agent for information.

No doubt in your reading and research, you'll come across articles that hold particular interest for you. It's apparent the writer is an expert and you'd give next week's football tickets to be able to visit with him or her. There may be a way! Why not write and ask? A suggested form letter follows. There are three possible ways to locate the expert. One is to find the person's or company's name and geographic location in the article. Then call information for an area code. Next call information again at 1 (area code) 555-1212 and try to get a phone number.

Another sleuthing trick that works well if the person is of some note is to call the library and ask them to check who's who directories and other reference works for the individual's name and address. A third detective

## FORM LETTER FOR RESEARCH

Date

Name
Address
City/State/Zip

*SPECIMEN*
*We encourage readers to photocopy these pages*

Dear _____:

    I'm writing because of an article entitled _____ that I saw in _____. It was very exciting to read about what you're doing.

    We are in the early planning stages of _____ _____. The knowledge and experience you've gathered on _____ _____ would be tremendously helpful. Hopefully, you will be kind enough to share some of it with us.

    Thanks so much for your interest and cooperation! For your convenience, I've enclosed a stamped, self-addressed envelope (or feel free to call me collect if that is more practical—Days: _____ , Evenings and Weekends: _____ ). I'm eagerly looking forward to hearing from you.

Sincerely,


Your Name

ploy is to write the person in care of the magazine or newspaper reporter and ask that the mail be forwarded.

Of course, when you receive the package from the chamber of commerce this opens additional opportunities. There are real estate offices to contact, plus banks and economic development agencies to approach if you plan to go into business. Don't be discouraged if the chamber doesn't reply. Our hit ratio was less than 50 percent. Try calling this time and reminding them it is a second request for relocation information.

## *Planning Your Visit*

You've pinpointed your places and done all the arm's-length research you can. Now it's time to plan your actual visit. A few words of caution: coordinate your visitation time carefully. Avoid holidays and peak vacation times when everything will be so hectic you won't get a real feel for the place, or people's undivided attention. If time constraints dictate you must fly, be sure to arrange for a rental car (preferably a 4-wheel drive vehicle) at the other end.

There are several ways to check out your dream destinations. The ideal is to take a sabbatical or leave of absence for several months while you really *experience* a place. This not only gives you plenty of time to make an informed choice but also assures you of ongoing income, should the test not be to your liking and you decide to return. Few of us live ideal lives.

If you're not currently tied to a job, consider caretaking or housesitting in the vicinity you're considering. The newsletter *Caretaker Gazette* (Box 342, Carpentersville, IL 60110) lists many provocative opportunities: free rent in an Ozark Foothills, Arkansas, cabin; a possible partnership in a farming venture in Spencer, Virginia; a primitive log cabin and board in exchange for caretaking 175 acres in Bristow, Indiana.

A more practical approach is to roam the countryside on weekends and vacations. This way you can set up a network of real estate contacts who know your needs and will contact you when something comes up. And you can see the place at different times of year. This is crucial information. A spot that's lovely in the fall may leave you wringing wet from the summer humidity—or up to your elbows in mud when the winter thaw hits in March. It's wise to sample the climate at its seasonal extremes.

Another good alternative is to do a vacation home swap. This economical idea allows you to be a temporary resident and quickly acquaints you with the true fabric of a community. You meet the neighbors (instead of the hotel maid), absorb their culture, and get their perspective on everyday life. And you can check a wide array of local businesses—from grocery stores to hair salons, banks to service stations. Often a vehicle (and sometimes the family pet) is part of these hospitable deals. This approach lets you evaluate the new area at your own pace before selling your home and burning your bridges. The typical swap lasts two or three weeks and is especially attractive to retirees and families with small children.

Exchanges are not necessarily "your place for my place" arrangements. There are exchange clubs with dues of under $50 that produce directories of available properties. To learn about the various clubs and their specialties, not to mention many exchanging tips, we recommend you get a copy of John Kimbrough's *The Vacation Home Exchange and Hospitality Guide*. Of course, you could also run an ad in the local newspaper where you want to locate. Don't do this in a really small town, however. It would label you as too unorthodox.

One practical solution is to take your lodging with you—in the form of a trailer, motor home, camper, or tent. Those who have traveled in this fashion often opt for the camper. It gives more freedom. You can easily take side roads without worrying if there will be room to turn around. And you can camp anywhere there is space for the length of a truck. Tent camping, while taking up valuable time to make and break camp, affords a sense of adventure and is more realistic for bigger families.

Of course, any town over 500 population will have a motel or hotel. Some of them are clean, restful places run by delightful people. Others feature sagging mattresses, noisy heaters or air conditioners, dingy carpeting, and proprietors with the tact of Madonna. Be sure you check out the room thoroughly *before* you plunk down your cash. A good way to assure yourself of reasonable standards is to stay in a Best Western motel or hotel. To find their lodging options as you travel, or get a free directory, call 800-528-1234.

Don't overlook bunking with friends or relatives. Well . . . maybe you should overlook it. When you're seriously searching for a new place to live—a whole new lifestyle—why get sidetracked by social obligations and unsolicited opinions?

One creative businessman we know had his family join him for a convention held in a town about 50 miles from where they were considering relocating. While he attended convention sessions, his wife and daughter took their rented car and checked out the area. The company paid for his lodging, so his family stayed free and he was able to piggyback two additional days at his own expense, but at the considerably reduced hotel convention rate.

Military retirees/officers can sometimes find economical accommodations on bases. Determine if there's a military base near your location and call their main number. Ask if they have a Guest House. Contact the Guest

House directly and ask for availability, costs, priorities, and the length of stay allowed. Check out any other rules concerning pets, children, food in rooms, etc. Or have them mail you a list of their regulations. Parameters vary widely, but it's well worth investigating. Base rates are cheaper than motels, and dining accommodations are usually close by.

Try to work in some fun activities, especially if you are taking children on the trip. Visiting a playground, park, museum, historical site, or other tourist attraction each day breaks the seriousness of the trip. It's a good idea to toss in some relaxing cassette tapes and a player too. And be sure to take comfortable shoes that allow for walking in all types of terrain. Other items might include sunscreen, insect repellent, a hat, backpack, and perhaps a walking stick if you plan to go really rural. If you have a hand-held cassette recorder, it is handy for recording your impressions or listing items for future follow-up. Short of that, take plenty of large pads, pens, and different colored Post-it Note pads so you can color code questions, different properties, etc.

Speaking of what to take, by all means include your camera—not to mention lots of film, extra batteries, flash attachment, plus zoom and telephoto lenses if you have them. It's a good idea to check out the camera before you leave, especially if you don't use it regularly. Shoot and develop a roll of film to be sure everything is working. Take some flash shots, some in normal light, and some as close-ups. When traveling remember not to shoot through the closed window or when the car is moving. Window glass plays havoc with auto-focus and a moving car often results in blurred pictures.

Finally, to check out the weather; you can do so anywhere in the U.S. for 95 cents a minute by calling 1-900-weather (932-8437). Then just enter "1" and the area code for the region you want to know about. Also be aware that even-numbered highways flow east and west; odd-numbered ones go north and south.

> Marilyn: *You probably already know that. This reminder is offered because, while I consider myself to be a fairly intelligent person, when it comes to reading road maps I'm a real dummy. Giving me a map is like giving pantyhose to a mermaid. Disaster!*

We hope we've given you the tools to find your way to your personal oasis. In the next chapter we'll explore doing a comprehensive on-site evaluation.

# 4

# Checking Out Rural Edens

People who want milk should not sit on a stool in the middle of a field in hopes a cow will back up to them. If you want to *know* a community, you'll need to be assertive, to cook up a strategy for relocation research. Whipping into town, looking at properties, and making an impulsive decision can lead to immense disappointment. (We know. That's what we did in First Try. We romanticized the place and were swayed by emotional urgings instead of sound logic.) Intuition should play a part—but only when leavened with analysis. That's what we help you do in this chapter: examine all the ingredients so you can create a life feast that will nourish you from now on. There are checklists and questionnaires culled from a combination of personal experiences and recommendations from others.

Probably the best place to head when you arrive in town is the chamber of commerce. Following is a list of questions we developed when relocating to Colorado. While you'll want to modify it somewhat, going over these questions with the chamber executive director will quickly give you a solid handle on what the community is like. Be honest about the type of business you're planning. Consider, however, that one of the main aims of this person is to recruit new residents. Some are so good at it they could sell eggs to a chicken! The ideal spot is fictional. Different locations attract different people. Focus on your needs and preferences and realize you may get a slightly skewed—but understandably justified—picture from chamber directors.

## QUESTIONS TO ASK
## AT THE CHAMBER OF COMMERCE

1) What is the population of the town? The surrounding area? Is it increasing or decreasing? Why?

2) What are the summer temperature highs and winter lows? How long is the growing season?

3) How far away is the closest college, junior college, or continuing education facility? Do you have a recent catalog of their classes?

4) What is the crime rate in comparison with other area towns? What's the most frequent problem in this area?

5) What are the hours of the local library? Does it encourage interlibrary loan? How in-depth is the reference section?

6) Is cable or satellite necessary for TV reception? Approximate costs?

7) What is the property tax rate? Sales tax base?

8) What recreational facilities or planned activities (festivals, special events, etc.) are available for fun?

9) What cultural opportunities are there?

10) How many grocery stores are there? Where do you shop for staples and sundries? How do prices compare with other Colorado towns?

11) What is the availability of small houses or apartments to rent? Will most accept pets?

12) What is the water supply source? Is it chlorinated? Do people pay a flat monthly fee or is it metered?

13) What religions are represented?

14) Is there a good supply of nearby lots or acreages for building sites?

15) What social clubs and service organizations are established?

16) What is the cost of living compared to other area towns?

17) How do your utility and phone rates compare with other areas?

18) Is there any air pollution? Noise pollution?

19) What is the least desirable characteristic of this area? The most favorable?

Checking Out Rural Edens

20) What is the teacher-pupil ratio in the schools? How extensive is the athletic program? Is there a music and/or drama department? How sophisticated is the computer technology being used?

21) Are there recycling programs? How far is the dump?

22) Get a street map of the town and surrounding area.

**Additional Business-Oriented Questions:**

1) Are there any zoning restrictions on home businesses? Any restrictions about living in commercially zoned buildings?

2) What incentives do you offer a company to relocate to your area?

3) Is there an available work force for my type of business?

4) What are typical monthly wages for secretaries?

5) What is the current unemployment rate? Is this rate rising or falling? Why? Is there a significant seasonal variance?

6) How well does the present telephone equipment work?

7) What role does the chamber play in helping new businesses?

8) How frequent are electrical power outages? Average duration?

9) What is the principal industry and/or agricultural emphasis?

10) Who are the primary employers? Are they stable?

11) Is there overnight mail, package delivery and pick-up? Does the post office have boxes available?

12) What businesses does the community really need? Are there any that would be unwelcome?

13) Is there an economic development office available and how can I contact them?

---

This session is almost guaranteed to leave the director bewildered; few people are so organized in their search for a new home as you have become. There will be several questions left unanswered. The following advice pinpoints more assistance.

## *Finding More Resources*

Of course, real estate offices specialize in knowing the answers to newcomers' questions. Since their specialty is rural property, we'd suggest you contact the United National Real Estate office in the area you're considering and have a chat with the agent. (If you followed our earlier advice, you already know of several interesting listings you want to pursue.) Fill in the blanks left from your chamber of commerce discussion. Discuss the properties you want to view. Really get acquainted.

There are more sources who will also prove useful. Check with local or college librarians. Introduce yourself to the editor of the daily or weekly newspaper. If you didn't previously subscribe, and you're really interested, spend some time in their archives going over back issues. Stories about proposed mines, new landfills, firms closing, planned recreational districts that will boost taxes (and offer more amenities), or news of barroom brawls and arrests all paint a vivid picture of the area's culture.

Pay a visit to the local banks and talk with the bank president or vice-president. (Yes, you can get to the head man or woman in small towns.) Inquire about real estate repossessions you might consider. Determine if their hours are convenient.

If you plan to open a retail or mail order business, ask about the availability of merchant credit card status so you can accept VISA and MasterCard orders. In metropolitan areas, new mail order companies find it virtually impossible to secure this status. We had no problem getting it here in Buena Vista. As a businessperson, you might also want to negotiate with the bank president to drop service charges on your accounts.

Charged with the mission of rural revitalization, the county extension service is another good resource. The USDA operates extension programs in all 3,165 U.S. counties. The area agent can help you with agricultural, water, and soil questions—plus job skill issues, career decisions, and expanded business opportunities.

If you're going to open a business (or even purchase an existing one), government agencies and regional economic development authorities can tell you about counseling and government funds available for business start-ups, on-the-job training programs for new hirees, and various incentive programs. And if you're considering purchasing an old building that needs repair, check with the local Historical Society about matching funds for preservation or special tax credits and incentives for restoration.

Migrating entrepreneurs will also want to talk with local business leaders, town council members, those who serve on the county board of supervisors, and other town boosters. (An abundance of additional business market researching tips are covered in Part II under "Researching for the Right Opportunity.")

To simplify your investigation and be sure you don't overlook important considerations, use the adjacent Ross Relocation Checklist.

## ROSS RELOCATION CHECKLIST
(check if high priority or major concern)

*SPECIMEN — We encourage readers to photocopy these pages*

**I. Education**
    A. Nursery school/day care facilities   ___
    B. Grade school   ___
    C. Middle school   ___
    D. High school
        1. sports program   ___
        2. music   ___
        3. drama   ___
        4. computers   ___
        5. gifted/remedial programs   ___
        6. dropout rate   ___
    E. Christian/private school   ___
    F. Vocational/technical school   ___
    G. Community/junior college   ___
    H. College or university   ___
    I. Continuing adult education   ___
    J. Private tutors/teachers
       (piano, violin, guitar, etc.)   ___
    K. Other_____

**II. Community**
    A. Churches   ___
    B. Professional organizations   ___
    C. Fraternal/sorority alumni groups   ___
    D. Service clubs   ___
    E. Senior citizen groups   ___
    F. Youth groups   ___
    G. Children's playground   ___
    H. Youth team sports   ___
    I. Veterans' clubs   ___
    J. Shopping facilities   ___
    K. Crime/fire protection   ___
    L. Responsive local government   ___

*Trade Your Business Suit Blues for Blue Jean Dreams™*

    M. Major industries  
    N. Per capita income  
    O. Unemployment rate  
    P. General acceptance of outsiders  
    Q. Proximity to major metropolitan area  
    R. Handicapped access  
    S. Other_____

### III. Resources
    A. Water supply  
        1. availability  
        2. treatment  
        3. taste  
        4. smell  
        5. well permit  
    B. Power supply  
        1. nuclear  
        2. electric  
        3. hydraulic  
        4. gas  
        5. propane  
    C. Other_____

### IV. Taxes
    A. City and county sales  
    B. State sales  
    C. State income  
    D. Inheritance  
    E. Gasoline  
    F. Other_____

### V. Climate
    A. Rainfall  
    B. Snowfall  
    C. Humidity  
    D. Winter lows  
    E. Summer highs  
    F. Average temperature  
    G. High winds  
    H. Percent of sunshine  
    I. Elevation  
    J. Other_____

SPECIMEN  
We encourage readers to photocopy these pages

Checking Out Rural Edens

## VI. Environment
  A. Parks/green spaces ____
  B. Trees ____
  C. Water
     1. ocean ____
     2. lake ____
     3. river ____
     4. creeks ____
  D. Cleanliness ____
  E. Recycling facilities ____
  F. Odor-free ____
  G. Noise pollution ____
  H. Air pollution ____
  I. Other_____

## VII. Transportation
  A. Distance to:
     1. airport ____
     2. train station ____
     3. bus terminal ____
  B. Public transportation system ____
  C. Taxis ____
  D. Handicapped assistance ____
  E. Commuting ease ____
  F. Bike routes ____
  G. Winter maintenance (snow plowing/sanding/salting) ____
  H. Other_____

## VIII. Cost of Living
  A. Real estate ____
  B. Food ____
  C. Clothing ____
  D. Fuel ____
  E. Utilities ____
  F. Insurance
     1. auto ____
     2. fire ____
     3. home ____
  G. Other_____

## IV. Culture/Entertainment
  A. Movies/theater ____
  B. Museum ____

*SPECIMEN — We encourage readers to photocopy these pages*

*Trade Your Business Suit Blues for Blue Jean Dreams™*

    C. Library    ———
    D. Bookstore    ———
    E. Nightclub    ———
    F. Restaurants    ———
    G. Aerobics/fitness center    ———
    H. Other outdoor pursuits
        1. golf course    ———
        2. tennis courts    ———
        3. swimming pool    ———
        4. softball field    ———
        5. raquetball courts    ———
    I. Athletic activities    ———
    J. Musical events    ———
    K. Nat'l Public Radio reception    ———
    L. Cable TV reception    ———
    M. Other_____

**X. Health Care**
    A. Hospital
        1. 24-hour emergency care    ———
        2. depth of facility    ———
        3. ambulance service    ———
    B. Doctor    ———
    C. Public Health Nurse    ———
    D. Medical specialist    ———
    E. Dentist    ———
    F. Optometrist/optician    ———
    G. Mental health care    ———
    H. Clinic    ———
    I. Chiropractor    ———
    J. Massage therapist    ———
    K. Emergency 911 number    ———
    L. Special support groups    ———
    M. Veterinarian    ———
    N. Other_____

**XI. Possible Undesirable Conditions**
    A. Environment
        1. nuclear power plant    ———
        2. dangerous waste site    ———
        3. well water contamination    ———
        4. flood plain    ———

*SPECIMEN — We encourage readers to photocopy these pages*

            5. radon
            6. allergens
        B. Elements
            1. hurricanes
            2. earthquakes
            3. tornados
            4. avalanches
        C. Community
            1. racial tension
            2. violent crime rate
            3. hate groups
            4. gangs
            5. high drug use
            6. nearby prison
        D. Location
            1. remote shipment
                a. old fruit/vegetables
                b. slow postal delivery service
            2. limited shopping
            3. inconvenient business hours
            4. scant entertainment
            5. lack of singles' activities
        E. Other_____

XII. **Considerations for the Mature**
        A. Public transportation
        B. Health care
            1. in-home assistance
            2. elder care program
            3. convalescent/nursing home
        C. Elevation
        D. Handicapped access
        E. AARP chapter
        F. Veteran's services officer
        G. Home delivered meals
        H. Communal meals
        I. Weatherization/LEAP program
        J. Community center activities

XIII. **Business Considerations**
        A. Enterprise Zone/economic development
        B. RTC/FDIC property available

*SPECIMEN — We encourage readers to photocopy these pages*

C. County/local tax incentives ___
D. Area labor pool ___
E. Phone system sophistication ___
   1. call waiting ___
   2. private lines ___
F. Temporary help/on-call secretarial ___
G. Services
   1. attorney ___
   2. CPA ___
   3. overnight pickup/delivery ___
H. Proximity to critical suppliers ___
I. Access for pick-up and delivery ___
J. Power reliability ___
K. Signage regulations ___
L. Parking availability ___
M. Chamber of commerce involvement ___
N. Zoning for in-home enterprises ___
O. Existing competition ___
P. Computer user groups ___
Q. Corporate taxes
R. Other_____

*SPECIMEN — We encourage readers to photocopy these pages*

## Tactics for Testing the Waters

Broaden your knowledge base by more firsthand explorations. But now instead of talking to various experts, you're getting to know the townsfolk. It's mingle time. You want to meet the natives on their own terms. So don't pull out a wad of bills or you label yourself a city sophisticate. On the other hand, ordering coffee at the local coffee shop and proclaiming, "What a great place to raise kids!" is sure to start up a dialogue.

To stimulate conversations, try using the *echo technique*. This encourages people to expand on what they previously said and helps you pull out information not normally shared. Here's how it works: you simply repeat the last few words the other person has said. For instance if Jane ends her comments with, " . . . and the heat is a problem." You pipe up with, "Problem . . . ?" She's likely to go on with something like, "Yes, the humidity gets so high in August we about die." Bingo! You've just gleaned data that may sway your whole decision.

Likewise if someone says, "Parker City is really an old-fashioned community," you come back with, "Old fashioned community . . . ?" And the other party will typically volunteer, "Oh, we have band concerts and parades for any occasion you can think of. And last summer everybody had a ball at the box lunch social." Here again you've uncovered valuable insight into the texture of this town's values. If traditional ways are important to you, this place appears to be a good match.

In the process of your informal interviews, also talk to recent migrants. What drew them here originally? Has the original attraction faded or bloomed? To what extent are they pleased with the move? Has the area improved or declined in meeting their needs? Just don't take everything you hear as gospel. Some people are as flaky as a good pie crust.

Successful relocation requires resourcefulness. Sometimes the most worthwhile information doesn't come to you directly, but rather through the conversations of others. Go to the restaurant with the most pickup trucks or sheriff's cars parked. This is the local hangout. It's the place you'll hear snatches of discussions about everything from the schools to local politics, farming to weather idiosyncracies, real news to plain gossip. And you'll find some of the best food in town. Another place to conduct eavesdropping reconnaissance is at the local bar. Tavern goers often get loose tongues in a hurry.

Additional hints include: strike up conversations with locals if you have a CB radio. Talk to vendors at roadside fruit, vegetable, or flower stands. Monitor any throw away newspapers or literature sitting on counter tops around town. Read posters in merchants' windows to get a sense of a locale's activities. Take pictures of places and people who hold particular interest for you. Make a game of keeping your antenna attuned to everything and everybody.

But don't let yourself get bogged down with analysis paralysis. After you've gathered the facts, it's how you *feel* about a place that counts. It may take two or three visits to establish a comfort level. That's fine. When all systems point to "go," move on as we discuss significant real estate purchasing pointers.

## *Choosing Your Specific Dream Home or Land*

Getting a good real estate deal in the location of your choice is like throwing the one-two punch to score a knockout. We've shown you how to scope out the community, now let's progress to finding an ideal property—and total victory.

One person's fantasy is another's albatross. You might hanker to own 40 or so acres where you can raise animals and grow crops. The family down the street may prefer to trade their condo for a house just outside a small town, while the retirees next door prefer a little place right in the middle of town close to all services. The career-driven yuppies a few streets over are looking for a second home in a recreational mecca where they can escape on long weekends. Each seeks a custom-made oasis.

People find their dreams take many shapes. Possibilities for shelter run the gamut. There are underground bermed homes, rustic cabins, grand Victorian ladies, sprawling ranch styles, peeled-log beauties, Swiss chalets, mountain A-frames, adobe haciendas, dome homes, and nondescript little houses. (By the way, we've discovered that a fair number of these exterior Plain Janes sport stunning interiors. It's a country quirk that some folks spend a lot more on the inside than the outside.)

Detached houses continue to be the most appealing to both urban and rural residents. Condominiums have also gone country. We have some here that sell for under $30,000. This is an ideal way out of the rental market for young couples, and a solution for mature adults who don't want the responsibility of a big house and yard.

Mobile homes, once thought of as tin boxes, have come into their own in the last few years. When making a transition onto bare land they are a wonderful alternative for quick housing. A 14 x 70-foot mobile offers nearly 1,000 square feet of living space. And some double wides have all the luxuries of conventional houses, including hot tubs and whirlpool baths. Once in place, these babies become stationary when the wheels, axle, and towing tongue are removed. Add a pitched shake roof, a porch or patio, some landscaping, and presto! Even the tax assessor may mistake a mobile home for a conventionally built house. We offer a caution when buying older mobiles though. It's difficult, sometimes impossible, to get insurance if a unit is more than 10 years old. So check with your insurance agent before investing in an older model. Also be sure the zoning laws allow mobiles where you plan to locate.

While we're doling out cautionary advice, let's talk briefly about subdivision lots. Disreputable real estate developers can make a tract of barren, parched earth or swampland look and sound like paradise. Each year they ring up billions of dollars in interstate land sales. *Always* visit property before you invest. Legislation enacted in 1984 offers some protection to buyers in larger subdivisions (over 100 lots and advertised in more than one state). But the byword is still *caveat emptor*. (Let the buyer beware.)

It's also a good idea to check Realtors' comments with the building department to verify that zoning, electrical, and other criteria meet your needs. Sometimes a building must have considerable upgrading to be used for a different purpose.

One of the issues that quickly surfaces when contemplating making a move is whether you buy or sell first. It's a shame to find the perfect country getaway, only to be handcuffed because all your capital is still tied up in your city property. Conversely, what a pity to sell your city home . . . and not have a country retreat to go to. There is no foolproof solution. It seems wise to us, however, once you've made the commitment to become an urban dropout and have narrowed your choices to a town or two, it's time to put your house on the market. If you find the ideal place at the right price, then you'll have one leg up on being able to purchase it.

Unless you have the cash to carry two places temporarily, make your offer on the new real estate *contingent* on the successful sale of your old residence. If this doesn't work, you might try renting with an option to buy until your capital frees up.

Depending on what the economy is like, it may take time to unload your metropolitan property. In 1980 when we tried to sell our 2400-square-foot home a couple of blocks from the beach, purchasers were as scarce as opera buffs at a Michael Jackson concert. We made the mistake of buying a second place before we sold the first. Finally we accepted a ludicrous offer on our San Diego property to get much needed cash to make payments on the ranch.

Don't rule out a fixer-upper, especially if you or a family member enjoy working with your hands. You can also hire construction help cheaper in the country. Be sure, however, to have an engineer check for structural integrity and a building inspector determine what it will take to conform to local building codes. We're now remodeling the church we bought to accommodate larger offices. It's an interesting experience. The church was built by volunteer labor. These willing, but unskilled, folks left us quite a challenge. The other day we overheard a workman muttering, "Isn't *anything* in this place square?!"

If you anticipate building a custom home, it's a good idea to rent first or purchase an interim property. Then you'll have time to become acquainted with a qualified architect and builder.

## *Working Through a Broker*

Especially when dealing with rural properties, it makes sense to work through a broker. Knowledge and familiarity with the area is vital. It isn't like suburban properties where it's easy to find comparable properties and know if you're getting a good value. Country property is spread out and more diverse in type and terrain. A competent real estate salesperson knows about problems unique to the area and distressed owners who need to bail out fast. He or she also knows better than to value country real estate through the eyes of suburbia.

By now you should have narrowed down those you'll work with to one or two. There's no need to deal with everyone. In most areas there are multiple listing services which catalog all real estate properties. Be sure to have detailed discussions with the real estate agents you choose so they know your individual likes and dislikes, wants and needs.

Owner financing has been a staple of country real estate markets for a half century. This is one of the advantages of buying rural property. Usually such loans can be arranged at rates below those quoted by banks and mortgage companies. Additionally, there are no points or loan fees, no detailed loan applications to complete, nor lengthy waits to see if you qualify. In fact, many owners financing their own properties never even check a buyer's credit, so someone cursed with a poor credit rating may be able to slip into a property.

What will you have to pay for rural real estate? By studying the United National Real Estate catalog (800-999-1020), area newspapers, and the *Rural Property Bulletin* (Box 4331, Prescott, AZ 86302, 602-775-5807), you can get a good sense of how area prices vary. Water is universally appealing—therefore a lake, river, stream, or pond automatically boosts the value. Trees are another drawing card. Property with a stand of timber will cost more than barren land. The closer to a large city, the higher the price. Statistics divulged at the National Association of Realtors' 1991 convention show the average house will sell for 16 percent below the original listing price. If you take your time, you're more likely to find a bargain than if you rush into making a purchase.

In small towns off the beaten path you can sometimes buy a *house* for what a nice car costs today. Prices in the $20,000 to $30,000 range can still be found. And remember you need a lot less income if your monthly mortgage payments are based on $16,000 or so (after a down payment), than if you're supporting a mortgage in excess of $100,000.

## *What to Look for in a Country Home*

City slickers who don't educate themselves can really get hurt when they buy in the sticks. Choosing property before you're informed is the human equivalent of a dog exposing its belly in surrender. A good book to help you avoid such pitfalls is *Finding the Good Life in Rural America* by Bob Bone. If you want to purchase a house or retail store rather than land, the following Quickie Rural Home/Store Evaluation Sheet is helpful.

## QUICKIE RURAL HOME/STORE EVALUATION SHEET

Address:

Name of broker or owner:　　　　　　Price: $

Down: $　　　　Terms:　　　　　　Annual taxes: $

How long has it been on the market?　　Size of lot/acreage:

Any other buildings on the property?

Total square footage:　　　　　　　　One story or two?

Condition of neighborhood:　　　　　　Landscaped?

Type of roof/condition:

Type of heating system/age:　　Average monthly utility bill: $

What is the water source?　　Well permits?　　Water rights?

Condition of plumbing:

Connected to sewer?　Septic tank?　How old?　Where located?

Condition of electrical system:

Telephone lines in/available?

Miles to town:　　　　　　Does county maintain road?

Overall condition:

Special **good** features of property:

Special **bad** aspects of property:

**Stores only:** Are fixtures included?　　Is inventory included?

*SPECIMEN — We encourage readers to photocopy these*

If you have any qualms about a piece of property, or are buying it directly from the owner, consider contacting a real estate agent in a neighboring town and hiring him or her to inspect it for $100 or $200. Also have them find out whether back taxes are paid and if the title is clear.

There's more to a house than meets the eye. In the city you can hire a home inspection service that will perform complete structural, wall, floor, ceiling, foundation, basement, and roof inspections. They'll also do a termite inspection; look at the plumbing, heating, and air conditioning systems; check the septic tank; do a radon measurement; even examine built-in appliances. In many small towns, however, no such service exists. (Maybe this is a part-time business idea for you!)

You can personally do some checking by talking with the people in the county courthouse and at the assessor's office. They know more than you'd imagine. Also chat with the neighbors. You'll quickly find out such details as what the roads are like in the winter and if the school bus comes by your front door.

It's been said that neighborhoods have personalities—even in small towns. Be sure to look not only at homes, but also at the surrounding clues. The house may be perfect. But if you have toddlers or school-aged children, an absence of bikes and basketball hoops may give you a hint about this area. When you visit with the neighbors ask open-ended questions. An older lady may complain about "all the kids in this neighborhood." If you have children, that's probably a positive remark. (Try to be around when the school bus arrives.) If you're a retired couple, you might choose to look elsewhere.

We knew a military family who tried this door-knocking technique. They thought they'd found the right house until they talked to a neighbor. She was describing the folks in surrounding homes. "Now those people are military," she remarked, pointing across the street. "They'll only be here a year or two so we don't think it's worth the effort to get to know them. They're so transient, you know." Needless to say, the house hunters filed this information away.

Consider other clues as you survey areas. If you're a gardener, you'll certainly notice the yards around you. Do these neighbors share the same values about their grounds? It doesn't have to be a perfect match, but if something is likely to get on your nerves, admit it. You're the one who'll see it every day. When you've narrowed it down to one or two houses, drive by several different times during the day to "feel the pulse" of the neighborhood. And be sure to take lots of pictures; family and friends will all want to see where you're going.

While it's simpler to get a feel for the size of a lot in suburbia, understanding larger parcels of land is a more difficult challenge. Purchasing land is foreign to most city residents. To help you get sizes in perspective, notice the visual titled A City Lot Versus Country Acreage. Acreage is most often sold in parcels of 5, 40, 160 (a quarter section), 320 (a half section), and 640 (a full section) acre increments. The smaller the parcel, the higher the cost per acre. For instance, you may pay $3,000 for five acres but be able to buy a 40-acre parcel for $16,000. Acreage can also be deceiving. Part of it may run up the side of a hill and be unusable, but you still pay for that by the acre.

Thousands of lovely farms with attractive buildings and good soil are for sale in regions that are not close to large metropolitan areas. They can be picked up at a fraction of their real value because the area is suffering from out-migration. If you want a bargain farm to play a large role in your future, check upstate New York, the upper Peninsula of Michigan, and the Ozarks.

## *Pointers for Picking Parcels of Unimproved Property*

As you contemplate buying unimproved country property, there are many things to consider.

**Number one is water.** Buying acreage without water rights is the equivalent of putting the fox in charge of the henhouse. And just because there is surface water on your land—a stream, river, lake, or pond—it does *not* necessarily mean you have the legal right to use it! Water rights are a commodity just like the acreage itself. One person can own the land, someone else the water rights. You need water not only for drinking and bathing, but also for animals and crops—so investigate this issue thoroughly. In our county you can't get a well permit for outside water use unless you have 35 or more acres of land. If you want a lawn, a garden, or a place to wash your car, you're out of luck without the acreage. And consider whether the flow will lessen or disappear during the hot summer months. If there aren't adequate water rights, get bids for drilling a well *before* you make an offer on the land. Know how deep you'll likely have to go to hit water and if it will be potable (safe for drinking).

**Look closely at zoning laws.** You can't always put a property to any use you want. There may be restrictions on whether a mobile home can serve as an interim residence, covenants in posh developments that restrict unsightly possessions or buildings, limitations on using your home as an

*Trade Your Business Suit Blues for Blue Jean Dreams™*

## A City Lot Versus Country Acreage

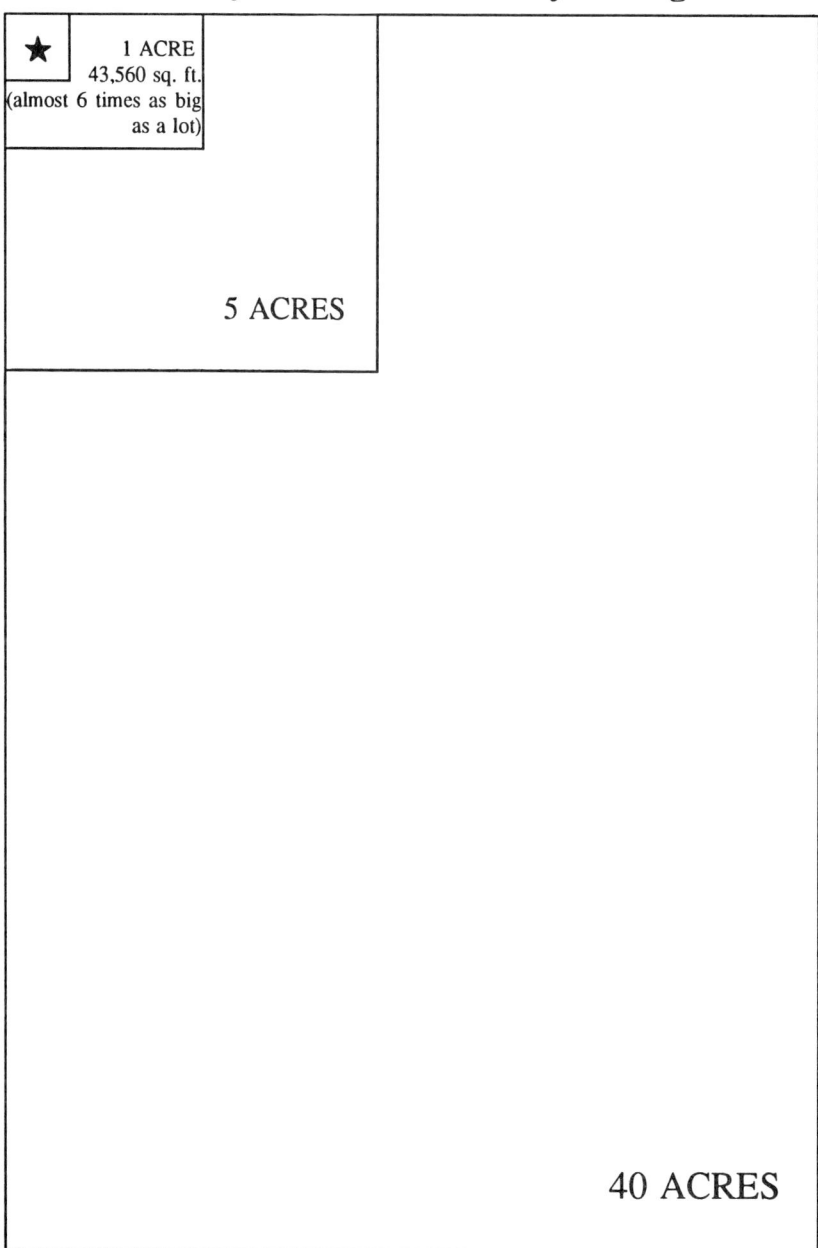

★ 1 ACRE
43,560 sq. ft.
(almost 6 times as big as a lot)

5 ACRES

40 ACRES

★ A typical city lot is 7,300 square feet

Checking Out Rural Edens

office. (We discuss overcoming this in the chapter on "Working From Home.") And if you're serious about farming, be sure the place is zoned for agricultural use. Likewise determine any zoning or deed restrictions that might prevent you from keeping certain types of animals.

*Will you need a septic system?* If you can't connect to a municipal sewer system, be sure the soil will accommodate a septic tank. Check this out by having a percolation test done.

*Investigate the soil.* Is it rich farm land? Tillable? Is there good drainage? What crops will grow best? Talk to the county extension agent about a soil analysis report to determine what kind of soil you have.

A rookie farmer or rancher might want to check with agricultural colleges such as those at Colorado State University or Texas A & M University. These and other universities hold a wealth of information and sometimes even have intern programs where junior, senior, or graduate students use their summers to work on farms. In this way you get the most up-to-date information available for very little cost. Room and board is necessary, and it's always thoughtful to include a little extra for spending money. The student will appreciate the experience and you've just gained a stronger footing in the agricultural industry.

*What's the "lay of the land?"* Is there a suitable home site or will expensive grading be required? Don't get stuck on a flood plain. And if you plan to have a great view from a hilltop, check to be sure it doesn't catch traffic noises. Sound carries remarkably well in the country, especially at night. Your frontier fantasy will be quickly dashed if the sound of roaring trucks permeates the evening breeze. If you want to use solar power, is there a good southern exposure—or do mountains limit the hours of sun? Is there a driveable road or would the existing jeep trail challenge the most stalwart Baja racer? Putting in access roads is expensive when you factor in grading, gravel, shoulders, and culverts to prevent washouts.

**Consider easements and encumbrances.** If the piece of land you want to buy doesn't have access to a public road, get an easement right to reach it without trespassing on your neighbor's land. And don't be surprised if the local utility company has an easement on your land giving them permission to run underground lines. Be sure to get a deed conveying clear title. If there is any question about encumbrances on the property, seek the counsel of an attorney. After all, you don't want a property dispute. What's a property dispute? *Ground beef* of course!

*What about mineral rights?* It's wise to insist on getting the mineral rights to your property. Seem like an insignificant point? Not so. One poor soul—who had built his dream home and planted orchards and gardens—came home one day to find his house bulldozed and his mature orchard being uprooted. Turns out the company that owned the mineral rights found coal on his land and he had no legal recourse. Additionally, mineral rights sometimes can add up to huge sums for you. We know one man who got $800,000 for the minerals on his property. Besides, who knows what raw materials will be of value several decades from now?

*Are there any natural hazards?* This might include excessive winds (terrific for generating windmill power, but difficult to live with), unstable soil and rock that could result in landslides, or steep terrain and thick brush that equal a fire hazard. Also consider any plans to develop nearby land. This could interfere greatly with your peace and quiet.

To simplify the selection process, use the following Rural Real Estate Checklist. It poses many questions to help you when romancing the soil.

## RURAL REAL ESTATE CHECK LIST

The following is a list of questions the prospective purchaser should know the answers to, before making a binding offer on country property.

Since there are special considerations which relate to one kind of property to the exclusion of others, concerns which are peculiar to a certain area of the country, or even to the buyers themselves, this is not to be construed as being a complete list.

In the writer's opinion, the concerns addressed by these questions fit most properties, most of the time, and for most buyers.

Some states, such as California, require a broker by law to obtain a disclosure statement from the seller for *residential* property. A copy of this disclosure must be delivered to the buyer of the property. It is becoming common practice for more and more brokers to obtain such disclosures from sellers even if the law does not require it. United National Real Estate brokers follow this guideline during their transactions. Such disclosures will answer many of the following questions.

Bob Bone

ZONING, BUILDING CODES, CC & R's
1. Is the property in compliance with **zoning and** setback regulations?
2. Is the owner aware of any health, **safety, or building** code violations?
3. Are there any notices of abatement or citations against the property other than the mortgage?
4. Read CC&R's if any. Are there any violations apparent?

PARCEL
1. Is the property in a flood plain or special study zone?
2. Is there any indication or does the owner know of any drainage problem?

3. Is there any indication or does the owner know of any water accumulation in the basement or on the property?
4. Has the parcel been surveyed? Are the corners identified?
5. If there is a stream, river, or lake, does the property line run to the center?
6. Are there any legal limitations of the use of any stream, river, ditch, or lake on the property?

## ROAD/RIGHTS OF WAYS
1. Is there deeded Right-of-Way to the property?
2. Is the road to the property public or private? Who maintains it? Snow removal?

## CONSTRUCTION
1. Is the owner aware of any structural or foundation problems?
2. To the owner's knowledge, does the property have any urea-formaldehyde or asbestos material used in its construction?
3. What type of roof? Age of roof? Any apparent leaking? Has the attic been checked?
4. Has the property suffered damage from a fire or flood?

## SYSTEMS/APPLIANCES
1. Are the following items in working order?

| Range | Trash Compactor | Air Conditioning | Sprinklers |
| --- | --- | --- | --- |
| Microwave | Garbage Disposal | Garage Door Opener(s) | Furnace |
| Dishwasher | Water Softeners/Filters | Refrigerator | Water Pump |

2. Is the owner aware of any problems affecting the plumbing, electrical, heating/cooling systems or the water heater?
3. What were the owner's heating and air conditioning costs for the past 12 months?
4. Is the sewage system public? If not, is there a septic system? To the owner's knowledge are there any blockages or breaks in the lines?
5. If there is a septic system, is the owner aware of any backup or overflowing of the tank?
6. Do any problems exist with permits, operation or system location?
7. What was the date the septic system was last pumped?

8. If the public sewage system is not hooked up, what would the cost be to hook it up?
9. If there isn't a septic tank in, what would the total cost for a system be for your family size?

WATER SOURCE
1. Is the water source public? Who is the water company? Approximate monthly cost for water?
2. If the water isn't in, what would the cost be to hook it up?
3. If the water source is public, is there any problem with the main line?
4. Is there a well? Public or private? Is there a maintenance agreement between all parties?
5. How deep is the well? Per the owner, what is the gallons per minute? Size of casting? What size horsepower is the pump on the well?
6. Has the owner had any problems with the water pressure or has the well ever run dry?
7. Is the owner aware of any contamination or other reason the water would not be potable?
8. Is there irrigation water? If so, what is the source? What is the cost to obtain it?

POWER
1. Is there power to the property? If not, how far is the property from power? What would the cost be to bring power to the property?

SERVICES
1. Schools. What type? How far away are the schools? Does the bus pick the children up?
2. Fire protection. How far away is the fire station?
3. Medical care. What is the distance to the nearest hospital? What about emergency care?
4. Is there mail delivery? If not, how do you obtain your mail?

LEGAL
1. Is there a Home Owners Association? If so, what are the dues per year?
2. Are there any disputes with neighbors regarding location or use of driveways, patios, fences, common walls, etc.?

3. Is the owner aware of any condition or situation which might result in an increase in assessment?

Reprinted from *Finding the Good Life in Rural America* by Bob Bone.

## *Living on the Land*

Some people dream of living off the land while they live on it. These homesteaders hope to generate enough income from vegetables, fruit trees, other crops, and meat they produce to make a living. It's tough. But it can be done—especially if you get enough capital from your city property to pay cash for your country spot.

Living simply, without electricity or a telephone, holds rewards for the hardy. Life can be rich: filled with your homegrown food, music, friends, and nature. Rather than an electric or gas range, you may use a cookstove fueled with firewood. Your refrigerator may be a cool natural spring.

Before our indoor plumbing was in place at the ranch, we rigged up a bathing arrangement that warmed the heart of every nonconformist. Imagine one five-gallon oil drum and kindling for a small fire. Add a bathtub, a gallon bucket, and one stream. Now start a fire under the oil drum. Use the bucket to dip water from the stream and half fill the oil drum. Transfer the warm water into the bathtub. BATHE! Pull the plug and water the creek bank. What an experience to cleanse yourself smack dab in the middle of nature—complete with birds chirping, a bubbling creek, and warm sunshine kissing your back.

However, some people (ourselves included) who have tried this "simple life" find it very difficult. You spend much of your time just surviving: chopping wood, stoking fires, boiling water, etc. You have to think and plan ahead. Nothing's immediate. You learn to organize yourself and your work in ways you never expected. It took us an hour's round trip to get into town for the mail or groceries. Substantial shopping had to be done in a distant town. That round trip consumed more than three hours.

Many others who have harbored the dream of self-sufficiency report the demands are too great. Fourteen-hour days, seven days a week, are not unusual if you're growing and preserving all your own food, making your clothes, plus providing for your own energy and heat.

> Marilyn: *Being a city girl, I proved myself in ways I wouldn't have dreamed of. It's funny the difference a pair of cowboy boots and work gloves make. Wearing those, I felt invincible. (Well most of the time.) I'll never forget the day Tom and our ranch hand had gone to an auction and I was alone. We had a mare ready to give birth—she had lost her foals the previous two years. When I went*

*out to check her, one of the baby's legs was already exposed. Panic engulfed me. How could I help her? Which way should I pull? What if she kicked me?*

*An hour—and many prayers—later, a gorgeous, spindly-legged newborn stood nursing. And I sat there in awe, rejoicing in the wonder of God's creation. There were other times I tested my mettle, other experiences that will always bring tears or a grin. I feel grateful and blessed to have had those opportunities to expand myself in fresh ways.*

Because we used computers, we had a generator and a bank of batteries to supply power. Something was always going wrong. Fortunately Tom used to earn his living as an electronics engineer, so he knows how to fix things. The typical city slicker would be lost trying to coexist with such obstinate systems. And that's just the tip of the iceberg. There are irrigation ditches to open (and close), tractors to get unstuck, animals to doctor, and much more. Trying to do all that—while maintaining two businesses—overwhelmed us. Though we have many cherished memories, the difficulties and inconveniences of home on the range just weren't worth it.

Although we miss the ranch and the animals, living in a small town with normal conveniences is much more realistic for us. So while we don't want to discourage those bent on being back-to-the-landers, in all honesty we must sound this solemn warning. Some people discover their dream of living in an isolated mountain cabin can become a nightmare. Sometimes it just doesn't mesh with their personalities, needs, and goals.

If you value your independence and still hanker for this rugged lifestyle, consider subscribing to *Mother Earth News, Harrowsmith Country Life, Country, Backwoods Home Magazine,* and *Country Journal.* And the beautiful *Countryside* magazine will make any city dweller drool. Their addresses are in the "Bibliography/Recommended Reading." Getting a power line to your remote dwelling can be a big challenge. Helpful resources on that subject include the 1992 edition of the *Alternative Energy Sourcebook,* edited by John Schaeffer; *Home Power Magazine;* and Backwoods Solar Electric Systems.

Now that you know the ins and outs of purchasing rural property, let's address the moving process itself. Relocation ranks among the top five stress producing activities, just below death and divorce. Yet many have made the transition happily. What's the key? Our next chapter has been gleaned from those who've been there. Fear not. Knowing how to do it *easily* will melt your resistance like a propane torch melts solder. With enough tips and know-how, it can truly be a *moving experience.*

# 5

# Making the Move— Without Making Yourself Crazy

So you've decided to make the move. Now the fun begins! A new home and job can be a wonderful adventure, filled with memories for years to come. The key to a successful relocation can be summed up in one word: *attitude*. Here's your opportunity to make some of those changes which up until now were only daydreams.

If you have children, you'll want to involve them in the move as soon as possible. Children key off of their parents' attitudes, so the more optimistic you are about the move, the more positive they'll be. Talk with them about why you're moving. Don't dwell on leaving your present location. Demonstrate your excitement about *going to* a new, exciting place. At the same time, leave room for dialogue about their feelings—hopes, fears, questions, and doubts. In whatever terms they'll understand, explain the time frame involved and what they can expect.

Now that you're armed with information about your new location, talk about the exciting things to look forward to. What nearby tourist attractions, special festivals, famous historic sights, and educational and cultural opportunities are available? How is the climate different? Can we look forward to skiing, sledding, and making snowmen—or will we find ourselves clamming, swimming, or surfboarding at a nearby beach? You've talked to people who live there and gleaned from their knowledge. Build on data you obtained from the chamber of commerce, etc.—not as if it were a school assignment but as you would devour brochures of the South Sea Islands while planning a vacation. Discovering exciting things to look forward to will help immensely in creating an upbeat attitude for the entire family.

## *Contract It Out or Do It Yourself?*

Getting a cost estimate will help you decide whether to use professionals or pull up stakes yourself. Moving companies will send someone out to your home to look at your goods and give you an estimate of moving costs. This amount will be impacted by whether you pack things yourself or have the company do it. The government regulates costs and rates of moving expenses, so most companies charge about the same. You'll want to talk with others who have moved to find out what different firms offer and who gives the best service. Remember that estimates of moving costs are not binding. Your final total will be based on the weight of your household goods.

Moving companies are busier in the summer months and at the end of each month, so as you plan the timing of your move, keep this in mind. Another advantage of contacting these firms early is that they can provide you with a wealth of information on everything from moving with children to tax deductible expenses. In researching this book, we found their brochures and free booklets filled with essential information and loaded with helpful hints. Be sure to take advantage of this expertise.

One caution: We've heard stories about movers who highly touted their professionalism and the care they gave your valued possessions. Yet when people used these firms, especially in very busy seasons, they found some packers and movers had been hired off the street just the day before! Be sure to verify workers have had training and experience with *this* company.

After getting a cost estimate and gathering other data, you may decide to move yourself. Vans, trailers, pads, packing boxes, ropes, and dollies are available to rent from several nationwide companies. They can also sell you insurance. (Keep receipts for everything in a central file.) Some companies furnish pamphlets on packing and tips for do-it-yourselfers, while others provide a video on what size truck to use and how to load it. The costs of moving yourself will probably be lower, but of course there's a lot more work involved. If you're thinking of towing a trailer, check to see if your car can handle the weight, and factor in the cost of a trailer hitch. Make sure your vehicle is in top condition.

For tax purposes you can write off all direct costs associated with moving, such as transporting yourselves and your household goods to the new site, if you meet certain qualifications. One IRS stipulation is that your new job must be at least 35 miles farther from your old home than your previous job was. Another is that you must work full time in your new position for at least 39 weeks during the 12 months after the move. Check with your accountant or tax consultant for current rulings.

## *List It—File It . . . but Don't Forget It*

One of the best things you can do for yourself at this point is to make a moving file. Preparation is to moving what a syringe is to a life-saving serum. Random action that isn't carefully planned is no more effective than a serum that can't be administered for lack of a syringe. Gather materials for a portable filing system, organizing information, records, and receipts concerning this move. One central place for these things will save you unnecessary stress in the weeks to come.

You'll also want to keep an ongoing list of every person, publication, or organization you'll need to notify about your move. Have change of address cards and stamps handy. As a bill or magazine comes in, send a card and check that name off the list. Health care providers and utility companies will need to be contacted. In your files, you'll also want to note records to be transferred. Medical, dental, and school records need to be gathered or sent. Some churches will provide a letter of transfer. These chores are like cats: if you dislike them and try to keep out of their way, they know it at once and land up in your lap. Most of this paperwork can be done ahead of time before everything really gets busy. And it will feel great to know you've already checked these things off of your list!

**Suggested File Headings**

    Dental/Orthodontic Records
    Housing Contracts, Leases, etc.
    Lists (See List of Lists)
    Medical Records
    Moving Company: estimates, contracts, payment
    Pet Records
    Receipts for tax purposes
    School Records
       -academic
       -birth certificates (photocopy)

-immunization records/copy of recent physicals
-letters of introduction or recommendation
-psychological testing records

Travel: coupons, hotel/motel information, maps, plane tickets, emergency phone numbers

Utilities Disconnect: contracts and deposit receipts

Utilities Connect: contracts and deposit receipts

Will: have at least one copy in files

## The ABC's of School Transfers

If you have school-aged children, transferring them to a new educational facility will be a major part of your move. Although choosing where they will attend school isn't the determining factor in deciding on a house, it certainly is something to investigate. Where you live usually determines where they will go to school. If a teenager is involved in a particular sport, be sure to check out opportunities for him or her at the new school. Participation in a sport a child is accustomed to will help greatly in his or her transition. If your offspring is obviously talented, don't discount the potential for a college scholarship; make sure the new school has a good program in that area.

Rural school options are often limited. However, there are private or church schools in many areas, as well as a growing population of "home schoolers" who network and pool resources. You'll want to consider all options and find the one that fits your needs. Once you've decided on a school situation, find out what the new school will require in terms of records and paperwork. Inquire about dress codes, transportation, school teams, etc.

In preparing for the school transition, there is necessary paperwork to gather. Younger children might need a birth certificate. You'll want to have a letter from your elementary school child's present teacher explaining his or her grading method, and describing the student's achievement level, interests, and needs for improvement. You might also want the teacher to add a short description of how your child interacts with other students in the class.

Academic records must be transferred. If you want records of psychological testing from the counselor's office, you'll have to make a specific written request for those to be sent.

Along with academic records, most schools require medical and immunization records if a child is participating in sports or physical education classes. Check on how current your records are. If an updated physical will be required, have it done before the move. Your child won't have to cope with an unfamiliar doctor at your new place, and you won't be pressured to search for an M.D. as soon as you get to town. While you're at it, have all family members' prescriptions refilled.

Consider, too, getting a letter for your student athlete. It's hard to break into a school team, particularly if the season has already started. A recommendation from his or her current coach will be an asset in making this entry. Then there are endorsements from past employers and teachers—especially if there's a college-bound teenager involved. These letters will serve as an introduction to the working community or the scholarship committee, as well as a boost to a teen's self-esteem.

Begin to gather this material as soon as you can. Make a separate school file for each child. Put this information in your moving files, and check it off your list.

## *Moving With Fido and Kitty*

Just as there are preparations for helping your children make a smooth change, there are certain details to cover when moving your pets. The first thing to consider is paperwork because it can be done early and added to your files. (One more thing you can check off!) Contact the state veterinarian in the capital city of your new state and find out about any special requirements. Your local vet can help you locate this office. Each state has laws applicable to pets' entry, so be informed. Nearly all states require an interstate health certificate for horses and dogs, and some require them for cats, birds, and other pets. Some states even want the certificate to precede your arrival. This document should have a description of the animal, list its immunizations and the dates, and state that your pet is healthy. Most states insist dogs have rabies shots, and many require them for cats. Rabies tags must be firmly attached to the pet's collar.

Allow time for treatment of any diseases and be sure to ask your vet for the name of a colleague in your new area. If your pet gets car sick or is easily excitable, also ask for a prescription for medication while traveling. In addition to a rabies tag, attach a large identification tag to the animal's collar during the move. (Luggage tags are great for this.) Include the pet's name, your name and new address, and someone to contact while you're en route. If you have horses or other large animals, ask about town or county regulations concerning how much space is required for them and how far away from your neighbors the barn or stable must be. (This is also helpful information if you're thinking of buying horses or other large animals once you move. Plan ahead.)

There are folks who send their pets ahead via air transportation. If you decide to go this route, the airlines will provide details. Since most people have to transfer at least one vehicle to the new locale, however, we recommend the family pet go with the vehicle driver. Animals feel the stress of a move too, and a little TLC helps their transitions. Besides, they're a comfort for children during this event.

In the case of a move which requires more than a day on the road, it will be necessary to make hotel or motel reservations at a place which permits pets. Check this out ahead of time. Most Marriotts and Holiday Inns allow well-behaved pets. Gaines Dog Research Center publishes a list of accommodations allowing pets. It's called, *Touring with Towser* and may be obtained by sending $1.00 to Touring With Towser, P.O. Box 1007, Kankakee, IL 60901.

Unless your pet is accustomed to traveling in the car, you should get him or her used to the idea by going for short drives before the move. Good travel manners taught during this time will circumvent your pooch's climbing all over everyone and barking at traffic. An excellent tip is to have your dog's nails or cat's claws clipped before the trip to prevent scratches on you or your car. Consider a travel kennel as a home away from home. When you stop for dinner, a rest, or a sightseeing respite—or a motel that doesn't welcome pets—you won't have to worry about chewed upholstery. If you're traveling with horses, check with the chamber of commerce in places where you'll spend the night. They can tell you about "horse motels."

Once you've arrived at your destination, keep dogs and cats confined for a week or so. They may tend to run off, trying to get back to their "real home." (Cats should be kept indoors for several weeks.) Use their familiar food and water dishes in the same place every day, and have their same toys out for play. Remember to have them licensed as soon as possible. Like the rest of the family, they'll get used to the fact that they, too, are home.

## *Saying Goodbye*

Plans are coming along and you're making headway. Good job. In taking care of all the "business details," be sure not to neglect the social and emotional implications of this move. No matter how wonderful your new place is going to be, you'll want to look back on your final time here with no regrets. Life gets very busy in the weeks before a move. Sit down now and make a list of people you really want to spend time with before you say *sayonara*. Scheduling your personal life at this point is every bit as important as scheduling the move.

When friends ask what they can do to help, don't demur, "Oh nothing, but thanks." Have a specific list ready. Perhaps you can combine personal visits with these necessary tasks. Some suggestions to include might be:

1) Bring lunch or dinner over on moving week. (Several can do this.)
2) Have us over to your house for dinner on moving day. (A sane home and dinner works wonders for a sagging morale and energy level!)
3) Let us spend the night at your home on moving day.
4) Babysit for me during the last week.
5) Help plan and host a children's party. (See below.)
6) Help me clean the house once it's empty.

While considering personal needs, don't forget the children will want to spend time with their friends too. Depending on their ages, you may want to plan a going away event for them. A skating party, pool party, or pizza party can be arranged with a minimum of effort. It will cost more than a home party—but it may be worth it not to have to prepare, host, then clean up when you have an already overloaded schedule. Another advantage of this type of party is that many ages can enjoy these activities. If you have children of different ages, they can each invite a few of their own friends to one big wing-ding, rather than feeling they have to have separate parties.

As we consider personal needs, think of aging parents. Having their children move to a distant location can be a cause of major stress. Talk to them about the possibility of relocating as well. Investigate senior centers, convalescent homes, or retirement complexes in your rural community, and discuss the options with your folks. If they decide to stay where they are, reassure them with phone calls, letters, news clippings, and pictures. And help them look forward to visiting you.

## *Taking the Panic Out of Packing*

Now that you have a concept of what your new home will be like, you have a better idea of what to keep and what to get rid of. Don't wait until the last minute to sort out belongings. Most moving companies will tell you that this is a good time to plan a garage sale and donate items to charity. (You may be able to get tax credit for goods donated to charity.)

In preparing for a garage sale, there are several steps you'll need to take. First of all, get out the family calendar and set a date. (With so much going on, you don't want to inadvertently plan it on Jimmy's soccer championship day or Easter weekend.) Some cities require garage sale licenses for a small fee. Call city hall to check.

The next thing is to identify a specific area for garage sale merchandise to accumulate—a bedroom corner or a closet. Make sure clothes and linens are clean and folded so they'll make the best possible display for the sale. Plan an outside staging area for shovels, hoses, barbecues, etc. Attack a room each week. Depending on their ages, the children can help sort through their belongings. Promise to let them keep the profits from their things—that's real motivation! (Specially colored price tags make it easier to mark and track their merchandise.) There's an old saying, "The mouse ate the elephant one bite at a time." You'll be surprised at your ongoing progress.

Consider major appliances. Is the washing machine struggling? Does the refrigerator need to be replaced soon? These are heavy objects, and you may want to weigh (no pun intended) the advantages and disadvantages of moving them. You'll be packing and unpacking—and paying for—everything you decide to take with you.

Do you have houseplants? Some states have agricultural restrictions on what can be brought in. Will you give plants to friends, take them with you, or sell them to others? A plant table at your garage sale can help fund new ones at your destination.

About a week ahead of time, place your ad in the newspaper. Tell all your friends. Make signs to post during the following week. (Be sure to note where you posted them so you can take them down after the sale.)

The week of the sale, have enough tables to display your items—and a "Plan B," if necessary, in case of rain. Display like articles together and attractively. Price everything. Help your children set up their table and prices. Go to the bank and get lots of coins for change as well as dollar bills. Decide whether or not you'll take checks and whether you'll negotiate prices. Get your money box and pens and notebook ready to record sales. Have a colored pen to record sales from the children's things and a regular one for yours. Expect "early birds" and decide ahead of time when you're willing to start selling.

When the sale is over, add what's leftover to your charity collection and call for pickup from Goodwill or the Salvation Army. Congratulations! You've just found a profitable way to lighten your load, and you're much better prepared to make the move now.

Weeks of preparation and anticipation have passed and moving day is approaching. Before you start packing, close your eyes and do some imagining. Get ready to make two more lists. The first is "What do I want to have with me the last day of moving out and the first day of moving in?" Items such as a coffeepot, the baby's favorite teddy bear and blanket, my files for this move, toothbrush and toilet articles, cleaning supplies, etc.

Try to mentally go through a day and think of what you absolutely must have at your disposal. Then assign a separate place in the house for these things. They will go with you in the car.

The second list is similar. These are things the movers will take with them; they're assigned last-thing-packed-and-first-thing-unpacked status. Pillows and bed linens, towels and washcloths, a shower curtain and hooks, a few tools, a box of basic kitchen utensils, pots and pans, the baby's crib, maybe the television set, and a favorite toy or two for younger children. Some moving companies even have brightly colored labels for these boxes, but it's up to you to separate these things and put them in a special grouping. Then watch them like a hawk!

Now let's look at some aspects of doing the packing yourself. Whether you have contracted with a moving company or not, you'll want to prepare some of your things for the move. Certain objects will require your own special brand of TLC. If you choose to do your own packing, begin to collect old newspapers and sturdy boxes for the move. The small amounts of money you save by being frugal can add up to big savings by the time you're done. Some folks choose to save money by shipping unbreakable articles, like books and tools, by slower and less expensive methods.

In addition to sturdy boxes and newspapers, you'll want to have tissue paper (newsprint will rub off and stain clothes and linens), plastic bags (for parts, bolts, etc.), a marking pen (for labels), and packing materials (popcorn or styrofoam peanuts) to fill up extra space. One trick we learned was to use extra sheets and towels as the packing material for good dishes and other breakables. Corrugated paper rolls will also help protect fragile items. Add to your list strong twine and gummed tape for sealing boxes. Pack heavier goods on the bottom and lighter ones on the top. Some companies advise, the heavier the item, the smaller the carton. And be sure to note "fragile" on appropriate boxes.

As you pack, do one room at a time starting as far ahead of the move as possible. You can begin with off-season clothes and Christmas decorations—things you won't be using until after you arrive. As you finish each box, label it with a number and designate which room it goes in. Have a spiral notebook with you to record the box number, room, and notes telling you something about the contents.

If the mover judges a box to be packed improperly, he may ask you to repack it or he may do it himself and charge you for it. This is because if it's damaged en route, he may be liable for the damage. So take care to do a good job the first time.

There are a few categories which require special preparation and care. Firearms and their serial numbers must be registered with your moving company. When you get down to the last items to be packed, note that flammables and combustibles will not be transported, so you'll need to dispose of them in a responsible manner. Be sure to drain the lawn mower, Weed Eater, barbecue propane tanks, and other items which normally contain fuel.

## *Mastering Moving Week*

What can I expect on packing and moving days? If you have contracted with a carrier to do your packing and moving, there will be two major stages of moving out: packing one day and loading the next. A different crew might do each job. (Depending on your contract, you may be packing some things yourself or the packers might do it all.) Your belongings will be placed into various sized cardboard boxes and labeled. Most companies will label cartons according to which room they're in. They'll also label in *generic* terms, such as linens (bath towels or sheets?) dishes (good china or pots and pans?) clothes (his, hers, Jimmy's or Lisa's?). Plan to have a couple of magic markers so you can go behind them and add your own details. Where they put "linens," you might want to add "MBR linens." Where they label "dishes," you might scrawl "crock pot." And where they write "clothes," make a note, "Jimmy's." It's not necessary to do this for all the boxes, but it saves a game of hide-and-seek to find the things you'll need early on. A few words of caution: Don't identify boxes as "Grandma's sterling silver" or "antique quilt." It's better not to advertise your valuables.

On moving day the loading crew will arrive and begin to put packed cartons as well as large furniture and major appliances on the van. (If you have a friend who's willing to be a "gopher," what a treasure—now's the time!) Be sure to record where spare parts are when packers disassemble things. Missing table legs or refrigerator hinges can cause great distress on the other end! Have someone carefully check the inventory list as the truck is being loaded (and unloaded on the other end of the move). If you can't do it, be sure to have someone you can depend on help you. This insures a record of what actually went on the truck in case you have a claim on the other end.

You'll be amazed how quickly the day goes by. It's not nearly as impossible as it seemed a week ago, and it will get done. Be positive—progress is being made!

One more bit of counsel: Although your material goods are dear to you, keep them in perspective. They are, after all, only things. People are important; relationships are important; things can be replaced.

Now the movers have left. The final step is ensuring the premises are left clean for the next people. Whether you're leaving a rental place or a home you're trying to sell, you'll want to leave it in good condition. Some people arrange for a cleaning team to come in after they move out; others clean it themselves. This decision should be made ahead of time because if you do it yourself you'll need to plan an extra day to finish up. It may not take a day, but plan for it. Once you're satisfied things are in order, you'll close the door for the last time. Think about the good things that happened while you lived here. Take the time to be thankful. Then start looking forward to what the future holds for you.

At this point we'd like to share our personal tale. Since we had an enormous amount of stuff—both personal and business—we elected to do it ourselves when relocating from the San Diego area. Never one to do the ordinary, Tom ferreted out a 1965 18-wheel gasoline tractor-trailer for the incredible price of $8,000. It was unpopular because it was powered by a gasoline rather than diesel engine. Then he and our son, Steve, got Class C driver's licenses and learned to pilot the monster.

> Marilyn: *To say the actual drive from California to Colorado was an adventure, is an understatement. At one point the truck blew a tire and gave poor Steve a bad scare and a challenge wrestling it safely to the side of the road. Thank God he's a well-muscled young man!*
>
> *During another stint, I was following the big rig in our four-wheel vehicle and pulling a trailer and got separated when everybody stopped to refuel. Since it takes a long time to pump 80 gallons into two tanks in the truck, I went ahead to a rest stop we knew of between Phoenix and Flagstaff. It was on a hill overlooking the freeway and the plan was we could connect there. Tom and Steve assumed I'd see them as the rig passed and would then join them. They cruised by, laid on the air horn, and anticipated seeing me soon pull in behind.*
>
> *After an hour or so, concern set in. We hadn't connected. Pulling the steep grade between Phoenix and Flagstaff in an underpowered gas rig is no picnic, so Tom and Steve had hesitated to turn around. Then their fuel switch, used to change from one tank to the other, failed—so they didn't have enough gas to make it back. It was on to Flagstaff for repairs and fuel. While Tom tended the truck, Steve watched the road. Still no Marilyn.*
>
> *I arrived some two hours later—while the freeway was being swept by Arizona troopers looking for me. It was with a lot of relief, and some embarrassment, that Tom called off the manhunt (womanhunt?). Communication is a wonderful thing. In this case,*

it failed completely. I'd been lazing in the winter sun at the rest stop . . . fully expecting the guys to pull in and stop when they caught up.

Tempers soothed and bellies full, our weary group hit the road again. Late that afternoon, after stopping for the day, we opened the back end of the trailer to get our Siamese cat, Kimba, out of his traveling cage and take him into the motel for some exercise and TLC. (Because he had a history of being a noisy and rambunctious traveler, we'd decided listening to him howl all across country was simply too much; thus he'd been banished to the trailer.) Well, Kimba is also a maverick. No confining cage for him! He had managed to claw his way out and was now howling from somewhere deep in the innards of the converted moving van. There was absolutely no way to unload a 30-foot trailer to rescue a cat, so we said a silent prayer that he would arrive intact.

By the way, we ultimately sold the tractor part of the 18-wheeler for more than we paid for it by using it as a trade-in on a new pickup. Then we took the trailer down off its axles, added a couple of windows, and used it as a shop on the ranch. (How's that for "recycling"?) While all this worked for us, we have to admit it certainly added another dimension to an already stressful transition. You probably want to do things more conventionally. And Kimba? Oh, he scampered happily out when we arrived at our destination and began unloading.

"When will we get there?" "Tell us again what it's like!" "The first thing I'm going to do is . . . " These are the sounds of adventurers. Dad is probably mentally organizing the garage as he drives, and Mom is grouping furniture. "Did we really do it?" "Is this really happening?" You bet it is! And moving into a new place is much more fun than moving out of the old one. There's an air of excitement, like the first day of school—you know it will be work, but it's loaded with surprises too.

The road trip marks a milestone—out with the old and in with the new. Traveling should be a wonderful interim between homes. Snacks, appropriate toys or games, and regular rest stops will make the trip more enjoyable. Youngsters can even pack their own backpacks with pajamas, toothbrushes, and favorite small toys and games. Whether you're traveling with or without children, make this time a semi-holiday rather than a tense journey. You've worked hard. Take time to smell the roses.

Soon enough you're at your destination and the moving van arrives—or you'll have it with you, as in our case. Your belongings have made the trip safe and sound. Boxes will be marked according to which room they'll be going into. Children can begin to unload some of their things and start to make their rooms home. Mom and Dad will probably spend the first day supervising and directing traffic.

Experienced movers suggest making one area or room a liveable retreat as soon as possible. That means amidst boxes and packing materials there's a spot—with a couch or chair, some magazines, and the television set—where a weary body can flop down and take a break from the chaos. This area will be a respite during your transition. A large box with a towel over it suffices as a coffee table, and a plant will lend some semblance of peace here too. There now, doesn't it already feel a bit homey?

Whether you're a couple, a single, or a large family, this period—before you've made new friends and started new involvements—can be a good time for reflection and pulling together. What will you do differently with your life this time around? In many ways it's like a clean sheet of paper. Think about the past. Take advantage of a fresh start. Set new goals as you drop old habits.

This can also be a treasured family or couple time. When you don't have the immediate demands of friends and prior commitments, it's a wonderful opportunity to talk of hopes and dreams for this new place, and to truly enjoy spending time with each other. Stick together like brand new dollar bills. There's a sort of you-and-me-against-the-world bonding that can take place, if you'll let it.

Talk to your children about a fresh start, new friends, sports opportunities, and other positive aspects of the new school environment. Perhaps a special breakfast the first day of school would be a good idea too. Make time to listen well the first few days of school. Share their adventures and help them make the change with enthusiasm, hugs, and a plate of cookies.

Think back now to long ago when the first inkling of a move tickled your fancy. How wild and impossible the idea seemed at the time. Now you're actually here. Yes, there are still some boxes to be unpacked, but rooms are taking shape. New friends are coming into your life and fresh opportunities beckon. You've found the grocery store. Already a daily routine is forming and the phone is beginning to ring. You've accomplished a lot these past weeks and months. Welcome to your new home. And welcome to the country!

## *A Calendar for Moving*

1) Plan tentative dates for moving. Gather brochures from moving companies.
2) If your business is moving you, verify what costs it will pay and what expenses are yours. Get estimates for moving yourself if you're thinking about it.
3) Go on a house-hunting/apartment-hunting trip. Check out schools and other important factors while you're there. Also, measure spaces where major appliances will go (refrigerators and washing machines). Will yours fit?
4) Confirm dates for packing, pickup, and delivery with your carrier.
5) Begin your file system, consulting lists at the end of this chapter. Call utilities and phone companies early and find out how and when to discontinue service. Mark these dates on your calendar or go ahead and set up a time now.
6) Contact your insurance agent about things to cover during this move. If you've bought a home, you'll want to check on that as well.
7) Plan and hold your garage sale.
8) Identify a staging area for give away items. Wait until after your garage sale to donate to charity. You'll surely have some leftover articles to add.
9) Make travel and housing arrangements. If you're flying, an advance booking will save you a bundle. Decide where you'll spend the nights during the moving process and make motel or hotel reservations, or firm up commitments with friends.
10) Gather personal records listed in your files or arrange to have them sent. Let your fingers do the walking whenever possible.
11) Re-check your lists and cross off everything you've taken care of. Set dates to discontinue services.
12) Arrange connection of utilities, or delivery of propane for your new home, if you haven't done so.
13) Arrange for phone referrals to your new number.
14) Register all firearms.
15) Drain oil and gas from all power equipment. Responsibly get rid of all flammables; they can't be moved.

**The last week:**

1) Defrost your freezer; give away any perishable food you won't be able to eat.
2) If you're not taking your plants, donate them to a loving home.

3) Make sure your car is in top condition.
4) Use paper plates and paper cups for a minimum of cleanup. Accept all offers by friends to prepare food!
5) Obtain traveler's checks and money to pay movers. (Payment is expected—cash, certified check, or money order—before they unload your goods.) Decide when to close out your bank account. Be sure you have adequate cash or traveler's checks for emergencies.
6) Empty and close out your safe deposit box.
7) Pack your luggage and those things you'll be taking in the car.
8) Be sure to let your mover know where you'll be, or a phone number to use as a message center in case of emergency. Reconfirm the date and time of delivery.
9) Leave your house or apartment in clean condition.
10) *Bon Voyage!*

## LIST OF LISTS

(Purchase a spiral notebook and make a heading on each page.)

A) **List of questions to ask the realtor and/or property owner**
B) **List of people to be contacted about this move**
C) **List of businesses to be contacted about this move**
    credit card companies
    magazines
    doctors
    dentist/orthodontist
    veterinarian
    phone company
    electric company
    gas company
    water company
    trash service
    post office
    newspaper delivery
    bank
    cable TV
D) **List of businesses to be contacted in the new town (see preceding list)**
E) **List of chores friends can help with**
F) **Checklist for garage sale**
    date decided
    license acquired
    tables to display merchandise

*Trade Your Business Suit Blues for Blue Jean Dreams™*

        plan in case of rain
        price tags on items
        newspaper ad
        signs distributed and noted
        money from bank for change
        pad and colored pens for recording sales
        phone number for charity after garage sale is over
        signs removed

G) **List of friends you want to spend time with**
H) **List of valuables**
I) **List of do-*not*-load items**
        toilet articles
        key to your new house
        medicines (have prescriptions refilled before you leave.)
        moving files
        coffeepot and coffee
        cleaning supplies
        suitcases
        fire extinguisher for car or truck
        first aid kit
        (add your own personal list)

J) **List of last-packed-first-unpacked essentials**
        pillows and bed linens
        towels and washcloths
        shower curtain and hooks
        basic tools
        basic kitchen utensils
        television
        school supplies for children
        baby's crib
        (add your own personal list)

K) **Travel list for baby or children**
L) **Travel list for pet**
        large identification tag and rabies tag
        food and water dishes
        can opener for pet food
        favorite toy or two
        medication and/or sedative prescribed by the vet
        paper towels or newspapers
        flea or tick repellent
        scooper and plastic bags

leash (always put it on before anyone opens a car or motel door!)
stake and chain or rope for outdoors
kennel

**M)** **List for After the Move**
Install a phone
List emergency numbers by telephone
Arrange for referral on old phone number (optional)
Register children in school (if applicable)
Get new driver's license if you moved out of state or change your address for an in-state move
Get new license plates and car registration if you moved out of state or change your current ones for an in-state move
Inquire about churches or places of worship (if appropriate)
Refer to Lists C and D

# 6

# Letting the Small Town Viewpoint Work for You

How exciting it is to live your vision! As you move to the country, you have dreams and anticipations of what it will be like. Those dreams are important. They are the impetus that spurred you on to this move. At the same time, it's vital to remember that nothing is exactly as we picture it will be. Many factors are beyond our control. If you look at this as an adventure—with open-ended possibilities rather than a list of expectations to check off—it will be much more fulfilling.

Just as you'd fasten your seat belt for a ride on the roller coaster, or take a deep breath before diving under water, prepare for relocating by looking forward to the unknown thrills ahead. Don't dwell on what you left behind. Above all, don't try to make your new surroundings a reflection of your past.

Remember the *Ugly American*? Although moving from the suburbs to the exurbs is different than visiting another country, the same principles apply. Too often people migrate, then radiate the feeling that locals are foreigners who should conform to the newcomer's ways. Be willing to change yourself. The countryside doesn't welcome transplants who insist on offering advice on how to live and do things, simply because that's the way the newcomer used to live and do things in the city. If it was so great, why did he leave?

Should your outlook differ from the local perspective, don't voice too many opinions. Intellectual sparks fly most easily when people of different backgrounds and viewpoints interact. Remember it was their town before it became yours. Be patient. It may take time to overcome their preconceived notions. Of course if you followed our advice, you didn't locate in an area hostile to newcomers.

*Givers get* is a sure-fire principle. Having a good life is a lot like a boomerang: You have to toss it out before it comes back to you. Zig Ziglar believes the best way to get what you want is to give others what they want. Maybe that's a jump-start when someone's battery fails. Certainly it's help when a motorist is stranded on a country highway. Or the offer of babysitting while harried parents enjoy a night out with each other.

Share what you have. When you pick berries or wild asparagus, get in the habit of gathering more than you need. Give some away. Plant a larger garden than your family will consume. Knit or crochet a baby sweater or afghan for a service club's fund-raising project.

## *Developing a Mind-Set for Change*

Let's be honest: the only person who really likes change is a wet baby. But if we want to adjust satisfactorily to a new community, we have to be willing to modify how we think and behave. The psychology of country living dictates that you must replace your urban mind-set with a rural one if you want to thrive. People are more easygoing. If you come bouncing in with brisk, rigid, sophisticated ways, you'll alienate the townsfolk.

We can manage our perspective as surely as we manage our time. When a closed mind re-opens, it's usually under new management. Moving means making adjustments. The difference in our reactions to new places, people, and customs depends on our expectations, awareness, and personality. If you're having trouble adjusting, reading *The Trauma of Moving* by psychotherapist Audrey T. McCollum might prove beneficial.

Moving is a profound opportunity for transformation. Realigning your thoughts can literally realign your life. Listen to your self-talk and identify any negative messages. (Research shows a whopping 87 percent of our thoughts are negative.) Replace these reflections with positive ones that tell you what's *good* instead of what's bad—what you *can* do, rather than what you can't.

Instead of wallowing in negativity, make a conscious decision to purify your thinking. Otherwise you'll get caught up in a down mood. When this happens it's as contagious as chicken pox. Pretty soon the whole family or entire store or office becomes cloaked in gloom. Our beliefs wield tremendous power. Ziglar gives us another wonderful quote to live by, "It's your attitude, not your aptitude, that determines your altitude." So imagine yourself being successful, making friends, fitting in.

In a mathematics equation there are constants and there are variables. The constants of our lives—our family priorities, our faith, our values, our personal gifts—add stability wherever we go. The variables—our career choice, our homes, what we do with our free time, the friendships we develop—add spice and momentum. It's important to have a sense of what we can or cannot change and still retain a sense of who we are.

How adaptable are you? Since things move more slowly in the country, you'll likely feel you've been plunked down in some foreign experimental laboratory at first.

> Marilyn: *When I moved from San Diego to First Try, it was major culture shock: a real socioquake! Everything was unfamiliar. All pretense was out. The old ground rules didn't apply. I flailed around like a fish out of water.*
>
> *It amazed me, for instance, when I learned we were perceived as a threat to the local weekly newspaper. Because it was known we did something with the written word, people jumped to the conclusion we might put this enterprise out of business. Who wants to extinguish a family-run firm that has been faithfully serving the community since practically the beginning of time?*

Habits are like cobwebs that turn into cables. Just because you've "always done it that way" doesn't mean you should continue in that fashion. *Flexibility* is the operative word here. Lifestyle changes pop up everywhere. Self-reliance is a big deal. Goods and services are not as immediately available as they were in the city. People are more informal and friendlier.

## *Attitudes: Yours and Theirs*

Certain values are different in the country. People are measured not so much by the size of their wallets, what they wear, or what work they do—but rather by their personal qualities, such as promptness, honesty, and resourcefulness. You can be yourself and be valued for that special self. There is typically less pressure to conform.

Rural people are also more in touch with the earth. They count on animals, crops, and weather for their livelihood. Sunrises and sunsets are important events to them.

The Knight of Lightning Speed never made it to the boonies. Being impatient won't get you anything but heartburn. Sure you ordered lumber to build that add-on last week, and the delivery was supposed to be here by noon today. Just because it's 4:00 P.M. and you've been killing time all day isn't going to change things. One of the sawyers may have had a sick cow to doctor, or the delivery driver might have had to plow his road before he could get out. Relax! Things happen in their own good time in the country. No amount of prodding on your part will alter that. All you'll do is get yourself more worked up. The lumber will be there, albeit tardy.

To get accepted may be as simple as a pleasant "howdy" when you meet. Asking residents for advice on local places or issues is also smart. It helps you get acclimated and it makes them feel important.

Realize that booms are threatening to small communities. On the other hand, orderly, planned growth that minimizes shock to the infrastructure and current systems is welcome. But problems occur when so many new people arrive that community services are stressed. Street paving and repair must be accelerated, sewage and garbage controlled, utilities and water provided, houses built, schools enlarged. This results in increased tax requirements and new stresses for the area. Managed intelligently, growth is a positive process. A strong citizenry contributes to a town, helping it expand and prosper.

## *Sorting It Out and Settling In*

Continuity gives us a sense of belonging. Your home is an extension of you, an expression of your self. It contains your individual imprint and embodies your personal and family history. Displaying certain mementos will give you, and other family members, comfort. These artifacts can pull us from the past into the present.

Another way to speed your re-connection is through sensory signals, smell in particular. Using the same kind of potpourri or cooking a family favorite meal with a tantalizing aroma signals "we're home!" People have reported when spring came in their new locale, the fragrance of lilacs blooming in a nearby garden gave them a sense that all was well.

Feeling at home speeds up when you know where to find things—goods and services within the community. Something as simple as learning how the aisles are arranged in a new supermarket is reassuring. It makes you feel you're more in control of your environment. Knowing where to get your clothes cleaned, finding a good place for a haircut, and discovering the best bakery in town are landmark occasions.

## *Overcoming Negative Feelings Towards Outsiders*

Some small towns are intolerant. Rigid thinking makes them very establishment-oriented. They shun gays and lesbians, for instance, and look down on hippie types until they prove themselves. City slickers who come on too strong also meet a chilly reception.

Ironically, sometimes so do the very tourists who are much of the lifeblood of the community. Townspeople love the money they infuse into the local economy, yet comment privately they "can't wait 'til the season's over and the tourists leave!" Shouldn't we rejoice when they're here? Aren't they what pay our bills and allow us to live this existence?

Anywhere you go, you'll find good people and bad people, those you like and those you don't. There's a story of a fellow who moved to a small town. When he asked a native what kind of folks lived in the town, the man replied, "What kind of folks did you leave?"

"Oh, they were selfish and bigoted, small-minded and petty," came the reply.

"Well, I reckon you'll find the same kind here," the native mused.

Another newcomer came along and asked the native the same question. "What kind of folks live here?"

Again the native asked, "What kind of folks did you leave?" The second person flashed a warm smile. "Oh, they were wonderful. Warm and friendly, generous and fun. Real neighbors, they were."

The native grinned. "Yep. You'll find the folks here are much the same," he said.

Circumstances constantly live up to our expectations. We have an acquaintance who's so pessimistic he has one CB radio in his car—and a second one in his trunk . . . waiting to replace the stolen one. Another acquaintance assumes life is "a bowl of cherries." For her it is. She constantly opens the door to serendipity and in walks something even greater than what she anticipated. Life continually delights her.

## *Losing Your Anonymity*

You won't even have begun unloading the moving van before the word spreads like wildfire: the new family is here! Newcomers are a big deal in a small town. It's an event. Besides, people are just naturally curious. Remember the old game where you got in a circle and the leader whispered something into the ear of the next person, then it was repeated all around the circle? What happened at the end? It was a totally different message than what was originally stated, wasn't it? That's the way it is in Small Town USA. Situations get jumbled because people love to talk.

One of the hardest adjustments for us was getting used to the gossip mill. Someone once said gossip is news in a red satin dress. I'd liken it more to a pair of grubby overalls with many pockets for stuffing tidbits. Sid Ascher observed, "A small town is a place where everyone knows whose check is good and whose husband is not." Gossip really flourishes where party line telephones still exist. In metropolitan areas most people don't have time to mind their neighbor's business. Let's face it, half the time they don't even know their neighbors.

> **Marilyn:** *In the boonies some tongues are malicious mischief makers. We encountered this in First Try. I've since learned, however, that gossip is a natural part of small town life, just like 4th of July picnics and summer band concerts. But to a city gal it was stifling at first when every move I made had an audience . . . and embellishment. This may be a difficult adjustment for you too.*

The advice we'd offer is not to get caught up in gossip yourself. A good neighbor has two ears and one mouth . . . and uses them proportionately. Be a protector rather than a perpetrator. (Actually you may be protecting yourself as well as others.) The majority of people in a small town are related. It may be via a distant cousin, but they are *family*. Woe to the person who makes a snide remark about some other member of the clan. Give folks the benefit of the doubt. If you don't make disparaging remarks about people, you won't be on the outs with their in-laws.

You'll also find it harder to slip into the post office undetected to pick up the mail. When you're rushed and need to get back to work, it's inevitable you'll bump into several people you know. A hurried hello may offend them. Visiting for a few minutes is part of the price you pay for good neighbors when the chips are down.

Urban and rural are as different as playing Old Maid with your grandchild and Bridge with your peers. Yet each has its attraction. Let's examine the trade-offs.

## *Playing the Big City/Small Town Trade-Off Game*

Tired of trendiness and materialism, Americans are rediscovering the joys of home life, basic values, and roots. They're rediscovering sentimental movies. Mixed-breed dogs. Push lawn mowers. Family reunions. Erector sets. They enjoy modest pleasures and homier values. They realize it's time to enjoy the little things, for one day we may realize they were the only big things.

## *Child Care in the Boonies*

And their children are becoming the number one priority. The National Commission on Children reported in late 1991 that 81 percent of parents say they don't spend enough time with their kids. Yuppie parents are trading the corporate culture for the family frontier in ever increasing numbers.

While both parents often still work in a country environment, child care is different. It's usually better. While there are fewer or no organized day care centers, informal home care providers offer several advantages. The adult-to-child ratio is normally lower. They are more willing to take a slightly ill child. The youngster is nurtured and allowed to form closer relationships. Meals are typically better as many substitute moms pride themselves on their cooking and baking skills. And if medications need to be given, they're not likely to be overlooked in the chaos of caring for countless numbers. In the winter, children are more likely allowed outdoors (it's easier to bundle and unbundle four little charges than 14). The overall environment is quieter; pleasures are simpler.

In the boondocks, a field trip may consist of watching cement being poured at a neighboring construction site or going down to Main Street to see the whole elementary school parade in their Halloween costumes. Kids also get to see the inner workings of another household. They're often taken along when the babysitter goes to decorate the church for an event, stops by the library to pick up books, or takes the car in for repairs. Such experiences enrich little lives more than remaining in a static environment.

In the city there is constant stimulation. It becomes a question of who can top whom. In a large nursery school, for instance, birthdays are frequent. So are clowns, elaborate cakes, and special treats. Parents try to outdo each other. Even show and tell becomes competitive.

With so much going on all day in nursery school, it's a letdown when the child comes home at night to parents drained from a hectic day. And one friend tells of her three-year-old daughter begging for OshKosh brand clothing "with a little character" because the other kids had it. What a sad critique on our society when such tiny tykes are preoccupied with status symbols.

Nothing is perfect. There are drawbacks to country day care arrangements too. It's hard to find alternative care when the sitter goes on vacation or gets sick. And there aren't as many field trips to the zoo, planetarium, etc. Some parents don't find this a deterrent, however. They'd rather their kids didn't expect every day to be action-packed. Continual activity warps youngsters and instills in them unrealistic anticipations about life.

## *More Differences*

While a city youth must officially wait until mid-teens to get behind the wheel with a learner's permit, there's a far different unwritten law for country kids. On farms, nine- and ten-year-olds drive four-by-four pickups and tractors all around the homestead. They learn to be responsible early.

Says Terry Barkett, a member of the Chaffee County Commissioners, "You need to be a little more creative to live here. One difference I see in working in a rural area is you have to handle new ideas carefully, and over a long period of time. Change isn't accepted as readily as in a metro area."

Choices are also limited in rural areas. You won't necessarily find the color, model, or style you had in mind. (You may be lucky to find the item at all.) Specialty stores are non-existent in tiny towns. Yet local merchants direly need your support. Buy locally whenever you can. When it isn't practical, make trips to the city count. Plan ahead. Buy in bulk. Save larger purchases for city shopping.

Consider shopping by mail. Browsing through catalogs trims shopping hassles and often saves money. (You don't need the tough skin of a rhinoceros to avoid temptation. You're less likely to make impulse buys when you can't actually see or touch objects.) Some 12 billion catalogs are mailed each year. Ninety million adults shop by mail or phone. Actually the service is frequently faster and better than shopping in person. Always check the company's guarantee and return policy before ordering. And don't send cash through the mail. Pay by credit card, check, or money order.

Wondering where you can find catalogs that carry what you need? A terrific source is *The Catalog of Catalogs*. It's an inexpensive and complete mail-order directory that lists more than 12,000 catalogs in 600 groups—everything from candles to yarn, brushes to trains. (See "Bibliography/Recommended Reading" for ordering information.)

Fun in the hinterland takes a new slant. You might play a Mozart tape or CD in your car while taking a long, leisurely drive in the country. You'll more likely enjoy wildlife instead of a wild life. Making friends with God's creatures brings rich rewards. A squirrel, deer, or raccoon will never ace you out of a parking spot or cut you off on a crowded freeway.

Speaking of animals, to help you talk rural lingo, we've included a chart showing the proper term for critters typically raised in the country.

## Correct Country Animal Terms

| Type | Horses | Cattle | Goats | Sheep | Swine (Pigs) | Poultry |
|---|---|---|---|---|---|---|
| Groups | Herd | Herd | Band | Flock | Drove | Flock |
| Newborn | Foal | Calf | Kid | Lamb | Pig | Chick |
| Young Male | Colt | Bullock | Buck Kid | Ram Lamb | Shoat | Chick |
| Young Female | Filly | Heifer | Doe Kid | Ewe Lamb | Gilt | Chick |
| Male of Breeding Age | Stud | Bull | Buck | Ram | Boar | Cock |
| Mature Female | Mare | Cow | Doe | Ewe | Sow | Hen |
| Unsexed Male | Gelding | Steer | Wether | Wether | Barrow | Capon |

We have a software design firm here in town that pulled off a coup they'd never have succeeded doing in suburbia. 2500 AD Software ships engineering programs all over the world. It's to their advantage to present a solid business image to these global customers. So Ray Billings is trying to convince the decision makers to *rename the street* on which their company faces. The rather innocuous Brookdale Avenue may become the prestigious-sounding 2500 AD Parkway.

Mark and Lindsay Dorio weren't that daring when they traded Los Angeles for Carson City, Nevada—a town of 39,400. While Mark's new job as a math teacher at Western Nevada Community College pays $32,000 (compared to his $44,000 with Xerox), the pluses far outweigh this minus. Auto insurance is half what they paid in Los Angeles. Since they stopped buying bottled water, that saves another $600 a year. And Lindsay no longer has to worry about keeping their two children indoors during smog alerts. Furthermore the crime rate is low and so is racial tension. But the biggest difference is in their home. What would have cost them $421,000 in Southern California, they purchased for $135,300 in Nevada!

## *Being a Big Fish in a Little Pond*

"I always wanted to be somebody, but I should have been more specific," quips Lily Tomlin. It's a lot easier to be somebody in a small town than in the big city. If you interact in the community, you automatically become known. It's but a step further to become renowned. For some individuals, there is a certain thrill to being in the limelight. If you hanker for such prominence, celebrity status here you come! But even if you don't seek prominence, you'll be noticed. And you will get a reputation . . . for better or worse.

Sarah Hemingway explains that when she and husband Tom moved to Buena Vista, they told their children, "In this town you're going to be a somebody. You can either be a good somebody or a bad somebody. But whatever you do, everyone will know about it." Life in a small town is life in a fishbowl. There are some positive aspects to that factor. It's a real incentive to live a worthy and good life. Another thing is when you're sick or hurting, the small town people tend to rally together like a family. Those are advantages to welcome.

"At the same time," she elaborates, "it's critical that you learn to keep a zip on your lip. Information—good or bad—travels like lightning in small towns. By the time you've picked up brochures at the travel agency, someone is calling to find out when you're leaving on vacation. Learn the value of keeping confidence and you'll be miles ahead."

You'll also settle in quicker socially if you follow the tips in the next chapter. It talks about developing a pleasant life and making new friends.

# 7

# Cultivating a Satisfying Social Life

In the city people ban together because they are white collar workers, they make a similar salary, work in the same industry or company, went to the same college, or live in a similar neighborhood. There's no such segregation in country companionship. Rural residents mix it up more. The reason is simple. There aren't enough people in any one group to constitute a self-contained social world. Differences in lifestyle, social standing, and educational level are accepted. You see people because you *like them*.

And you entertain at home more, cocooning and surrounding yourself with soothing, congenial compatriots. Things are casual, sometimes spontaneous. Blue jeans replace cocktail attire most of the time. Bringing out the crystal and silver is an occasion, rather than what's normally expected. People live in a more relaxed atmosphere, visiting the city when they want stimulation—yet being protected from its everyday evils.

A move to the country is a move away from the hustle and bustle of city life. While many people understand this intellectually, they still find themselves wishing for the best of both worlds. Country workplaces can be every bit as busy and stimulating as those in the city, but when it's "Miller time," the options for recreation and culture are much more limited. Country entertaining centers more around people and friendships than around happenings and events. There isn't a weekend edition of the newspaper offering new movies, musicals, exhibits, plays, and gourmet restaurants. More often the paper will tell of new babies, traffic violations, and school lunch menus. So perhaps it's time to take a personal inventory and look at your social needs.

## *What's Your F.Q. (Fun Quotient)?*

How do you go about deciding which leisure opportunities are best suited to you? Perhaps you feel like the mosquito that accidentally wandered into the nudist camp. He immediately recognized there was plenty to do—but *where* should he begin? The following Fun Quotient Quiz will help answer that question for you by probing your personal interests. We suggest you copy it so each family member can participate. (You are given permission to photocopy this quiz, but not other parts of the book.) The Fun Quotient Quiz was created with the help of Dr. James Conant, a psychologist on the staff of Fullerton State College, Fullerton, California.

It's not a test. There are no right or wrong answers. What excites one person will bore another. Just be *honest* with your responses. Wonderful new leisure doors will open if your responses are candid and thoughtful. Possible answers range from 4 (which means yes or almost always) to 3 (usually) to 2 (sometimes) down to 1 (which means no or hardly ever). Now grab a pen and discover your F.Q.!

### "Fun Quotient" Quiz

| KEY ||
|---|---|
| **1** = *hardly ever or no* | **2** = *sometimes* |
| **3** = *usually* | **4** = *almost always or yes* |

| | |
|---|---|
| 1. Do you like to think about new ideas and concepts? | |
| 2. Do you enjoy working with your hands? | |
| 3. Do you consider yourself adventuresome? | |
| 4. Do you like to guide others such as a teacher, speaker, manager, or presiding officer does? | |
| 5. Do you spend much time enjoying nature? | |
| 6. Is it easy for you to go to a party alone? | |
| 7. Do you find it hard to make new friends? | |

| | |
|---|---|
| 8. | Do you enjoy collecting items like stamps, miniatures, bottles, antiques, etc.? |
| 9. | Would you give time to a cause you feel strongly about? |
| 10. | Do you like quiet surroundings more than a bustling atmosphere? |
| 11. | Are cultural events and fine arts pleasing to you? |
| 12. | Do you like to invent things or systems? |
| 13. | Do you feel it's more fun to do things on impulse rather than something you've planned? |
| 14. | Are you skillful at getting people to do things? |
| 15. | Do you consciously strive to have a stronger, healthier body? |
| 16. | Are you more likely to be a participant rather than a spectator? |
| 17. | Do you wish you were more open and free . . . less "uptight?" |
| 18. | Would you prefer to deal with things rather than people? |
| 19. | Do you enjoy helping others? |
| 20. | Do you often get "roped into things" you'd rather not do? |
| 21. | Do self-improvement pursuits stimulate you? |
| 22. | Do you like to tinker and discover what makes objects tick? |
| 23. | Do you get a thrill out of doing things that are considered risky? |
| 24. | Do you have a lot of self-confidence? |
| 25. | Would you rather be outdoors than inside? |
| 26. | Are you active in one or more clubs? |
| 27. | Do you prefer being alone the majority of the time? |
| 28. | Does precise, detail-type work agree with you? |
| 29. | Are you a good listener? |
| 30. | Would you rather associate with people similar to you or those who are different? |

| | |
|---|---|
| 31. | Do you consider yourself an active reader? |
| 32. | Do you enjoy doing things around your home such as wallpapering, puttering, or gourmet cooking? |
| 33. | Do you write poetry or keep a journal? |
| 34. | Does it please you to influence others? |
| 35. | Do you consider yourself to be an active person rather than sedentary? |
| 36. | In your opinion, do most people like you? |
| 37. | Do you dislike crowds? |
| 38. | Are your possessions extremely important to you? |
| 39. | Are you persistent when you take on a task? |
| 40. | Does it bother you to be involved in several things at once? |
| 41. | Do you like challenging, thought-provoking activities? |
| 42. | Do you have a specific hobby area such as a workbench, sewing spot, special reading chair, etc.? |
| 43. | Do you feel the need to do something creative such as painting a picture, arranging flowers, sculpting or crocheting? |
| 44. | Do you assume responsibility eagerly? |
| 45. | Do you like animals, pets, or birds? |
| 46. | Do you prefer being part of a team or group as opposed to solitary activity? |
| 47. | Do others seem to think you're standoffish or unfriendly? |
| 48. | Are you frequently let down by people? |
| 49. | Do you like to teach others about something you do well? |
| 50. | Do you prefer routine and continuity over frequent change? |
| 51. | Are you happiest literally "doing nothing?" |
| 52. | Do you feel you're a self-disciplined person? |
| 53. | Do you like classical music? |
| 54. | Are you interested in sports? |

*SPECIMEN*
*We encourage readers to photocopy these pages*

| | |
|---|---|
| 55. | Do you enjoy competing with others? |
| 56. | Do you enjoy traveling in foreign countries? |
| 57. | Are you easily managed by other people? |
| 58. | Do you get bored quickly? |
| 59. | Does history interest you? |
| 60. | Are family-oriented activities important to you? |

The Fun Quotient quiz was designed to stimulate thinking and help people take a fresh look at themselves. It will assist in deciding what leisure activities are likely to provide you the most enjoyment.

Let's evaluate the patterns that emerge from your answers. Record the numbers you gave for each question in the corresponding blanks below. Total the scores for each set; then check them against the tables to determine your interest level. Now turn to the Interest Analysis to find what personal characteristics emerged.

| Total points and interest ranges in Sets 1-6 (Total possible: 20) || **High** interest level: 20-15 |||||
|---|---|---|---|---|---|---|
| ^ | ^ | **Medium** interest level: 14-10 |||||
| ^ | ^ | **Low** interest level: 9-5 |||||
| SET 1 | SET 2 | SET 3 | SET 4 | SET 5 | SET 6 |
| 1 ___ | 5 ___ | 4 ___ | 6 ___ | 7 ___ | 2 ___ |
| 21 ___ | 10 ___ | 9 ___ | 16 ___ | 17 ___ | 12 ___ |
| 31 ___ | 25 ___ | 19 ___ | 26 ___ | 27 ___ | 32 ___ |
| 41 ___ | 45 ___ | 29 ___ | 36 ___ | 37 ___ | 33 ___ |
| 59 ___ | 60 ___ | 49 ___ | 49 ___ | 47 ___ | 43 ___ |
| TOTAL | TOTAL | TOTAL | TOTAL | TOTAL | TOTAL |

SPECIMEN
We encourage readers to photocopy these pages

COUNTRY BOUND!™

| Total points and interest ranges in Sets 7-9 (Total possible: 20) | SET 7 | SET 8 | SET 9 |
|---|---|---|---|
| | 4 ___ | 15 ___ | 11 ___ |
| | 14 ___ | 16 ___ | 31 ___ |
| | 24 ___ | 25 ___ | 43 ___ |
| | 34 ___ | 35 ___ | 53 ___ |
| **High** interest level: 20-15 | 44 ___ | 54 ___ | 56 ___ |
| **Medium** interest level: 14-10 | TOTAL | TOTAL | TOTAL |
| **Low** interest level: 9-5 | | | |

| Total points and interest ranges in Sets 10 and 11 (Total possible: 24) | SET 10 | SET 11 |
|---|---|---|
| | 2 ___ | 3 ___ |
| | 8 ___ | 13 ___ |
| | 12 ___ | 16 ___ |
| | 18 ___ | 23 ___ |
| | 22 ___ | 53 ___ |
| **High** interest level: 24-18 | 38 ___ | |
| **Medium** interest level: 17-12 | TOTAL | TOTAL |
| **Low** interest level: 11-6 | | |

## INTEREST ANALYSIS

**SET 1**
Characteristic: You tend to have intellectual interests.
**SET 2**
Characteristic: You enjoy nature.
**SET 3**
Characteristic: You enjoy helping others.
**SET 4**
Characteristic: You tend to be an extroverted, people-oriented individual.
**SET 5**
Characteristic: You tend to be an introverted, shy person.
**SET 6**

Characteristic: You are creative, imaginative, and sensitive.
**SET 7**
Characteristic: You have strong leadership abilities and interests.
**SET 8**
Characteristic: You enjoy sports.
**SET 9**
Characteristic: Cultural pursuits are important to you.
**SET 10**
Characteristic: You prefer working more with things than with people.
**SET 11**
Characteristic: You are an adventuresome person.

Now let's take the F. Q. Quiz "Interest Analysis" a step further and do a little brainstorming. Suppose you tested high in Set 5. For someone who's shy, taking up contesting and the wonderful world of sweepstake entries might be fun. Or you could enjoy hobbies like crocheting or model railroading. The person with strong numbers in Set 7 is a natural community leader. Why not get involved in politics on the local level, assume a key role in a volunteer activity, or become an officer in a service club?

An adventuresome individual (Set 11) is a natural for backpacking or mountain climbing . . . or perhaps participating in the next rodeo that comes to town. Of course if you tested high in Set 2, being surrounded by nature is a real treat. Be sure to take time to enjoy this new blessing. If you really shined in Set 3, read on in this chapter where we talk about volunteering.

Looking at your answers to individual questions can also be revealing. Enjoy doing nothing (question 51)? Indulge yourself! Give yourself permission to lie back, watch the clouds, meditate, experience, just be lazy—without feeling guilty. And if question 59 tickled a dormant interest in history, why not trace your ancestors by studying genealogy, or get acquainted with local history buffs and learn the heritage of the area? There are many options.

## *Recreation and Entertainment Tips*

So what, specifically, does one do for recreation and entertainment? Take a look around. What about your specific area is unique? If people come there for vacations, what attracts them? Also learn from those who have lived in your area awhile. What do they do for fun? Try it. You may like it. For instance, we have the annual "Hookers Ball" where the women get dressed up as ladies of the evening.

This week our paper reports tryouts are going on for the production of *Annie*. What fun to go and watch the youngsters . . . and their "stage" mothers. Of course, you could audition for a role yourself. Don't want to be part of the cast? Fine. Backstage workers to help with sets, props, and costumes are always in demand.

On a more athletic front, you might want to work out alone or with a companion. If you prefer the latter, look for an aerobics class or a dance class. Softball, small towns, and summer go together like Peter, Paul, and Mary. The competition is fierce and it's a good way for both men and women to get acquainted as there are usually co-ed teams too. Of course it's free entertainment if you're on the spectator side. Our local horseshoe group has a tournament which goes all season; prizes for points accumulated range from a new rifle or shotgun to money and everyone enjoys the big feed at the end. Billiards and bowling are popular, as is supporting high school sporting events. Square dancing is projected to charm greater numbers this decade. It's a fun activity, helps keep weight down, and attracts wholesome people.

In some areas a visit to the farmers' market is a weekly ritual. Not only will you find vine-ripened melons and fruit just in from the orchards, but also fresh-picked veggies and country-fresh eggs. And the proprietors are usually a talkative bunch who intersperse hawking their produce with local wisdom and friendly advice. There are over 2,000 farmers markets scattered around America. They come in all guises, from covered semi-permanent stalls to farmers selling produce off the tailgates of their pickups. They're usually worth a detour.

For singles, we project there's a new love byte on the horizon. It's already happening in San Francisco where romance is blooming on computer screens. This occurs via a coffeehouse network called SF Net. Shy souls who hesitate to flirt face to face can visit anonymously with like-minded others. This certainly takes personal classified ads into the computer age.

But finding a convivial computer conference appeals to more than those seeking dates or mates. It's actually a remarkable way to connect people heart to heart, not just screen to screen. Distressed parents are reassured by their computer compatriots, insomniacs have lively late-night discussions, homesteaders suffering from cabin fever discover stimulating companions. And those interested in various causes—such as ecology, politics, or peace—can have discourses with other spirited converts all across the nation. All it takes is a computer, modem, and telecommunications software. Such computer networking revives a safe and sane way of relating to strangers. It's like sitting on the porch in Grandma's rocking chair on a lovely moonlit evening and philosophizing with a kindred soul. And it brings the world to your doorstep!

There are two main companies that facilitate these nurturing interpersonal relationships and therapeutic support. The WELL (The Whole Earth 'Lectric Link) has an electronic bulletin board that provides a forum for thousands of simultaneous on-line conversations. For details, reach them at 27 Gate Five Road, Sausalito, CA 94965, or phone 415-332-4335. Their New York City based counterpart is ECHO (East Coast Hang Out). You can contact them at 97 Perry Street, Suite 13, New York, NY 10014, or phone 212-255-3839.

When Faith Popcorn looks futureforward, she also sees computers giving us other forms of entertainment. She predicts it won't be long before we have such fantasy adventures as mind-trips to Africa, the Brazilian rain forest, and the Himalayas. Or time-travel back to the French Revolution or the time our grandparents lived.

## *Dealing with the Family Issue*

Severing family ties is never easy, as we've said. One way to stay connected is to call more frequently. Plan to invest a little more in your phone bill during those first months. Another idea is to send videos of the new house, town, and surrounding area. Make the rest of the family a part of your new adventure. And consider launching a Continuing Cassette Program. This is where you add to an audio cassette snippets of intriguing tidbits and happenings as you think of them, toss in lots of love, then send it "home" every week or so. Thinking of You cards are another caring touch to ease the transition for those left behind.

It's also important *for your sake* to keep close contact with old friends and family during this time. They'll remind you of how special and loved you are on days you feel rejected or lonely. Absence doesn't necessarily make the heart grow fonder. It can make it grow forgetful. So keep loved ones close in mind and spirit. Memories missed and precious pasts shouldn't be ignored.

Yet sometimes it's good to get some space between you and your relatives (*his* or *her* relatives?). Then grandma or auntie can't routinely badger poor junior or discipline the other kids in ways you disapprove of. Nor do you have to listen to unsolicited advice about how to live your life. Or put up with uninvited visits just when you're ready to snuggle into a comfy chair and read a book or watch your favorite sitcom.

Visits will come in bigger chunks, otherwise known as vacations. (*Theirs* not yours.) If this area was captivating enough to entice you away from the city, it must have many redeeming qualities. Before too long those left behind will probably journey to your new environs. In fact, branches of the family tree you didn't even know existed could show up to check out your new digs.

So will your friends. When you move to the country, everybody wants to visit: some, once to satisfy their curiosity; others, frequently to escape their lifestyle . . . and enjoy yours. You'll need to establish some rules. Nobody just shows up. They must call and arrange a suitable time first. And if you're a busy homesteader with animals and crops to tend, you may want to make it clear they will *participate*. Handled properly, having friends and loved ones come for short visits is a wonderful way to keep in touch and enrich everyone's life.

One of the pluses about leaving family behind is that you can now create your own traditions. Instead of following the wishes of your parents at Christmas or Hanukkah, you can make up your own customs. And this doesn't just go for yuletide rituals. You can establish new habits for Thanksgiving, Easter, Memorial Day, Labor Day, or the Fourth of July too.

## *Making New Friends*

Take time and choose your friends carefully. Those who are anti-outsiders probably won't change. Why waste time on them? You'll find plenty of other folks to laugh with and enjoy. Just don't be in a hurry to please everyone.

Since a vibrant social life will not likely come knocking at your door, it's up to you to make things happen. When you find people you think you'd like to know better, invite them over for Sunday brunch or dinner. Prepare one of your specialties or something unique to the area you came from. Ask questions of them—why they came here, where to shop for so-and-so, what's their favorite family outing. Before you know it, friendships will blossom. But don't be discouraged if every attempt doesn't pan out. You have lots of time to develop rapport. Go with what works.

What worked for Bill Seavey and his wife was to sponsor their own party. When they moved to Bend, Oregon, in 1981 they decided the best way to get to know the neighbors quickly was to have a potluck. "Worked wonders," Bill reports.

One of the lessons we learned is how important it is to *respond* when someone does reach out. When we first moved to First Try, there simply weren't enough hours in the day to run three businesses and have any social life. So the first couple of party invitations we received were declined. Rejecting those offers of friendship proved to be a social blunder. The invitations came to an abrupt halt. Though it was never our intention, the locals decided we didn't want to mix with them. Once such word gets around, your fate is sealed.

A similar situation is reported by a woman who moved to advance her career. Colleagues invited her to special discussion groups, but she was preoccupied with her work and failed to attend or reciprocate. The invitations dwindled. Clearly, this had been a critical period for her to make friends and she let it pass.

It's tough to be outgoing and vivacious, to mobilize energies already sapped by the other tasks of moving. Yet those early weeks are so important. It's worth reaching down in your personal reserves to muster the time and energy to respond, to be available. People who do welcome you warmly expect their gestures to be met with some initiative on your part. But many of us are anxious and afraid of being rebuffed. We miss our old comfortable relationships. That's only natural. Yet making the right contacts now can relieve loneliness and ignite purpose. Try to extend yourself.

Clubs and classes are fertile friendship fields. These spontaneous joinings bring together people with common interests.

> Marilyn: *I met two of my best friends in San Diego through a writing class. Similar concerns and goals were the glue that cemented our relationships. If there is a Newcomers' Club, by all means attend. While some people shun such groups because they want to penetrate the "in crowd" of long-time residents, attending newcomer functions is an excellent non-threatening introductory step. Often there are sub-groups, such as those interested in gourmet cooking, bicycle riding, or crafts. If no such club exists, you might consider starting one. Or at least investigate enrichment classes like music appreciation, quilting, painting, literature, etc.*

Once you're settled in, one way to find special friends is to become a fate shaper. A fate shaper gives destiny a nudge. One imaginative widow who had sold her big home and wanted to move to a smaller town set out to rent a *way of life* instead of an address. Finding a suitable looking apartment complex, Gladys asked about the make-up of the residents. The manager explained there were six widows among the 30 tenants. Her next action was to call on each of the widows and ask candidly if they were interested in playing bridge, having morning coffee, or going for a Dutch-treat dinner occasionally. Four of the women were elated that somebody was moving in who could be a companion.

Lauri devised a clever way to encourage others to get acquainted with her. Whenever she and her sons went to the park, she always took along fate shaping *props*: a tiny chess set, a cribbage board, and a current best-seller. She never read the book, however. It laid on the blanket in full view of anyone who wanted to use it as a peg on which to hang an introductory conversation. Of course the chess set and crib board were also unspoken invitations.

Frank uses his hobby to meet all kinds of interesting people. Known as the "Golden Ram," he's a CB enthusiast. Citizen band radio not only provided him with a leisure outlet, it gave him the chance to talk with "Ding-A-Ling." Each liked what they heard so well, the two joined forces and became Mr. and Mrs. KOQ7026!

Another way to attract others is to become an expert. Then when someone wants information or help in your field, you're the natural resource. This also allows you to get involved in such pursuits as school activities where the students can benefit from being exposed to your expertise.

There is one element within you, however, that will attract people more than any single action. That's a good self image: the quality of truly liking yourself, of knowing you're a valuable human being. When you possess that characteristic, you give off a glow of self-confidence and serenity. Combine that with a welcoming smile and you're sure to captivate people.

As Robert Fulghum says in *It Was on Fire When I Lay Down on It*, "The grass is not, in fact, always greener on the other side of the fence. No, not at all. Fences have nothing to do with it. The grass is greenest where it is watered." To have a friend, you must first be one. Be *genuinely* interested in other people—sympathetic to their troubles, excited about their triumphs. Offer your friendship without expecting anything in return. If you do kind things because you want to make people feel indebted to you, they'll know it and resent you.

How do we go about showing a friend that he or she is cherished? Be a good listener. Listening attentively, instead of letting your mind wander or thinking about what you want to say next, shows support for the other person. Learn to tune into feelings as well as words and to demonstrate to friends how much you value them. Why is it so easy to say "I love you" in some situations . . . and so difficult in others?

If we can find a way to verbalize our caring, it will go far towards stabilizing friendships. Love can be shown in many ways. If you have trouble saying these words, write a note or find a greeting card that expresses your feelings.

Giving of our time and self promotes lasting goodwill. Stopping by to see a friend in the hospital (even though her jaw is wired shut) is an act of love. So is leaving a football game to help a buddy tow his car home.

Volunteering to watch a couple's children occasionally—or their puppy when they go away for the weekend: these are also acts of love. So is starting a plant from a slip of your prize-winning fuchsia. Or clipping an article you know your chum would love to read. Such are the unselfish acts of true fellowship. Wonderful, intimate companionship awaits you in your new town. Just give it a little time, and a gentle nudge, and you're sure to find people with whom you have an affinity.

## *The Virtues of Volunteering*

Over the last decade volunteerism has been gussied up—hair done, nails polished, and jewelry in place—to catch a beau. No longer does she offer only routine tasks like filing and envelope-stuffing. And her suitors are no slouches either. They come with ties on straight, socks matching, and flowers in hand.

This romance between community needs and willing individuals will blossom even more in the last years of this century. People feel a need to contribute. They're hungry to nurture our world and the people in it. Some even see it as a calling.

Today's volunteers serve in a myriad of ways. They present guided tours at museums, write publicity releases, tutor a needy child, plan gala charity events, or serve on town councils and advisory committees. Others counsel prison inmates, coordinate fund-raising campaigns, coach a sports team, plant trees, do outdoor community beautification, even perform musical extravaganzas for the elderly.

Volunteer vistas are popping their buttons in every direction. The result? Meaningful involvement beckons many.

Elizabeth describes herself as a "career volunteer." She explains in a competent tone, "That title gives weight to the value of my experience." Elizabeth is one of many active women who are finding that their expertise and achievement in challenging unpaid service puts them on equal footing with professionals. They exert tremendous influence in their fields. And they do it at times and on a schedule which meets *their* needs. Consequently they have the mental stimulation of a satisfying career, a sense of knowing they add meaning to the lives of others, and the flexibility to pursue important family activities and private pleasures.

Finding the right service niche is very personal. We each have some things we do better than others, special inborn qualities and talents. So the first step towards courting the lovely lady of volunteerism is a self-inventory.

## VOLUNTEER SELF-EVALUATION

- Do you enjoy working more with people or with things?
- If you prefer people, would you most like to associate with children, youth, adults, or older folks?
- Are you at ease around someone with a handicap?
- Do you have a car or access to public transportation?
- Are you willing to give time on a consistent basis, or would spontaneous or one-shot activities be more suitable?
- Want to offer your service behind the scenes rather than on the firing line?
- Do you speak a foreign language?
- Play a musical instrument?
- Excel at a particular hobby or craft?
- Do you participate in a sport?
- What do people always compliment you on and say you do best?

Virtually any skill you have can be put to good use in volunteer activities. They are your rebellion against enforced and empty idleness. And if you suffer from intellectual atrophy, there's a sure cure in volunteer work. It's a wonderful springboard to something new. It gives you a chance to try different pursuits in a semi-protected environment.

Now that you have some idea of what you are most qualified for, and want to do, it's just a case of wedding you to the right volunteer opportunity. Some places you might check are the school, hospital, nursing home, and the Cooperative Extension Service. Of course your pastor, priest, or rabbi will leap at a question of how you might help. Any political candidate or party will find you an assignment as quickly as a comet streaks across the heavens. Health and welfare agencies, plus service and civic clubs are also likely candidates.

Volunteering is an ideal atmosphere for making new friends and feeling the joy that comes from knowing you enhanced the life of another. It gives an opportunity to refurbish skills grown rusty from lack of use, or master new ones. It puts purpose in life. Invest yourself. The dividends may exceed your wildest dreams.

## *Ingenious Ways to Enrich Your Life*

The challenge is to stay rooted and not rutted.

We find nourishing ourselves spiritually is important. Just as our bodies need food, so do our minds and souls. By reading spiritual materials—or listening to uplifting tapes—we submerge our subconscious in positive ideas and constructive action. When you feed your spirit wholesome fare, your entire being feasts.

In rural settings, one of the foremost centers of activity and fun is a local church. Sunday many people come into town and enjoy worshipping together. Those who depend on the weather for their livelihood tend to place a high priority on faith. In our town a local church sponsors potlucks, interesting speakers, open gym nights, activities for teens and young children, and musical entertainment.

They even have Christmas decorating parties—complete with rooms full of pine boughs, staple guns, baby's breath, glue guns, and plaid ribbon. These activities provide not only something to do, but opportunities for everyone to contribute their unique talents while cementing friendships. To get acquainted with her church family more quickly, one newcomer we know goes with the pastor's wife when she makes house calls.

For many the backyard is replacing the boardroom. Eastern ex-apartment dwellers, who never had a plot of ground of their own, are enchanted with gardening. They cultivate tomatoes and squash as enthusiastically as they used to cultivate mentors and bosses. Outdoor barbecues supplant cocktail parties.

You might also think of things you've done, or seen done, in other communities and try them out in your new locale. Create a unique type of party, or decoration, or recipe. People love something different. The key is to try new things out on small groups. (To attempt to change a *town's* tradition is quite another story!) In everything, remember you have something to contribute and something to learn. Be open-minded and open-hearted.

Just because you live in the country, don't think you have to find everything right there. If you've enjoyed symphonies, ballets, and theater productions before, continue to enjoy them. Surely you have a city within a few hours' drive. Check out their fine arts options and make an investment—in both time and money—for occasional tickets. Take a mini-vacation. A long weekend every two months or so does wonders for the soul. Make hotel or motel reservations and eat at a fancy restaurant one night. Salve your financial conscience by doing your city errands on the same trip. The break in your routine and surroundings will be welcome, and you'll find yourself refreshed and eager to head back to "the sticks."

Another excellent investment is a quality stereo system with a collection of fine music. You won't find Rachmaninoff on many country western stations. Sometimes you won't find jazz or classical selections to your liking either, so having a record collection, tapes, or CDs of your preferred music gives you a soothing sense of continuity. Don't try so hard to blend in that you forget what you liked before the move.

The Teaching Company (1555 Wilson Blvd, Suite 300, Rosslyn, VA 22209, 703-875-8727), has begun a program that will please well-educated and curious rural adults. They hired professors from such top universities as Yale and Dartmouth to deliver eight hours of lectures before a live audience at the Smithsonian Institution. The lectures were taped and are available in either audio or video formats. Current topics include philosophy, religion, poetry, history, politics, psychology, and literature. You can learn about modernist theater, Shakespeare, or Agatha Christie, to mention a few of their offerings. What an easy way to bring culture into your life. Perhaps inviting a few friends to enjoy one with you would make for a lively discussion afterwards. It could even lead to an informal educational arrangement where people take turns purchasing the tapes and leading the critique.

You can also turn your computer into a classroom and get your B.A., B.S., or M.B.A. by enrolling in an electronic degree program. Geared for working adults, the online classes are intensive and taken one at a time. For more information call 800-888-4935, or write to Online Program of the University of Phoenix, 101 California Street, Suite 505, San Francisco, CA 94111.

For retiring minds, AARP has a new *Directory of Centers for Older Learners*, which lists state-by-state information on 254 education programs around the country designed for mature students. For a free copy, request stock number D13973 from AARP Fulfillment, EE0233, P.O. Box 2400, Long Beach, CA 90801-2400.

We know one local family who entertains fascinating guests from all over the world. They are a host-home for SERVAS, an organization that encourages international travelers to visit in private homes across the globe. SERVAS, which means "serve" in the international language of Esperanto, is dedicated to fostering harmony and peace on earth. Says one older couple who can't travel themselves, "SERVAS brings the world into our living room through the visits of friendly, enthusiastic people from every continent."

Visits are usually for only two or three days and the guests participate as one of the family: working, playing, and sharing activities. What a unique opportunity for personal contact with people of diverse cultures and backgrounds! And these visits often lead to lasting friendships . . . with the welcome mat out when *you* travel abroad. For more information contact their international office at 321 West 24th Street, Apt. 7C, New York, NY 10011, 212-242-1163.

Think of your relocation as an adventure. Slow down. Enjoy every minute. Take time to fantasize about how much happier you're going to be and how positive change can be. Understand you're weaving new threads into the fabric of your life, while old ones ravel and fray. Sure you face an unknown future. So did our ancestors. Yet with vision and courage they accomplished remarkable feats. So can you. Let your spirit soar!

# Part II
## Business Aspects

# 8

# Evaluating Your Entrepreneurial Options

Being self-employed can make you feel a little like Christopher Columbus sailing off into the unknown. It's both exciting and scary. Those with an entrepreneurial spirit have their heads above the crowd. They're risk takers who see economic freedom. Statistics show that more than one out of every four people would start their own business if they won a million dollars. You can do so for a whole lot less. But starting a business is only the beginning. Keeping it going year after year is no small feat.

The startling facts are that 65 percent of all new businesses fail within five years. That's the bad news. The good news is many are extremely successful, especially when they're led by people like you who *educate themselves before taking the plunge.* That education is the focus of the entire Part II of *Country Bound!* So if you want to BYOB (Be Your Own Boss), rather than being in occupational limbo, read on! It has been said the best way to predict the future is to invent it.

We'll explore what personal characteristics it takes to run a company well. (Not everyone has them.) And we'll be your brainstorming partner, helping you become a master at foreseeing your ideal future and initiating positive change. Here you'll uncover how to determine windows of opportunity, turn a hobby into a living, and create your ideal "cashing out" career. We're off on a journey to discover a brave new entrepreneurial world!

## *Determining if You Have Self-Employment Potential*

Striking out on your own takes equal amounts of moxie and motivation. If one or both of your parents were in business for themselves, you're already a step ahead. Studies show those who come from such families have a greater tendency to be successful themselves. Some feel having a close relative who was an entrepreneur is the single most telling indicator. You benefit from having these role models. All that shop talk over the dinner table wears off. You may have been in an apprenticeship program and didn't even realize it!

Take a look at the following Characteristics of Entrepreneurs. If you don't have most of these qualities, it could be wise to jump ahead to the chapter on "Finding a Rural Job."

Go-getters typically start early in life. They have newspaper routes, set up lemonade or vegetable stands, do babysitting, help with haying, mow lawns, etc. They like to earn their own money.

> Tom: *After working on the family farm six days a week (the draft horses had to rest . . . not so the humans), I rode the range on Sundays "cowboying" for nearby ranchers. I made $5 a day counting cattle, herding, branding, and bronc riding to break horses when I was 14 years old. That's how I earned the money for my first full size saddle.*

> Marilyn: *I began earning money regularly when I was nine years old. I had a loom and wove potholders, then sold them door-to-door around the neighborhood. I soon discovered this "product line" was too limited, however. So I also bought and re-sold kitchen gadgets, small gift items, and boxes of greeting cards.*

## CHARACTERISTICS OF AN ENTREPRENEUR

- Self-directed with a strong internal focus of control
- Highly independent
- Lots of energy
- A futuristic outlook
- Often got poor grades and was rowdy in school
- Careful about money

- Persistent—to the point of being obsessive
- Creative, supports experimentation
- Earned own money at an early age
- Has vision, intellectual creativity
- As an employee, arrived on the job early and often left late
- Street smart
- A high tolerance for ambiguity
- Willing to take risks
- Competed in sports, debate, etc. in school
- Little need for peer approval
- A low tolerance for frustration, little patience
- Enjoys having power
- A sales personality, good communication skills
- Anxious to take on responsibility
- Focused, strong ability to concentrate well
- Devotes more time to work than hobbies
- Dissatisfaction with bureaucracy and "the system"
- A decisive self-starter
- Intuitive, willing to go with hunches
- Not afraid of change

Why do people go into business for themselves? Money is secondary. "When you become your own boss, the only orders you take are for more business," remarked one individual who recently left a large company. Another quipped, "I'm recovering from major surgery. I just had the boss removed from my back."

Freedom . . . having command over their own destiny, is the major reason given by those who have shunned employee status. A 1991 MasterCard BusinessCard Small Business Survey polled 405 owners of small businesses. Eighty percent had left jobs at other companies. The main reason for 35 percent of them was to be their own boss and have more control over their work and lives. Surprisingly, only 24 percent of them did it for the money.

For many small-business owners, control over their lives also means less leisure time. Fifty-eight percent of those polled above said they have less free time now. But you really only have to work half a day. It makes no difference which half: It can be either the first 12 hours or the last 12 hours. Entrepreneurs are a hard working bunch, but they're basically content with their lot.

In discussing this book with Jeanne, a Realtor who specializes in selling rural property, she observed that often what people would *like* to do is vastly different from what they're *equipped* to do. Many want to play, not work, at a new business. The very times they need to be there are when they want to be gone. For example, the guy who loves fishing buys a tackle shop . . . then resents having to open it on weekends when *he* wants to be out fishing. One alternative to this predicament is to go into business with another person or couple.

Most people who start their own small businesses are technical experts. They know their product or service intimately and can design, create, and perform at a high level of proficiency. While many have college degrees and some sport MBAs, education doesn't seem to be the critical factor. A survey by the National Federation of Independent Business found that 40 percent of those studied had no college training. Eight percent were even high school dropouts. The vital factor was the knowledge they sought before going into business. The seed for success is adult education. This is what develops the pioneers of small business, the true heroes of the American economy.

It was once unusual for people over 50 to launch a new business. Today this daring mid-life venture is played out in every state in the union. The Roper Organization forecasts the next major wave of entrepreneurs will include an unusually high proportion of older Americans. Many of these people have been forced out of jobs by early retirement. Close to 20 percent of start-ups are begun by men and women age 50 or over. Folks in their sixties and seventies are retiring from one career, then starting in an entirely new field—finally doing what they've dreamed of all their lives.

Age often works *for* them. They're less impetuous, have wisdom gleaned from years in the work force, and know themselves better than their younger counterparts do. And when it comes to international trade, maturity is respected abroad—especially in Japan. It is imperative, however, that older entrepreneurs take all precautions to do everything right. If the business turns sour, it's infinitely more difficult to start over at 55 or 65 than at 35.

No doubt about it—whatever your age—you'll encounter physical, emotional, and financial strains when you start a new business. Below are some penetrating questions. Answer them honestly.

1)  Are you aware that running your own business may require you to work 12-16 hours a day, six days a week? Are you prepared to work even Sundays and holidays if necessary?

2)  Do you have the physical stamina and energy to handle such a workload?

3)  What about emotional strength? Can you withstand the strain?

4)  Are you prepared, if needed, to temporarily lower your standard of living until your business gets firmly established? (This may be especially relevant if you refuse to work such long hours.)

5)  What about your family? Are they willing to go along with the strains they too must bear?

6)  Have you faced the fact that you could lose your savings?

Some people join the ranks of entrepreneurship for the wrong (or at least questionable) reason: lose job—start business. As we've tried to show, not everyone is suited to being his or her own boss, either by temperament, background, or discipline. People who've always had their work lined out for them—and a supervisor or manager telling them what, when, and how to proceed—will likely be overwhelmed with all the added responsibility. A few naive souls even think starting their own business will be *easier* than job hunting!

## *Exploring the Alternatives*

Perhaps what you're now doing can be accomplished from anywhere. If you relocate an established business to a rural area, you and your company inject capital into the economy. You're then bringing something to the table. If you already have a going concern, the question then becomes: Is your business relocatable? That depends on the business and the new site you choose. It's certainly easier to pick up where you left off than to start new. Some enterprises can be run from anywhere. If you're a freelance writer, artist, craftsperson, or publisher, lucky you. Light manufacturing and some consulting often fall into this category as well.

But let's suppose you're a massage therapist contemplating moving to a town of 4,000 where no one currently offers this service. A visit with the local chiropractor and M.D. shows they are receptive to referring certain patients to you. Bingo! You have a transportable skill.

Or imagine you have an accounting firm. Maybe you don't want to move too far away and can set up a mobile van to service your existing clients from your new, more remote location.

To be successful, offer products or services your prospective new town would really love to have available. Ask key townsfolk, "What do you *need* here?" Also find out what businesses have come and gone in the last five years and why. Such information can be quite revealing.

What kind of enterprises are most likely to make it in the country? According to David Birch of Cognetics, Inc.—who wrote an excellent book called *Job Creation in America*—"Remote start-ups and success stories (tend) to be a little different from the mix found in metropolitan America. Generally," he says, "they fall into four groups . . . 1) satisfy fundamental needs, 2) revolve around natural resources, 3) are needed because of an area's remoteness, or 4) would be practical no matter how remotely situated."

Perhaps the last is the most viable. These consist of mail-order firms, specialty manufacturing, and others not dependent on the local economy for their well-being. Our two consulting firms—one specializing in writing and publishing books, the other in publicizing and marketing small businesses and professional practices—serve clients from coast to coast. While we occasionally assist a local, that's a rarity. Yet we infuse the area with tax dollars and provide jobs and paychecks that further enrich the local economy.

As Ralph Waldo Emerson observed, "If a man can write a better book, preach a better sermon, or make a better mouse trap than his neighbor, though he builds his house in the woods, the world will make a beaten path to his door." Where you are isn't as important as *who* and *what* you are. This was proven to us a few years ago just after we moved to the ranch.

In our zeal to *finally* live on the land we'd bought, we moved too soon. There was a mobile home and a partially-finished log structure for the office. What there wasn't, was running water or indoor plumbing. We hauled buckets of water from the creek and heated it on the wood stove. And we rented a porta-potty, which was installed in a grove of aspens across a clearing from the trailer. (This made for mighty cold trips that chilly February.)

One day soon after we'd moved, a gentleman called on the cellular phone wanting to meet with us. We said fine. We'd be traveling to Denver the following week and could meet him any place he desired. (While we're rural at heart, we own a snazzy car, have a business wardrobe, and make a reasonable impression.) "No," he said. "I want to come out and meet you and see your operation." Oops! No amount of talking could dissuade him. So we gave him directions for finding our gravel road and held our breath.

Marilyn: *Two days later he pulled up, got out of his BMW, grabbed his alligator briefcase, and headed for the trailer. After shaking hands, he asked to use the bathroom. "Right across the* clearing," I said, smiling wanly and pointing to the south. "No," he replied, "I said 'bathroom.'" I smiled once more, nodded my head affirmatively, and gestured south again . . . After meeting for four hours we took him away from a New York PR firm. (He later told us he figured if we could make it out there, we had to be good.) *Countrypreneuring at its zenith!*

A lot of us would rather trade a buttoned-down indoor existence in the big city for an outdoor adventure in the hinterlands. Here are some ideas for developing a business that capitalizes on fresh air: off-road, trail bike, or all-terrain vehicle rentals—boat rentals, taking out charters, canoe or raft operator—rock hounding and lapidary work—RV renting, campground and RV park management—hunting guide and outfitter.

Too often people open new storefronts that directly compete with existing establishments. That's not a good way to win friends or stay financially healthy. Small towns can only support a given number of like establishments. While the owners of two different flower shops may be making a living, for instance, if a third opens and siphons off part of the trade, everybody is in trouble.

There's a higher degree of risk if you open a new competing retail outlet than if you purchase an existing one. That's like buying yourself a living. If you've always wanted to operate a gift shop, talk to local real estate brokers and the owners of current gift shops in town. It's doubly difficult to tackle a new environment and a new venture at the same time. Maybe you'd be more comfortable studying the chapter on "Buying an Existing Business or Professional Practice."

Another entrance to career change is moonlighting. It also provides a buffer against the unemployment that results from corporate roulette. With companies merging and purging employees as fast as they do databases, moonlighting offers a safety net.

The ideal time to position yourself to launch a business is while you're still on the payroll. Sure this means working extra evenings and on weekends. Many ambitious moonlighters also use vacation days, sick leave, and lunch hours to pursue their second job.

Starting a business while you still have a regular paycheck allows you to test your business plan, line up clients, and establish cash flow—all without taking any risks. You can build relationships in your industry and go the extra mile with people in your field. It also gives you time for training, both in your field and as a new businessperson. *Gradually* testing your entrepreneurial skills is like learning to ride a bike with training wheels. Once the wheels are removed you have the experience and confidence to zip right along.

A bonfire of corporate layoffs has been turning up the heat on middle managers for over three years. When corporate downsizing hit record levels in 1991, middle managers and executives bore the brunt of it. And with the collapse of the savings and loan industry, major bank mergers, plus trouble in defense and computer firms, thousands of high-level jobs are still in jeopardy. Dan Lacey, editor of the newsletter *Workplace Trends*, projects jobs could be slashed by almost 700,000 by the end of 1992 if the current wave continues. According to the American Management Association nearly ¼ of U.S. firms expect to continue downsizing in 1992. (You didn't realize when they told you you'd be on the cutting edge of the company, they meant your *head* would be on the chopping block, did you?)

But then you may have already decided the fast track is the wrong track for you. As baby boomers reach middle management, there are signs they are rejecting corporate cultures that suck them dry. One authority recently observed in *The New York Times* that the "Me" generation is turning into the "Flee" generation as executives watch the best years of their lives slip into the corporate black hole.

According to figures from the National Federation of Independent Business, 43 percent of people get their business ideas from their prior jobs. One corporate escapee warns that life on the "outside" is very different, however. "It's easy to become mesmerized at a large company and lose any idea of what life is like on the outside," reports engineering consultant David Hudson. A helpful book on surviving and thriving the ups and downs of being your own boss is *Making It On Your Own* by Sarah and Paul Edwards.

Perhaps you've found the perfect place to live and need to come up with a way to make a living. You may require a primary income or perhaps your desire is to merely supplement a retirement income or pension. If this is your approach, you'll want to take a look at a unique book, *Offbeat Careers—The Directory of Unusual Work* by Al Sacharov. Though not all of these occupations are viable in a country setting, many are ideal for an adventuresome spirit. You could be an herbalist, clown, pipemaker, or windsmith. This little book is full of novel suggestions for someone who desires a change of pace.

These days, developing a business that appeals to the more mature market is like betting on a sure thing. It's the "age" of opportunity. Between 1990 and the year 2000, the number of people between 45 and 64 will increase by a whopping 26 percent. By 2000 there will be an astonishing 61,700,000 individuals in this group. Not only are these numbers impressive, so are the ones in their bank accounts! This segment of the population controls approximately 75 percent of the financial assets in America.

What does that mean to you? Think about what graying baby boomers will want and need. Real estate, recreational equipment and clothing, entertainment, personal services, and health care lead the pack. Entrepreneurs who know how to catch this age wave will prosper far beyond the norm. Thousands of new products will be invented to make these people more comfortable as they age. Service opportunities sprout like wildflowers after a spring rain. Jeff Ostroff, business consultant and author of *An Aging Market: How Businesses Can Prosper*, pinpoints seven kinds of businesses which stand to benefit most from our aging population. These are endeavors oriented to the home, health care, leisure, counseling, education, managing finances, and slowing the aging process.

Here's another intriguing angle to this aging society: There are about 53 million grandparents in America. The average grandparent has 3.4 grandchildren. In 1990 a fourth of all the toys purchased were bought by you-know-who. And they purchased the most expensive ones too. Does this give you any ideas? What about opening a toy store near a *retirement community*? Make it easy for all those doting grandparents to shop for their grandchildren.

The migrating elderly are revitalizing dozens of small towns. Between social security, pensions, and investment incomes a "mailbox economy" is emerging as unprecedented numbers of mature Americans head for the hills. They need real estate, home cleaning services, transportation and delivery services, bookkeeping help, financial planning, travel agencies, and auto repair—to toss out a few possibilities. And restaurants smart enough to develop inviting menus with smaller servings at reduced prices will get out of the starting gate fast.

Those who are pushing 70 in the '90s aren't like our grandparents. Today's mature people are much more active and energetic. They like to travel and be involved, to look and feel good. Cater to these needs and you'll be as fortunate as Cinderella when the prince discovered the glass slipper fit *her* foot.

Businesses in the boonies are often shared by husband and wife. Entrepreneurial couples run mom and pop grocery stores, bed and breakfast inns, motels, restaurants, home-based enterprises, and a wide variety of shops. They also farm together.

Sharing work and life can be both a blessing and a curse. You'd better have a strong marriage. There's no doubt being in business together will add stress to the relationship. And it's ideal if you possess complementary skills. Both of you having similar abilities and being responsible for the same area is likely to be as volatile as two male cats wooing the same feline female. On the other hand, if you love being around each other, it affords great opportunity for togetherness. There's also a special bonding when both of you pull together for a common work goal.

Country business owners are wise to be especially service-oriented. "Even people in smaller country towns are busy," says William L. Seavey of the Greener Pastures Institute. "And while they are more self-sufficient than city folks, they will still buy services like housecleaning, computerized bookkeeping, diet programs, consignment clothing, auto repairs, vitamins, resumé writing, pet grooming, etc. If there is no, or little, competition in these things," he continues, "a person has a basis to succeed."

Rural people usually go to an urban area to buy the majority of their purchases because they believe they'll get better prices in the city. That's tough competition. Most successful rural businesses are *non*-dependent on the area economy—or they serve as a local convenience. You'll find service stations, hardware stores, lumberyards, convenience stores, dry cleaners, feed stores, florists, coffee shops, gift shops, beauty salons, auto parts stores, small engine repair, clothing stores, bars—all commodities used by the residents. One study shows such firms get 40 percent of their sales from customers within 10 miles of their business site. Sixty-three percent of their patrons are within 20 miles.

Remember that in Small Town USA, you aren't just selling resources, you're also selling relationships. People go out of their way to trade with folks they like. That doesn't preclude the fact, however, that for retail stores location is often everything. Many shops depend on foot traffic for survival. Parking is also a big consideration. Potential customers will become frustrated and take their business elsewhere if they encounter a hassle finding a parking spot. For planning purposes, also factor in seasonal variances. If you relocate to a tourist town, for instance, 60 percent of your business may be done during the three summer months.

Locally dependent businesses are limited, however. While they usually provide adequate incomes, a broader base is necessary to make it big. The kind of expansion typical in the city—opening additional branches—isn't practical. More creative ways of blossoming are needed. A printer, for instance, might also carry office or art supplies. We'll discuss more about how you can diversify to multiply later.

Most self-employed people we interviewed are satisfied with the performance of their firms. They wouldn't consider working for someone else for a higher salary. These proprietors experience yin and yang harmony between their lifestyles and their careers.

## *Brainstorming to Break Your Barriers*

How do you get from the itch to the idea? It's one thing to want to move to the country, quite another to support yourself once there.

One of the best ways to generate a whole host of possibilities is to invite a group of people to help you think of ideas for a business opportunity. Set an initial time period, maybe two or three hours, and explain the procedures. (See the following Brainstorming Guidelines.) Set a positive tone. You might start out by reminding everyone that "No one of us is as powerful as all of us."

In a brainstorming session, each participant generates as many options as possible. All ideas are welcome, even if they sound kooky, impractical, or wild. The point of this exercise is to explore a range of possibilities, not to sell any one perspective. Brainstorming stretches the imagination and produces acres of ideas from which you can harvest the best.

## BRAINSTORMING GUIDELINES

- *Appoint someone to serve as a facilitator.* It's this person's job to ensure that everyone gets a chance to discuss their ideas. It helps when the facilitator summarizes the previous participant's contributions before the next person speaks. Use a blackboard or flip chart to record what's said so it is visible to everyone.

- *Reinforce and encourage all suggestions.* Don't worry about details at this point. Concentrate on producing as many ideas as possible. Encourage people to participate quickly without evaluating their own or others' thoughts.

- *There are no wrong ideas.* Don't be judgmental. If you must comment, limit your remarks to how a proposal might be improved.

- *Listen to the full explanation of an idea.* Don't interrupt others—wait until they're finished talking.

- *Nobody has all the answers.* Group success depends upon every member sharing opinions and observations. Encourage all to contribute and avoid promoting your own agenda.

- *Sort out the best suggestions.* At the end of the time, have the participants divide the ideas into three groups: 1) those with excellent potential, 2) fair options, 3) unacceptable suggestions.

- *Focus attention on the most promising in group 1.* Refine these ideas. Further brainstorm why they're a good match for you and how they might be implemented. Look for ways to put a more profitable spin on them.

- *Bank the best of the rest.* Keep an inventory of other potentially useable possibilities. This might take the form of 3 x 5 cards, notes jotted on scraps of paper, articles, etc. Deposit them in a manila folder, large envelope, shoe box, computer file, or whatever makes sense for you. But keep them so if times turn sour, you have a waiting account from which you can withdraw inspiration. One of them will serve as a catalyst to mobilize your creative thinking.

---

It isn't necessary to have a room full of people to accomplish wondrous acts though. You can take other approaches by yourself with a pencil and paper or computer keyboard. One method is called Freewriting. Sit down for 15 minutes and write anything and everything that comes into your head. No fair stopping or crossing out words. And don't worry about spelling or punctuation. The object is to lose control, to reach your intense inner thoughts so you can harness that energy.

Another dynamite doorway to your mind is called Clustering. This is a magic key for getting in touch with your secret reserves of imaginative power. Clustering is a nonlinear personal brainstorming process similar to free association. It's like writing a map of ideas, beginning with a core word or statement, then branching out with associated ideas in many directions.

Starting with a main idea in the center, give your mind free reign and radiate thoughts and images out from this nucleus. Write new ideas in circles—which, in turn—are connected by lines to other circles. Ideas spill out with lightning fast speed. They form associations that allow patterns and solutions to emerge. Chaos becomes order as ideas surface in a gradual map that accesses our interior landscape of thoughts. It's an easy, flowing process. There's no right or wrong place to start; nothing is forced. While this is an excellent solo exercise, it can also be effective done as a group.

When searching for a new idea, look from all angles. Successful businesses are often simply a different application of an existing concept.

Can you reverse something? (Look at the huge new industry of fragrances for men. Twenty years ago guys wouldn't touch perfume.) When using "reverse psychology," think about not only the opposite sex, but young to old, right-handed to left-handed, etc.

Minimizing or maximizing may hold the key to your entrepreneurial triumph. The computer field gives us a perfect example of how minimizing has led to new profit centers. From PCs that sat on our desks, they went down to portables, then to laptops, and now to notebooks. Small is beautiful. So is big. Our aging population, for instance, will increase demand for large print books in the years to come. Can you capitalize on less or more?

Combining two or more things may be your cure-all. For instance, a clever person put clocks together with radios several years ago and developed a whole new line of merchandise. In the service arena, some upscale beauty salons are now converting into mini-spas where a woman can be pampered from head to toe for a day.

Many successful new ventures offer only a slight variation on a proven market leader—just enough to establish an identity and a profitable market niche. Look how PC compatibles and clones quickly nipped at the heels of the IBM PC, and how overnight delivery services flourished once Federal Express proved it was possible.

When inventing your own business, try to improve on something for which there is already an established market, rather than beginning from scratch. Reverse it. Minimize it. Maximize it. Combine it. Examine the possibilities from every perspective.

## *Occupational Variety to Add Spice to Your Life*

Is the advice business for you? Consulting is a promising field for rural entrepreneurs. It's no secret that the information explosion is upon us. While we started as hunters/gatherers, went to farming, then became factory workers—now we're in the knowledge age. Are you sometimes overwhelmed by the increasing number of things you know less and less about? Join the crowd. Yet most of us are an *expert* at something. Find that something and capitalize on it!

As corporate downsizing continues, it bolsters the demand for subcontractors. When layoffs occur, corporations sometimes hire former employees on contract to perform needed services. Hiring consultants is often less expensive for the company than maintaining an employee full time and paying fringe benefits. Often the work can be done from a remote location.

Enter you. It's entirely possible you can serve your current or previous employer as an outside consultant . . . doing much the same tasks you did while on the payroll. This is just the pad needed to launch a consulting practice. Some people are even convinced they have as much security outside the corporate structure as within when they turn their previous employer into their first major customer.

Consulting is a broad term. People with expertise in widely divergent fields all fall under this heading. Perhaps you have skills in an occupational category that's in demand. The following list of Consulting Areas will give you an idea of the variety.

## CONSULTING AREAS

| | |
|---|---|
| Accounting | Labor relations |
| Advertising | Legal matters |
| Appraising | Mail order |
| Architectural | Management |
| Child care | Manufacturing |
| Collections | Marketing |
| Communication | Material handling |
| Computers | Meetings management |
| Construction | Nutrition |
| Cost benefit ratios | Office design |
| Data processing | Organization |
| Education | Package design |
| Employee training | Plant design |
| Employee safety | Printing |
| Energy | Product development |
| Fashion | Production/Productivity |
| Finances | Public relations |
| Fitness | Publishing |
| Food preparation | Restaurants |
| Forms design | Sales training |
| Freight handling | Security |
| Government work | Substance abuse |
| Graphics design | Telephone systems |
| Health care | Testing methods |
| Import/Export | Transportation |
| Industrial methods | Warehousing |

Consultants should like people. You have to be able to sell yourself and your abilities, then interface with organization personnel. You must be capable of putting together a compelling proposal, not to mention meeting deadlines. In addition to the marketing strategies needed to launch any business, it's important you price your services properly. An excellent book on this subject is *How to Set Your Fees and Get Them* by Kate Kelly. (See the "Bibliography/Recommended Reading" section for ordering information.) If this idea appeals to you, also get a copy of Brian Smith's *The Country Consultant*.

Those health professionals with a serious case of urban plague may find a move to the country a real shot in the arm. Rural areas are hungry for the kindly Dr. Kildares and Marcus Welbys of yesterday. There is a doctor shortage so family practitioners are in demand. Says Dr. William Featherston, "I like following a whole family, not just seeing people maybe a couple of times and never again. I don't think that people looking for family practice are looking for economics," he continues. "That's not the deciding factor. You make more money in a specialty." But, like other citizens, some physicians are turning their backs on lucrative specialties, opting instead for the quality of life available in the country.

To help them in this quest, the National Health Service Corps has boosted their recruitment budget to $49 million. This federal program offers scholarships to students in medical school, or helps repay other loans after school is over if doctors work in rural or underserved areas. Recipients serve a year for every school year funded by the government. In addition, all the corps' doctors are paid salaries by the clinics or hospitals that employ them. To further encourage doctors to hang out a shingle in Small Town America, medical school admission policies give preference to people from rural and underserved areas, and are instituting curriculum changes to add a rural emphasis.

Running a country inn appeals to many city dwellers. Bed and breakfasts (B&Bs) have boomed in the last decade. Today there are over 7,000 commercial country B&Bs.

It's estimated one in seven of them is on the market at any given time, so there are many to choose from. Prices range from $20,000 to $100,000 per guest room and figures from a recent survey report that those with 11 to 20 rooms are more profitable than smaller establishments. The February 1992 issue of *Kiplinger's Personal Finance Magazine* reports now may be the time to buy. Vacancies are high (the entire lodging industry is crippled by the recession) and buyers are few, which drives prices down.

The hot spot for starting an inn is the Midwest. The Sunbelt runs a close second, while New England and California continue strong. Having a B&B is a lot of fun if you enjoy people and making them comfortable. Guests become friends who return year after year, becoming almost extended family. Innkeeping is also a lot of work.

Because the field is extremely competitive, you may want to offer something extra, such as catering to families with small children. In this case you'd have cribs and high chairs available, provide a space for preparing formula, have toys on hand, and childproof the house. Of course, being able to arrange babysitting is an added benefit for traveling parents.

The recipe for innkeeping success is one part personal touch, one part lovingly restored antiques, one part delicious food, and seven parts location. Ambiance is everything. But guests want their country atmosphere mixed with a generous dollop of luxury. To test drive this business idea, stay at several inns yourself. Talk to the proprietors. Once they understand you're seriously considering buying, most will gladly share their joys and woes. Also check your local library or bookstore. There are several good books out on the subject.

The restaurant business is the denim dream of a lot of people. Beware of this industry. People romanticize about owning a restaurant; it's really a lot of work. But of more concern, the failure rate is phenomenal. Even experienced restaurateurs are going under. For the first time since the trade journal *Restaurant Business* started tracking trends in 1980, the number of closings exceeded the number of openings in 1990. Believe us, waiting around for someone to patronize your eating establishment is about as much fun as watching paint dry.

On the other hand, recreation and entertainment-oriented businesses flourish in tourist areas. These also can be fun. If you love white water rafting, horseback riding, or dune buggying, for instance, perhaps you can turn your bliss into a business. Active recreation runs the gamut from fishing to hunting, water sports to snow skiing, desert diversions to mountain activities. A golf enthusiast might open a miniature golf course, a surfing buff a surf shop—complete with lessons. Bait and tackle shops, taxidermy work, sporting goods stores, boat sales and storage—the list of potentials goes on and on.

Concocting gift baskets is another intriguing alternative. This can be both creative and lucrative. They retail for between $25 and $50 and contain food, wine, tea, gourmet coffees, snacks, gift items, useful articles, fun prankster objects, you name it. Style sells. Since the presentation is very important, this vocation taps your artistic abilities. You buy in bulk and enhance your baskets with ribbons, greenery, natural-looking reeds, and theme balloons.

Why would anyone buy a gift basket? For birthdays, anniversaries, showers, thank-yous, get wells, new homes, retirement, thinking of you, grand openings, corporate promotions, nostalgia, virtually any occasion—or for no occasion. Naturally these gorgeous delights are popular for holidays like Christmas, Valentine's Day, and Mother's Day. There are even masculine themes such as baskets for handymen, gardeners, fishermen, and sports fanatics.

A charming alternative to traditional floral bouquets, gift baskets have lasting value. Some clever gift basket creators even have bridal registries and mail all across the country, thus they're not dependent on the local economy. Of course that doesn't rule out making local deliveries as well. For more information contact Basket Source Reports, c/o All the Best, Inc., P.O. Box 627, Burtonsville, MD 20866, 301-604-2378. We'd also suggest you subscribe to *Gift Basket Review*, c/o Festivities Publications, Inc., 1205 W. Forsyth Street, Jacksonville, FL 32204, 904-634-1902.

The list of manufacturing possibilities is almost endless. We know of one rural area that is trying to recruit sporting goods manufacturing, medical and dental equipment manufacturing, plus geothermal users such as greenhouses and fish farms. Another manufacturing likelihood is clothing. Small towns like clean industries that won't pollute their environment. If you're considering making a product, be sure there is a suitable local labor pool. Otherwise you'll have a production line that turns out widgits similar to snowflakes . . . no two will be alike.

Then there are bowling alleys, secondhand stores, camera shops, campgrounds and RV parks, bakeries, craft shops, car washes, laundromats, and taverns. What about well drilling and septic tank sales? Construction companies and subcontractors, concrete, carpet sales, and real estate agencies are more prospects. Look in the Yellow Pages if you need to spark your imagination.

And for some, back to the land is their call of the wild. They go into tree farming, or raise berries, grapes, or other crops. Some develop a massive garden and become truck farmers. Of course, there are chickens, turkeys, hogs, cattle, horses, sheep, and goats to raise—not to mention exotics like alligators, ostriches, and llamas.

> Marilyn: *We tried our hand at this while living at the ranch. We weren't big-time farmers or ranchers—but we had some frustrating, funny, and humbling experiences. We raised our own meat: a few cattle and a pair of hogs. I'll never forget the time Tom came home with two new pigs. These little critters had been raised indoors on a concrete floor. When they came out of the horse trailer and hit the dirt, they froze like statues. Pigs are smart. They just knew this pebbly stuff underfoot meant no good. We convinced them to move around and their fear soon vanished.*
>
> *But by the next day they had another problem. These were pure white pigs that had never seen the light of day before. Their little white bodies had turned a rosy red. They were sunburned! (Porky and Petunia got even with us when we were trying to catch them*

*for butchering. They led me on the chase of my life! And they weren't even greased.)*

Another time I was helping Tom catch a young bull that needed doctoring. Tom had him roped and the rope attached to a sturdy tree. Being the epitome of a naive city girl, I made the mistake of getting between the bull and the tree. The beast made a few fast turns and pinned me against that tree faster than cowboys rope steers. Feeling a rope cutting into your body as it tightens makes you wish for suburbia in a hurry. Fortunately Tom intervened and we finally got me rescued, doctored the darn thing's ear, and turned him loose.

Only slightly less adventuresome was teaching a calf to drink from a bucket. (For you citified folk, you do this when you're milking the mother cow. The calf gets fed via bucket; you get the rest to drink, make butter, etc.) You straddle the calf, or back him into a corner, so you can get his head in the bucket of warm milk. Knowing this is totally unnatural, he fights you with the strength of a gorilla. Usually he wins. The bucket of milk dumps all over you and you get to start again. Once you have him settled down a little, the easiest way is to use your finger to simulate the mother's teat and get him to suck. If you've never felt the rough tongue of a calf, you've really missed something.

After doing this twice a day for a week or so, your back has a semi-permanent kink. The reward? The calf greets you with bawling anticipation as soon as he sees you approaching with a pail. You still need to hang onto your wits—and perhaps a fence—however. Once the pail is empty, he's likely to root it right out of your hands looking for more. (An aside I'd never have believed if I hadn't done it: bag balm—used to treat a cow's sore udder—makes the most soothing hand lotion.)

Rocks also proved a quandary for me. We did what is called "rock picking." That means you get all the rocks out of a nice meadow so the equipment can come in and cut the hay easily at harvest time. I did this diligently the first year. That meadow was as smooth as a baby's bottom.

After the hay crew finished, I went out to look again at my clean meadow. But it wasn't. Fresh rocks had appeared! It was then I learned another country truism: rocks grow. Somehow the earth shifts and new rocks settle up to the top. Unreasonable. Unfathomable. And certainly unfair!

*Rocks got the best of me another time too—or rather they were helped by our dog, Bandit. It was spring and time to clean out the debris and rocks so the creek and irrigation ditches would flow freely. Being one to tackle life with gusto, I was in the creek grabbing a rock in each hand and flinging them out behind me. Then I heard Tom laughing. It seems Bandit thought this was great sport . . . and was gleefully fetching the rocks and dumping them back in the creek.*

*When it came time to turn off the irrigation ditches in the fall, there were always a few little trout left flopping about in the trickle of water. Now fishing isn't normally my thing. It takes too much patience for nothing to happen. But this was different! The heck with poles, reels, and bait. I soon had a brookie in each hand and was dumping them into a bucket. Boy, that was some good eatin'.*

*Another thing baffled me in my early country days. People referred to mealtimes by odd names. They would say "dinner" and I'd think of the evening meal and be all set. But they meant lunch. Why didn't they just say "lunch" I reasoned, relying on my southern California upbringing. To further complicate the issue, "supper" was served in the evening. What ever happened to* <u>lunch</u> *boxes?*

While the ranch turned out to be the wrong road to the right destination, it gave us wonderful memories. But enough of our escapades. A useful and folksy reference for those who want to go back to the land is the *Small Farmer's Journal*. Get information on this quarterly magazine by writing P.O. Box 2805, Eugene, OR 97402-0318, 503-683-6486.

Do you love horses? What about setting up a horse motel? (Yes, you read right.) Horses being trailered to shows, auctions, or new owners often need overnight accommodations. Or perhaps you could open a stable, tack shop, or become a horseshoer.

Maybe you have in mind to invent something. There are some 11 different government departments and agencies that offer more than $475 million each year in grant money to small businesses and individual entrepreneurs working on new ideas. How do you get yours? Try contacting the Office of Innovation, Research and Technology, U.S. Small Business Administration, 1441 L Street, N.W., Washington, DC 20416, 202-205-6450. Another funding source is the Energy Related Inventions Program, National Institute of Standards and Technology, Building 411, Room A115, Gaithersburg, MD 20899, 301-975-5500.

And here's a quick and cheap way to protect your invention for two years: Get a disclosure statement for $6. While not a full patent, this tactic gives you time to maneuver and see if you have a saleable idea. To show evidence of the dates of conception of your invention, contact the Patent and Trademark Office, U.S. Department of Commerce, 2121 Crystal Drive, Arlington, VA 22202, 703-557-3225. Ask for a disclosure statement.

Mail order is an ideal boonies business too. Properly approached, it can thrive regardless of what happens locally. Ads in various national magazines and newspapers put dollars in your mailbox. Or you can rent mailing lists of prospects interested in your product. What do you sell? The options are infinite: crafts you make, items you purchase for resale, books you publish.

Speaking of publishing, many country folks make a nice living writing and publishing books, booklets, and newsletters. With the recent technological advances in desktop publishing, it has become very cost-effective. For everything you need to know to write, publish, promote, and sell your own book, look in the "Bibliography/Recommended Reading" section for information on how to order our *Complete Guide to Self-Publishing*. We also offer free guidelines to help new writers get started. For a copy send a self-addressed stamped envelope to Writer's Guidelines, Box 1500-CB, Buena Vista, CO 81211.

Personal services are popular with countrypreneurs. Perhaps the town you're considering needs a taxi, limo, or shuttle service. With a fleet of one vehicle, you can keep busy all day. In some states dental hygienists can work from their homes, as can some beauticians.

As people live longer, elder care for their parents is becoming a big concern for many baby boomers. With the cost of convalescent homes and private duty nurses skyrocketing, the market for senior day care centers is excellent. Perhaps you would feel personally fulfilled creating a supervised setting for frail senior adults.

Businesses need service providers too. Ever thought of offering a professional billing service? With the right software, knowledge, and marketing, you can be serving small businesses all over the county. And this could lead to doing other accounting and tax work.

Many small towns could benefit from having temporary secretarial and word processing help available. If your skills fall in this area, consider offering vacation relief, coverage during illness, and aid with overload projects. And you can probably pick up work from fledgling firms that can't yet afford a regular secretary, but need help a few hours a week. Develop a core of loyal customers and they will provide you with an ever-increasing stream of profits.

We know of one elderly gentleman who runs a regional clipping service. He scours area newspapers and magazines for such clients as attorneys, doctors, bridal consultants, and an office furniture dealer. This gives him purpose to maintain his self-esteem and profits to augment his social security.

Another man has a mobile washing service. Using his power washing equipment, he's cleaned driveways, parking lots, restaurant freezers, telephone booths, boats, signs, shopping carts, dumpsters, awnings, even airplanes. His motto? "We wash anything, anywhere, anytime."

If you want help advertising, publicizing, or maximizing your service business, get a copy of our *Big Marketing Ideas for Small Service Businesses*. It's listed in the "Bibliography/Recommended Reading" and contains 229 ideas to make your life easier and your business more profitable.

## *Turning Avocational Pastimes into Regular Paydays*

By looking at what gives you pleasure—your hobbies and personal interests—you may find a wonderful career opportunity waiting in the wings. This is the second largest source for business ideas. Eighteen percent of people use a hobby to get a handle on the world of work. They grease the slide for change in a multitude of ways.

A computer buff begins to repair computers, gives training, serves as a consultant, or writes software programs. A man who's enthusiastic about using his video camera brushes up his skills and "angles" jobs videotaping weddings, graduations, and special events. A homemaker who re-covered her sofa and love seat turns commercial and begins earning money reupholstering furniture for others.

Many skills used to run a home can be translated into paying professions. What about becoming an event planner? Even in small towns, some people are too busy to plan their own social or corporate activities. With research, organizational insight, and chutzpa you're set to coordinate weddings, anniversary bashes, mini-conventions, meetings, reunions, charity events, and gala parties.

Do you win raves for your cooking and baking? Joann Roth always had a dream of being a caterer. Her business began when she catered a series of small dinner parties from her clients' kitchens. You might prepare a luxurious breakfast in bed for 2, elegant gourmet dinners for 20, or traditional wedding suppers for 300. Maybe your forte will be special occasion cakes.

Or nutritious home cooked meals for busy working couples. You line up 10 or 12 couples who purchase your service two or three times a week, prepare that evening's dinner in bulk, then deliver it on beautifully presented trays. We'd wager in a town of any size, there are many overloaded entrepreneurs who would pay for such a healthy convenience.

For a lot of people, a rut is a grave with the ends kicked out. Ron Fuller became very disillusioned with his corporate rut. Although he was in upper management in a Michigan furniture company, he had all kinds of responsibility—but no authority. So he left the corporate world in the dust.

"I always liked to work on cars," reminisces Fuller. "I've got several friends who race and I have pitted for them . . . changed tires, worked on engines, a little bit of everything." All this came in handy when he accepted a job managing Mountain View Motor Sports Park in Mead, Colorado. The 1.7-mile racetrack accommodates everything from roller blades to Indy cars. He does it all around the track: maintenance, cutting the grass, fixing wires and speakers, phone work, greeting folks, and safety inspections. "There are two things that I like about this job," says Ron. "One is being outside and two is the people." Ron used his avocational interests to escape the corporate rut.

So did Phil Albin. Tired of being a securities broker in Houston, he turned to his hobby of fixing things. He knew how hard it was to get competent repairs done, so Albin launched The House Doctor as a maintenance and repair service targeted primarily to absentee owners.

His first job was weeding a flower bed for $3.75 an hour. The owner kept asking him, "Are you sure you're a gardener?" Today The House Doctor has a gross annual income of $150,000—divided between Albin, one part-time helper, and occasional subcontractors.

Margaret Day of Watch Hill, Rhode Island, is a musician. Initially she only played her harp for family, friends, and at occasional weddings. Recently she began playing professionally. Business is booming and has developed into a full-time career for her.

Irene Burrows' work has been saluted around the world. She spends part of every day making flags for domestic and international customers. Her creations have gone to the U.S. Department of Education, the Securities and Exchange Commission, AT&T, the Netherlands Air Force, the Cotton Bowl, and the NCAA basketball tournament. Leaving a job with J.C. Penney, she eventually formed the Independence Flag and Banner Company to capitalize on her seamstress skills. "I just love it," says Burrows of her Buena Vista-based business.

Several other successful artisans operate here in Chaffee County. Jackieanne Shepherd is a former fine arts teacher who left the classroom for wheat weavings, dough ornaments, corn dolls, and canvas rabbits dubbed Wild Hares. "You can't rely on a local market or even the summer tourist market if you expect to make a business of crafts," she counsels. "Much of my exposure comes through shows in Denver, Colorado Springs, Grand Junction, and New Mexico." She feels it is critical to keep ahead of the trends and on top of whatever is the latest in crafts.

Donna Harmon designs wreaths for a living. Not just evergreen holiday wreaths, but also ones for all seasons. A big challenge is coming up with innovative designs. To trim costs, Harmon grows many of the materials she uses in her wreaths, such as miniature pumpkins, baby's breath, and wheat. In addition to local outlets, she displays at shows to generate more orders.

Cheri and Curt Welty also turned their hobbies into a business. "It's nice to be able to make a living doing what you love to do," says Cheri. Their enterprise includes Curt's stained-glass windows, lamp shades, and wall hangings, plus mugs he creates with designs for skiers and rafters. Cheri's contribution includes weavings and classes. Additionally, she has introduced a line of high-quality yarns.

One gentleman was responsible for commercializing his wife's lifelong hobby of fine-needle, baroque textile embellishment—an astoundingly beautiful amalgam of embroidery and needlepoint crafts. He started by getting several locals to pay for textile decorating lessons taught by his wife. The pair also developed a mail-order business offering supplies, patterns, and instructions for this craft.

Getting known and established is perhaps the most difficult part of making a living from one's art. Though the work is good, it's tough to get going until you've developed a reputation. And it's hard to know what is the best way to merchandise your wares. Options include direct sales, craft shops, galleries, mail order craft catalogs, home parties, craft cooperatives, and through sales representatives.

Of course pricing is another challenge. Figuring out what the traffic will bear sometimes requires a crystal ball. Short of that, we'd suggest you pick up a copy of Barbara Brabec's *Creative Cash*. It tells how to sell your crafts, needlework, designs and know-how. This definitive guide to making money can be ordered in the "Bibliography/Recommended Reading" section. Another interesting source for help is The Front Room Publishers. Request their Learning Extension Catalog—which is brimming with useful information—from P. O. Box 1541, Clifton, NJ 07015-1541.

## *What's Your Passion?*

"Those whose work and play are one, are fortune's favorite children," said Winston Churchill. For some of us a nagging displeasure with work begins to consume us, a stoic acceptance numbs our senses and reduces our productivity. When that happens, it's time to leave. Maybe you're asking yourself all over again: *What do I want to be when I grow up?* Since we spend more of our adult lives working than doing just about anything else, that work experience should yield a major return on our investment. If you're experiencing a negative emotional cash flow, liberation here you come!

God has given each of us a gift. Some people term it a *calling*. We experience great joy when we let this light shine, when we give to life on earth something no one else can contribute in quite the same way. But finding your mission in life, what you're most enthusiastic about, isn't always easy.

If you're having trouble identifying your passion, scheduling a few sessions with a career counselor knowledgeable in entrepreneurial topics makes sense. These individuals have personal insight and professional experience in guiding people into satisfying livelihoods. Their unbiased individualized assessment can prove extremely helpful. You'll find them in the Yellow Pages under "Career & Vocational Counseling." (This may also prove a wise strategy for relocating spouses unsure of which way to turn if their skills aren't in demand in the new town.)

You'll probably be encouraged to take an aptitude test. This gives you an inward view, yielding an objective profile of your natural abilities. In many jobs we end up denying a part of ourselves. When we do this, we get antsy and antagonistic. Aptitude testing confirms the enormous variety of human talent. Though somewhat expensive, it may be the price of admission to a happy and rewarding new life.

In the end *you* will be the cornerstone of your business. So know thyself. It's your interest, fervor, energy, skill, time, and effort that make a new enterprise happen. Before you make decisions, take a personal inventory.

What are your skills? Literally submit a resumé to yourself. And don't be shy. List all work experience. Note any areas of competency that relate to a business. Write down your volunteer work, hobbies, and other activities. Look at your education, both formal and informal. Have you taken special courses or attended useful seminars?

Now inventory your likes. What would you do for free? If there were no financial requirements or other constraints how would your days go? How do you spend your time off? Do you enjoy gardening? Computers? Tinkering with your car? Making handicrafts? Writing? Helping people? Go back and look at your Fun Quotient Quiz from the chapter on "Cultivating a Satisfying Social Life" for additional ideas.

Next look over your two lists and make a third one of your strongest skills and greatest likes. This final tabulation provides a good basis for helping to decide the type of business to start. Of course, there must be a marriage between what you want to do and what people are willing to pay you for.

Another valuable measurement is to get input from 20 friends, relatives, or colleagues. Ask each to tell you *one* thing you do well. You might be amazed at the results. They may see your abilities differently than you do. After trying this exercise, one man who planned to open an advertising agency reported, "I've got a great list. But there's one funny thing. No one I spoke with mentioned advertising as one of my strengths!" What revealing feedback. This could open wonderful new horizons . . . or save you from a horrible mistake.

Don't become so enamored with *your* likes, however, that you fail to measure them against reality. We're reminded of a Michigan couple who enjoyed fine wine and good food so much they opened a gourmet wine and food shop in Flint. Only after they lost their $60,000 investment did they realize most of Flint's wine drinkers patronized the one-stop-shopping supermarkets where they bought their libations along with their groceries. When you're considering opening a new business dependent on the local economy, a good question to ask is "Why doesn't _____ already have such a place?" The answers are often penetratingly revealing.

If no one else is offering what you have in mind, why not? Perhaps you've hit on a brilliant idea. Or maybe others have already tried it and failed. Ask around. Don't be surprised if your ideas change, Welcome these modifications; they often lead to the ideal solution. Give this input serious consideration. You may find starting a certain kind of business in the country makes about as much sense as opening a tanning salon in a desert.

As you further refine your business options, creating a personal Balance Sheet might make sense. Let's suppose you and your spouse are considering purchasing a specific restaurant. You might list your assets and liabilities as follows:

| *Assets* | *Liabilities* |
|---|---|
| Gloria's a wonderful cook | They don't know the restaurant business |
| Cliff does a great job of baking | Used to forty-hour weeks |
| Both in their forties | Unaccustomed to performing tasks |
| High energy people | The restaurant has been closed a year |
| Cliff's handy and can fix plumbing, etc. | Decor needs to be jazzed up |
| He can do initial remodeling carpentry | |
| Gloria is excellent with people | |
| She's experienced with ads/promotion | |
| She knows how to keep books | |
| They have adequate down payment | |

Want a foolproof way to check out a business before you plunk down your dollars? Volunteer to work there for free! Or if this seems too blatant, offer your services gratis to a similar business in another town, perhaps where you're currently living. Although this won't give you the local flavor, it will provide heaps of insider information about buying strategies, customer service, vendors, industry policies, etc.

Chris Meyer traded Los Angeles for tiny Scottsville, Virginia. She also wanted to trade a career in video production for one in drama therapy. Working the phones from California, Meyer landed an unpaid internship with Jan Goodrich, a pioneer in the field. By donating her time she will quickly learn if this field is really for her. We cover many more sophisticated methods for researching an industry and a geographic area in the next chapter.

"Either we're prisoners of change or we'll use it to our competitive advantage," states futurist and technology forecaster Daniel Burrus. But how do we "use change"? And how does the smart budding entrepreneur struggle through an endless sea of information to discover *the* innovation that will launch a cutting-edge business? One way is to get Burrus' book, *The New Tools of Technology*, listed in the "Bibliography/Recommended Reading" section.

He shows how to gain a strategic advantage in such areas as computer science, biotechnology, optoelectronics, communications, energy production, and materials science. Fortune 500 companies hire Burrus to tell them how to integrate the discoveries outlined in this book into their corporate plans. Now you can tap into this futuristic problem-solver.

Also investigate the upcoming chapters on "Working From Home: The 'Information Age' Option" and "Telecommuting: A Growing Solution to Urban Blues." Both address using technology to your advantage.

The following Occupational Satisfaction Scale was adapted from a model in *How to Uncover and Create Business Opportunities* by Dr. Dale Rusnell and Bill Gibson. This is an excellent book for generating start-up ideas. The scale will serve as a barometer to help clarify your personal needs.

So you've pinpointed your passion. Now it's time to focus on accomplishing it. There are several techniques to help accomplish this. One is to visualize yourself in your new career, actually performing the tasks involved. Close your eyes. See and feel your dream. Smell the hay if that's what you want to raise. Feel the fabric in the garments if it's a clothing store you yearn to own. Hear the music if teaching piano is your vision. Apply all the senses to your dream. Go through the daily process in your mind's eye. By repeatedly seeing ourselves doing what we want, we condition our subconscious mind to accept this as reality.

## Occupational Satisfaction Scale

| Indoor | 1 2 3 4 5 6 7 8 9 10 | Outdoor |
|---|---|---|
| At Home | 1 2 3 4 5 6 7 8 9 10 | In Office/Store |
| Physical | 1 2 3 4 5 6 7 8 9 10 | Mental |
| With Others | 1 2 3 4 5 6 7 8 9 10 | Alone |
| High Travel | 1 2 3 4 5 6 7 8 9 10 | Stationary |
| Fixed Schedule | 1 2 3 4 5 6 7 8 9 10 | Flexible Schedule |
| Routine Activities | 1 2 3 4 5 6 7 8 9 10 | Diverse Activities |

Another proven route to success is to affirm what you want. Write out a statement about your new career. Phrase it in the present tense, as though you *already have* what you want. Rather than saying you're "going" to do such and such, state it as if you already own the store or do the thing you aspire to. Write this affirmation several times each morning and evening. It's also a good idea to repeat it aloud. When we truly *believe* something, it is ours.

Look at the big picture. A new business in a small town is an event. Sometimes projects rise or fall due to the personalities of the people in charge and what they intend to do. How might the community perceive your venture? List any groups, businesses, or individuals your enterprise might antagonize. How would it harm them? Can these effects be offset? List key people who could oppose you. Why would they do so? How can you shape what you have in mind to get their support, or at least keep them **neutral?**

Now think of groups, businesses, or people who might receive special benefits. What resources, effort, or support might they give you? This kind of perception forecasting can be invaluable. It allows you to get into the heads of people and figure out how to fashion win-win liaisons in advance.

## *900 Phone Numbers Open New Doors*

They've gotten a bad rap, these 900 pay-per-call phone numbers. And many of the complaints were justified. But as the industry matures, a second generation of them are emerging—respectable players offering valuable services. There will be a new level of consumer acceptance—and legitimate profits. In fact, millions of dollars ($975 million in 1991—more than doubling in two years) are being made in the 900 business. Pay-per-call telephone programs give you a chance to reap amazing profits for a minimal investment, especially if you have information to sell.

The lease rates have come tumbling down like Humpty Dumpty over the last few years. Working through what is called a "service bureau" makes it even more affordable. These are firms that serve as intermediaries between you and the telephone companies. Many believe 900 numbers are the marketing wave of the future.

We see them as a practical way for people to take their expertise to the hinterlands, to become remote information providers. In 1991 35.6 percent of all calls were for information. A *Chicago Tribune* study suggests that by 1996 informational and business purposes will mushroom to 45.6 percent. With some 900 numbers, callers talk live to individuals. In other situations, they hear pre-recorded messages. Often there's a selection of various messages they can access.

Legitimate areas of successful pay-per-call operations include a wide range. There's business and finance—general news and information—newspaper, magazine, and television hotlines—horoscopes and fortunes—games, humor and entertainment—promotions—sports— plus public service and fund raising.

And dialing 900 is getting a professional twist. Doctors, lawyers, financial planners, pharmacists, insurance agents, even certified social work counselors have already climbed on this bandwagon. These phone pros charge about $3 a minute.

Tele-Lawyer was begun by a California attorney, Michael Cane. He and his staff dispense legal advice via the telephone. They field over 100 calls per day covering divorce, taxes, even how to file for bankruptcy. The average cost is $21—quite a consumer savings over typical attorney fees of $150-$200 an hour. Yet at $3 a minute, times 60 minutes, the revenue generated still holds up for the lawyer. (Give you barristers out there fed up with city life any ideas?)

Dial-a-doctor has also débuted. Over-the-phone medical consultations now allow people to talk with a licensed physician. The average call lasts five minutes and puts a $15 charge on the patient's phone bill. The doctors on call answer basic questions about pediatrics, geriatrics, sex therapy, cardiology, and emergency medicine. They work in tandem with a computer database of medical information. This service appeals especially to people who don't want to discuss sensitive problems with their regular physician. It's also useful for those who don't understand why certain tests were ordered or who don't have a regular doctor.

There's also a 900 service for animal health and behavior information. The number appears on a directory distributed in veterinary offices and in packages of pet food. (That's clever marketing—the key to 900 success.) The directory contains 300 pet topics from which callers can choose.

Extrapolating from this, we predict many kinds of experts will encourage prospective clients or customers to initiate phone consultation services. This has electrifying possibilities. No longer do you have to dial a 900 number and just listen. The technology has become much more sophisticated. With today's interactive programs, you can now use your telephone's touch-tone pad to choose from many additional menu items.

Taking our About Books, Inc. as an example, here's how it might work: You first get a welcoming message (which, by law, must include the cost per minute). Then a menu of possibilities is announced and you plug into whatever fits your individual needs.

There would be separate extensions dealing with various topics: how to find an agent, write a book proposal, and negotiate a contract. Other possible subjects could include finding a good printer, writing a winning ad, launching a marketing campaign, how to behave for media appearances, selling to book clubs, etc. See what we mean?

This is a way to *start* a business or *layer* an existing one. A newsletter publisher, for instance, could use 900 to impart individualized, high-value information to his or her subscribers. Certain facts are of only peripheral interest to all subscribers, yet of paramount value to some people. These numbers expand possibilities for immediacy and timeliness.

Remember how great it used to be when you could go into a music store and *sample* selections you were considering buying? Now technology has brought back listening booths . . . only they're in your own home and over the telephone. An Omaha, Nebraska, music company has set up a $2-per-minute line to allow prospective customers to listen to tunes they might

## Trade Your Business Suit Blues for Blue Jean Dreams™

want to buy. Purchasers deduct the $2 from their bill. The company first tried an 800 number. They were deluged with calls (at *their* expense) but only converted about 2 percent of those to sales. With the 900 number the amount of inquiries naturally lessened. But they are converting an impressive 30 percent of those callers.

With many of these applications you can be an "absentee owner." Maybe you spend half a day twice a week programming your information. The rest of the time the automated calls handle everything in your absence—turning calls into income seven days a week, 24 hours a day. This concept offers practically all the advantages of mail order without any of the associated hassles. It even works for you while you're on vacation. All you need is a phone from which to download your messages.

"And even if the rural telephone company doesn't offer touch-tone service, you can get a hand-help touch-tone dialer to tell the central 900 number computer to download, play back, or save your 900 messages," explains Ron Hanus. He's the author of *Power Up Your Profits Report,* a useful monologue on the subject of pay-per-call. "Using a cellular phone, you could even operate a 900 number business where there are no phone lines at all," Hanus continues. See the "Bibliography/Recommended Reading" for ordering information on his intriguing report.

Here's another spin on using 900 numbers: Let's say you're an appliance repair person. Often you can coach a person through a minor repair over the phone for $15 or $20, in contrast to the usual $60 house call. And you can do this from Timbuctoo! (You might even inventory and ship the most commonly needed parts to make additional revenue.)

Of course nothing is a panacea. While you have no billing problems because charges go directly on the caller's phone bill, there are holdbacks or chargebacks to cover people who refuse to pay. That typically runs in the neighborhood of 15 percent. And, unless you're working through a firm which fronts the operation, it usually takes from three to four months for the first check to roll in.

To avoid the previous abuses and police the industry, there are a host of new legislative initiatives, primarily at the state level. About 10 states have enacted laws which impose specific requirements for 900 number advertisers. There is talk that a few states also plan to put a limit on what you can charge per minute or per call. This will curtail some opportunities.

The Federal Trade Commission is the federal body responsible for protecting the public in this area. They are particularly concerned about cost disclosure requirements. What's emerging overall is a patchwork of confusing and often contradictory federal and state advertising standards, so be sure to investigate thoroughly before you invest.

Like any business, with a 900 line you must drum up customers. This requires aggressive promotion or advertising to get the number publicized and circulated nationally. Alliances with related products or services can lead to a pot of telecom gold at the end of the phone line. Remember the pet food packages mentioned above that promoted a 900 number? So can a well orchestrated and timely PR hook.

We think 900 numbers (maybe even 1,000 numbers) have terrific potential. Through them, you can help people glean tips on dealing with everything from their golfer's slice to financial woes, from fixing their computers to patching up their marital problems. A free booklet, "900 Service From A to $", gives an introduction to the possibilities. You can order it from Comtec at 800-832-0123.

For those who want to seriously investigate this opportunity, we recommend *The Power of 900* by Rick Parkhill. This unique sourcebook lists 96 service bureaus and over 600 pay-per-call numbers. It also contains chapters on pursuing this as a business opportunity, gives a cash flow model, industry forecast, advertising and promotion pointers, plus hard-to-find facts. To order this sophisticated manual, see the "Bibliography/Recommended Reading" section.

Visions of the future also include significant new ways telephones and computers will be linked. Recent lifting of restrictions on the Baby Bells will allow them to generate, acquire, store, transform, process, retrieve, use, or make available information conveyed via telecommunications.

This information gateway resembles a shopping mall containing a variety of service providers. Some are big like the anchor stores; others small like the boutiques. They will allow consumers to shop, learn, and conduct business from home. This future is coming fast. If you feel such advanced technology might play an important role in your business plans, see the listing in Part III called Where to Ring the Baby Bells.

## *Making the Most of Your Money*

Severance pay, lump sums from retirement plans, and golden parachutes are allowing thousands of Fortune 500 executives to pull the rip cord on corporate life and launch careers of their own. If you're laid off, get as much of a cushion as you can. Some companies offer "reduction-in-force" policies about once a year. Be patient and maneuver until you qualify for such a plan. Most planned layoffs give you several weeks of severance, medical coverage, and insurance.

When someone starting a business has a lot of money, however, it can be a deterrent believes Paul Hawken, author of the excellent *Growing A Business*. "Most small businesses fail due to lack of imagination rather than capital," he says. The temptation to *buy* solutions is overwhelming. Yet ideas don't come with check stubs attached to them. "Necessity nurtures invention," contends Hawken. (If you suffer from the opposite dilemma—no capital—take heart. We devote a full future chapter to "Generating Capital to Launch Your Venture.")

"Many professionals are equity rich," says David Savageau, author of *Places Rated Almanac* and *Retirement Places Rated*. "Now they want to split and look for a nice countrified place. Lots are coming out of southern California. They are individuals who have capital and are willing to take the risk. Quality of life is their prime consideration." Savageau advises a business should require less than $150,000 to start or buy and should operate with fewer than four employees. He points out that beginning a small manufacturing firm may appeal to engineers who want to make a part or a circuit.

It's not unusual for fledgling firms to be undercapitalized. The basic money rule is to have enough to get the doors open and keep the business going for at least 90 days—with absolutely no cash income. And don't count on credit from your suppliers to stock your inventory. It's ideal to have a reserve above this amount, or a prospective partner who can be brought in if the business turns out to be a late-bloomer.

Few first-time entrepreneurs are prepared for clients or customers who pay their bills late—or not at all. Meanwhile the company must meet its financial obligations and may not have enough cash to purchase goods or services to satisfy new orders, or cover payroll. If possible, structure your payment schedule so at least half the amount owed is paid *before* the goods or services are delivered.

Our consulting agreement requires that all funds be paid when the work is begun. Rarely does anyone quibble with this policy. If they do, we simply refuse to work with them. We create intellectual properties customized to meet individual client needs. It isn't like manufacturing a chair which can be sold to someone else, should the original order fall through.

Speaking of money, one of the severest blows comes when you find out what health insurance costs. Barbara Brabec, editor and publisher of the *National Home Business Report*, tells of premiums that skyrocketed from $2,400 one year to $6,000 the next. When contemplating self-employment, be sure to take this into consideration. (And try to use it as a bargaining chip to continue coverage when leaving a large corporate employer.)

A couple of other cautions: don't lock yourself into a long lease initially. We just had dinner with a couple who lamented having to keep a dying business in operation until they could escape a five-year lease. And be careful of putting a lot of money into remodeling right away. You may need that extra cash to tide you over during slow times.

Also allow for "shrinkage." If you're in the restaurant business, that may mean a cook who takes a side of beef or slips butter out the back door. In a retail store it is the merchandise that's stolen by innocent looking customers. In a bar, it's the liquor the bartender or servers tote home. Of course cash registers can come up short too. Even in manufacturing environments this goes on. Quantities of either raw materials or the finished product disappear.

## *Diversify to Multiply*

Synergy—the combined effect of two or more things working together—may be what allows you to make a living in the country. Rural folk often wear as many hats as Imelda has shoes. They have to. There simply isn't a large enough population base to support just one endeavor. Besides it's more fun when you have your fingers in several pies.

A barber we know uses the extra space in his 3-chair shop to sell potted plants. His customers feel as if they're getting their hair cut in a garden. They tell their wives, who come in and buy plants at attractive prices. In turn, the ladies often bring the kids back for a haircut.

Laundromats have really capitalized on this idea. They are now operated in conjunction with bars, restaurants, exercise rooms, tanning salons, video game arcades, video rentals while you wash, you name it. Some even offer dry cleaning and tailoring . . . certainly natural additions.

We know of one funeral home that doubles as a wedding chapel. "We want to be part of more than just the final event in a person's life. Whether it's a wedding, a seminar, or just a get-together, we want to provide a warm, friendly place for people to meet," says a company spokesperson. Their Abundant Living Center serves the community and brings in extra revenue for the company.

One smart motel operator located near a ski and rafting area put together a deal that keeps her "no vacancy" sign on most of the time. She worked with nearby resort and recreation operators to create getaway packages that work both winter and summer. A family campground stimulated more business by buying a few horses and offering riding (at no less than $60 a day), pack trips, hay rides, and an evening steak ride via horseback.

When we owned the hotel in First Try, we scrambled to think of practical add-on money makers. Since it was a historic hotel, in keeping with the period, we didn't have phones in the rooms. But we did discover we could keep half the revenue from an on-premise pay telephone. That proved profitable. We also installed some video games in a part of the lobby. They brought in a sizeable chunk of change each month.

We contemplated becoming the local bus depot and serving as the UPS or Federal Express pick up point. It was decided, however, these activities would interrupt our main focus too much. But when we started thinking about *Country Bound!*, we purposely focused on additional spinoffs that would interest our readers. We came up with a newsletter, *The Country Bound!*™ *Connection*, to keep people better informed about the trends in this fascinating movement. And we had so much favorable feedback on the cover of this book that we designed colorful T-shirts to incorporate the drawing, plus the words: "Country Bound!™" and "Trade Your Business Suit Blues for Blue Jean Dreams™". Want one? See the Order Blank at the end of the book!

The list of options goes on and on: A music store owner sells recorded music, sheet music, strings, reeds, and can special order larger instruments. To be different, he also tunes pianos. A bookstore promotes several sidelines: church supplies, audio tapes, and greeting cards. A real estate office carries maps and regional guidebooks. A maid service offers plant care, pet care, and housewatching for their traveling customers.

Diversification of business equals multiplication of dollars. You might start a new sideline business that relates to your original company, calls for similar skills and know-how, attracts the same customer or client base, or utilizes similar facilities. For instance, combining child care and elder care might make an excellent merger.

Farmers and ranchers always look for ways to augment their primary income. They have many irons in a crowded fire. Some set up fruit, vegetable, or flower stands—offer breeding services—raise earthworms—fix fences for their neighbors—or lease grazing rights for part of their land.

In some states they also make money off hunting rights, charging $300 to $400 per person for hunters to have permission to come on their property to hunt deer, ducks, geese, etc. In most farm households canning is as common as quilts. Pickles, relishes, chutneys, chili sauce, and preserves are sold at flea markets, or given as gifts.

Those into horses often break others' animals, shoe them, or offer riding lessons. They also sometimes serve as guides and outfitters, taking out groups of hunters unfamiliar with the territory. Some even butcher the meat and do taxidermy work. Many farmers with fruit or vegetable crops set up popular "pick-your-own" operations where area residents pay a fee to garner all the produce they can personally pick.

Fee fishing is also an alternative for those with ponds. Farmers stock their ponds, then allow the public to indulge themselves for a flat fee, or pay for the fish they catch. This is a painless way to expand your income. Of course equipment also can be rented or leased, or the owner can perform services himself—such as snow removal, welding, or custom haying. We had a backhoe we planned to use for jobs beyond our own needs, but it didn't work out quite that way.

> **Tom:** *A couple of our ranch hands had broken down the transaxle on our backhoe to repair it one summer, then got pulled away on an emergency job and never returned to the backhoe task. Fall came and went, then winter descended. As you might guess, we suddenly needed the backhoe.*
>
> *I set up shop in the old stable behind the hotel. Wind whistled through the cracks, but a kerosene heater kept my fingers from freezing. After much thinking and trying to figure out the configuration, I finally got the transaxle together, hoping everything was right. I really had no reference since I hadn't taken it apart. Besides, a year had elapsed!*
>
> *So one bitter cold January day Marilyn and I went out to install the transaxle in the backhoe and finish the job. Wouldn't you know the rest of the parts had been left strewn all over the ground. No big deal in summer. BIG deal in winter—with a foot of snow to paw through. We lit a fire in a five-gallon oil drum to thaw our frozen hands and proceeded with the job. It was a long, miserable day crawling around in the snow trying to find minute nuts, bolts, and other parts.*
>
> *But we finally got the transaxle and beast back together, gave each other a conquering smile, and lit 'er off. I climbed up on the driver's seat and shifted into gear. The backhoe lunged . . . in the wrong direction. I had installed the ring and pinion backwards! The backhoe now had 10 reverse gears and 2 forward ones! (Needless to say, we never rented it out. We only share this story with you because you can't see our red faces.)*

We sometimes think our son, Steve, is the champion of diversification derby days. He runs a multiplicity of small businesses. While his main emphasis is selling tires, he also retails auto supplies—does auto repair—gathers, cuts, and hauls firewood—buys and resells an occasional vehicle—rents out himself and his backhoe and homemade crane—and carries hunting supplies during hunting season. And, now that the local hardware store went under, he also carries a line of hardware and lumber.

In *The Popcorn Report*, Faith Popcorn predicts the watchword for the streamlined '90s will be *multi-function*. (Do you suppose Steve qualifies?) Related services will be clustered. Instead of traipsing to the dry cleaner's, then to the shoemaker's, and finally to the tailor's—these functions will be brought together for one-stop-shopping. Already in Seattle there is Espresso Dental. It's a combination dentist's office, espresso bar, and massage parlor. Leisure time and dental hygiene are collapsed into one time slot. Any service that saves time, money, or aggravation will have a lot going for it.

Some businesses are considered seasonal income producers, or year-round ventures that are only part-time. In that case you'd darn well better combine two or more ideas or you'll starve (look how popular cranapple juice is). We know of one operation, the Pool and Yule Shop, that blends swimming pool maintenance and supplies in the summer with a Christmas shop in the winter. Someone adept at helping people with their taxes might be a ski instructor in the off season. Get creative. There are many complementary pursuits that go together like biscuits and gravy.

Lastly we'd like to introduce you to something we've dubbed Link-Think. In this concept you get together with other businesses and set up a cooperative approach to encourage the customer to purchase a chain of items.

For instance, when a real estate agent sells a home, there are several other businesses he or she might alert to this prospect. They could include an interior decorator, a carpet and drapery salesperson, an insurance agent, and a landscape architect or gardener.

If the new residents have children, the list might also include a diaper service, day care facility, private school, etc. For this to be a win-win situation, the referred business could pay a small fee to the real estate agent. Get the idea? With LinkThinking entrepreneurs can forge strong chains of prosperity with each other.

Now let's move ahead and scrutinize ways to thoroughly examine the industry and geographic area you contemplate joining. Knowledge is power. Get set for some mighty astute maneuvers to arm yourself with lots of both.

# 9

# Researching for the Right Opportunity

Depending on hearsay to evaluate what business you should be in makes about as much sense as using a yardstick to measure temperature. You'll need to do your research systematically and intelligently. Yet "research" is a scary term. It sounds intimidating. Expensive. Boring. It needn't be any of these. In fact, it can be as exciting as going on a treasure hunt—a hunt for nuggets of information to help you establish a solid enterprise.

You'll want to map out your strategy for gathering facts. Use tools that are economical and effective. Explore the market intelligently. Our aim is to illuminate innovative ways you can accomplish this so that someone else doesn't mine the gold while you get the shaft. The information here is of primary value to those who want to have their own business, but job hunters will also find it worthwhile. In this chapter you'll learn two things: ingenious ways to discover inside intelligence about an industry and methods to shadow potential companies and competitors. We'll show you how to extract a quarry of vital information as frank as a "Candid Camera" shot.

For some people, research involves priorities: Do we decide *where* to live, then figure out how to earn a livelihood? Or do we take the opposite approach and look for a place that *needs* what we have to offer? David Savageau—co-author of *Places Rated Almanac* and owner of

PreLOCATION, a personal relocation consulting firm—advises to identify the business first, the location second. If you have a specialized skill, we agree finding the place is probably the wisest choice. But perhaps you're like many folks who don't have a definite career path. Then what?

## *Taking the First Easy Step*

To show you just how simple market research can be, let's create a hypothetical case. Suppose you're an avid fisherman and the idea of opening your own tackle and equipment store makes your pulse race almost as fast as hooking a five-pound trout. First you need to know how many other tackle shops are in the area. How stiff is the competition? To find out, it's back to the trusty Yellow Pages. Congratulations, you've taken the first step in research. (No, it won't always be that easy. For more sophisticated businesses, the investigation is naturally more complex.)

Now you might visit the competition as a customer. In this role you can determine such details as whether the location seems ideal, how complete the inventory is, and what prices are like. You can also gauge how accommodating and knowledgeable the proprietor is. This is of particular importance in a small town.

Don't be surprised to find yourself at the chamber of commerce next. There you'll glean particulars on the number of residents within the town's trading area, their average income, and their age level. What an encouraging sign, for example, if there are many retirees or pre-retirees. These people have plenty of time to fish. You can also find out tourist figures—a primary consideration for your type of business. If you choose to reveal your plans, you can also ask if anyone else is talking about opening a similar business. Or how progressive the existing competition is. (Remember how fast word travels in rural places, however. If you don't want it known you're contemplating opening a certain kind of business, talk in generalities. You would be looking at entering the "recreation industry.")

Research comes in two varieties: primary and secondary. Primary research is the snooping you do yourself. It often takes the form of surveys or interviews. Secondary research depends on material already available. In it, you analyze existing information. That might include databases, corporate reports, government documents, magazine and newspaper stories, etc. Trying to conduct an investigation by using only one of these techniques is like having a body without a head.

When our fisherman embarks on secondary research, a logical place to contact is the trade association to which other similar entrepreneurs belong. There is an association for virtually *every* interest or endeavor. They can be located in two ways: Contact the American Society of Association

Executives, 1575 Eye Street N.W., Washington, DC 20005, 202-626-2723. An even more complete list can be found at your local library (as can many of the reference works we mention in this chapter) in the three-volume *Encyclopedia of Associations*. Start in Part 3 with the name and keyword index. When we look under "fish" there are many options. Reading the names of the associations quickly narrows the field of candidates, however. Then go to the proper number in Part 1 and 2 to learn more about the mission of each association and how to reach it.

What can associations do for you? Lots! They provide much relevant information. They conduct surveys about salaries and revenue generated, and they can put you in touch with suppliers, for starters. In addition, they publish newsletters or magazines with useful how-to articles. Ask to speak with both the membership coordinator and the public information director. Explain you're considering joining the industry and ask how they can help.

Another source to check is *Directories in Print*. The 1992 ninth edition contains about 14,000 significant directories divided into 26 easy-to-scan subject chapters. This is a good place to prospect for supplier directories and reference works containing industry-specific information.

To see how well a business might do in a particular geographical area, check the *U.S. Census of Retail Trade* for the average number of inhabitants per type of store. Let's say you want to open a women's clothing shop. According to this publication, such a business takes 5,000 residents. A bookstore, on the other hand, needs 26,000 inhabitants to support it. Next determine the population and number of similar retail operations in the area you're considering. If the enterprise you're interested in starting would be under the recommended ratio of people to type of retail store, be cautious. But don't let this undermine your plans entirely. Many businesses are successful in spite of ratios far under the desired ones.

## *Tracking the Trends*

It may behoove you to get into a cutting-edge business rather than doing something traditional. Here are some ideas to help you predict the future.

The Department of Commerce publishes the *U.S. Industrial Outlook* annually. It traces the growth of 200 industries and provides five-year forecasts for each. Another potentially helpful publication is the *U.S. Statistical Abstract*. It's a compilation of data, reports, and charts from various federal agencies. The government is constantly conducting studies on industries, new technology, and social trends. These and many other helpful publications are on sale from the Superintendent of Documents, U.S. Government Printing Office, Washington, DC 20402. Write for a free catalog.

The Rochester Institute of Technology released a list of 12 fields it describes as "hot career choices for the remainder of the 1990s and the start of the next century." They are: information technology, environmental management, imaging science, microelectronic engineering, packaging science, telecommunications, food marketing and distribution, biotechnology, travel management, allied health sciences, electronic still photography, and biomedical photographic communications.

We devote a considerable portion of another chapter to the Gray Market (the aging population) as an important trend. And globalization is making us all neighbors, providing new opportunities for many companies. Niche marketing is another important tendency. General interest magazines, for instance, are floundering. Yet those that target a special pocket of the population are racking up impressive circulation numbers.

How can you personally tune in to the trends? What are ways you can stay alert to the hidden needs of America? Use your eyes and ears. Review our following list for Reading Your Way to the Hot Careers. Watching television commercials keeps your finger on the pulse of what people want. So do shows like Donahue and Oprah, plus the various exposé programs. Attending trade shows is a further way to stay informed.

In the mid-seventies a lady by the name of Mable Hoffman did just that. She noticed several manufacturers' exhibits were introducing a small appliance called a crock pot. She reasoned consumers would need new recipes and guidance on how to use their new cookware. This trend-conscious lady went home and wrote a book called *Crockery Cookery*. The last time we checked, it had sold over 3 million copies!

Be sure, however, you are tuning into trends not fads. A fad is here today and gone tomorrow, like the hula hoop. Ignore these transient crazes. Don't let a turkey gobble your time and capital. Look for trends that have staying power. Before we started writing *Country Bound!*, we tracked the fact that several major magazines carried cover stories about Americans' desire to escape big cities.

## READING YOUR WAY TO THE HOT CAREERS

Following are books, magazines, newsletters, and newspapers to help you stay abreast of trends and create exciting new business opportunities.

*The Popcorn Report,* by Faith Popcorn, not only pinpoints consumer moods but is just plain fascinating reading.

*Megatrends 2000*, by John Naisbitt and Patricia Aburdene, details 10 new directions for the '90s.

*Powershift,* by Alvin Toffler, is both entertaining and profound as it serves up insights we need to survive in the future.

*The Lifestyle Odyssey: 2,001 Ways Americans' Lives Are Changing,* by the editors of Research Alert, pinpoints six principles—and their ramifications—that will shape our lives in this century.

*The New Tools of Technology,* edited by Daniel Burrus and Patti Thomsen, cites 20 key technologies entrepreneurs can use and discloses 520 of the latest advances.

*Trend Tracking: The System to Profit from Today's Trends,* by Gerald Celente with Tom Milton, offers a formula for trend analysis that people can apply independently for business survival and growth.

*Advertising Age* or *Ad Weekly* magazines help you get a feel for what new products, consumer interest trends, and ad agency advance plans are on the horizon.

*American Demographics* magazine forecasts consumer trends for business leaders. Back issues on specific topics are also useful.

*Entrepreneur* magazine interviews forward-thinking small businesspeople and is a good idea generator.

*Publishers Weekly* is the bible of the book industry. By studying the spring and fall issues you can get a feel for upcoming consumer interests.

*The Wall Street Journal* gives an excellent overview of breaking business news.

*USA Today* runs cover stories plus interesting "snapshots" of statistics and how people feel about issues.

*The Futurist* is a journal of forecasts, trends, and ideas about the future. (Global in scope, it's available only through membership in the World Future Society.)

*John Naisbitt's Trend Letter* offers cutting-edge news on a variety of topics twice monthly.

## Sleuthing as You Schmooze

Once you've determined the industry you're going to enter, it's time to interview others in that same business. Naturally you'll pick someone in another town who is not a direct competitor. Schmoozing is a real door opener. People love to talk about themselves, so you should have little trouble finding folks to visit with. Especially if you play your cards right. Intelligence is like money . . . if you don't let on how little you've got, people will treat you as though you have a lot. Start with general questions, then move gradually to more specific inquiries.

Go armed with a fistful of well constructed questions designed to ferret out answers to the tough inquiries. You want to know what has been their biggest stumbling block. Would they do it all again? How much money did it take? Would it be more today? What's the biggest mistake people just entering this business make? Don't go for "yes" or "no" answers. If your aim is to loosen lips, keep the conversation open-ended so people will elaborate.

There are many other individuals who can contribute to your information arsenal. Think about sales and support personnel from companies with complementary services. What about chatting with past employees or alumni from competitors? Talk to distributors, dealers, and franchisees serving your potential customer or client base. Get in touch with the County Extension Agent.

How about key industry vendors? Most industries have major suppliers who must know about the industry they serve and the companies within that field because of repercussions to their own business. Cooperative vendors can provide you with timely and valuable research and development details. They know who's in financial trouble, which company has management problems, who is planning to expand, etc.

Don't overlook the local newspaper. The managing editor is usually a repository of knowledge. Place a phone call, stop in to converse briefly, or even extend an invitation for lunch. (Be sensitive to deadlines, however. If the paper comes out on Thursday, Tuesday and Wednesday are frantic times.) Also check the paper's archives for articles about competitors or industry-related stories. Then contact the reporter who did the piece. He or she probably has additional background information that could shield you from making a mistake. While you're at the paper, also monitor classified advertisements to see hiring patterns.

In addition to gleaning considerably from the chamber of commerce, another resource is your local economic development group. This is an umbrella organization and clearinghouse for area business information. Request a list of all companies who recently relocated to the area. You want the *whole list*, not select names. Then you can pick entrepreneurs at random to interview. This gives a more balanced view than if you are provided just the names of known town boosters.

Also ask about any proposed interstate highway changes or plans to add or alter other major thoroughfares. Many downtown sections became ghost towns when the freeway bypassed them. You don't want to situate in an undesirable location. Is the business you plan to open currently missing from the local scene? Inquire why. There may be a valid reason your type of business has been unsuccessful in this locale before.

Talk to people. Any people. All people. This informal research is sure to uncover some interesting prejudices and beneficial advice. Big corporations conduct "focus groups" where they pick people's brains. You're taking a less formal and costly route to the same destination.

## *Detection Methods Worth a Fine Ransom*

Shortly, we'll show you ingenious ways to track your quarry through the paperwork maze. But nothing is so revealing as reality immersion—being there yourself. If you've ever participated in a police "ride-along" program, for example, you know what an eye opener it is to spend a night on the beat with a cop.

Try to find a way to get direct experience in the business opportunity you're exploring. Beyond being a customer, consider taking a job in the industry for a short time. Or volunteer to work for nothing for a few days to get a feel for things. If you're determined to own a restaurant, find a sales representative for a food wholesaler who will let you tag along as he or she makes calls. You'll have a whole new respect for restaurateurs—not to mention traveling sales reps—at the end of a week.

Cushion your entry into a new business with knowledge. Study the competition. Intensely. "Most people don't do enough of this type of homework," says William Dunkelberg, dean of the School of Business at Temple University in Philadelphia. "If others are doing something similar to what you plan to do, go watch them—even if they're in another town."

Reading trade journals devoted to your proposed field is another way to hit the information jackpot. You probably received a copy when you contacted the association related to your interest. Study it carefully, not only from an editorial perspective but also by looking at the advertising. You can learn a lot by reading the ads. Additionally, ask about any special issues. These highlight developments, trends, and leaders in the industry. *Inc.* magazine does an annual special issue called "The Inc. 100," in which the fastest growing businesses in the U.S. are featured. Also go to a major library and ask about the various periodical indexes. They will lead you to more written bonanzas.

It's been said those who want advice the most, like it the least. Yet expert advice when launching a new business is an invaluable aid. There are many places to find individual experts. Federal Information Centers are one such source. You can unearth a free government expert on any topic, some 700,000 of them estimates Matthew Lesko in his excellent reference book *Lesko's Info-Power*. (See ordering information in the "Bibliography/Recommended Reading.") To locate the Federal Information Center nearest you, look in the telephone directory.

Penn State publishes a directory of faculty and staff contacts for the media. They have individuals proficient in the areas of farm management, self-employment, construction management, nutrition education, fiber optics and lasers, mushrooms, employing older workers, you name it. To find out about these experts, call their office of public information at 814-865-7517.

There's even a *Directory of Experts, Authorities & Spokespersons*. This encyclopedia of sources lists individuals, associations, and clearinghouses for a myriad of topics.

Can you guess one final intriguing place for locating a guru on a specific topic? Doctoral dissertations! University Microfilms International (800-521-0600) offers a free catalog of more than 1 million dissertations available for purchase. Much of this information has never been in print before. For about $55 you can get a paperbound copy of the dissertation of your choice.

It may be even more useful to contact the creator of the dissertation to get your questions answered. We can tell you from personal experience that an author has a lot more research and knowledge at his or her fingertips than ever reaches a manuscript page. What appears there is often only the tip of the iceberg. Hiring the author of a work as a consultant might be an extremely shrewd move.

A good checkpoint for overall business intelligence can be found in the following list of State Agencies Administering Franchise Disclosure Laws. In 15 different states, franchising companies must file detailed financial information. This is perfect for gathering competitive and marketing data—even if you have *no intention* of opening a franchise!

How so? If you want to know insider particulars about running a cleaning service, auto tune up, or printing business, for instance, look up the details of franchises in that line of work. To obtain agreements and financial data from the 15 states that require such disclosure, simply contact the office listed and request information by specific company name. If they operate in that state, it's yours for the asking. Photocopies are normally available for a nominal fee.

Also be aware that if the state to which you're planning to move doesn't require disclosure, you can get pertinent information on a national franchise from one of the states that does. (We go into detail about franchising in the upcoming chapter on that subject.)

## STATE AGENCIES ADMINISTRATING FRANCHISE DISCLOSURE LAWS

**California** - filing required
Franchise Division
Department of Corporations
3700 Wilshire Blvd., Suite 600
Los Angeles, CA 90010
213-620-6515

**Hawaii** - filing required
Franchise and Securities Division
State Department of Commerce
1010 Richards Street
Honolulu, HI 96813
808-548-2021

**Illinois** - filing required
Franchise Division
Office of Attorney General
500 South Second Street
Springfield, IL 62706
217-782-1279

**Indiana** - filing required
Franchise Division
Office of Secretary of State
One North Capitol Street,
Suite 560
Indianapolis, IN 46204
317-232-6681

**Maryland** - filing required
Franchise Office
Division of Securities
200 St. Paul Place, 20th Floor
Baltimore, MD 21202
301-576-6360

**Michigan** - filing required
Antitrust and Franchise Unit
Office of Attorney General
670 Law Building
Lansing, MI 48913
517-373-7117

**Minnesota** - filing required
Franchise Division
Department of Commerce
133 East Seventh Street
St. Paul, MN 55101
612-296-6328

**New York** - filing required
Franchise and Securities Division
State Department of Law
120 Broadway
New York, NY 10271
212-341-2211

**North Dakota** - filing required
Franchise Division
Office of Securities Commission
600 East Boulevard, 5th floor
Bismarck, ND 58505
701-224-4712

**Oregon** - no filing
Corporate and Securities Division
Department of Insurance
and Finance
Labor and Industries Bldg.
Salem, OR 97310
503-378-4387

**Rhode Island** - filing required
Franchise Office
Division of Securities
233 Richmond St., Suite 232
Providence RI 02903
401-277-3048

**South Dakota** - filing required
Franchise Office
Division of Securities
910 East Sioux Ave.
Pierre, SD 57501
605-773-4013

**Virginia** - filing required
Franchise Office
State Corporation Commission
1220 Bank St., 4th floor
Richmond, VA 23219
804-786-7751

**Washington** - filing required
Franchise Office
Business License Services
State Securities Division
P.O. Box 648
Olympia, WA 98504
206-753-6928

**Wisconsin** - filing required
Franchise Office
Wisconsin Securities Commission
P.O. Box 1768
Madison, WI 53701
608-266-8559

Source: *Reprinted from Government Giveaways for Entrepreneurs by Matthew Lesko, published by Information USA, Inc.*

Another checkpoint of interest to some entrepreneurs is the Environmental Protection Agencies and offices. In larger towns they provide information on proposed new plant and office construction, environmental impact, size, production, capacities, employees and financing. For details, contact the Public Information Reference Unit, Environmental Protection Agency, 401 M Street, SW, Washington, DC 20460, 202-475-7751.

The county courthouse holds as many secrets as a locked diary. Yet you can legally pick that lock and gain access to many court records. In most jurisdictions the clerk of the court keeps chronological indexes that record charges or complaints. They also include the names of the defendants and plaintiffs, the date of filing, a case number, and disposition, if resolved. Armed with the case number you can track down and look at these files. Often proprietary information—details not normally released to the public—are contained within. Some firms even reveal their annual sales figures, other private financial data, or research and development (R&D) plans during a court battle.

While we don't recommend going to this extreme, we're also aware of one man who got so caught up in scrutinizing his potential competition that he checked their dumpster nightly. From bits of trash, he pieced together a revealing picture of their corporate health.

## *Flushing Out Sophisticated Facts*

To follow a more conventional paper trail, one place to look is the state corporation office. If a company is incorporated, the state will have details on the nature of the business, names of directors and officers, location, and capitalization.

Local, state, and federal government agencies can be a mother lode of information. To unveil competitor activities, *backtrack* by asking yourself what you have to fill out to be in business and meet the requirements of various agencies. Then seek copies of identical kinds of paperwork for your competitors.

When you start doing heavy duty researching you're likely to run into two acronyms: SIC and DOT. SIC stands for Standard Industrial Classifications, which are contained in—you guessed it—the *Standard Industrial Classifications Manual*. It contains detailed listings of all industries, their codes, and their definitions . . . which will take a reference librarian to interpret for you. The SIC system facilitates the analysis of data on all industries in the U.S. by individual establishment. If you look in the alphabetical index in the back, for example, you'll find a shoe repair shop is 7251, while shoe stores, retail is 5661. Once you've mastered using this bugger, it's a noble brainstorming partner.

The *Dictionary of Occupational Titles* (DOT) is a catalog of almost 13,000 occupations known to exist in this country at present. It's also a horror to work with. Richard Nelson Bolles, in his wonderful *What Color is Your Parachute?*, suggests you first go to the *Dictionary of Holland Occupational Codes: A Comprehensive Cross-Index of Holland's RIASEC Codes with 12,000 DOT Occupations*. Whew! "It gives a comprehensive list of occupations which your 'code' suggests," explains Bolles, "plus the DOT number for each of the 12,860 occupations, thus enabling you to go to the *Dictionary of Occupational Titles* and look up more detailed information on each occupation that's of interest." If you're at a loss for what career route to take, cuddling up with this monster for a few hours could prove extremely beneficial.

Want more details about individual counties you're considering starting a business in? Coming right up. Let's scrutinize a series of publications from the U.S. Department of Commerce called *County Business Patterns 1989*. (This is the most current data available as we go to press.) There is a separate report for each state. The particulars contained here can be extremely useful for making basic economic studies of small areas. Under Colorado, we looked up Chaffee County where we live.

Let's say you're interested in moving your general building contractor business. You'll find there are 14 existing "general contractors and operative builders." Most of them are small: 10 have 4 or less employees, two have 5-9 on the payroll, and two have 10 to 19 employees. You'll also find such statistics as the total number of workers in that industry, plus the overall annual payroll. Maybe you want to open a service station. There are already 16 of them in this county and they divide among them an annual payroll of $839,000. Hanker to buy a motel, hotel, or other lodging place? You'll be competing with 28 other establishments who hire a total of 220 employees.

Want even more definitive information? Have we got a gem for you! Just off the press is *The Sourcebook of ZIP Code Demographics*. Volume One is the Census Edition with engrossing recaps of the 1990 figures. It weighs no less than *seven pounds* and is the most current and specific reference anywhere covering the latest demographic and marketing information. Here you'll discover facts on population, housing, and household data—plus income estimates. Zip codes are each profiled by more than 80 variables. With zips you can get even more exact than with counties. Now we can look at the two primary towns in Chaffee County—Salida and Buena Vista—separately.

Household and family income projections can be decisive in deciding where to locate your business, especially if your product or service depends on discretionary income. Here you have at your fingertips these figures for every zip code in America. Age distribution tables cover five-year increments. If your enterprise caters to a certain age group—perhaps teenagers or the mature market—here are dynamite statistics to guide you. You'll find the percentage of households with children and those with single people. Ethnic mix is also addressed. Race percentages are shown for Whites, Blacks, American Indians, Asians, and those of Hispanic origin.

Under the housing category, you'll learn the dollar value of specified owner-occupied units. If you're debating between several locations, this will be helpful information. So might the vacancy percentage. And the percentage of those whose primary home is elsewhere draws a picture of how many residents live there year-round. There's even a state-by-state comparison for each of the above categories in the back of the book.

Dialing for databases is another research method. If you have a telephone, computer, modem, and telecommunications software, you can go on-line to do your investigative work. (If you don't own these items, most libraries are equipped to perform the service for a fee.) Popular database services for this purpose are Nexis, Dialog, CompuServe, Prodigy, and Bibliographical Retrieval Services (BRS). The trick is knowing which of the hundreds of individual databases to check for appropriate questions, key words, and subjects. If you're stuck, talk with a business librarian for guidance.

State-operated on-line electronic information systems (OEIS) allow you to capture little-publicized demographic files. Thirty-one states currently have such databases. They allow you to gain speedy access to such economic development data as population and income statistics in municipalities, counties, and states. In some states you can even find out about sales tax records and construction statistics. This is incredibly helpful to small businesses, not only in the initial stages but for future marketing decisions. Says one user, "Research that used to take me all day now takes me 20 minutes." For more information see the following table of State Publicly-Accessible Databases.

## State Publicly-Accessible Databases

| State | Contact | Agency | Phone |
|---|---|---|---|
| AK | William Paulick | Department of Commerce & Economic Development | (907) 465-2017 |
| CO | Mark Krudwig | Colorado Division of Local Government | (303) 866-2156 |
| DE | Judy McKinney Cherry | Delaware Development Office | (302) 739-4271 |
| FL | Ed Perron | Florida Department of Commerce | (904) 488-4255 |
| HI | Glenn Ifuku | Economic Planning Information Systems | (808) 586-2485 |
| IN | Carol Rogers | Indiana Business Research Center | (317) 274-2205 |
| IA | Steve Rosenow | Department of Economic Development | (515) 242-4881 |
| KY | Beverly Daly | Urban Studies Center | (502) 588-7990 |
| LA | Rajiv Gupte | Northeast Louisiana University | (318) 342-1215 |
| ME | Jean Martin | Maine Department of Labor | (207) 289-2271 |
| MD | John Kozarski | Maryland Department of State | (301) 225-4450 |

| MA | John Gaviglio | Institute for Social & Economic Research | (413) 545-0176 |
| MI | Jane Benke | Michigan State University | (517) 353-3255 |
| MN | Jim Ramstrom | Land Management Information Center | (612) 296-2559 |
| MO | John Blodgett | Urban Resource Center | (314) 553-6014 |
| MT | Dave Elenbaas | Department of Commerce | (406) 444-2463 |
| NE | Tim Himberger | Center for App. Urban Research | (402) 595-2311 |
| NV | Annie Kelly | Nevada State Library | (702) 687-5160 |
| NJ | Doug Moore | New Jersey State Data Center | (609) 292-0076 |
| NM | Juliana Boyle | Bureau of Business & Economic Research | (505) 277-2216 |
| NY | Lenny Gaines | New York State Data Center | (518) 474-6005 |
| NC | Joel Sigmon | State Library of NC | (919) 733-3270 |
| OH | Mark Shaff | SOICC | (614) 644-2689 |
| OK | Jeff Wallace | Commerce Dept. (SDC) | (405) 841-5137 |
| PA | Erin Shannon | Pennsylvania State Data Center | (717) 948-6336 |
| TX | Tom Linehan | Texas Department of Commerce | (512) 472-5059 |
| VA | Sam Kaplan | Center for Public Service | (804) 924-4102 |
| WA | Tim Norris | Employment Security Department | (206) 438-3163 |
| WV | Ed McMin | Business Industrial Data Center | (304) 348-3810 |
| WV | Linda Culp | The Center for Economic Research | (304) 293-5837 |
| WI | Paul Voss | Applied Population Lab | (608) 262-9526 |

Source: *The Pennsylvania State Data Centers Second Annual National Survey on Publicly Accessible Online Electronic Information Systems.*

If you need really complicated reconnaissance and are willing to pay the price, there are several options. You could contact the American Association for Public Opinion Research at P. O. Box 17, Princeton, NJ 08542, 609-924-8670. Outside firms that do secondary research are listed in *Burwell's Directory of Fee-Based Information Services.* This directory describes hundreds of information brokers in the U.S. and abroad.

*Findex, the Directory of Market Research Reports, Studies and Surveys* contains both industry and company reports. Studies by think tanks and social research organizations complement those from Wall Street and research firms around the world. Prices vary widely. You'll pay $50 for "Trends in Production of Lead and Zinc," $995 for "Market for Collectible Dolls," and a staggering $15,000 for "Amorphous Silicon: Non-solar Applications."

Of course once your information is gathered, it must be processed, analyzed, and interpreted in a systematic and objective way. Try not to let your emotions overrule your logic. Being in the right business in the right rural location can be a lucrative, exciting adventure . . . or a life sentence. Do your homework and research carefully. The future belongs to the prepared.

But maybe you're not prepared to start from scratch. You want to buy a business or professional practice that's already up and running—a proven success. Then keep reading because that is the subject of the next chapter. (Or skip ahead if you plan to import a business.)

# 10

# Buying an Existing Business or Professional Practice

Purchasing an existing retail store, service business, or professional practice removes much of the risk. It's like taking an ocean voyage on a seaworthy vessel . . . as opposed to launching your excursion in an untested dingy. Current establishments already have a following, a customer or client base on which you can build. Locals are in the habit of doing business in particular places. When you buy that place, you also gain their loyalty—to a degree. (We'll discuss how to solidify—and boost—that degree later.) Naturally, some cash flow is also guaranteed.

## *Finding a Suitable Business*

While virtually every hamlet has a general store, gas station, bar, and restaurant, few of us want to go that remote. A greater population base brings more diversity. There are likely to be beauty shops, a lumberyard, antique shop, cleaners/laundromat, flower shop, hobby/craft store, real estate offices, bookstore, recreational facilities, travel agency, various retail stores, plus some light manufacturing. This is in addition to health practitioners, attorneys, CPAs, and various consultants. The options run a wide gamut.

Think about what you want to do—and what you abhor.

You may have been a middle manager used to delegating routine jobs. If you buy a country business, chances are *you* will be the one doing those jobs—plus cleaning the john and shoveling snow off the sidewalk. At least at first. Are the trade-offs worth it to you? Does hefting fifty-pound sacks of feed or concrete bother you? If so, stay away from those kinds of businesses. If you contemplate purchasing a bakery, are you willing to get up at 3 A.M. to start the ovens?

Does the idea of cleaning guest rooms turn you off? Then don't buy an inn, motel, or hotel. Guaranteed—the time will come when you're the only one available to change the linens and tidy the rooms. On the other hand, if you enjoy playing host or hostess, this occasional downside is a small price to pay for having a livelihood you love. Resist the urge to start a restaurant if you know nothing about this industry. Statistics show this profession has the highest rate of failure.

Boy can we vouch for that! When we began operating the hotel and restaurant we bought in First Try, it seemed so simple: just hire a qualified staff, serve good food, and get the word out. "Qualified staff" are the operative words here. Reliable cooks are as hard to come by as a cool breeze in Death Valley. In our experience, most people who follow this profession also tip the bottle—often and industriously. Or they specialize in things like cold strawberry soup, hardly "in demand" fare in a sparsely populated village.

You recall the adage, "If you want something done right, do it yourself" don't you? We modified that to "If you want it done at all, do it yourself!" First Tom took his turn at cooking while Marilyn acted as both hostess and waitress. But his patience quickly evaporated. "This is not why I came to the country!" he announced, giving notice that his last day was coming soon.

> Marilyn: *So I also became the cook. The first time I had to prepare a banquet I really agonized. We had reservations for 46. I'd done dinner parties before, but this was ridiculous! How in the world did one judge how much to prepare? Well I wasn't about to dish up 43 servings, 44 servings, 45 servings . . . and then run out. So I made plenty. Did I ever—we ate beef stroganoff for weeks afterwards!*
>
> *And in the process of being rural restaurant keepers, we learned several tricks . . . not the least of which was how to slam-dunk eggs. Many restaurants fail because all their profits go out the back door in waste. Offer a sparse, pared down menu. Create*

interesting daily specials that recycle left overs. Keep your steaks frozen until you get an order (no spoilage that way). Audit the bus trays to see what's coming back; that's a clear signal people don't like something. Find a way to become known for something special.

We began a special Sunday brunch. People traveled up to 100 miles to partake of our historic ambiance, friendly service, and tasty food. One of the menu items we featured was quiche. I'll never forget the day a gentleman studied the menu, then ordered a "quickie." Little did I know when we left San Diego, that I'd own a hotel and restaurant and become known for my "quickies."

Some businesses are almost recession-proof. No matter how bad the economy gets, people still have to eat, so grocery stores are good possibilities. And during tough times folks fix things rather than buying new ones. Thus auto mechanics, shoemakers, and appliance repair people will be in demand. And the worse things get, the more taverns flourish.

There are some firms that specialize in rural properties. United National Real Estate has commercial as well as residential offerings. Their semi-annual catalog tells of farms, ranches, business opportunities, and commercial properties from coast to coast. To receive a copy call 800-999-1020. Once you provide them with your specific needs, they offer a free search among their thousands of properties. Strout Realty also specializes in the country scene. Look for them in your Yellow Pages.

Another possibility is *Business Opportunities Journal*, Box 60762, San Diego, CA 92106. And don't overlook classifieds in the *Wall Street Journal* and *USA Today*. While usually lean or non-existent, the "Business Opportunities" or "Investments" classifieds in the local newspaper of your destination area may also provide some leads. So might the nearest big daily paper where boonies businesses advertise to attract metro money.

When sleuthing around town it's best to leave your city slicker ways back home. Drive the jeep rather than the BMW. *Be* smart. Just *don't show it*. And bring every ounce of common sense you can muster. Just because someone has rented a store front and hung out a shingle doesn't mean he or she has a viable business. While many of the business owners you'll be dealing with aren't sophisticated, they have a savvy all their own.

When it comes to actually locating possible businesses, often the best buys are also the best kept secrets. Many stores and firms shun posting "For Sale" signs in their windows. "'Tain't good for business," observed one old timer. That doesn't mean there aren't owners eager to sell. Your challenge is to find them. Become a detective! When something interests you, go in and ask to speak to the owner. Find a secluded corner and explain you're new in town and looking for a business to purchase. Interested proprietors will take it from there.

## *Evaluating Prospective Ventures*

What appears to be a sterling buy may turn out to be fool's gold when you dig deeper. And dig you must to be sure you're not investing in a marginal undertaking. First find out why they want to sell. Don't always take what you're told at face value. Perhaps the owner is indeed ready to retire or has a health problem. On the other hand, he or she may also have less benevolent reasons for wanting to sell: new competition, supplier problems, a declining local economy, or a planned freeway which will bypass the town.

Sift out the obvious by talking to people. Assume a relaxed, easygoing manner. Things don't happen at lightning speed in the country. Visiting with townsfolk is the most valuable research you can do. All sorts of useful tidbits will emerge. Especially hone in on members of local service clubs such as Kiwanis, Rotary, Lions, and Elks. These are the business leaders.

Systematically analyze all aspects. This won't be easy. In cities you can look at "comps": comparable businesses and what they sold for. But in rural areas no such numbers exist. Don't let your emotions overload your intellect. Buy with your head not your heart. That darlin' little antique shoppe could be the biggest albatross in town. And get professional help. Be wary, however, of hiring the same accountant or attorney as the business owner uses. That's like putting the fox in charge of the henhouse.

Stop by the library and look in the *Encyclopedia of Associations.* Find out what associations similar businesses belong to. Call them for norms, membership information, and industry surveys. See if they can recommend a member in a non-competitive, similar area whom you could phone and chat with.

Check the competition. How long have they—and the business you're considering—been in business? Is there enough for all of you? Three video stores in a town of 3,000, for instance, is probably two too many. Has the business been profitable? If not, what's the reason? Can you *really* do something to turn it around? Do you honestly have the money, ideas, personality, stamina, and skills to transform it into a moneymaker? Are you smart enough to compete against your competition's *weaknesses* rather than their strengths?

There's another intriguing facet to doing business in Small Town America. In many situations, living quarters are part of the package. There's an apartment above the store or a house behind the shop. This can prove very economical. In such cases your living quarters' mortgage payments, utilities, taxes, and insurance are often shielded under the business umbrella. And if you purchase an inn or similar establishment, food and auto expenses are also sheltered. When you start racking up these costs in an urban setting, pulling up stakes for the country may equal prospering in paradise.

Many rural businesses are family run. This can stir up a witch's caldron of trouble—or be a practical, solidifying blessing—depending on the family. What about your other half? Does he or she have the skills—and the temperament—to supplement or complement your abilities? For parents seeking to teach their youngsters a sound work ethic, there is much to be said for a country family business. It's not unusual to see three or four generations helping out in rural enterprises.

One detracting aspect of rural entrepreneurism is your personal life isn't your own. Most people in town know where you live—whether it's above the store or out on County Road 364. They're your friends, your neighbors, your acquaintances. And the unwritten country code is you help your neighbors.

This means getting a carburetor for Larry's pickup so he can get his little girl to her physical therapy appointment early tomorrow morning—even though you officially closed two hours ago. It means opening the restaurant to make hot chocolate and sandwiches for the Search and Rescue Team when they're called out at 4:00 A.M. on a dreary Sunday morning. It means going down to the shop to find a spool of turquoise thread so Mable can finish the bridesmaid dresses she needs for the wedding tomorrow. It means being part of other people's lives—and allowing them to be part of yours. Not such a bad trade really.

When it comes to the purchase agreement, be sure you understand what it encompasses. Is the actual land the business is located on included? What about the building itself? If not, what are the terms and restrictions of the lease? Is it transferable? Is the business name included? All the inventory? Equipment? Fixtures? Be sure the exact terms of the sale are clearly spelled out and you know about existing contracts that affect the business's operation.

For instance, who's responsible for any debts? Are there ongoing contracts, like a lease on a copier or telephone equipment, you must assume? Are there any outstanding claims or loans on the inventory, equipment, or fixtures? What about liens on the property? Don't just ask the seller. Also check with the county clerk and at the recorder's office in both the county where the business is located and the one where the owner lives. You may even want to conduct a UCC search to be sure no liens are filed against the property or assets of the business. This is typically done through the Uniform Commercial Code Section of the secretary of state's office.

In addition to studying the seller's books, also ask to see actual tax returns—personal as well as business. If there's a discrepancy between the owner's salary as stated in the company books and his personal income tax, this bears close scrutiny. Sometimes owners "fudge" on their books. This can have disastrous ramifications for the new purchaser. One man recommends dividing the down payment into three chunks. One is paid immediately, one midyear, and the last portion at the end of the year. You'll know by the end of the first increment if the books were honest. If not, you've only lost ⅓ of your money. Sales revenues and owners' salaries are easily manipulated. Your diagnostic work will include such research as whether the profit picture reflects steady growth. The previous owner's attitude or poor health could have sapped a growing business. It's amazing how *one* simple idea can change the direction of a venture. In a retail shop, does the inventory turnover (meaning how fast it sells and must be replaced) match national averages? New systems of managing inventory can make an enormous difference in retailing. And providing outstanding customer assistance may be the key for a service business.

## *A Warning to the Wise Is Sufficient . . .*

Investigate before you celebrate. Be sure you don't inherit a bucket of worms. The Environmental Protection Agency, for instance, in their zeal to protect ground water supplies, is clamping down on gas stations across the U.S. Many service station operators are being forced to close because their underground gasoline tanks don't meet EPA regulations. Woe to the poor soul who buys such a station.

Another area to watch is "grandfathering." No, we don't refer to the jolly older man. In this case grandfathering means a rule or law that is waived for the present owner. Let's say there is a new sign code enacted, but Joe Smith is allowed to keep his big, flashy sign because it was already in place when the law went into effect. Often, however, this latitude is not extended to the new owner. What a blow that could be if one of the primary reasons you bought Joe's place was because of the dominant advertising sign!

In many businesses, such as vocational schools and factories, OSHA is a consideration. OSHA stands for the U.S. Labor Department's Occupational Safety and Health Administration. This agency is charged with making sure work premises are safe and healthy for employees. Meeting requirements can cost thousands of dollars. Be sure any plant you anticipate purchasing already meets their exacting standards.

In certain endeavors it's wise to budget way ahead and take into consideration seasonal lulls. Rural businesses often fluctuate between soaring highs and disheartening lows. If you blow all your cash from a good month, you may not have enough to carry you over in a bad one. Seasonal businesses that depend on tourism are especially vulnerable. We know one motel owner who had such a profitable summer he went out and bought a new Cadillac to celebrate. Then winter came. Business plummeted. Because he hadn't put something aside to see him through the lean season, he lost his place when he couldn't pay the taxes and insurance in the off-season.

In retailing, figure the money you invest in inventory is gone. "What?!" you exclaim in horror. Think about it. You never actually recoup that money until you sell the business. Why? Because you must constantly replenish the inventory! A dwindling inventory means sagging sales. Sure you make a profit when you sell merchandise, and you may learn to buy more shrewdly, but the bulk of those original inventory dollars will remain tied up in your goods.

## *What's a Body to Pay?*

Reckoning the true value of a business is about as scientific as catching catfish with a bamboo pole, string, and a safety pin. Some say a going concern is worth the value of its equipment, plus the wholesale cost of its inventory, plus one or more year's anticipated profit. Most small businesses are rarely sold for more than a year's gross sales. This, of course, may be two to three times higher than the annual pre-tax income.

Then there is the issue of measuring goodwill. Let's say you're wanting to buy a service station. How can you figure a fair price for the business that takes into account goodwill and business contacts, in addition to the value of the equipment and inventory? Many methods can be used. The bottom line is you're trying to set a value on the assets and earnings record of the firm. The simplest way is to determine the "payback period." This is usually two or three years. That is, the net profit for two years would equal the goodwill value. Goodwill, while an intangible quality, means a lot. Community support and individual patronage can make or break a business.

And speaking of paying, one of the delightful aspects of buying a rural business is that the owner is often willing to finance the sale. With a decent down payment, many sellers will carry the paper themselves.

We know of one situation where a business was purchased with no money down. The buyer pledged a percentage of the profits on a monthly basis until a specified figure was reached. This arrangement worked well for both parties. The seller avoided a lump sum tax liability. Because he also charged 11 percent interest, he realized more overall than if he had gotten the purchase price in full initially. And the deal was structured so the seller's investment was secured by a note on the assets of the business.

Another important way the previous owner can aid you is by agreeing to stay on for a period of time and "teach you the ropes." He or she can introduce you to suppliers, take you on buying trips, and explain how to display items for faster turnover. More importantly, the seller can introduce you to customers and fill you in on their idiosyncracies. This kind of reconnaissance is as valuable as a fraternity brother's little black book.

If you can't involve the seller in your financing package, ask the local bank if they will consider the business itself as collateral. Then you can get a chattel mortgage. This puts a dollar amount on all the business assets (excluding real estate) and requires that you not dispose of any of them until it is paid off.

While we're on the subject of money, never *never* invest all your liquid assets in a business. Keep some cash in reserve. Probably 20 to 30 percent. You don't know when broken water pipes will hit you with a devastating plumbing bill, when the furnace will conk out, or when a dismal quarter will require you to dip into your reserves for living expenses.

For guidance on locating suppliers and recruiting employees, refer to the chapter on "Pivotal Start-Up Considerations." And an excellent book for further reference is Frank Kirkpatrick's *How to Find and Buy Your Business in the Country.*

But maybe you're leery of taking the do-it-all-yourself plunge. If so, the next chapter offers tips on effective job-hunting techniques in rural America.

# 11

# Investigating the Franchise Alternative

With the recent white collar layoffs, most people realize the days of the protective parental company are over. No longer can we depend on our employers to safeguard our positions. The era of twenty-five year watches is swiftly drawing to an end. The alternative is for individuals to create success for themselves.

If building a business from the ground up sounds a bit too risky for your taste, franchising may be a viable solution. With less than a 5 percent failure rate, it provides the enterprising countrypreneur with a welcome safety net. Franchising is a practice in which the company owner (the franchisor) licenses the right to use the name, product or service, and procedures of the company to an investor (the franchisee). It's a multi-billion dollar industry that appeals especially to ex-corporate middle managers who appreciate having some structure. Ever-increasing participation fuels the franchising frenzy.

It provides an easy-entry opportunity for small investors to get into business. Franchise owners are not cookie-cutter people. Variety can be found in every area from the type of franchise purchased to the style of doing business. If you're a risk taker, it can be your route to a business empire. It has been said the only difference between a franchisee and an independent businessperson is that the franchisee is smarter. Approached properly, this business concept is almost recession-proof.

Franchisees have training, marketing expertise, and business consulting at their fingertips. Investing in a franchise offers many advantages including having a *proven* product or service at your disposal. Identification with a brand name offers instant credibility. And start-up costs will typically be lower than those in an independent business because of volume purchasing power for products or equipment.

Before deciding if franchising is for you, consider a couple of important points. With this method of conducting business, investors pay for the right to use the existing system and market existing products or services. If yours is a total entrepreneurial mind-set, think carefully about whether following someone else's guidelines works for you. Though there is plenty of room for creativity, you are buying into an already tried and established idea.

Another point worth considering is the expense involved in buying into a franchise. Those interested in this sort of opportunity can expect to pay an initial fee, royalty, or both. Initial investments run anywhere from $5,000 to $500,000. Royalty fees range from 3 to 10 percent of gross sales. Additionally there can sometimes be a advertising fee of 2 to 5 percent. Potential participants should plan to provide part of the capital themselves. The wise new businessperson also creates a personal cash cushion to cover the first year of start-up. This way more money can be funneled through the infant franchise, creating more growth at a faster rate.

## *Fertile Fields*

The recent expansion in this area is phenomenal. Franchising added 400,000 new jobs to the economy between 1987 and 1989. In 1990 alone sales from franchised business services surged 14.4 percent. From 1990 to the present date, franchising has continued to multiply profits for savvy folks who had the foresight to become involved.

The International Franchise Association's (IFA) Naisbitt Report predicts that: "By the year 2000, franchise sales will account for half of all retail sales. Almost any service imaginable can be franchised . . . " According to the IFA, a new franchise store opens every 16 minutes, bringing the number of outlets to more than half a million. Franchised outlets account for more than ⅓ of all retail sales in the United States, compared with 1/10 only 10 years ago. Will this growth include rural America? You bet!

Although some organizations choose to limit themselves to upscale malls, many flourish in Small Town America. One of the advantages of taking a franchise rural is the excellent word-of-mouth advertising. Citizens of these areas share new finds freely, so remember to make a dynamite first impression on them. With this in mind, you'll find that small populations yield rapid market penetration. Networking is easier because of strong community ties, and a healthy work ethic among prospective employees makes finding good help a simple task.

One of the franchises going to the country is Mr. Rooter. More people are on septic systems and few plumbing companies think of locating in remote areas. Locals appreciate franchises setting up shop in their areas. It gives them access to services they've not had in the past. Previously they had to drive long distances and pay high fees.

Another franchise booming in remote regions is Express Mart. Mark Maher, Director of Franchising for Express Mart says that 60 to 65 percent of all their locations are rural. They've found a strong need for the combination of gas pumps and convenience stores there. The company has also taken advantage of the fast food void in such areas. Now they're raking in the benefits. Other familiar rural franchise names include Dairy Queen, Sonic drive-ins, and Pizza Hut.

## *Separating the Wheat from the Chaff*

With franchising, being in business for yourself doesn't mean being *by* yourself. Support networks are vast. Most franchisors offer advertising guidance, training and professional advice, marketing and accounting know-how—even advice on start-up procedures, finance avenues, and location choice for your new business. Products and services are tried and proven. Operations are in place; problems already faced and handled. You'll find a kaleidoscope of opportunities—finding one to fit your dreams will take some time. But with such limitless prospects the new franchisee is bound to find a niche personally customized to his or her needs.

While some are skeptical of the market for franchises in rural America, most are singing its praises. Not all potential choices would work, of course, but many could thrive in the fertile soil of America's hinterland. Base your choice on your present skills: what do you already enjoy doing? This will be a long-term time investment, so whether you enjoy performing the services rendered should be a major component in making your choice.

After you've narrowed down the list of possibilities, figure out what your proposed community needs. Our dry cleaners burned a few years ago. A replacement would certainly be a welcome addition here. In a village of 2,000, another accounting service may not be a very good idea if they already have two or three. Choose something that fills a void and your success will be much greater. A small town will view a new service as an exciting event. Folks will drop by to see what you're about. If no one else offers what you do, you have the local market sewn up.

If your chosen area draws tourists, explore recreational franchises. Sweeten the deal by starting up a candy franchise. These go over like gangbusters in tourist towns.

Many small towns don't have janitorial services. Oh sure, there are those who profess to be housecleaners. But there's no quality control, no standards of operation, and many aren't reliable. In addition, those working independently in this area have to find their own clients. Bringing in an established franchise and offering training to these people, working around their schedules, putting them on salary, and giving them encouragement and support might just be the ticket to improving their situations. And higher standards of service would certainly be an asset in clients' eyes.

Looking at market inclinations in franchising is helpful in guiding you to your choice. This is a hotbed of change, so be sure you're looking at a trend versus a fad. Is your choice something that will have high demand ten years down the road? Or will it flash and burn like a shooting star?

Environmental franchises are an up-and-coming idea in remote areas. Many folks have never had the convenience of dropping off recyclables in town. Either locals don't recycle at all, or they save mounds—then make a monthly trip into the city to dispose of them.

And don't overlook the fastest growing segment of our population. Senior citizens will soon be the largest slice of the American pie. Many flock to rural areas for retirement. If exercise programs are a favorite, look into Take Time, Incorporated, an exercise chain for mature consumers. Other franchises that cater to this group include travel agencies, interior decorating, home services (i.e., lawn care and maid service), accounting and tax assistance, health aids, and recreation.

Other hot franchising opportunities include diet centers, quick automotive services, children's goods, party supplies, temporary services, house inspection, carpet cleaning, pest control, and chimney sweeping. Explore all businesses that interest you, but make sure you look to the needs of your new neighbors. Giving them a service they've previously had to drive miles to get will make you a valued new asset in your community. Be unique, but practical.

## *If Home Is Where Your Heart Is*

A cost saving alternative is the home-based franchise. Extremely practical, start-up costs here can be limited in some cases to just a computer program and training. Franchise fees for a home-based business can be under $10,000. Working out of your house not only saves the overhead of another location, it's a tax deduction as well.

If this lights the fire beneath your motivation, look for a customized product or service and deliver it to your clients' homes. A clever entrepreneur with a decorating bug could have samples organized in a van, while keeping base operations at home. Companies handling glass and marble lend themselves MARBLEously to delivery and home service. Again be imaginative. Very few rural citizens have access to home services. If you handle it with pizazz, you'll find yourself in high demand.

## *Matchmaker, Matchmaker*

Finding the franchise that's just right for you can be a challenge. But if you follow a selection system, you can make the job much easier. If there is something you don't have much experience with but you have a strong interest in, don't limit yourself. Travel Agents International, for example, prefers to recruit people who have no experience. As we've counseled before, prioritize your life. If you want to spend evenings and weekends with your family, then don't go into the hospitality industry. Weekends mean big money for this field. Folks wanting success here need to make their full energy available when it is most needed.

Look at the priorities of the franchisors. If God, family, and country are important to them—and these are your priorities as well—you'll find it easier to align your lifestyle with the company values. Make sure those you are considering have been around for awhile. One of the advantages of going with franchising is the product and the market have been proven. If you go with someone too new in the field, you could be setting yourself up for failure.

If you're more adventuresome and have a desire to cash in big, you may look at buying additional franchises down the road. Adding more salespeople or additional units is one avenue to increased profits. This freedom is great for the person who isn't happy with a plateau. When your first location reaches its peak, continue to grow. Go to surrounding areas opening the same type of business, or stay where you are and open complementary organizations.

For example if you go with Mr. Rooter, you might think of opening other home improvement franchises. Some ideas could be painting, interior decorating, or cabinetry. You can perform many services for the same client base. In this way you can boost your opportunities for increased earnings.

Use the resources available in looking for your location. Remember that most franchisors offer this service. And don't feel restricted because of your remote location. What they look for is accessibility. Can 20,000 people comfortably reach the location by car? Traffic counts are key factors in deciding this important point.

## *Finding Specific Help*

There are many excellent tools available to smooth out the wrinkles in your quest for the ideal franchise. By far the most valuable resource we've found to date is the International Franchise Association (IFA). Anyone checking into buying a franchise should contact this organization. They offer several inexpensive publications. *Investigate Before Investing* is a booklet with tips on evaluating a franchise. *Answers to the 21 Most Commonly Asked Questions About Franchising* is vital to newcomers in the field.

They also publish the comprehensive *Franchise Opportunities Guide.* It lists IFA members, all other franchises, plus additional important information. Updated twice a year, it always has the most current data available. It's a marvelous place to prospect. After looking through it carefully, you may come up with a list of 20 possibilities initially. This directory includes tips on choosing a franchise and what to do before you invest. IFA is also a ready source for advice and encouragement on finding the right franchise. Ask for their *Publications and Products Catalog.* You'll find everything you need from books to audio cassettes.

If computer software is more your style, their *Franchise Finder* works with either IBM-compatible or Macintosh computers to help you peruse more than 500 franchisors. Just input such priorities as: how much you want to invest, is it a workable option for the country, categories of businesses you're interested in pursuing, etc. Once you've fed it information important to you, it will cross-reference and spit out a list of choices fitting your criteria. It sells for $79 plus $5 shipping. Latch onto this and other IFA tools by writing IFA Publications, 1350 New York Avenue NW, Suite 900, Washington, DC 20005. Or call 202-628-8000 for further information.

The Bureau of Consumer Protection publishes several free resources designed to aid compliance with federal guidelines. When writing to this source ask for *Franchise and Business Opportunities, The Franchise Rule: Questions and Answers,* and *Franchise Rule Summary.* Write to: Federal Trade Commission, Bureau of Consumer Protection, Division of Enforcement, Pennsylvania Avenue at 6th Street NW, Washington, DC 20580.

Use franchise experts such as Brian Bond at the Business Development Office of the Small Business Administration—409 3rd Street SW, Washington, DC 20416-0001. People like Brian are available to answer your questions and guide you to resources that will make your planning easier. You'll find additional listings of these consultants in IFA's *Franchise Opportunities Guide.*

*The Franchise Annual* is a comprehensive guide covering a total of 4,783 franchises in its 1991 edition. It's chock-full of advice on the technical aspects of becoming a franchisee. Help is available in checking agreements and interpreting laws on earnings claims here too. You can find it at Info Press, Inc., Box 550, Lewiston, NY 14092.

The *Directory of Franchising Organizations* published by Pilot Books, Pilot Industries, Inc., 103 Cooper Street, Babylon, NY 11702, offers a listing of franchise opportunities. They give addresses and approximations of initial investments, classified according to industry. This information makes easy work of narrowing the field of choices. Simply choose areas of interest within your individual investment range and write for information.

For recent veterans, we've discovered a wonderful bonus. A new program called VetFran (Veterans Transition Franchise Initiative) introduces previous Armed Forces personnel to business opportunities in the franchise industry. This plan makes it possible for qualified veterans to get substantial discounts and financing of up to 50 percent of the franchising fee from participating franchisors. More than 100 companies have endorsed VetFran so far. The list is expected to triple by year's end. To receive a list of participating franchisors and more particulars, send $1 and a stamped, self-addressed envelope to VetFran, P.O. Box 3146, Waco, TX 76707. The deadline to apply for funding is August 15, 1993.

## *Putting Franchisors under the Microscope*

In the 1850s Singer accidentally developed the first franchise network to distribute and sell sewing machines. But it wasn't until the 1950s and 1960s that the practice was actively pursued. Companies getting in on this initial surge were Holiday Inn, Dunkin' Donuts, Roto-Rooter, McDonald's, Burger King, Midas, and 7-Eleven. Unfortunately at that time there was very little regulation and many fly-by-night organizations took advantage of small businessmen looking for big opportunities. As a response to this problem the Federal Trade Commission developed the Uniform Franchise Offering Circular (UFOC). It is required by the federal government. If you have a difficult time getting this document from a prospective company, it's likely not a safe choice.

Ask for the franchisor's UFOC. It puts in writing the company's history, principles, business experience, and franchise program. It covers everything from accurate earnings claims to forecasted sales. You'll find out what restrictions to expect on goods and services offered by the franchisee. This document also spells out what obligations, assistance, and supervision can be expected from the franchisor. An outline of fees and royalties is included. You'll find a virtual who's who of the company. Biographical and professional information on these officers is complete and up-to-date.

You can also examine the franchisor's profit and loss statements. Peruse annual reports. Seek documents that offer a wealth of information such as: initial fees, financing arrangements, territorial rights, past bankruptcies, and standard operating statements. Also look for listings of privately held franchises versus company-owned outlets, plus copies of contracts and agreements. Check with the state attorney general's office to see if there is any record of complaints against the franchisor.

Above all be informed. Be sure to have a lawyer who understands this area review the information. Consulting with an accountant who specializes in franchise agreements is also a wise move. Trusting those who know always works best. Do your research and hire expert advice.

The UFOC will also have a listing of current franchises. Spend time talking with these people. Ask lots of questions! Listen carefully to their answers. What kind of training did they receive? How's business? Are they able to meet desired goals? How well does the franchisor work with them?

You can get invaluable "insider information" by chatting informally with a franchisee in a noncompetitive location. To get a feel for things, befriend someone in an area similar to yours and ask to take a look at their franchise agreement. You can find out how much it will cost you to open your franchise and sometimes even expected salary levels.

Once you've narrowed the field, consider going to work for one of the existing franchises. Whether done openly or incognito, this can be a source like no other for finding out how well franchisors work with franchisees, what training and support really is available, and how much freedom there is to grow.

Always visit the franchisor's headquarters. Meet the management. Find out if you agree with their business philosophy. See the quality of work at home base. If the atmosphere is disorganized and unproductive, beware! If there are problems with the heart of the corporation, the extremities will surely suffer.

While you're there, ask to audit their training program. Is it meaty? Realistic? Upbeat? Be sure headquarters is committed to ongoing support of their franchisees. Their concern with providing for success assures you continued, expert guidance. If your chosen franchise is a member of IFA, you can be comfortable with the professional standards to which the company adheres. Members have agreed to abide by the IFA Code of Ethics.

For many the "extended family" aspect of franchising is the key to success. Working with a team that cares about how your business is progressing is always encouraging. If this is the avenue for you, fully exploring all possibilities will yield satisfaction and opportunities for great prosperity. In a crowded market, franchising is the key to market share and profitability. You can catch the wave of this burgeoning field and ride the crest to success and financial security in your new country home.

We discuss creative financing elsewhere. Just remember that the best alternatives don't always come from a bank. Some franchisors offer aid to prospective franchisees. Investigate that option. And spend time digesting the information in the upcoming chapter on "Persuasive Marketing Strategies." They will help you excel.

## A FRANCHISE EVALUATION EXAM

- Do you have a complete description of the business?
- Does the franchisor have a proven success record of at least 5 years in actual franchising?
- How many franchises has the company sold?
- What are the total costs for entering the franchise (including initial investment, equipment purchase or rental, training costs . . . )?
- Does this fit with your ability to invest? Don't forget to include the costs of a building site, storefront, needed vehicle, etc.
- Did the company supply you with an up-to-date UFOC?
- Is the company strong financially?
- Is it interested in a long-term relationship?
- Does the company have a good reputation and credit rating?
- How fierce is local competition?
- Does the product or service meet a local need?
- Is territorial protection defined and guaranteed?
- Have you checked with other franchisees concerning the business ethics and continuing support of the franchisor?
- From whom will you purchase inventory and supplies?
- Who handles advertising?
- If it's the franchisee, do you have the capital and know-how to back this up? Does the franchisor tack on an extra fee?

- What fees are required? Is this too big a cut from your anticipated profits?
- Are most franchises in the system succeeding?
- What are the continuing costs for maintaining the franchisor/franchisee relationship?
- Under what conditions can the relationship be renewed or ended?
- Have many franchisees left the system? When? Why?
- Will you have the power to sell your franchise?
- Did your attorney and accountant review the contract?
- Have you found out if the state attorney general's office has any record of complaints against the franchisor?

Some people prefer working from their home. The next chapter gives you the inside scoop on accomplishing near miracles without setting foot outside your house.

# 12

# Working from Home: "The Information Age" Option

What do Domino's Pizza, Hallmark Cards, Nike, Playboy, Amway, and Baskin-Robbins have in common? They all started as home businesses! According to Link Resources, 44.7 million people now work at home at least part of the time. Twenty-eight percent of them run a full-time home-based business, while 29 percent operate a part-time enterprise. By the middle of this decade, it's projected that 50 million people will have agreed "there's no place like home." What used to be perceived as a humble industry now enjoys newly-found prestige.

Who are those participating in this 10-second commute? Most are around 40, married with a child or two, well-educated, and have an average household income of slightly over $50,000 a year. Fully 99 percent of the readers polled by *Home Office Computing* in their 1991 survey say they are happier working on their own, and 98 percent would recommend it to others.

## *Who's Doing It and Why?*

Why did they escape corporate confines where office politics are filled with quibbling rivalry? "I wanted to be my own boss," report 64 percent;

50 percent say, "I wanted more control over my life." Only after these two reasons does money influence decision. The desire to meld family obligations with work responsibilities is a recurring theme among home-office enthusiasts. Thirty-one percent made the change to spend more time with their loved ones. Some believe home-based businesses (HBBs) are doing more to restore family unity than education, philosophy, and social service put together.

A Montana mother of small children living 25 miles from the nearest town couldn't justify commuting and babysitting costs, especially when most jobs offered only minimum wage. She created a home business as a telemarketing service bureau that's mentally stimulating and income producing.

"There is work beyond 'day care and crafts' for mothers who want to remain home with their children," observes Jane Williams. In 1986, she launched Bluestocking Press from Placerville, California, a town of 8,000 located in the Sierra Nevada foothills. With the help of her family, she publishes educationally-oriented books and a 50-page book catalog.

Her children, Katie aged 11 and Ann aged 8, have always been home schooled. "This means we interact within each other's working and living environments throughout the day," says Williams. "The kids understand what work is, what it takes to put food on the table. They participate in those jobs they're skilled enough to do. Katie is a dynamic phone receptionist and handles customer service work. Ann fills book orders."

This mother is an outspoken advocate of home schooling. "It brings the real world into children's lives more effectively than conventional education," she observes. Williams—who can be reached at Bluestocking Press, P. O. Box 1014, Placerville, CA 95667, 916-621-1123—sells books on the subject. For more information on home schooling, see the Private Sector Help section of Part III.

This is a familiar refrain as baby boomers hunger to sink deeper family roots. Couples with children can better balance family and dual careers if one or both parents work at home. This also gives career-oriented women who want to nurture their children the opportunity to plant a foot in both worlds.

Judith Wunderlich thought she had it all . . . until she realized that she had less of what mattered. Wunderlich rarely saw her baby. Supermom would rise at 4:30 A.M. for an hour-long commute to her fast-track management job in insurance, then return home about 7:30 in the evening. Frustrated and exhausted, she finally quit and started a home typesetting business in Bartlett, Illinois. Today Wunderlich runs a $300,000-a-year temporary employment service out of her home. Her two children play in an adjacent room.

What other sorts of businesses are run from the home? Virtually everything. Notice on the following recap from *Home Office Computing*, an excellent magazine, that consulting leads the pack. In this age of corporate retrenchment, budget-conscious companies are keeping a lid on costs by using more freelancers or independent contractors. Mail order and desktop publishing also flourish in home environments. Of course, so do B&Bs—not to mention day care, gift basket services, janitorial firms, and public relations agencies.

## TOP 10 BUSINESSES

1) Consulting
2) Computer services/programming
3) Business support/services
4) Financial support/services
5) Independent sales
6) Graphic, visual, or fine arts
7) Writing
8) Marketing/advertising
9) Construction/repair
10) Real Estate

Source: © *1991, Home-Office Computing Magazine.*

While traditionally work-at-home people have been writers, artists, and others whose occupations required they work alone, that's changing. The ranks are swelling like a cresting river. Teri Ross of Minnetonka, Minnesota, designs sportswear at home. Those offering financial counseling services have a rosy future too. Clients who prefer to cocoon needn't even leave their homes. Everything can be taken care of by phone, fax, computer, or mail.

Word processors who work from home say their business is recession-proof. When the economy turns down, companies cut back on secretarial help and use outside services like theirs. Personal shopping services are thriving. Reports one lady who runs such a business, "With fewer employees, those who still have jobs are often asked to work overtime . . . They're reluctant to (refuse) for fear of losing their jobs. So they hire me to shop for them."

In North Dakota, home-based manufacturing is as busy as a plant running three shifts. People knit sweaters, create jewelry, and fire pots. And they're learning how to take their products to market all across the USA. Home-based franchises—such as Pet Nannies, Decorating Den, and Computertots—perform services at the client's site.

Multi-level marketing (MLM), once castigated as pyramid scams, has cleaned up her act and is making millionaires out of ordinary people. Today she dresses in fine suits, wears tantalizing perfume, and exudes an aura of respectability. She's even changed her name. Now many call her "Network Selling." The secret of MLM is individual contact, done out of homes and apartments across the land. The potential for profits is geometric growth. With the right product and the right organization, it can be an extremely viable HBB. After all, in the new millennium, we won't go to the store—the store will come to us.

## *Achieving the Three "F's"*

People set up home businesses to get the "Three F's": freedom, flexibility, and financial independence.

Having freedom is a wonderfully liberating feeling. Anyone who works in a city has two choices: live in the city and face high rents, congestion, crime, and noise—or move to the suburbs and endure long daily commutes. Entrepreneurs who work at home can live almost anywhere. Sophisticated ad agencies are run from farmhouses. In-demand consultants, some of whom have an international client base, operate out of posh country homes.

Flexibility is another plus. You don't have to battle the elements, the traffic . . . or the clock. You can work any hours you want. Have young children who need attention during the day? Work evenings or weekends. Or while older kids attend school. Flexibility applies in other ways as well. You might start your HBB as a sideline or do it part-time while you hold down another job to earn a base income. This allows you to build clientele and cash flow. In some cases, it's practical to start a home-based endeavor while still located in the city, then transfer clients' or customers' work when you move.

There's also financial independence. When you work out of your home, the price for office space is always right. You can operate on a shoestring when combining your work and your residence. "If you have a problem," advises one home-business operator, "don't throw money at it; throw your mind, your energy—your spirit." Besides overhead and start-up costs being lower, multiple tax breaks are also available.

The secret to the IRS space odyssey? Devote one area of your home *solely* to business. Then you can deduct rent and utilities for that portion.

This makes good sense anyway. Trying to mix work in the same room with personal living is like mixing oil and water . . . they just don't blend. You need a separate office, showroom, or studio that's strictly for business.

Keep good records: letters, calendars of meetings, copies of proposals or bids, notes about contacts, anything that proves you are actually "in business"—even if you don't show immediate revenue. When it comes to remodeling for a work area, it may make sense to do it *after* you've started the business. Check with a tax consultant, accountant, CPA, or the IRS before you call in the carpenters. There are some quirks in the government's rules on home improvement. It's always wise to get professional advice on any tax planning.

The Tom Scheibal family of St. Helena, California, runs an antique shop and B&B out of their home. Scheibal reports, "With the expense and tax write-offs I get on a place that's also my home, I do a lot better financially than I could on a regular job."

We also know of a source of inexpensive crime insurance for your business equipment when you're home-based. In the case of burglary, residents in many states are eligible for a federal crime insurance program that actually subsidizes the cost of insurance. This lowers the premium because Uncle Sam pays part of the bill if your place is burglarized. To see if your state qualifies, call 800-638-8780. Chances are you can get a rider added to your homeowner's insurance to cover computer equipment and business furnishings. You may also want to investigate business interruption insurance, disability income protection, and business life insurance.

Two excellent books on the subject of HBB are *Working from Home*, by Paul and Sarah Edwards, and *Homemade Money* by Barbara Brabec. She also edits and publishes the *National Home Business Report* for those who want ongoing information and inspiration. For ordering information see the "Bibliography/Recommended Reading."

## *Making It Work for You*

When people go from the corporation to the cottage, many need an "attitude adjustment" (though not the kind Hank Williams, Jr. sings about). What we refer to is an upbeat outlook that expects—and projects—excellence.

It's especially important to alleviate any shreds of amateurism. To look and feel your professional best, dress the part. You can slouch around in a bathroom only so long before an important business contact shows up unannounced—and catches you looking like you're heading to the bedroom rather than the boardroom. Forget high heels or a necktie, but do be presentable.

Consider spending a bit extra on your written materials. A snazzy business card, letterhead, and brochure *shout professionalism*—rather than whispering it. For a home-based business, these are your windows to the world. Be sure they sparkle! Carry business cards with you everywhere. Marilyn made a good contact at a hotel swimming pool one day . . . and was able to fish out a card from between the sunscreen and room key in her fanny pack.

There are other actions that can help establish you as a serious countrypreneur. If it's possible to set up a separate business entrance, do so. This is especially true if clients will be coming to your home. And be sure the yard, porch, and foyer aren't littered with toys, coats, shoes, or other inappropriate items. Make sure, too, the family dog doesn't ward off would-be clients.

You may want to make arrangements for UPS or Federal Express to pick up letters and parcels from your home. Additionally, it's a good idea to think of your mail carrier as part of your team. He or she will be delivering more than usual to your address. Be kind, patient, and generous with this person. By the way, if you live in an apartment, consider referring to your apartment number as your *suite number*. The post office doesn't object and it comes across so businesslike.

Some HBBs affix a lockbox outside for the convenience of their clients or customers—not to mention themselves. Good accounts receive a key. These people regularly drop off work to be completed and retrieve it when done. This cuts down the interruption factor.

Reinvent routine. Even if you didn't punch a company time clock, you were expected to be at work at a designated time. You may find it helps to establish regular office hours. Then when the urge to do the laundry, tidy the house, or lie down for a nap seems overwhelming . . . check and see if you're "off work." Maintaining a schedule makes it easier to get into a productive rhythm.

And setting firm deadlines for having projects finished will keep you out of trouble. Making "to do" lists is another good strategy. Put the task you *least* like to do at the top, then reward yourself when you've accomplished it. Play with the dog, eat a frozen yogurt, or listen to a few minutes of your favorite music. Remember, you're the boss.

Give yourself permission to enjoy yourself! This is your chance to finally try your wings. Yes, at times you'll be on an emotional roller coaster. One day you're elated because you just put together a big deal; the next day you feel overwhelmed by all the work to be done. But you'll get through those times.

Of course you need to know your personal bottom line. If you nurture your business well, chances are it will flourish. This could present a real dilemma. Do you want to expand beyond your home? Will the prospects for extra profits be worth what you'll give up? There are definite trade-offs.

> Marilyn: *When I worked out of my home, I was a lot more freewheeling. If it was a beautiful day and I wanted to sunbathe or putter in the yard, I did it. That night I might work until 1:00 A.M. Since I met my clients elsewhere, I also had the latitude to work in sweats and be completely comfortable.*
>
> *Now that we've grown to a staff of eight and moved into office quarters, it's a different story. I feel obligated to be at work when everyone else is. While my country lifestyle still permits some informality, sweats and slippers would be stretching it.*

## *Using Equipment as Your Staff*

Does it seem impossible you'll be able to perform dozens of tasks all by yourself? Can you handle correspondence, market for new prospects, track bills, cut invoices, take inventory, do the bookkeeping, update the mailing list, service the business you generate, and perform other record-keeping tasks? Yes! With several electronic helpers. A telephone and a computer allow you to deliver the one-two punch that knocks out these chores like they were rank amateurs.

Many entrepreneurs take it a step further. Their "electronic cottages" are the ultimate in high-tech wizardry. The phone has several lines and sophisticated features. The computer sports a modem, fax capability, and software with the latest bells and whistles. Complement this with a laser printer, and they have a state-of-the-art office right in their homes. Those who are doing desktop publishing from home might add a scanner to the list of equipment helpers. Some HBBs find a copier a tremendous help, rather than having to dash out to make photocopies. (Others *welcome* a quick break to make copies, do banking, and run by the post office.) Some individuals find using a hand-held tape recorder allows them to capture ideas no matter where they are.

How expensive is setting up such an office? Dan Janal left his job with a mid-sized New York PR firm three years ago. He invested $5,000 in equipment. "My income has more than doubled," reports Janal. In fact, he now has to hire freelancers to handle the extra workload. Would you believe all this is happening out of a *hallway*! He turned the long hall from his kitchen to his bedroom into Janal Communications.

When you live in the boonies, the telephone is your lifeline to the world. When you work out of your home, it becomes doubly important. Handled properly, prospects need never know you're comfortably ensconced in the spare bedroom, looking out at the horses in the pasture while nibbling on a bagel. By all means, get a separate line for your business. Nothing is less professional than calling a business long-distance and getting a four-year-old who wants to chat. Answering "hello" also brands you as a novice. Talk with phone representatives and learn what options are available to make your work easier and more efficient. Automatic dialing, for instance, is a real time saver when you repeatedly call the same people. Call conferencing might be useful. You may want call waiting.

Also give considerable thought to how the phone is handled when you're not home. If you use an answering machine, be sure it allows unlimited length messages. It's a good idea to get one equipped so you can pick up messages remotely. Voice mail on your computer is a preferable alternative, and answering services are better yet . . . and more expensive. People, however, prefer to talk to other people. A further option is to make a deal with another local business or neighbor to answer your calls. You pay them to take messages and set appointments for you. To do this you'll need a call-forwarding device, which requires two phone lines.

## *Designing Your Perfect Office and Getting Organized*

A home-based office can be professional, functional, and great-looking. Your office is a tool, just like the telephone and computer. So consider ergonomics—the relationship between people and their environment—when setting up shop. Home offices are becoming so popular, Faith Popcorn coined a new word to describe them: hoffices. She forecasts they will be the newest real estate development. As if in answer to that prediction, a recent *Denver Post* article quoted Andy Ades of Ades Design as saying, "We're probably putting offices in more than half the homes we're building in the Evergreen (Colorado) area."

No longer relegated to the back of the house, today's office in new home construction is usually in a main part of the house, often close to the entry. This preserves privacy for the living area and allows easy access for business visitors. An adjacent private bathroom is important too if the business will have outside visitors. The traditional study/library feel is popular. Features like a bay window, wood paneling, and bookshelves provide a special ambiance. French doors with beveled glass give the room a "grand" look and permit regular guests to peek in—without encouraging them to enter the business domain.

When constructing an office space, beefed-up electrical wiring is an important consideration. The handful of typical wall outlets can't handle today's office needs. You may want to add floor plugs to accommodate a desk in the middle of the room. It's a good idea to include a closet for resale value. With built-in shelving, it can store office supplies out of sight and have hooks for prospects' coats. Think about lighting too. Recessed and track lighting, which can be clustered over computer work stations, functions well.

The more windows the better. They help combat feelings of isolation. Blinds—rather than drapes, curtains, or shades—are the foremost window cover. You can tilt them slightly, or completely, and change the whole mood of the room. We had fun decorating one home office with shutters which created a similar effect.

Size is all in the way you look at it. What one person calls a "compact office" another dubs a "walk-in desk." Be assured, however, you'll expand to fill the space. Any space. Make it as large as possible.

The physical layout should be arranged to accommodate your work style. Having two desks—or an adjacent work surface—is extremely helpful when approaching a big project. If you want to churn out the work, forget high-backed chairs with arms. While imposing looking, and outstanding for napping, these plush monsters aren't practical unless your job is just thinking. A sturdy steno chair gives you greater movement and better back support. Comfort increases productivity. One other tip: keep the phone away from the printer. Otherwise the rat-tat-tat will drown out your conversations.

The atmosphere you create in your office is very important to your psychic well-being. You can transform a plain room into an enchanting oasis with thought, planning, and imagination. Surround yourself with things you love. Maybe it's a few exquisite antique pieces, or perhaps a quality stereo player and classical CDs. Include photos of loved ones. It's refreshing to look up and see the face of someone dear. Don't treat your workplace one-dimensionally. Include memorabilia, a collection of treasures, houseplants, an aquarium . . . whatever delights you.

To break the monotony of staring at a computer screen all day, Barbara Brabec filled an entire wall with artwork and photographs of Bengal tigers. To her, this is the most exquisite wild animal in the world. "When my eyes are tired and I need a stretch, I lean back and gaze into all those beautiful amber eyes staring back at me and feel a sense of peace that is hard to describe," relates Brabac.

Clutter is to a home office what an accident is to a freeway. It impedes the flow, causing movement to grind almost to a halt. Clear your work area of all non-essential items; handle only work-related tasks in this area. It's easy to be distracted when you work at home. That's one of the reasons you want to organize yourself well. Police paper relentlessly. As you open mail, sort it into appropriate stacks: to do, to pay, to file, to read. If in doubt, trash it. Reading materials grow like bacteria in a friendly culture.

Don't agonize, organize! To be productive, establish "action needed" and "pending" files. Decide on a way to file things so you can retrieve them quickly. Set up a tickler system to remind you of items or tasks needing follow-up. Find out your personal *peak time*—when you are most creative—and handle the toughest jobs then. By taking these simple precautions, you'll boost your efficiency manyfold.

## *Cottage Industry Coexistence: Melding Business and Personal*

While using your residence as your office has many advantages, it also has drawbacks. Sometimes it's a mine field waiting to shatter your serenity.

Take chatty neighbors, for instance. (Yes, please take them!) They figure when you're home, you're not *really* working. In their eyes, you're fair game for coffee and gossip and favors. Now you get to use all your diplomatic skills. Try to keep on good terms while you explain firmly that you have important obligations and can't get your work done when there are unnecessary interruptions. Be careful not to encourage them in the beginning, however, because *you* miss the water cooler chats.

Friends also need to be educated to reconsider every time they want to contact you. Set aside an hour in the day when you're least productive and designate that as "caller time." Train your friends to phone during that period. And help them realize you can't take off to join them to fish, or go to an auction or fashion show. (And maybe you can—especially if you make an arrangement with the boss [you] to make up the time evenings or on the weekend.)

Of an even greater challenge is your family. It's impossible to make a two-year-old understand that mommy isn't to be bothered. With children that young, your choices are to hire child care, work when they're asleep, or get your mate to babysit. That is, unless your job requires little concentration and can be done while Lindsey or Christopher is toddling around the house chattering like a magpie. As they get older, youngsters can participate in the business itself. Then instead of feeling alienated, they feel included.

**Marilyn:** *When I began my freelance article-writing career some 20 years ago, I got my sons involved. They both took typing in school. I would write a standard query letter soliciting an article assignment, then have the boys retype the letter with different editors' names and addresses. This allowed me to send out multiple, customized queries. And it gave the kids spending money since they made 35 cents per letter. (Wow! What a difference computers have made in our lives.)*

Family privacy and lifestyle patterns are disturbed by a HBB. Your teenage daughter will resent having to keep the stereo low because you're meeting with a client in the next room. Your husband won't look kindly on you when he can't get to the Ping Pong table in the rec room because you've confiscated it to lay out a wedding gown pattern. Or your wife may not understand why you can't fix the leaky faucet today. After all, you're just shuffling a lot of papers. Furthermore, your son may be testy when you won't stop to fry the fish he just caught.

## *All That Glitters Isn't Gold*

Besides the above, other traps wait to ensnare HBB operators.

Sometimes it's difficult to separate your business from your personal life. The office is so handy, you're tempted to dash in and finish that project. Thus workaholics are born. Overwork is a habit prevalent among entrepreneurs. We love to lavish attention on our enterprises. It's even more seductive when the office is only a few feet away. Shut the door and hang a "Closed" sign if necessary. That takes self-discipline.

On the flip side of the coin, so does *making yourself work*! There is no longer company structure to shape your day. When the business is in the boudoir, the enticements to get sidetracked are many. You notice a houseplant drooping slightly and decide they all need watering. Or you look out the window and the grass seems unusually long. Better get to it. You remember the pot roast left over from last night and long for a snack. The commercial for Oprah said today's theme is right up your alley. Friends call your business number during office hours and you don't have the heart to cut them off. A neighbor arrives with a plate of brownies hot from the oven. It's distraction with a capital "D."

To combat this productivity gobbler, take yourself seriously. Other people will adhere to your rules about work only if you do. Stay focused. Limit personal calls and other interruptions. Have friends telephone during your designated lunch hour or after work. (Or put on the answering machine to screen calls. Only acknowledge business callers.) Discourage visits from neighbors. Handle routine household chores in your off hours. Stay away from the TV. When you get interested in Donahue, your mind isn't on your work. Avoid nibbling. Many new HBB operators gain weight when they first start working from home.

Explain to your school-aged children early on about this being your new work and why it's important they not interrupt you unless it's an emergency. (Help them define what an emergency consists of.) Lay out snacks for them when you make your own lunch, then take around 30 minutes when they arrive home to hear about their day. They'll sense if you're "squeezing them in" so relax and be prepared to listen. Once they've been heard, they'll happily go their own way. If they feel rushed, however, you can bet they'll find an urgent need for you within the hour . . . that's how children are!

Perhaps the most difficult aspect of working from home is the isolation factor. Most of us who come from a busy office or store environment go through withdrawal; we're struck by feelings of exile and loneliness. Being alone in a home office is unfamiliar. There is no one to bounce ideas off of. No one to praise our work or share a story with. The quiet and inactivity engulfs us.

The best antidote for these feelings of separateness is to become part of something. Get out among your peers on a regular basis! Join a local service club that meets weekly for breakfast or lunch. Get involved in your trade association and attend out-of-town workshops, conventions, and trade shows. Consider organizing a local brainstorming group of four or five other countrypreneurs with whom you can kick around ideas and discuss problems. Or find a buddy and set up an informal mentor program. Don't forget to include your spouse. He or she can be your greatest supporter—sounding board—strength.

You'll also feel less isolated if you treat occasions to run business errands as mini social functions. Visit with the bank teller as you make a deposit, stop and chat a few minutes when you bump into acquaintances at the post office. And tease the UPS or Federal Express courier when he or she comes with a delivery.

Company can also be as close as your computer's "on" switch. As we've mentioned before, various electronic bulletin boards allow you to tap into special interest groups. Here you can conference with distant colleagues, send messages, and trade tips with other small business owners. There's even Home Office Message Echo, a bulletin board that attracts HBB operators from all across the U.S. and Canada. That's in addition to CompuServe's Working-from-Home Forum.

Another way to combat the blahs is to get a pet. A dog, cat, or bird is good company and makes the house seem less empty. And have you ever thought about *appreciating* that quiet? Turn negative emotions into positive ones by acknowledging how nice it is not to be constantly interrupted by co-workers.

## Zapping the Zoning Ordeal

Zoning restrictions can present another hurdle. Many communities have strict laws about the *secondary* (or business) use of a home. These rules vary. One town may allow professionals—whom they consider to be doctors, lawyers, dentists, etc.—to work from home. (There is much controversy today about which additional occupations qualify as "professional.") Other places permit virtually anyone to run a business from his or her home as long as it doesn't become a neighborhood nuisance. Still others prohibit HBBs completely.

If you plan to use your residence as your office, it pays to check out local regulations carefully. In small villages, contact town hall. Other sources for information are the planning department, zoning administration, or building inspector. Don't take the word of a real estate salesperson. Determine for yourself that the zoning is appropriate.

If it isn't, there's hope. Your recourse is to apply for a variance. This means you ask the ruling body to make an exception in your case. If your business enterprise won't markedly increase the neighborhood traffic flow—cause a parking problem—be noisy, odoriferous, or dusty—or require unsightly signs or storage facilities, you'll probably get your way. Most neighborhoods have a "live and let live" attitude if you keep your premises neat, are quiet, and don't create undue activity. Naturally a computer operator is much more likely to get a zoning variance than someone who plans to do mechanic work. Most of us wouldn't want to live next door to a person who tunes up hot rods all day.

Do be aware that many towns limit the number of employees you can have working at your home. In some cases, it can only be the owners; in others, one employee is allowed. More lenient laws permit as many as three people. A few HBB operators stretch that by having more workers, but using them part time, rationalizing that two half-time people equal one full-time position.

Some proponents of home occupations complain that archaic zoning laws, irate neighbors, even unions, have combined to thwart their intentions. In extreme cases, assertive entrepreneurs have been known to contact their Congressperson to intervene in their behalf.

If you contemplate purchasing property in an exclusive subdivision, watch out for CC&Rs. That stands for conditions, covenants, and restrictions. The deed to your house may prohibit running a business out of your home. Sometimes you can even get around this. But don't count on it. Contact the homeowners association and request a special dispensation or ask them to amend the restrictions.

For those interested in starting a manufacturing enterprise at their residence, it's of interest that the federal Industrial Home Work Act of 1943 was repealed in November of 1988. That opened the door for doing certain kinds of garment manufacturing in your home. Some experts feel it has far-reaching implications and will nullify many local zoning regulations.

We'd advise you not to proceed illegally. If you operate a business in violation of zoning ordinances, chances are excellent that a disgruntled neighbor will report you. This can result in an injunction to cease business, forcing you to close up shop that very day!

On the other hand, some communities are actually launching subdivisions targeted to *attracting* HBBs. Market Place in Oak Creek, Wisconsin, for instance, consists of 20 homes built especially to accommodate home occupations ranging from dentists' offices to craft studios. And each home in the Eaglecrest subdivision in Foresthill, California, was designed to include a teleport containing a personal computer and modem so occupants can link to computers—and employment.

A village in Lynwood, Illinois, has taken this concept a step further. There a development has one-acre lots in which the front is zoned for a single-family residence and the rear is dual-zoned to encourage commercial use. Residents have drafted restrictive covenants governing the neighborhood businesses and find the roomy lots give their neighborhood a country atmosphere. That's progressive zoning!

And restrictions are being relaxed elsewhere. In Cochise County, Arizona, they passed a law permitting "minor home occupations" (whatever *that* means) which have no outdoor signs or outside employees, and take up only a limited space. Owners of such businesses will no longer have to go through zoning hearings. And Davis, California—which prides itself on fostering energy efficiency—is considered very permissive toward home businesses. Air pollution is greatly reduced when cars never leave home.

To fully prepare yourself for launching a successful HBB, we recommend you also study Part III for more home-based business resources to make your heart race. Also get into the other chapters in this part of *Country Bound!*. They contain valuable tips on starting your business, becoming an entrepreneur, marketing your new venture, plus staying prosperous and personally content. Pay particular attention to "Telecommuting: A Growing Solution to Urban Blues." Now let's move ahead and get the jump on how to find a rural job, should you not want to work for yourself.

# 13

# Finding a Rural Job: Gutsy Strategies Mother Never Told You

Americans have been pulling up stakes and pursuing prosperity elsewhere since the days of the Conestoga wagon. An estimated 1.3 million heads of household moved annually during the 1980s. Many people are tired of working at the wrong job (not doing what they love) for the right reasons (money, benefits, and security). Plant closings and massive layoffs are snuffing out the livelihoods of others. And each month thousands of tenured managers find themselves among the unemployed as a result of hostile takeovers and corporate downsizing.

Many of these individuals don't have the temperament or desire to run their own businesses. Or they're spouses from two-career families involved in a move to better their mate. They want to find a good job quickly in their new surroundings. If you fit this description, listen up. We give you tips to spin your fantasy of straw into a reality of gold. This chapter contains dozens of gutsy strategies for finding a satisfying rural job.

## *Getting Off on the Right Foot*

Let's look at some overall recommendations first. Find out if you can stay connected to your old job through telecommuting. Being electronically employed is a growing phenomenon. In this situation, you're linked to the home office via computer, telephone, and perhaps a modem and fax machine. Catalog sales, outbound telemarketing, and credit and collections are just a sample of the kinds of jobs being performed from homes located at remote destinations. (See the next chapter on "Telecommuting: A Growing Solution to Urban Blues.")

Even while the whole country sputters in a recession, regional job markets often thrive. It's wise, however, not to locate in a town dependent on only one industry. If it fails, the area economy goes into a tailspin. And remember our previous encouragement to situate in a place with a significant proportion of *non*-natives. Otherwise, you may be an outcast.

Government jobs are more secure and often pay better than private industry. Consider not only federal and state positions, but also those with county or town governments. (With this in mind, you may want to locate in the county seat if you seek a stable clerical job.) Sure you'll probably have to pass a civil service exam. But if you develop a rapport with the hiring manager, he or she will help guide you through the examination maze.

In addition to asking around locally and countywide, check out the bimonthly *Federal Jobs Digest*. Also investigate *Federal Career Opportunities*, which lists available jobs plus application instructions. Then there is Daniel Lauber's *The Compleat Guide to Finding Jobs in Government*. He covers finding both professional and non-professional positions. Check your local library for these references.

"The next best employer to work for is the aggressive manufacturing or service firm with a national market," believes relocation expert William Seavey. "These types of businesses are much less affected by the ebbs and flows of the local economy." He feels those jobs that offer inherent fringe benefits beyond minimum wage—such as waitress or waiter in a resort, cab driver, or ranch manager—include useful perks. Servers get tips and a ranch manager probably has free living accommodations.

Perhaps you're a retiree seeking to supplement your income. Maybe you recently got out of the military, or you received early retirement from your company. Possibly your Social Security benefits just kicked in.

Statistics show that nearly one in four people continues to work part-time for a few years immediately after they start receiving Social Security. And an additional 25 percent say they would do so too, if they found a good opportunity. What you can earn without being penalized depends on your age. If you're under 65, the maximum amount you can earn in 1992 without a cut in benefits is $7,440. That figure rises to $10,200 for those between 65 and 69. And once you hit 69, the sky's the limit. (See, older does get better in some ways!)

Many mature people prefer temporary, seasonal, or part-time jobs. Unfortunately, most of these pay little more than minimum wage. When applying for such a position, stress your reliability, experience in the work world, and good judgement. Employers get tired of hiring and training young people over and over again. Once you're in, we'd wager you'll soon be getting raises, promotions, and pleas to work permanent, full-time hours.

If you're not willing to settle for this, fantasize! Imagine your fairy godmother will give you any job you want. What would it be? Write down your wish. Then ask yourself what you're doing to move yourself in that direction. If getting your ideal seems unrealistic, break it down into components, suggests psychologist and career-change speaker, Dr. Lawrence Le Shan. If being a doctor is your dream, but you're too old for medical school, think about another health-care position. For some, employment after retirement is a chance to finally get paid for doing what they've always dreamed of.

## *Molding Your Career Focus*

Some skills are transferable almost anywhere. Generic occupations—like teaching, nursing, and secretarial work—fall into this category. Electricians, plumbers, mechanics, and hairdressers can usually earn a living almost anywhere. And doctors are in demand in rural America.

Your career will often be molded into a different shape in the country. A truly rural nurse, for instance, isn't as likely to deal with severely ill people. They will be in the hospital. Instead she or he works in health promotion and prevention of illness. Also family planning, school physicals, and infant care occupy a lot of time. Sometimes there are other differences. Noel Ekin, a licensed practical nurse who traded Houston, Texas, for Salida, Colorado, doesn't mind a daily 140-mile round trip drive to work. She bought a camera and leaves plenty of time to stop and take pictures of sunrises, sunsets, elk, antelope and deer along the way.

A friend who taught at Lamar Community College felt like she was part of Little House on the Prairie, compared to the megauniversity where she was before. But once she got her foot in the door of this community of 10,000, she ended up teaching classes in English Composition, Business English, Business Communication, and Speech.

Bob Nelson had taught in several large schools in Washington and Oregon. But he missed having the opportunity to make a difference in kids' lives—he wanted to give his students more one-on-one attention. Now he's in Seneca, Oregon, with a population of 170. At the Seneca Elementary

School where he teaches, he has lots of personal contact with everybody. "It's like teaching family," Nelson says. When he opens school at 7:30 each morning, several parents drop by for a cup of coffee on their way to work. His only regret? "That I didn't do this sooner."

If you're an educator who'd rather switch than fight, think about who you want to teach. Will it be elementary, middle, or high school? Perhaps college or adult continuing education classes sound more fulfilling, or maybe you want to leave this specialty entirely. Two interesting books on that subject are *Teachers in New Careers* by Frances Bastress, and *Alternative Careers for Teachers* by Marna L. Beard and Michael J. McGahey.

On the other hand, many people are *entering* the teaching profession from other nontraditional fields. "Alternative certification programs, designed for career-switchers and other college graduates who lack education degrees, are gathering steam," reports *John Naisbitt's Trend Letter*. Over the last five years thousands of former lawyers, computer analysts, engineers, and other professionals have entered teaching. And it's an occupation expected to draw heavily from the military sector as the Department of Defense downsizes in the coming years. Two factors contribute to this surge of interest in teaching: people want to make a lasting contribution and salaries have increased. In 1991 the average public school instructor made $33,015. For more information, contact the National Center for Education Information at 202-362-3444.

Some people feel it's a poor act of stewardship not to use the gifts God gave them to care for their brother or sister. Jobs dealing with social change are attracting greater numbers. People in these public service positions often work with the underprivileged or the handicapped. They also serve as city planners, recreation directors, or gerontology specialists.

## *Resources to Ease Your Quest*

Urban opt-outs who drool over jobs that keep them outdoors or in the heat of adventure will enjoy James Joseph's *Complete Out-of-Doors Job, Business and Professional Guide*. It runs the gamut from game warden to archeologist, RV campground manager to forest ranger, timber grower to professional rockhound. And if your quest is excitement, consider being a forest fireman, yacht delivery person, wilderness outfitter, or ski instructor.

More possibilities for outdoorsy types are listed in *The Caretaker Gazette* (Box 342, Carpentersville, IL 60110). In one issue we noticed an ad for free rent if you pay for repairs and upkeep, a farming venture that promised possible partnership, and use of a fully equipped cabin and sauna for two months in exchange for caretaking. (Caretaking can be a great way to determine if you can hack remoteness. That particular cabin had no phone or power and involved a ⅓ mile walk to reach it!) Another opportunity involved not only free housing and utilities, but also a stipend of $150 a month for feeding the horses and chickens. Under their heading for "Environmental Positions" the gazette lists scientific and supervisory positions, plus intriguing internships.

Yearn to grab your hat and bedroll and move 'em out? For a nominal fee, Agri-Jobs will send you three months of listings from ranchers and farmers seeking help. Jobs range from ranch hands to managers and include barn personnel, ranch cooks, tree planters, house parents, horse trainers, grooms, wranglers, sheep herders, you name it. If cowboying tickles your fancy, this may be the answer. Write the Agri-Jobs Newsletter Service at P. O. Box 30236, Amarillo, TX 79120.

On a slightly less horsy note, *The Rocky Mountain Employment Newsletter* also covers jobs in farm and ranch work. Yet forestry, teaching, resorts and recreation, seasonal employment, government jobs, clerical positions, construction, the ski industry, and many more fields are also listed. They concentrate on Colorado, Wyoming, Arizona, New Mexico, Idaho, and Montana. For subscription information, contact Intermountain Publishing & Referral Service Inc., 703 S. Broadway, Suite 100, Denver, CO 80209.

While we're making recommendations, another ideal national source for high caliber professionals is the *National Business Employment Weekly*. Published by *The Wall Street Journal*, it combines a week's worth of help-wanted advertisements from all the regional editions. While many of these jobs are in major metropolitan areas, some are located in more secluded places. Especially strong as a recruitment tool in the financial field, the paper also covers health care, high-tech, managerial, and executive opportunities. Additionally, it breaks the country into four regions and lists seminars and events for job seekers in the Weekly Calendar of Events. Helpful articles are also part of the package. For subscribing information, call 800-JOB-HUNT (800-562-4868).

Another potential is *The National Ad Search*, a weekly publication listing jobs from 75 Sunday classified ad sections across the USA. Their number in Wisconsin is 899-992-2832.

Career women might find it useful to join the National Association of Female Executives. For $29 a year you get a directory of 500 local chapters that can serve as instant networking links. Naturally, many are headquartered in major cities, but we also recognize several towns of 5,000 or so among the chapters. Additionally, they publish a magazine and offer other benefits. For information, contact NAFE at 127 W. 24th Street, New York,

NY 10011, 212-645-0770. Think about other professional organizations to which you belong. Many, such as Toastmasters and Swap Clubs, will have branches in or near your new destination. Look up members in the national directory or roster and call them for advance help.

Consider associations where you hold membership when you're job hunting. For instance, the American Institute of Architects, the American Institute of Chemical Engineers, and Women in Communication all have nationwide databases to match job-hunting members with employers.

And lest we forget, this chapter would be incomplete without a hearty endorsement for Richard Nelson Bolles' *What Color is Your Parachute?*. Without question, this is the premier book for any job hunter or career changer. It's updated each year and has sold over 4 million copies. We defy even the most seasoned pro not to find some useful information here.

For many folks, rural relocation means they shift the approach to their careers. A Houston developer sold his business to become a carpenter. A geologist caught in Colorado's oil bust in the '80s now applies her critical thinking skills to her job as a career counselor. An east coast corporate meeting planner converted her organizational savvy into a less sophisticated wedding and event planning service. A southern California stockbroker left his hectic lifestyle to join a most unusual brokerage house: Edward D. Jones. This firm, which believes that well-heeled investors can be found almost anywhere among the hills and dales of America, has over 1,200 brokers living and working in towns of less than 25,000 people.

As we've suggested throughout this book, you need to probe your avocations as well as your vocations, determine your likes and dislikes, and take a skills inventory. Everybody is good at several things. That's as true if you've been a homemaker all your life as it is if you've run a company that employed 200 people.

If you've supervised a home, you have been involved in purchasing (all those trips to the market), budgeting (making money stretch from paycheck to paycheck), and coordination (organizing car pools, preparing meals, doing laundry, cleaning, correlating kids' activities, running errands). Cooking is no doubt one of your competencies. Flower arranging, sewing, furniture placement, and other such activities may have given you a leg up on interior design. And when you organized and wrote all those PTA reports, or oversaw the whole Junior League cookbook project, you developed talents that have value in the job marketplace.

## *Planning Your Job Search*

Most likely you come from a large company where the corporate culture is very different from that of small, rural firms. In Fortune 1,000 companies there are personnel departments and many layers of buffers between where a person is hired and where he or she ultimately works. In our opinion, this breeds negligent hiring practices. Interviewers in Goliath firms have little vested interest in the company. They're influenced by degrees, prestigious schools, and impressive former titles.

Not so the small businessperson. These Davids are concerned with *results*. They want to know if you can do the job and how you'll make or save them money. It's a whole different mind-set. They often base decisions on gut feelings. Credentials are secondary. Be sure to tune into this significant difference when planning your job search.

Also be prepared for the reaction that you're "overqualified." It's probably a reasonable concern. Your challenge is to convince a prospective employer that he or she is foolish not to hire you. Don't come on too strong. Underplay your achievements. Make it clear you don't expect to earn the same salary in the country that you collected in the city. If you're moving because you want more time with your spouse and kids, it's completely legitimate to say something like: "Although I made a substantial income last year, I also had to travel 60 percent of the time. I personally consider lower compensation with no travel to be a fair trade-off. Time with my family is a high personal priority." Then, without sounding like a cocky hotshot, describe how you can contribute.

Blend into the community and identify with its rhythms, needs, and wants. Reposition yourself both mentally and physically for this new environment. If you're an experienced executive used to responsibility and power, do some role playing to take the edge off your super sophisticated airs. Foremost in the minds of those making hiring decisions is "will this person *fit* into our team?"

To better connect with the individual who's interviewing you, evaluate his or her style—then mirror it. If he's about as upbeat as an undertaker, try to match this behavior. If she's warm and cordial, return her friendly demeanor. We're not saying change like a chameleon from one job interview to the next. But it is smart to take into consideration the mannerisms and attitudes of those in a position to offer you a job.

You can learn how to write a resumé in many books on that subject if you need help. A functional, rather than a chronological, one probably works best for the country, however. A functional resumé catalogs your most important skills, then illustrates how you acquired and honed them. It's especially useful if you have a unique talent you want to showcase.

Think through what supporting materials you can provide. You've gotten letters of recommendation on company letterhead from former bosses. Right? What about personal letters of reference? (Especially if you're weak in the former.) Have you received any awards or certificates of merit? Are there favorable performance reviews you can make copies of? If you're a writer, photographer, or artist certainly you have a portfolio of samples to show.

The meek may inherit the earth . . . but only after it's been picked clean. Be ready to address the salary issue. "You must have a figure in mind," advises Richard N. Diggs in *Finding Your Ideal Job*. That means doing your homework. Find out what the usual wage is for your kind of work *in this area*. The last three words are the operative ones. It doesn't matter a crumb what people make for doing what you do in Los Angeles or Chicago or New York. In small towns the salaries are considerably less. But then so are the living expenses. One way of checking out the going rate is to ask key people, "If you were applying for a position as a _____, what would you consider a good starting wage?" Also be sure you know how the cost of living differs from what you're used to.

Diggs advises when you're asked, "What salary are you looking for?" to counter with, "Is there a set wage for this position?" If the answer is "No," you need to parry. You might say, "I feel I'm worth $_____ as a starting salary. But since *you* can't be sure of that yet, I'll place my request in the range of from $_____ to $_____." Put the first figure at something that's realistic for the area and that you can afford to live on. The second figure is what you'd *like* to have. (By the way, management thinks in terms of monthly or annual salaries for key personnel, not hourly pay. If you seek a high-powered position, you label yourself as a rookie when you give an hourly figure.)

Feel good about the company and the job? Then don't leave without asking for it! That's called closing the sale. Every successful salesperson does it. You might say something like, "I'm impressed with what you do here and know I can contribute to your growth. I can start this week or next. Which will be most convenient for you?" Remember most entrepreneurs or small business managers are put off by indecision. They'll assume if you're indecisive at the interview, that characteristic will also prevail on the job.

Don't forget there are other considerations besides salary. Will you get a company car? Free meals? Are good tips likely? Are stock options available; what about a bonus plan? What are the employee benefits? It may come as a blow that many small-town firms don't provide health insurance. (By the way, if you've recently stopped working for a company with 20 or more workers, federal law requires that your medical coverage be extended at least 18 months. Although *you* must pay the premium, this is a convenient way to keep cost-effective coverage until you have time to shop for a new policy.)

Don't expect highfalutin titles in the boonies, unless you're working with a firm that has a national clientele. Bestowing titles is perceived as a waste of time in many small towns. People there are "just folks."

Job seekers who take a passive stance after the interview are usually left waiting on the curb. Be proactive rather than reactive. Send a prompt, (error-free!) thank-you letter to the person who interviewed you. Typed is best, but handwritten is better than nothing. (Do this even if you *don't* want the job. Why? Because this courtesy is so seldom extended it will set you apart. Small town business owners talk to each other. Ralph Mercer may well mention you to Diane Bell . . . who just happens to need a new employee.) Not only is sending a thank you gracious, it also serves as a reminder of your past meeting. It's a good idea to include one additional strength or accomplishment you didn't bring up in the interview. If you haven't heard anything in a week, follow up with a phone call.

Be politely persistent. Ask if you can provide any additional information. Calvin Coolidge had the right idea when he wrote, "Nothing in this world can take the place of persistence. Talent will not; nothing is more common than unsuccessful men with talent. Genius will not; unrewarded genius is almost a proverb. Education will not. The world is full of educated derelicts. Persistence and determination alone are omnipotent. The slogan 'press on' has solved and always will solve the problems of the human race."

When John F. Kennedy ran for the Senate in 1952, he collected 262,324 nomination signatures from all over Massachusetts. Only 2,500 were required. Persistence often prevails over talent in a job search.

Right beside persistence is networking. These two go together like salsa dip and tortilla chips. It's estimated about 75 percent of available jobs are never advertised. Personal contacts are the best sources of job leads.

Networking isn't just letting people you know, know—it's creating a ripple effect: contacting *their* contacts. Ask friends and acquaintances for referrals, for people they think might have some ideas. Talk with town leaders. Get permission to use their names when you contact the new lead. The best approach is not to ask strangers for a *job,* but rather for *advice* on how to go about your job search. This takes the pressure off them, yet it accomplishes the same thing.

And if they can't help, keep the ripple going by asking them for referrals to others. Executive search consultants coach their clients to try for three new names from every contact they canvass. This jump-starts the search from linear to geometric proportions. The secret to job-finding success often lies in pursuing people you don't know. (For further hints on how to network effectively, see the upcoming chapter on "Tactics for *Staying* Prosperous and Happy.")

## *Some Random Thoughts . . .*

People ask us where the jobs are. Nevada is definitely a hot spot. The Sagebrush State led all 50 in the number of new jobs added in 1990. Some 35,500 people joined their working ranks. The Northeast finished dead last, losing a whopping 328,100 jobs. If construction is your field, head for Idaho, Alaska, or Oregon. Should manufacturing attract you, consider Wyoming, North Dakota, or Utah—in addition to Nevada.

Some people increase their chances of finding the ideal position by using a technique called visualization. They imagine in great detail every aspect of the interview, being hired, and performing well on the job.

Suppose you're an artist, writer, photographer, dancer, or have some other talent you're not using fully at the moment. When our real love is different from the job that pays the bills, we sometimes give our talent short shrift. When people ask what you do, get in the habit of saying, "I'm a writer" or "I'm an artist." This not only validates and fortifies it in your own mind, but plants seeds in the minds of others that you have this ability. When they need someone to write a brochure or handle an artistic assignment, they may think of you.

It may make sense to inform yourself about federally funded placement programs like JTPA (Job Training Partnership Act). Why do *you* need to know about this? Because potential employers may not, and it could be the edge that gets you a job. You see, when someone qualifies for JTPA, the employer gets help paying them for the first six months. This usually amounts to a savings for the company of several thousands of dollars. The point of JTPA is to get jobless workers quickly into permanent, self-sustaining employment.

While their requirements are that a person be economically disadvantaged, dislocated, or face significant employment barriers, in reality many people qualify. We hired a very competent administrative assistant through this program. Hugh relocated here after a several-month stint of not working. He also lacked any knowledge of our particular industry. JTPA even paid for him to take classes to learn how to use WordPerfect.

We've spoken about volunteering elsewhere in the book, but want to reinforce it as a job-hunting technique here. Working as a volunteer or unpaid intern has opened many career doors in the past. You get on-site and visible, your cheery smile and efficient ways are a constant reminder of how valuable you are. And what you learn—Wow! One volunteer joined Habitat for Humanity so she "could learn carpentry and dry walling while building for the homeless." She then used these skills to do a lot of the construction on her own home.

Don't let yourself get discouraged. If you're having trouble finding an ideal position, look for a temporary job. Or put a classified ad in the paper and see if you can pick up some freelance work. People hire data processors, housecleaners, home care helpers for the aged, and handymen—to name a few possibilities—all the time.

## 23 More Tips to Enhance Your Chances

Below is a list of additional tactics. While some are general, most work especially well in small towns. Included are suggestions for trailing spouses anxious to find employment in a new locale.

* **Read the trade journal for your industry.** Most have classified ad sections that list job openings around the country.
* **Get on the phone to anyone you know at your new destination.** (Or anyone who has a friend who might know a friend there.) Find out how your skills fit the needs of your potential new home.
* **Subscribe to the local newspaper *and* the Sunday paper from the nearest large city.** Sometimes important jobs are advertised in the city rather than the local rag. Or a headquarters office may hire district representatives to cover the area where you want to live.
* **Look into state certification or licensing requirements.** If your profession requires this, and you expect to move out of state, determine the new requirements immediately.
* **If you're planning a career change and your education is irrelevant or (gasp) lacking, take a course ahead of time.** You don't need a B.A. or an M.B.A. But be able to say you're "studying" business or marketing or finance or whatever. Employers are impressed with adults who go back to school. It shows a conscientious, get-ahead attitude.
* **Get some experience . . . somehow.** So you've never worked in this new field. Have you read books about it? Pored over the industry trade

journals? Gone to a relevant conference? Talked to people in the profession? Learned the jargon? Can you *talk* the business?

* **Make an appointment with the personnel director of your spouse's firm.** Ask about possible employment at the new branch (if they don't frown on nepotism). Also request names of reliable employment agencies, search firms, or temporary help services they can recommend.
* **If you're a relocating spouse, be sure potential employers realize your moving expenses will be borne by your mate's company.** This allows you to compete more fairly with local applicants.
* **Check first in the hot industries**—services, retail trade, plus finance, insurance, and real estate (known as FIRE). This is where the majority of the action will be this century.
* **Connect with the college placement office.** In additional to having lists of available jobs, they'll also know of any upcoming job fairs. And they can tell you things it would take you weeks to chase down yourself.
* **Identify the local power brokers.** While many will hold elective office, some are simply respected old-timers who wield unusual clout.
* **Attend chamber of commerce mixers and meetings of any economic development group.** This is where small town business leaders network. If you socialize well, chances are you'll meet someone with an opening—or someone who knows about a position coming up.
* **Look for a church affiliation early.** Religious organizations are a wonderful place to harvest job referrals. People will be anxious to help you. They want you to stay and be part of their church family.
* **Watch for *hidden* opportunities.** Announcements appearing in the newspaper or chamber newsletter about new business developments or personnel changes often flag openings. Read these publications as soon as they're available and act immediately.
* **Find out where the regulars hang out.** Go there yourself and eavesdrop on what's happening around town.
* **Consider renting a local post office box and hiring an answering service.** If you're going to be writing or calling companies before arriving in town, make it *easy* for them to respond.
* **Plan a vacation to check possibilities out personally.** Pound the pavement; it's the only true way to find out what's going on.
* **Study the Yellow Pages for leads.** If it isn't clear what a business does, call and ask.

★ **Tap into any personal information network you've developed.** Ask for help from your real estate salesperson, insurance agent, lawyer, banker, etc.

★ **Respond to all possible ads.** That gets you in the door. If you don't qualify for this position, perhaps you can convince them to create a spot where your skills *will* be useful.

★ **If the town is large enough to have one, register with any employment agency or temporary help firm.** Working as a temp is an excellent way to check out potential employers and pick up gossip about jobs coming up.

★ **Notice if the local newspaper does a column on "New Faces" or something similar.** If so, send in a black and white photo and a brief profile stressing your professional abilities.

★ **Take *something* ... even if it isn't your ideal.** This eases the pressure and will give you a chance to get acquainted and look around while having a salary coming in.

## *Choosing a Company That's Right for You*

Whether you go to work for an employer or not is as much your decision as it is theirs. Big career leaps should be made carefully. And in some cases, you'll have more than one job offer. So how do you decide between firm A and firm B—or if you want to go to work for either? You profile both prospective employers. Thanks to a cache of reports, news items, and inventive inquiries, you can compile stacks of information. Together, these items provide a portrait that's as descriptive as a paint-by-numbers picture.

Start by calling the area Better Business Bureau. If there are a lot of unresolved consumer complaints, you better believe they won't be pleasant to work for! The BBB frequently has company histories on file which show the date of incorporation, who the owners are, and basically what the company does.

If your interview didn't give you this opportunity, finagle a firsthand look at the company in operation. Deliver something. Seek directions. Make every second count while you're on the premises. What image is projected? Is the atmosphere conservative or progressive? Cluttered or organized? Informal or rigid? Are there plaques or awards on the walls that give clues about their reputation or sense of pride? What reading materials are in the lobby? Of particular note is how employees relate to each other—and you! Ask yourself if this is an environment in which you could flourish.

Also check the largest area library. There may be annual reports on file, newspaper articles about their accomplishments or indiscretions, even copies of their promotional literature. Look up the owner or manager in various who's who directories, especially regional ones like *Who's Who in the West*. This often yields intriguing personal information like religious affiliation, alma mater, hobbies, etc. (Of course, doing this research *before* a prime interview will equip you with information for asking the right questions and developing rapport.)

If the firm has a net worth of from $500,000 to $1,000,000, it'll probably be listed in Dun and Bradstreet's *Middle Markets*. Here you'll find out about their main office location, any subsidiaries, names and functions of corporate officers and directors, annual sales volume, number of employees, and their SIC classification.

If the company you're checking out is a public corporation, it must file with the Securities and Exchange Commission (SEC). One of the following SEC document retrieval companies can clarify if the firm is public. Call either 800-231-3282 or 800-951-1300. If it is public, the SEC will have its annual report (known as a 10-K). This describes overall activities and reveals its financial status.

You can also verify information through Dun and Bradstreet (D&B). Most bankers will do this for a small fee. Realize this information is primarily financial. While the government can jail people for not telling the truth, D&B has no such leverage. Consequently, the data may be a sanitized version. Very small firms are not usually registered with D&B.

Look in the earlier chapter on "Researching for the Right Opportunity" for additional sleuthing ideas. Every employment interview has a double purpose. The company will probably check your qualifications. You owe it to yourself to make sure *they* measure up.

We promised earlier to tell you about a fascinating concept called telecommuting. Your time has come. Turn the page and learn about this modern-day way to stay connected, yet separate.

# 14

# Telecommuting: A Growing Solution for Urban Blues

"Who will ever use it?" people asked in 1878 when Alexander Graham Bell published the first phone book. "Who wants a letter in one day?" others scoffed when Fred Smith started Federal Express. "Nobody needs a computer on their desk!" ridiculed some when Steve Jobs and Steve Wozniak launched Apple Computers. "How will I manage my people?" supervisors wondered in the '80s when forward-thinking employees pleaded for the option to telecommute.

## *Understanding What It Is*

Exactly what is "telecommuting?" The term was coined in 1973 by Jack Nilles. It is the process of transmitting, or communicating, information electronically. While there are varying definitions, most agree telecommuters are people who are employed by companies—but who do much of their work at home. They are connected to their corporate offices by computer-network phone lines. This term is synonymous with the moving of work to people, rather than people to work. Of course, position responsibilities *and* individual personalities must mesh if this technology is to be truly exploited.

Many believe working for a salary without leaving the house is the shape of the future work force. It's much more than the separation of worker from office. Ultimately, it will be a total transformation of the structure of the work force. Teams of employees meet for conferences, lunches, or training sessions (or gossip over video screens). Smaller corporate headquarters bring them all together several times a year for rallies or retreats. Roving secretaries supply day-to-day support. Telecommuting has significant potential to protect the environment, improve economic competitiveness, bring families closer together, and enhance quality of life.

Until a decade or so ago, the only practical method for communicating quickly over long distances was by telephone. Today fax machines enable us to send printed sheets, handwritten notes, graphs, drawings, and photographs across the country almost instantly. Modems allow computers in one location to send, receive, and access information from computers and databases in other areas. And affordable video conferencing will soon permit participants in various locations to view a document on the screen, then work on it simultaneously.

This technology allows *anyone* to do almost *anything* virtually *anywhere*. Location is no longer a limitation. Occupants of households hundreds of miles from headquarters can process insurance claims, reorganize financial data, or answer 800 number calls. A major catalog sales firm has more than 100 employees working out of their homes accepting long distance orders. From a farmhouse outside a small Colorado town, a computer program designer serves clients on six continents. A speech writer telecommutes instead of braving Manhattan traffic each day. Decentralization is here. The options are infinite.

## *How Telecommuting Answers Personal Needs*

This opens stimulating alternatives to dreary daily commutes under gridlock conditions. Such travel becomes much more tolerable when it occurs only one or two days a week. Parking fees drop too. And many can move further from their workplaces—finally becoming *Country Bound!*

The more affluent will find this new structure allows them complete latitude to make non-location-specific decisions. They can relocate anywhere! And they'll simply catch a plane into the office the few times each month they must make a personal appearance. A new breed of worker will emerge: people who are cosmopolitan, yet proudly provincial.

## Trade Your Business Suit Blues for Blue Jean Dreams™

Telecommuting supports family values. When one or more parents work at home, the children feel more connected. There is more quality family time. This increased family interaction is typically coupled with reduced stress. But you can't expect to concentrate on work and still care for preschoolers by yourself. Once children are in school, however, some telecommuting parents save considerably on babysitting costs.

Flexible work schedules contribute to this. In some positions it doesn't matter when the work gets done, as long as it's accomplished in a timely fashion. Enter flextime. Maybe you'll work evenings or weekends sometimes. The choice is yours.

Another plus includes controlling your work atmosphere. You fellas don't have to shave. Ladies, if you feel like running around in shorts, a halter top, and barefoot—go for it! To get an idea of some practical home-based positions, see the following Sampling of Ideal Telecommuting Jobs.

## A SAMPLING OF IDEAL TELECOMMUTING JOBS

| | |
|---|---|
| accountant | programmer |
| analyst | public relations |
| booking agent | person |
| customer service rep | purchasing agent |
| data-entry clerk | parts orderer |
| dispatcher | reporter |
| editor | researcher |
| engineer | salesperson |
| fundraiser | secretary |
| insurance claims rep | stockbroker |
| lawyer | telemarketer |
| order processor | typesetter |

Some large companies—AT&T, Johnson & Johnson, Sears, Roebuck & Company, Wendy's International, Inc., American Express, Levi Strauss & Co., and J.C. Penney—have instituted telecommuting programs for certain positions. And a few progressive government bodies—the City of Los Angeles and the State of California Franchise Tax Board, for instance—have climbed on the bandwagon. The highest concentration of telecommuting is in the southern California area. Companies there were encouraged to start programs in the early '80s to cut down on traffic congestion. But this movement is still largely a national oddity.

We foresee growing legions of individuals chanting "home sweet office." People who love their jobs don't want to get away from it all. They want to bring it with them. If you yearn to be part of this, chances are *you* will need to take the initiative. You'll have to cut your own deal with your boss. Think through the concept and put together a benefit-laden proposal to convince your current employer to let you telecommute in your present job.

Tell your boss how telecommuting will reduce absenteeism, since you can be "on the job" at home, in spite of minor illnesses or family emergencies. Encourage your firm to offer this as an employee benefit to motivate workers and decrease turnover. (For more ammunition, closely study the company advantages outlined in the next section.)

Many in the corporate world are reluctant to endorse telecommuting. Their greatest fear centers around how they manage—and measure—employees who perform tasks off-site. Supervisors are understandably more secure when they can see people work. They're intimidated by absentee workers, feeling a little like a traffic cop at a kamikaze convention. Another concern is that "everybody" will want to do it.

And many feel it will create administrative hassles. This is partially true. Yet there is a price to pay for everything. Have these same managers looked at the escalating cost of office space or the eroding effect of absenteeism? Both are minimized by telecommuting. Even more promising, studies repeatedly show that productivity goes up when employees work from their homes.

Of course, every situation has its downside. This is no exception. As we explained in the chapter on "Working From Home—The 'Information Age' Option" (which you should probably re-read), you may suffer from feelings of isolation. The company grapevine is partially severed. There is no other person present to bounce ideas off of. You may miss out on knowledge disseminated through informal channels and observation. Be sure both the job *and your personality* translate well to a home environment. Some people wilt when they're removed from the bustle of typical office surroundings. Others need the *motivation* provided by a busy office atmosphere.

A few companies try to switch employees' status by converting them to self-employed independent contractors or paying them on a piecework basis. Beware of this; it will deprive you of benefits and might lessen your income as well.

Some feel telecommuting leads to career plateauing. It's true, not being visible can hinder advancement. This is a valid concern. It's up to you to be creative about being noticed. Send frequent computer memos. Copy strategic people. Use the technology at your fingertips to position yourself as a "doer." Be sure information about any awards you've received or articles or books you've written lands in your personnel file. When you do journey to headquarters, be professional, prepared . . . and vocal.

An excellent reference is *The Telecommuter's Handbook* by Brad Schepp. It coaches readers on how to make a case to convince their present employers to let them telecommute. Furthermore, it lists companies that have formal programs in place, or that allow telecommuting in certain situations. For additional references on telecommuting resources and consultants, see the "Private Sector Help" section of Part III.

## *From the Corporate Perspective*

From a company's viewpoint, increased productivity is a major advantage of telecommuting. Travelers Insurance Company, which has a telecommuting staff of 80, cites productivity increases of 20 percent. This is no fictional figure plucked from a dreamer's head. The human resources department determined this number by examining the amount of actual lines of code generated by programmers.

Workers see the improvement themselves. They have greater efficiency. Some report being less distracted by chatting co-workers, ringing phones, and a constant flow of office interruptions. Others love being less captive to time-wasting meetings. And parents can keep an eye on a sick child, for instance, while working at home. With traditional office arrangements, they would have to be absent from their jobs.

Alvin Toffler observed, "In a country that has been moaning about low productivity and searching for new ways to increase it, the single most anti-productive thing we do is to ship millions of workers back and forth across the landscape every morning and evening." Perhaps we're finally beginning to hear his clarion call.

The two "R's" offer more reasons telecommuting is gaining in popularity. They are *recruitment* and *retention*.

In our increasingly competitive job market, the ability to attract prime people is a serious consideration. Many professionals would prefer spending a majority of their work time at home, rather than having their off-hours gobbled up by long commutes. "Recruitment is a prime reason for offering work-at-home [arrangements] to employees," reports Travelers' Diane Bengston. The geographic boundaries of a company's hiring pool widen since candidates need not live near the worksite. This is an innovative way to entice talented people and take advantage of a broadened range of skills.

Travelers' retention statistics are impressive. After two years in the program, 28 of 35 participants remained. Says a spokesperson for Blue

Cross, "We have a waiting list a mile long, the error rate has plummeted, and no one has ever quit as a cottage coder or keyer." Telecommuting appeals to employees as a benefit. It's perceived as a "perk."

This non-traditional workplace strategy also lowers overhead by cutting facility expenses. Most of tomorrow's office workers will "likely go to a corporate office as little as once or twice a week," says Richard Romm of SCR, a firm specializing in corporate office design. Therefore corporate buildings will be smaller, serving as satellite work stations. "Most of our time will be spent at home in front of a bank of video terminals," predicts Romm. "From there we'll communicate via modems and fax machines to co-workers who may be in a different city—or country."

In addition to saving on rent, lease, or mortgage payments, companies will find other costs dropping: utility and janitorial bills, for instance. And because many telecommuters will work evenings and weekends, a mainframe computer in demand during regular working hours will be more readily accessible.

Says Henry E. Kates, president and CEO of Mutual Benefit Life, "Fiber optics will change the makeup of cities. Employees will be able to serve their companies from miles away, thus reducing the requirement for large urban office masses."

Fast electronic switching systems, fiber optics, and powerful user-friendly desktop computers make it possible. This means places like New York and North Dakota, or California and Kansas, are only a fraction of a second apart. And even more sophisticated new voice, data, and video services and products are hitting the street almost daily. With this greater use of technology, however, will come increased risks of untimely disclosures. Confidentiality and security issues will present new complications.

Especially in metropolitan areas, companies must comply with public aims to improve air quality, employ the disabled, and reduce traffic congestion. This movement helps with ordinances, legislation, and regulation covering all three mandates. California's Regulation 15 requires companies with 100 or more employees to develop commuting options for their workers. Obeying these trip-reduction and air-quality statutes must go far beyond ride sharing.

How practical is telecommuting? A survey conducted by JALA Associates indicates 20 to 30 percent of workers have location-specific jobs requiring they be in a particular place. This firm, which consults with corporations interested in telecommuting, predicts 20 to 30 percent could work part-time at home. About half of the overall work force could work at home or in a regional office, they say.

What are the criteria for this method of accomplishing tasks? First, the job has to be physically portable and require a minimum of unscheduled face-to-face contact. Second, it must be measurable, with a definite beginning and end. Otherwise managers have no reasonable way to gauge how their people are doing.

Supervisors will be additionally challenged. They must hold a tight reign on scheduling. And it's vital their out-of-office people be kept informed. Managers should also focus on results rather than processes.

Most larger firms have found specific training helpful in preparing workers and managers for a successful journey into this new job-handling adventure. Managers improve communication and planning skills. They learn to overcome their reluctance to allow employees to work without close supervision. One supervisor comments, "I do a lot of management by wandering around. I just do it [now] through remote telecommunications. I think I am still a pat-on-the-back coach." Another observes he can count on his people to give him at least 40 hours a week. "Maybe not 9:00 to 5:00," he says, "but I don't enforce that."

Experienced workers make the best candidates. "Usually telecommuters are people who have been on the job long enough to solve their own problems," says Gil Gordon of Gil Gordon Associates, a New Jersey-based management consulting firm. "They must be confident and intelligent enough to function independently."

Link Resources National Work at Home Survey data shows that telecommuting is growing rapidly among several key groups. They include large organizations with more than 1,000 employees and small firms with less than 10 employees. This form of work also appeals to business executives, managers, engineers, and scientists. Strangely, few mid-sized firms participate.

Business guru Tom Peters admits to being a broken record: "Don't just bash hierarchy, destroy it—if you want to survive," he challenges managers. In his *On Achieving Excellence* newsletter, he calls telecommuting "perhaps the ultimate bureaucracy-bashing tool." Peters practices what he preaches. He confesses to spending ⅔ of his year in Vermont—as the telecommuting manager/owner of his businesses, which are headquartered in Palo Alto, California.

## *Communities Also Benefit*

This workplace strategy addresses several hot national issues: air pollution, traffic congestion, employee recruitment, and improved child care options. These are tough challenges for civic leaders in both the private and public sectors.

Telecommuting is being spurred on by stressed-out commuters, a growing concern for the environment, plus federal and state government initiatives. It decreases the need for mass transit, reduces fuel consumption, limits the demand for transportation infrastructures, and improves air quality. Environmental impact can be significant. It also offers increased employment opportunities for those with limited mobility.

In a speech presented at the University of California—Irvine on July 16, 1991, John Niles—president of Global Telematics—stated, "The telecommuting phenomenon gives economic development activists a new option for long-run regional improvement." He pointed out that not only growth, but *quality*, should be considered by sophisticated economic development proponents. Niles explained that *5.5 million* people telecommute today. And the number is growing so rapidly it will double by 1995!

What are some tangible results? If only 5 percent of commuters in Los Angeles County telecommuted only one day each week, have you any idea the travel saved? A trip to the sun plus 18 round trips to the moon: 205 million miles! They'd put 47,000 fewer tons of pollution into the atmosphere. And they'd save 9.5 million gallons of gasoline a year.

From immense Los Angeles, California, to tiny Telluride, Colorado is a huge leap. Yet when it comes to technology, they're as close as a new bride and groom. Telluride, with a population of slightly over 1,200, may even have the edge. Perched in these 10,000-foot-high mountains is the state-of-the-art home of John Naisbitt and Patricia Aburdene. From what Naisbitt calls his "control center" (he hasn't been in his Washington, DC, office for years), he reaches into many countries each day to pluck information and monitor global trends.

Telluride is also planning a telecommunity of 800 households called Sky Field. Every unit will be wired to fiber-optic telephone lines, satellite uplinks, and other fancy gadgetry that will change as technology evolves. "The world is moving steadily toward digital work forms," says Link Resources' Tom Miller. "Once you make that transition, where you work is almost an afterthought."

From President George Bush we hear, "Telecommuting is a concept that is emerging from the grassroots of America, and its time has come. Across the nation, both employers and employees are recognizing the many benefits . . . " He continues by observing, "Most important, perhaps, telecommuting benefits families as well as business. In today's changing labor force, telecommuting helps to meet the needs of working parents. It fosters productivity and improves morale by allowing parents to work closer to the people that they're really working for: their children."

*Trade Your Business Suit Blues for Blue Jean Dreams™*

Ironically, this chapter could also be called "Telecommuting: A Growing Solution for *Rural* Blues." Telecommunications has been hailed as having as dramatic a potential for rural America in the 1990s—as did railroads in the 1870s and interstate highways in the 1950s. As the traditional staples of rural economies—agriculture, mining, and manufacturing—falter, telecommunications can infuse these idyllic isolated places with new life.

People who are free to perform their work from any location will often pick more bucolic surroundings. Like Alexander Graham Bell, Fred Smith, and Steve Jobs, the pioneers in this exciting field are pointing the way to the future. There's no question telecommuting holds the key to freeing millions of frustrated workers . . . and reviving thousands of dying country communities.

# 15

# Generating Capital to Launch Your Venture

Going into business without adequate preparation is like trying to determine the nature of the ocean by studying a cup of water. You need the right tools . . . whether they be money, expertise, or imagination. This chapter is about all three.

Now that you know you want to go into business for yourself, creating "adventure" capital to make your dream come true is the first step. There are more ways to generate cash than there are instruments in an orchestra. Some are more viable than others for the person desiring to set up a rural enterprise. You're sure to find innovative ideas for raising money as we explore and exploit these methods.

Some of the most visible possibilities—banks, government programs, and venture capitalists—may be the *least* important sources of business capital. Most new firms gain financial support one of two ways: through their owners or via private investors. The role of the private investor is underestimated and undervalued because it is neither institutionalized nor documented.

How much do you really need to get started? The amount may not be as much as you thought. According to a study done by the National Federation of Independent Business, one out of three new businesses start with $10,000 or less. And you can use that to leverage a venture in the

$50,000 to $100,000 range. The next most common capital investment amount is from $20,000 to $49,000.

## *Tapping into Personal Resources*

You may want to refer to the section on Cashing Out with Your Urban Equity in Chapter 3. For many of us, our metropolitan real estate is just the nest egg needed to launch a country business.

Have a passbook savings account, CDs, or annuities? Most people are tempted to use these to start new businesses. Don't. Once it's gone, it's gone. On the other hand, there's an old axiom that says, "Thems that got, gets." Never was this more true than when approaching your banker for a loan. If you have $7,000 in savings, there is little hassle in borrowing another $7,000. The lending institution probably won't even require your account as collateral. Now you have $7,000 of other people's money (OPM), plus your original $7,000 (less the amount of interest on the debt, of course). If you reverse the process, though—spending the $7,000, then trying to borrow that amount—you have about as much chance for success as the guy who went bear hunting with a switch.

There may be other assets you can use to capitalize your business. Do you receive rents from real estate or dividends from stock? What about royalties from a book, song, computer software, or invention? One acquaintance used her hefty divorce settlement to start a new rural life.

According to the October 6, 1991, edition of the *Boston Globe*, baby boomers may *inherit* the nest egg needed to start a business. Due to historic gains in the stock market, high real estate prices, and the growth of millions of family-owned businesses, baby boomers can expect to inherit an estimated $8 trillion in cash and other assets over the next 20 years!

In the meantime, consider your credit cards. Many a creative financier has breathed life into a small business thanks to multiple MasterCards or VISAs. In fact, some folks plan years ahead to use this strategy. They amass as many cards as possible, use them regularly, and pay punctually. As a reward, the card companies keep raising their limit. We know of one person who borrowed almost $30,000 on his credit cards. The downside is interest rates for this money are exorbitant. The debt service cost could be devastating.

Building a good personal credit history will go a long way toward helping you in business. Borrowing increasingly larger amounts from your bank, S&L, or credit union—and repaying promptly—is a good start. If you anticipate doing your own thing, get any personal loans *before* you quit your present job. Bankers are understandably skeptical of the newly self-employed. Business start-ups usually can't get unsecured loans. In most cases, the business owner must put up collateral—his or her home, plus a combination of other personal or business assets. And most banks require your personal guarantee, sometimes even that of your spouse if the collateral assets are jointly owned. Often your individual financial statement becomes the basis for the loan.

Be aware there are different levels of bank officers. While a regular loan officer at a branch may have a limit of $10,000, a senior loan officer at the main location can go much higher without requiring committee approval. Usually the higher you begin, the better your chances. If you dead-end at the local level, ask how to contact a regional investment bank specializing in financing small companies. There you'll gain access to a wide range of lenders and investors, including pension funds and insurance companies.

An acquaintance of ours used another approach. We don't recommend it, but you be the judge. Mike told his banker he wanted a loan to go into business. He was turned down. Later Mike learned if he'd asked for a "home improvement" loan or a "vacation" loan, it would have been approved.

Perhaps you have a vested interest in a retirement fund or pension plan. They often make loans at reasonable rates. Consider this as a revenue source.

If you're a mature person, lump-sum retirement benefits may well pave the way to an exciting new enterprise. There are all sorts of annuities: IRAs, Keogh Plans, plus a myriad of private and government pension plans. Some 6,000 government plans cover federal civil service, the military, state, and municipal employees. Of course, each has different rules about the years of service required, age of eligibility, payouts, etc.

Ex-executives laid off as a result of mergers and downsizing sometimes receive a cash settlement called a *golden parachute*. It is meant to ease the bumpy ride back to employment. Instead, a golden parachute often aids the leap to freedom. Out-placement specialists estimate that more than 20 percent of the people they see as a result of downsizing go into business on their own. Many executives open consulting practices, thus capitalizing on expertise developed in the corporate world.

Life insurance is another funding option. Possibly a sizeable chunk is lying there in cash value. Presto, magic! Such loans require no qualification and carry attractive interest rates. If you took out a policy before 1965, for instance, you can typically borrow an amount equal to the policy's cash value for about six percent interest.

But what if you've got lousy credit and need an infusion of quick cash? One non-traditional answer for a loan might be a pawn shop. Yes, you read right. You won't get big bucks here and the neighborhood may make you feel about as welcome as a furrier at an animal rights convention. Yet if you need a few hundred or a thousand to shoestring an idea, it's a possibility. Such assets as stereo systems, expensive watches, diamond rings, sterling silver sets, musical instruments, guns, and family heirlooms are most likely to turn the most cash.

Another unorthodox seed money source is unemployment insurance. In Washington they've started a pilot program with 500 unemployed applicants. Called the Self-Employment Demonstration Project, it lets jobless workers use their unemployment checks to start their own businesses—up to a maximum of $7,000. The aim is to reduce unemployment and boost small business development.

## Reaching Beyond Yourself

In these days of troubled S&Ls, many potential small businesspeople turn to F&Fs: Family and Friends. In 65 percent of the cases, the start-up capital needed for a new business is obtained from personal savings, relatives, and friends. Yet many people shun approaching their relatives and friends. If you believe in the business enough to put yourself on the line, is it fair to *protect* your loved ones from participating? Try to find family, neighbors, colleagues, and buddies who are on your wavelength . . . *and are soft touches*. Sure some will give you a reception as cool as the backside of a pillow. But you'll never know unless you ask.

There are various ways of structuring such arrangements. Do prepare a written document specifying terms and conditions. It must be clear whether the lender will get equity in the new business, sit on the board of directors, or have any say in day-to-day operations. Family-owned businesses are enjoying a resurgence. Just be sure yours doesn't have so many strings attached it braids into a noose around your neck.

## Money from Heaven

Another popular source of start-up money is to find an *angel*. This term refers to a private venture capitalist not affiliated with any institution. Often these people are successful entrepreneurs who yearn to re-live the thrill of the chase. Usually an angel won't require you to put up any collateral; rather he or she will want a piece of the action. In his book *Finding Private Venture Capital for Your Firm*, author Robert Gaston estimates there are some 720,000 angels committing somewhere in the range of $56 billion annually. The angel's average equity investment is $64,000.

That's in sharp contrast to professional venture capitalists, who more typically finance companies seeking upwards of $2 million. Some are interested in smaller potatoes, however. If you need large amounts of money, a $90 financial computer program called *VenCap Data Quest* has an interactive directory of all U.S. venture capital sources that manage legitimate funds and are currently making investments.

But let's get back to angels. An additional way an angel can serve as your guardian is by offering advice. Those who enjoy the challenges of start-ups can help a fledgling entrepreneur ask all the right questions.

So where do you find these investment cherubs? Go through your Rolodex. Ask around your professional community. Talk with lawyers, bankers, and CPAs. Search out people in your industry who have made money. Or visit one of the 100 or so venture capital clubs around the nation. You can get the *Directory of Venture Capital Clubs* by sending $9.95 to the International Venture Capital Institute, Inc., P. O. Box 1333, Stamford, CT 06904, 203-323-3143. These groups hold regular informal meetings. Here guest speakers give presentations, angels hear your proposition, and lots of networking goes on. Some folks even find their angel by advertising in the "Business Opportunities" classified section in newspapers and business magazines.

These informal investors form a diverse group, but there are some common denominators. They're usually above average in age, education, and affluence. A study of 463 investors, prepared for the Small Business Administration, revealed that few are millionaires. In fact, a third had family incomes below $60,000. How much do they invest in a single entrepreneurial deal? Twenty-one percent of them put in less than $10,000, 43 percent less than $25,000, and 64 percent less than $50,000.

Angels usually want returns of three to five times their investment in about five years. (They are not just *financing* your operation in return for a simple payback on the loan.) Angels are *investors*. They expect substantial ownership in a company and strong growth potential. That can present a problem. Some start-ups give away too large a slice of the pie and ultimately harm themselves. Know, and be able to articulate, the difference if you want to appear credible.

## *Securing Conventional Bank Financing*

Money is expensive any way you look at it. There would be no problem if you were a Fortune 500 company and could borrow at the prime rate. But you're not. So the banker will expect to get several percent above prime as a precautionary way to hedge his or her bet and protect the bank's investors. When someone quotes 5 percent above prime, that means if prime is 12.0 you will pay 17.0. Today variable interest rates are popular because they allow lending institutions to further protect their profits.

There are techniques for talking your way into money. One is to practice giving a 20-minute presentation. Ideally, rehearse with a video camera. Short of that, stand in front of a mirror and use an audio cassette recorder. Monitor your eye contact, comfort level, and voice projection. Dress conservatively for your interview. Bankers are known to be a restrained group. Don't inflate your numbers, it smacks of amateurism. If you're selling a product, be sure to take samples with you or prepare an impressive "dummy" mock-up.

Not every bank feels the same, so if you're appalled by what one says, try another. Geography also impacts your ability to borrow. In high growth parts of the country, money is easier to get. Some states have laws that prevent banks from taking actions that other states encourage.

In many places, rural banks don't handle commercial loans. They aren't simple like car and residential loans that turn over fast. Yet counter to expectations, research shows some local rural banks taking a strong role in providing start-up capital for new businesses in their area.

It's wise to apply a dual strategy: work through local lenders, but also take additional steps to access federal and state financing programs. Secure as many diverse sources of capital as possible. Cultivate them deliberately and vigorously. Use the following Financing Structure Worksheet to help you keep track of your use of funds and potential sources. It's important to match the figure in the Monthly Debt Service column against your monthly cash flow. You must have adequate income to cover this debt. Look at each month individually and make any necessary adjustments promptly. Also take into consideration seasonal changes, especially if you're in a tourist-oriented business that has wide income swings from season to season.

Finally, don't rely on a handshake. Always get commitments on paper. Then your dream isn't vulnerable to the whims of banks or investors. Everything is subject to change. Rates vary. Policies are revamped. Bank officers retire. And hopefully your negotiation acumen improves.

If they're unwilling to give you a real estate mortgage, inquire about a chattel mortgage on your equipment or inventory (if applicable). Equipment is typically financed over three to five years. There's no way you'll get a 10-year loan on a piece of equipment that only has a value (life) of two years. Working capital is usually financed over three years, buildings and land over seven.

You may be able to convince a banker to go with deferred payments. This option takes into consideration business swings and is especially helpful for tourist-oriented enterprises. You pay more during the good months and less during the slow ones. This helps you get over a hump until

# Financing Structure Worksheet

**SPECIMEN**
We encourage readers to photocopy these pages

| Use of Funds | | Source of Funds | | | | | |
|---|---|---|---|---|---|---|---|
| Use | Amount | Lender's Home | Term of Loan | Estimated Interest Rate | ** Collateral | Amount of Loan | *** Monthly Debt Service |
| Land | $ | | | | | | |
| Bldg. Construction/Renovation | $ | | | | | | |
| Machinery & Equipment | $ | | | | | | |
| Furniture & Fixtures | $ | | | | | | |
| * Leasehold Improvements | $ | | | | | | |
| Contingencies/Emergencies | $ | | | | | | |
| Working Capital/Inventory | $ | | | | | | |
| TOTAL COST | $ | | | | TOTAL SOURCES = $ | | $ |

* Improvements to the physical property. ** Property or securities pledged by the borrower. *** Cost of principal, interest, and possibly taxes and insurance.

the cash flow comes in line to cover the dept service. Payments may be structured 75/25, for instance, with the highest amount due during the seasonal tourist time.

How much can you get? At the max, 70 percent of the total price. And then only if you've put together a dynamite business plan (discussed shortly) and have a strong personal financial history. If you're purchasing real property, the terms of the mortgage can vary significantly. Naturally the longer the loan, the less your monthly payments—but the more overall interest you'll pay.

Here's one strategy that works beautifully for some people. Take as long a term loan as you possibly can . . . even if you think you could handle a shorter one with a higher payback arrangement. Then *double* your payments every month. That extra money goes towards the principle and retires the loan faster, saving you a fortune in interest. It also gives you a safety valve. If business gets sluggish, you aren't stuck with arbitrary high monthly mortgage payments.

Be wary of *balloons*. Unlike the colorful toys of your youth, this means a massive payment which comes due at a distant point. It can quickly drain all the color out of your future. When the time comes, you must either fork up all the cash or pay to refinance.

For a list called Lending Sources, see the Private Sector Help section of Part III.

# *Franchise Financing: Using the Team Approach*

In spite of recent economic woes, franchisors are bullish about financing. Banks and other lending institutions recognize these businesses as solid investments. They realize the franchisor has a vested interest in the franchisee. This interest translates into support. And it's that support which gives new franchises their excellent chance for success.

Some companies provide expert guidance for their potential investors. A Dallas-based franchise, I Can't Believe It's Yogurt, employs a full-time staff member to help qualified franchisees find financing. They even work with a special lender who knows all about their track record. Other franchisors also address the complicated chore of completing applications, aiding prospective franchisees in wading through loan paperwork. And some headquarters have aligned themselves with large leasing companies that help their affiliates finance equipment and vehicles.

When Gina and Mark Edwards decided to buy a franchise in Apopka, Florida, it was a struggle to come up with the required amount. Their choice, Pak Mail, stepped in to assist in several ways. They helped negotiate the shopping mall lease, putting in penalty clauses if the project didn't finish on time. And the Pak Mail area distributor waited for his fee of $7,000 until the couple's store was operating. "We were fortunate to have a good franchise like Pak Mail behind us because they did some things that helped us get through that first year," says Gina Edwards.

Even more exciting, many franchisors are digging into their own pockets to bolster prospective recruits. Don Dwyer—president of the Waco, Texas, Dwyer Group—says, "We will finance ¾ of the initial franchise fee, allowing our franchisees to pay us back $50 a week at 12 percent interest." Another franchisor that will fund a large portion of the franchisee's investment is Steamatic, Inc. of Dallas, Texas. "We finance up to $15,000 for hard assets," explains Vice President Bill Sims.

Debra Janos learned her business from the ground up. She joined Merry Maids as a part-time cleaning person eight years ago. Soon she was working full-time, then managing the office. Janos quickly realized the potential and set about to buy a franchise. Although she worked three jobs, she couldn't come up with the needed $28,000. So Merry Maid's parent corporation, Service Master, stepped in with $10,000 in direct financing, enabling Debra to set up shop in Las Vegas.

Franchise financing can be achieved in other ways too. Dan Smith wanted to open a Juicy Lucy's outlet in Naples, Florida. But he couldn't handle the hefty $325,000 to $375,000 fee. So he got creative with the developer of a strip shopping center he determined would be a good location. He formed a partnership, working out a build-to-suit arrangement in which the mall developer incurred the cost to construct the fast food outlet, then charged Smith a monthly rental.

In this arrangement, the developer assumes the risk. In exchange the developer gets "a solid tenant who generates an instant income flow in their center even before the rest of the project is completed," says Smith. His investment amounted to the $25,000 franchise fee, $25,000 for working capital, plus a $95,000 loan package for equipment leasing. Comments Smith, "My liability is half of what it would be if I had bought the franchise outright." Which all goes to prove franchise financing is alive and well . . . and using the team approach to partner for profit.

## *Getting the Government on Your Side*

Seed capital from Uncle Sam—or his state, county, or local counterparts—has financed many a fledgling business. Government funding programs are especially accessible to women, minorities, the handicapped, and companies who create new jobs to escalate the area's economy.

**SBA loans** are negotiated through a conventional lender (also known as a sponsor), but guaranteed up to 90 percent by the Small Business Administration (SBA). The new SBA administrator, Patricia Saiki, says the major loan program volume has jumped 28 percent over the five months since September, 1991. This makes the Small Business Administration the small firms' lender of *first* resort. During 1991, more than 40,000 entrepreneurs sought 7a loans (which can't exceed $750,000). Almost 19,500 applications won approval.

Loans must be paid back in eight years and carry interest rates slightly lower than a commercial loan, usually two or three points above prime. But just because it's government backed, doesn't make it easy to get. You'll still need a powerful business plan to get you in the door with bankers or to attract investors. Cash flow projections are also necessary. The paperwork you do almost guarantees you'll have the answers for bankers too.

Want to know quickly if you're eligible for an SBA loan? The SBA and the National Business Association recently teamed up to offer a free, time-saving software program called *First Time Review*. It's available for either IBM or Apple Macintosh from the National Business Association, P. O. Box 870728, Dallas, TX 75287, 800-456-0440.

The SBA also licenses **Small Business Investment Companies (SBICs)**. These are private investor firms which can borrow up to four dollars from the SBA for each dollar of private capital they have. They move quickly and are relatively uncomplicated to deal with. For a list of SBICs and their specialties, write to the National Association of SBICs, 1156 Fifteenth Street NW, Suite 1101, Washington, DC 20005, 202-833-8230.

**State funds** are another source. All 50 states have some sort of program designed to help small businesses raise capital. They're competing with each other to make their business climates more attractive to smaller firms. This adds jobs and boosts tax revenues.

Pennsylvania's Ben Franklin Partnership Program hands out seed grants up to $35,000 to qualified companies doing product research in technology. "One of the principal activities of the Ben Franklin program," explains Andrew T. Greenberg, Pennsylvania's executive deputy secretary of commerce, "is to provide grants for cooperative research and new product development between businesses and universities in our state." Their grants typically range between $5,000 and $50,000 and are available to individuals or companies for early-stage research. Recipients must match the funds.

Ohio has a similar plan dubbed the Thomas Edison Seed Development Fund. Once an entrepreneur's research project receives approval, the seed program directs the funds to an Ohio academic institution—which conducts the research for and with the entrepreneur.

To find information on state funding contact the National Council of State Legislatures, 1050 Seventeenth Street, Denver, CO 80265, 303-623-7800.

And to tap into a wonderful road map of 9,000 sources for free help, information, and *money*, get a copy of *Government Giveaways for Entrepreneurs* by Matthew Lesko. Next year more than 150,000 businesses are going to get funds from the government to start or expand a business. You can be one of them! See the "Bibliography/Recommended Reading" section for ordering information.

**The United States Department of Agriculture** (USDA) is responsible for about 29 money programs which entrepreneurs can use to begin or enlarge a business. For example, the Business and Industrial Loan Program can be used to start almost any kind of business as long as it is in a town of fewer than 50,000 people. And the USDA's Farmers Home Administration wants to promote economic stability and job creation in rural areas. It guarantees loans up to 90 percent of the principal advanced, to bolster weak rural economies and create jobs. For more information, call 202-720-4323.

## *Enterprise Zones: Waiting Bonanzas*

Another intriguing option available to some budding entrepreneurs is enterprise zones. Currently there are about 500 state zones in 37 states. And the federal government is expected to set up about 100 federal enterprise zones soon, one-third of which will be in rural areas. The concept is to create a pro-business atmosphere and bolster lagging area economies. These zones encompass tax incentives and credits offered to businesses which expand or locate within certain areas around the country.

Cuba, Missouri—a village of 2,100 people located 75 miles southwest of St. Louis—is one example of how this program turned a town from gloom to boom. When two factories closed in 1984, unemployment soared to 18 percent. Enterprise zone incentives coaxed more than a dozen new industries into Cuba. They, in turn, spawned 750 additional jobs.

Missouri has 33 rural and urban enterprise zones. They provide a variety of tax incentives for new jobs, investments, and training. And local property tax abatements run for 10 to 25 years.

Although not all businesses qualify for all incentives, here's a sampling of some tax breaks: triple investment tax credit and new business facility job credits. These are for firms that create new jobs, add value to agricultural products, or provide health insurance to their employees. Other inducements include state sales tax and use tax exemptions for manufacturing equipment, tax credits for research and development or the rehabilitation of vacant buildings, even local government tax incentives. For more information contact the American Association of Enterprise Zones at 1420 Sixteenth Street NW, Suite 103, Washington, DC 20036, 202-466-2687.

While financing a fledgling business is never easy, there is another source that may be willing to back your start-up. Community development funds are available in some areas. These are for businesses likely to have a direct and positive impact on the community, such as job creation. If you find this source, investigate the ratio of dollars lent to jobs created. Organizations that manage such funds provide loans at or above prime, or sometimes money in exchange for stock.

In Wiscasset, Maine, Coastal Enterprises Inc. raises funds from private foundations and corporations as well as from the state itself. In turn, it dispenses loans and puts together equity investments in small businesses. Since 1977 it has raised about $9 million and financed some 150 enterprises with credit of up to $50,000. To determine where such funding is available, contact the National Congress of Community Economic Development, 1612 K Street NW, Suite 510, Washington, DC 20006, 202-659-8411.

## *Developing a Business Plan*

No matter where you go for funding, chances are you'll need a well-thought-out business plan to unlock the vaults of the financial community. This is a formal walk-through on paper of everything you and a potential investor or lender need to know about your venture. It should provide a detailed description of your company, its products or services, management, market, competition, history, and forecasts.

Fuel their interest. Tell why your company is special, why your product or service is unique, and why you expect success. Any financial institution or individual investor wants to know there is meaning, purpose, and commitment behind a company seeking funding.

And if you're purchasing an existing building or business that has been appraised, study that appraisal. They often contain errors. Look for flaws; check the overall level of accuracy. A solid appraisal attracts financing just as the Indy 500 attracts racing wannabees.

Including appropriate financial documents will automatically raise your octane rating in their eyes. These documents should encompass profit-and-loss and cash-flow statements, and a balance sheet showing assets and liabilities for the next three to five years. Experiment with different growth rates: high and low scenarios. If you're still in the red, you'll also need a break-even analysis.

Of course for new businesses, conservatively calculated estimates must suffice for much of this information. Remember when creating your business plan that sound, stable management strategies go further than pie-in-the-sky projections.

And pay attention to the physical presentation package. Your plan is a direct reflection of you. Give it clout by providing an attractive, well-organized, easy-to-read proposal. This favorably affects decision makers. For help in preparing a business plan, call your local SBA office for the nearest location of the Service Corps of Retired Executives (SCORE) and the Small Business Development Center. Most SCORE and SBDC services are free. Local universities and community colleges also offer useful courses.

The area economic development group may also be of help. Their whole purpose is to entice businesses to their area, so it only makes sense that they assist worthy ventures in obtaining necessary start-up loans. Coordinate your visitation time to avoid holidays, peak vacation times, or weekends. Ask very specific questions. Rather than saying, "Do you have any ideas on how I can finance this business?" go with something like, "What three local avenues do you feel are most viable for potential financing?" and "Who should I see there?"

## *More Funding Ideas*

When searching for capital—creativity, persistence, and action are the keys. Here are a few random thoughts on other possibilities.

What about using sympathetic suppliers as a form of short-term financing? A major vendor that will wait 90 days to be paid may be just what you need to get a new establishment off the ground. If you're looking into a franchise, talk with the franchisor about providing financing.

If you're a super salesperson, you may be able to convince a banker to finance *purchase orders* for your product. (They sometimes do this on receivables for established customers.) Here's how it worked for one firm: When they got a purchase order, it went to their outside accountants who verified that the order was accurate and the purchaser was credit worthy. Then the bank advanced them 40 percent of the value of the order. This equaled their production cost. When they billed the customer, they faxed a copy to the bank, which sent them another 40 percent. Finally, when the customer paid, the bank took its 80 percent of the bill, plus interest, and sent them the rest—which was their profit. In effect, they pledged their purchase orders as collateral to gain short-term financing.

Are you a start-up technology company? Corporate giants and global conglomerates are a rich source of capital. While it's difficult to find the key players, once you've identified the corporations most likely interested in your technology, contact the corporate development director. But be wary. More than one inventor has inherited heartache along with hard cash by climbing in bed with a giant corporation.

Grassroots peer-group lending programs are cropping up around the country to help low and moderate income individuals become self-employed. They are especially prevalent in areas suffering from severe unemployment. Many of these aim at home-based or garage-based entrepreneurs.

One such alternative program is The Good Faith Fund in southeastern Arkansas. It makes small loans to anybody with an idea and four friends who also might need to borrow a modest amount. Borrowers—who require no collateral, work experience, or credit rating—can get from $500 to $5,000. It operates on the simple principle of people helping people and being responsible to one another and the fund. For information on this and other similar experiments in economic development, contact Julia Vindasius, Director, Good Faith Fund, 1210 Cherry Street, Suite 9, Pine Bluff, AR 71601, 501-535-6233.

Another option for aspiring entrepreneurs is *bootstrapping*. While you won't get any money here, you may save a bundle and help cover your start-up expenses. This is an arrangement to supply something other than funding to a new business. Such strategic alliances frequently come as a result of good networking. Companies that would benefit from your success, or individuals who simply support you in what you're trying to do, may be willing to loan you an office... or let you use their production facilities or computer system after hours. Perhaps a colleague will give you access to her conference room if you need to impress clients. Maybe a business associate will have his secretary accept phone calls for you. The opportunities here are bound only by your imagination, contacts, and chutzpa.

Of course, if you're buying an established business, one of the best sources for financing is the present owner. This is especially true when times are tough and money is tight. After all, who's better acquainted with its potential? (Short of that, talk with area real estate personnel about other local businesspeople who might be receptive to a shared risk proposition.)

Sellers are often anxious to make installment sales to postpone or reduce their capital gains tax on the sale. Have you noticed ads that say "only 29 percent down?" That's a tip off that the owner wants to spread the actual proceeds of the sale over a period of years to avoid IRS penalties. The

Internal Revenue Service regulation allows the seller to report income in the year of actual payment if he or she receives less than 30 percent of the total amount in the year the sale occurred.

> **Marilyn:** *Being a good detective can pay big dividends. That was so in our case. When our telephone communication was abruptly interrupted on the remote ranch we operated from in southern Colorado, we had no choice but to make a hasty retreat, or lose all our clients. We pinpointed five other Colorado communities to consider, then hastily began looking for real estate. The odds weren't good. We had no time to sell our ranch, thus no down payment for new property.*
>
> *By calling the Federal Deposit Insurance Corporation (FDIC) and inquiring about the towns we were considering, I learned that Buena Vista had suffered a bank failure a couple of years previously. After making friends with the area coordinator, I discovered a few pieces of property still on the FDIC's rolls. I ended up knowing more about them than any of the local real estate brokers.*
>
> *As it turned out, one was a 4,000-square-foot church with an accompanying rectory. Since it was a unique property and they'd been unable to sell it, the price was amazingly low. It was perfect for our needs. We could convert the church into offices and live in the rectory. Because we had an excellent company credit rating, and Tom was a relentless negotiator, we purchased the church and accompanying house in our corporate name—without even a personal guarantee. We offered $5,000 less than the asking price and a 15 percent down payment, which we scraped from corporate funds. Miracles do still happen. You just have to give them a nudge!*

To explore properties available through this resource, prepare yourself to wind through miles of red tape. Start your journey by calling the FDIC regional or consolidated office in the area where you want to relocate. A list appears in Part III. Ask for the Owned Real Estate Department.

Another source for seized properties is the Resolution Trust Corporation (RTC). It is the official body for handling commercial and residential real estate liquidated from savings and loans after January, 1989. As you can imagine, this federal S&L bailout program has a huge inventory! The sad fact is the U.S. government is becoming our nation's biggest property owner.

While officials tell us they typically want to sell property for more than the appraisal value, which is the current market price, you can occasionally pick up a bargain. This is especially true in depressed areas. One real estate broker spoke of property going for 85 percent of the appraised value. A list of the RTC Sales Centers also appears in Part III.

With both the FDIC and RTC you purchase property "as is." For instance, we had to install a new furnace in the building we bought. You also receive only a quit claim deed, which might concern some people. Both agencies prefer buyers who come with financing in hand, but they do underwrite loans in some situations.

Also, don't overlook the possibility of finding a great piece of property at a bargain price by scanning the local paper for tax sales. Auctions are a common event in country areas and sometimes a way to acquire real estate cheaply.

A company can always make it through thick and thin . . . providing the thick isn't the owner's head and the thin isn't the capital! We hope you've found ideas here to fatten your funding. Now that you have a grasp of your financing options, let's move on to discussing all the particulars that go into setting up a successful business.

# 16

# Pivotal Start-Up Considerations

Now that you've pinpointed precisely *what* you want to do, let's explore *how* best to do it. We'll decipher all the damnable details—chop the elephant-sized job of start-up considerations into easily digested, bite-sized pieces.

Going from paycheck to president can be one of the most exciting—and potentially intimidating—adventures you'll ever embark upon. Our goal in this chapter is to equip you with the gear to make your pilgrimage easy and successful. Hindsight is a tragic teacher. Here we outfit you with the foresight essential for gaining prosperity.

We'll look at the structure your enterprise might take—sole proprietorship, partnership, or corporation—plus registration and licensing procedures. Business incubators will be examined. So will creating a mission statement and business plan, and deciding on a location. Additionally, the subjects of finding reliable suppliers, not to mention qualified employees, will be addressed.

## *Business Structure Options*

One of the first decisions to be made involves what business classification to use. A 1989 report showed that 13.2 million businesses were organized as proprietorships, 4 million as corporations, and 1.6 million as partnerships. Let's briefly examine the pros and cons of these three options:

In a **Sole Proprietorship** you operate as a self-employed individual. The majority of fledgling businesses begin this way because there are no legal setup fees and you alone call the shots. Profits or losses are considered part of your personal income. Even if you begin this way, you can always incorporate later.

If your plans are large-scale and aggressive, **Incorporation** probably makes sense. The drawbacks include setup costs and annual fees, greater regulations from state and federal authorities, more complicated accounting procedures, unemployment taxes covering yourself as an employee, higher social security taxes, plus loss of the ability to operate in a freewheeling way. There are also distinct advantages. The normal (Chapter C) corporation can pay many of the legitimate business expenses from pre-tax dollars. These include medical and disability coverage, liability insurance, perhaps even a portion of life insurance—all of which can be written off as a cost of doing business. And you can participate in employee benefits not available to unincorporated owner-operators: tax-sheltered pension plans, profit sharing, and bonuses.

Incorporating also typically gives you personal protection. As a legal entity, it shields you against individual liability, thus protecting personal property that could be considered fair game in a lawsuit. Once incorporated, you can also attract investors by selling shares in the business. (Be sure to get expert advice when doing this.) One further consideration: if a sole proprietor or partner dies, the business is legally dissolved and must be reorganized to continue. Not so with a corporation. It has permanency.

Some small businesses use a simplified **Subchapter S** corporation. While this offers some tax advantages, it doesn't let you write off insurance costs. This structure does, however, allow profits to flow directly through to shareholders. It is especially useful as a tax shelter when losses are involved, providing there is other income to shelter. In this variation on the corporate theme, the IRS allows business owners to declare all income and losses on their individual returns.

**General Partnerships** work for some people. They can also be fraught with problems. In a general partnership, each person is completely responsible for the debts and obligations of the whole partnership. What that means is your partner can incur bills and make promises you don't even know about, and *you* will be held financially responsible. If the relationship turns sour, your partner can really do you in!

In a **Limited Partnership** there is at least one general partner and one limited partner. The general partner is fully liable for all obligations and controls the business. The limited partners have just that—limited liability and rights of control.

It's wise to hire an accountant or attorney to advise you about the most advantageous business structure for your individual needs. Each person's requirements are different. Saving money here can end up costing you a great deal in the long run.

## *Name Registration Requirements*

Naming your business is an exciting, creative activity we cover fully in the upcoming chapter on "Creating Attention Getters and Revenue Reapers." But be aware that once you've decided on a name, in most states you have to register it. Get particulars from the state corporation office, the county clerk, or your attorney. If you are using anything but your full legal name, you are operating under a "fictitious" name. Sometimes this is also called a "dba," which means Doing Business As.

Many states also require you to publish this proposed trade name to allow anyone already using such a name to object to it. The process takes longer than growing your hair long. Several weeks elapse as the notice must appear repeatedly. Find a small weekly newspaper where many other fictitious name ads appear. It will be cheaper to advertise there.

## *Licensing and Regulatory Procedures*

Talk with the local chamber of commerce to determine what steps must be taken—and places contacted—to get yourself properly taxed, licensed, and regulated. (That one should have to request help with such dastardly duties!) Procedures vary from state to state, county to county, town to town. Some states have a business start-up kit which condenses the process and allows you to fill out all your papers at once.

In some places, occupations like barbers, taxi drivers, psychologists, kennel owners, child care providers, plumbers, and architects all require a special license, examination, and/or approval from an appropriate state agency. If your new enterprise involves food or liquor you can definitely count on needing a state license. The same probably holds true if what you plan involves **haz**ardous substances or could pollute the air or water. Additionally, check with your city clerk's office to verify whether your new occupation falls under any special city licensing regulations.

Every business must have a federal tax employer identification number. This number is needed for filing tax returns and will be requested by other firms with whom you do business. It is obtained free from the nearest IRS office.

Most municipalities also require you to have a local business license. Costs are usually between $20 and $100 and must be renewed annually. Check at the town hall for details.

And if you're opening a retail establishment, or purchasing goods to be resold, you'll need a resale tax number. This lets you buy merchandise for resale without paying tax. You will, of course, need to collect taxes when you sell the item, then later remit that tax to the state. For more information contact the state tax office.

When you apply for a seller's permit you'll be asked to estimate your anticipated revenue. This is a time to be humble. If you indicate you expect terrific sales, you'll likely be instructed to leave a hefty deposit against future taxes, plus file quarterly tax reports. On the other hand, those who expect meager sales often dodge the deposit completely and need only report annually. For more information about tax laws and how they'll affect your new business—plus good general financial advice—you'll want to get your hands on *Small Time Operator: How to Start Your Own Small Business, Keep Your Books, Pay Your Taxes, & Stay Out of Trouble!* by Bernard Kamoroff, CPA. Look in our "Bibliography/Recommended Reading" for ordering information.

There may be some advantage to registering your business as a trademark, such as we've done for *Country Bound!*™. For information on this subject, contact the U.S Department of Commerce, Patents and Trademarks Office, Washington, DC 20231. Or look for professional help in the Yellow Pages.

## *The Telephone: Lifeline to Opportunity*

Telephones can ring up huge profits for most businesses. You'll probably want a business, rather than a residential line. While business lines cost more, they also give you a listing in the Yellow Pages—usually an important asset. In most areas there is also a feature dubbed "call waiting." This little technological option is both a blessing and a curse. Although it allows you to know when another caller is on the line, it's also a rude interruption of the original conversation. It may make more sense to have two lines installed—one primarily for outgoing calls.

Some folks on shoestring budgets opt to have a residential phone installed and answer it simply with the phone number or "good morning/good afternoon." While this is definitely a cost savings since you can also take advantage of low long-distance rates, technically it may be illegal in some places and cuts you out of Yellow Page listing opportunities.

Phones also give the little business a way to appear big. You can get remote call forwarding (also called a foreign exchange) where it appears to customers you have a local number. In actuality, you pay a flat monthly service fee to have those calls forwarded to you—but the customer never knows the difference. You may be 100 miles away and have a local phone number. Think about how you're going to advertise and whether this would be advantageous.

Professionals and some other businesses will want a dedicated phone line for their fax machines. As fax communications grow ever more popular, it will become less and less attractive to have this machine sharing your regular telephone line.

In Arkansas, Texas, and Oklahoma a new service is ringing up impressive demand. Personalized Ring gives an existing phone number additional flexibility by allowing two additional distinctive rings. What this means is you could conceivably operate three different businesses from the same phone number. You'd know which company was being called because each would have a different sounding ring. This new business feature costs from $7 to $10 per month and includes a White Pages directory listing at no additional fee. It's now available in most Southwestern Bell Telephone markets, from US West Communications, and some other baby bells. With this custom ringing feature it's like being on a party line with yourself.

If you're seeking regional or national orders, an 800 number garners extra inquiries and sales. Many companies also use them for customer service. Costs have plunged the last few years. Today installation charges typically range from zero to $50, monthly fees go from $6 to $20, and rates per minute vary from 16 to 31 cents. In this highly competitive market sometimes unadvertised specials make it even more attractive. Ask around about deals. The ultimate cost depends on usage. Naturally if those calls are racking up sales, the more the merrier.

However, toll-free numbers aren't always necessary. While they're a plus when trying to entice the average consumer who has to pay his or her own phone bill, if your prospects are in the corporate sector, don't bother. They'll pay for the calls because it isn't coming out of their pocket. (We explore the wisdom of using 900 numbers in a future chapter.)

And what's available for those who must spend a lot of time on the road and want to get really sophisticated? Today there are cellular phone connections, fax machines, computers, modems, even message centers in automobiles to turn the business traveler into an entrepreneurial whirlwind. And paging units allow you to offer prompt customer service as well.

## *Location, Location, Location*

For most retail stores, restaurants, and lodging accommodations the key to success hangs on a hook labeled "location, location, location." If you're in any of these three fields, deciding precisely where in your new community to situate your business will have a profound impact on your survival.

Retail stores in small towns depend largely on foot traffic. Who your potential neighbors are may be more important than your store site itself. You're looking for retail compatibility. Planning on opening a women's shop? If you find a suitable spot next to a busy beauty salon, grab it! You'll automatically have a certain number of women passing each day. A fabric shop, drugstore, children's shop, five and dime, or craft store are other desirable neighbors. It works in reverse if you want to open a hardware store. Find a location that's adjacent to a sporting goods store, men's wear store, barber, auto supply store, etc.

Downtown versus a strip mall is a decision many new businesses face. Take a careful look at each and think about the purpose of your business. If you're selling carpet, appliances, or furniture, for instance, the mall—or even a remote location—is probably the best bet. People will make a special trip to visit your facility when they need one of these high-ticket items.

On the other hand, if you're dependent on getting many of your sales from impulsive drop-in trade, better take a hard look at downtown. The sad fact is, however, in many small towns the downtown section is a depressing collection of boarded up buildings and discouraged merchants hanging on by their fingernails. Think long before you join such a group, even though the price seems ridiculously low. You're better off paying more and being where the action is.

Speaking of action, especially if you're wavering between downtown and a mall, investigate if either has an active Merchants' Association. This is usually separate from the chamber of commerce. An association strengthens your business though group advertising programs, group insurance plans, and collective security measures. They can be especially effective coordinating common themes or events and promoting special activities during holiday seasons. Affiliating with an association gives you more clout. Very active ones have been known to get grants for civic improvements and to successfully lobby for highway exit changes.

Grocery stores, service stations, and other outlets at intersections will out-pull those in the middle of the block because they can depend on two distinct traffic streams and more window area. For certain stores, window display area is a big consideration.

If you don't have enough of your own, consider doing what we recommended to one of our clients. Contact nearby stores that don't need their display space and put together an informal lease where you pay them a little each month to show your merchandise in their window. Simply add a sign directing passerbys to your establishment. This is also smart advertising reinforcement.

When you're evaluating traffic flow, pay attention not only to the number of cars (or people) who pass by, notice also *when* they pass through, and if they appear to be your kind of customer. Heavy early morning and late afternoon traffic is great for gas stations and convenience stores, but it does little for specialty retailers. Those in the entertainment industry would look for a surge during evenings and weekends.

Design a worksheet for yourself and keep accurate records. Analysis of the characteristics of passing traffic often reveals patterns and variations not apparent from casual observation. If a traffic study is important to you, try contacting the planning commission, state highway department, city engineer, or an outdoor advertising company to see what data they can provide. And if you're making a pedestrian survey, be sure not to count people twice.

One final bit of advice for those opening stores: conduct a site history. Ask surrounding merchants what businesses operated in the location you're considering and how long they were there. If you discover a series of failures at a particular site, either back off or investigate very thoroughly to be sure you won't be the most recent in a long list of losers.

If you're a professional or a company seeking office space, much of what we've said still applies. A new attorney or CPA would do well to locate in a spot where he or she is very visible to the locals. But nothing too radical. People expect these professions to have traditional offices. Ad agencies and writers, on the other hand, might set up shop in a loft, a renovated Victorian home, a remodeled barn, or the second story quarters over a retail store. For larger firms wanting to make the right move, we recommend the *Company Relocation Handbook* by William Gary Ward and Sharon Kaye Ward. (See "Bibliography/Recommended Reading.")

The one remaining issue is whether to lease or buy. That's a personal decision that will be partly dictated by your financial capability, tax situation, and future plans. If you chose to lease, here are some pointers:

1) The higher the vacancy rate, the cheaper the price.

2) If the landlord isn't willing and cooperative in the beginning, it will only get worse.

3) Cost per square foot depends on your location within a larger building (upper floor, corner office vs. the basement, etc.).

4) Is there a clause that allows you to sublease?

5) The longer the lease, the lower the rate.
6) Can you negotiate a lease with an option to buy?
7) Is the lease flexible with a realistic option to renew after a specified number of years?
8) Is the landlord willing to put in writing any special promises regarding repairs, remodeling, and maintenance?

Is a drive-in service in your future? Be sure you're easily accessible to automobile traffic. Or maybe you're one of the fortunate ones who will work at home. We coached you about making intelligent residential selections earlier in the book. Be sure to apply that same intelligence when you look for business property.

Don't decide on a location based on your personal preference. Because it's within walking distance to home, is such a darling place, or belongs to a friend are not valid criteria. Your first consideration should be for your customer or client. Consider where you situate your firm carefully. Otherwise you may live up to the adage, "Locate in haste, repent at leisure."

## *Miscellaneous Details*

Develop a mission statement for your business. In 30 to 40 words, capture the essence of your objective. Who will you serve? What will you provide them? How will you do it? This should be a carefully crafted, well thought out, realistic plan. It describes the products or services you plan to provide and the intended market. It will help you get—and stay—focused.

Write a business plan defining your long and short range goals. It should include cash flow projections and profit and loss forecasts for at least two years. Prepare what you hope to accomplish, based on reasonable, conservative projections . . . and also a worst case scenario. There are excellent books devoted to this subject—and the SBA and many accounting firms hand out free brochures with detailed information—so we won't go into depth here. Not only will this vital written plan help you see where you're going, it's mandatory if you hope to interest investors in your enterprise. Be precise and conscientious. Don't use the SWAG (Scientific Wild Ass Guess) method. You'll find it's about as practical as trying to eat Jell-O with chopsticks.

People often ask us what is the most important thing in starting a business. We answer in two words: cash flow. You can have the greatest idea since the pet rock—but if you can't stay afloat until it catches on, all is lost. In the early life of a business you should be lean and mean both personally and professionally. This is not the time for extravagance. On the other hand, don't fail to calculate all you need for start-up costs. A common problem is not borrowing quite enough and having no cushion. It isn't necessary to *spend* it all, but be sure to request adequate financing.

Of course cash flow is impacted by what you charge. If you're going into a retail business, the markup is usually double the wholesale price. For those manufacturing a product, determining how much to charge is a prickly decision. It's influenced by four factors: 1) your direct and indirect costs, 2) the profit you want to make, 3) your competitors' prices, and 4) urgency in the marketplace.

Here's a formula for computing a fair price. First, look at your direct material costs for a month. What do you have to pay for the raw material used to make an item? (You may need to divide batches to get the price of a single item.) Second, what are your direct labor costs? What do you pay employees—or yourself—to produce the item? Don't forget to factor in fringe benefits; they usually equal about ⅓ of the salary again. Now figure your monthly overhead expenses, such as rent, utilities, insurance, packing and shipping supplies, delivery, etc. List all overhead items and total them. Then divide that figure by the number of items produced by month. So you have:

$$\frac{\text{Materials} + \text{Labor} + \text{Overhead}}{\text{Number of items per month}} = \text{Total cost per item}$$

Now it's time to add something for profit. Find out what the competition is charging. If you have a new, rare, or handmade product—or needed personalized service—people may be willing to pay a little more.

We talk about zoning restrictions in the chapter on home-based businesses. But be sure you don't overlook this consideration. Only certain parts of a town are zoned for commercial use. While sometimes you can get a variance, this involves red tape and lapsed time.

Naturally your new entity deserves its own checking account. We advise getting all the other necessary registrations and paperwork out of the way first though. Most banks will want to see your articles of incorporation (if your company is a corporation), your fictitious name registration, and your Federal I.D. number. By the way, when dealing with the banker, this is *not* a time to be humble. Because we started our companies with sizeable deposits and indicated hefty anticipated monthly activity, Tom was able to negotiate corporate checking accounts without any service charges. Perhaps you can too.

Select a banker, accountant, lawyer, and insurance agent whom you trust. Their expert advice at this stage can save you thousands of dollars later. Establish a bookkeeping system in advance so you have everything in place *before* you open for business. And don't forget to include insurance premiums when figuring start-up costs.

You may also want to hire a business or marketing consultant. A major advantage of hiring a consultant is that he or she brings fresh and objective expertise to the table. Perhaps you need help setting up a computer system, developing a business plan to present to the banker, or creating a results-oriented marketing campaign. Through our firm, Accelerated Business Images, we've been called on to execute each of these functions for small business owners. When working with a consultant, explain what you need and ask for a proposal outlining costs and time lines to accomplish your goals. A competent expert can help you think though your venture and avoid problems before they arise. Otherwise, you can pop into trouble as fast as a cork from a bottle.

Another option for guidance includes the Small Business Administration (SBA). Their national toll-free number for the Answer Desk is 800-368-5855. This is an information hotline that provides personalized attention to your business needs or refers you to the proper person or place. For your local SBA office, see the blue government pages of your phone book or call 800-UASK-SBA. They publish tons of useful brochures and books, sponsor conferences and seminars, and offer free counseling and training services through SCORE and ACE.

Additionally, they have district and regional offices (see Part III under "Government Sources"), sponsor Small Business Development Centers (SBDCs) in partnership with other entities, and have Small Business Institutes (SBIs) at more than 500 college campuses that provide student and faculty help to small business clients. Contact the SBA resources in your area to find out how they can assist you. Or write U.S. Small Business Administration, Office of Business Development, Room 317, 1441 L Street, NW, Washington, DC 20416, for more information or to order a directory of business development publications.

Also check with local colleges and universities to see what business courses they offer. And if you're a computer buff, don't overlook going on-line to ask questions. You'll get immediate feedback.

To pull everything together, review the following Start-Up Stimulator Checklist. It will serve as a memory jog to help you take into consideration various possible items or functions. Not all points will apply, but it should keep you from overlooking essentials.

## START-UP STIMULATOR CHECKLIST

- ✓ Accounting/Bookkeeping/Tax Preparation
- ✓ Advertising/PR Plan
- ✓ Alarms/Security Systems
- ✓ Answering Machine/Service
- ✓ Auto Renting/Leasing
- ✓ Banking Services
- ✓ Business Consulting Plan
- ✓ Chamber of Commerce/Other Memberships
- ✓ Computer Consulting
- ✓ Computer Equipment/Supplies
- ✓ Computer Repair/Service
- ✓ Copy Machine
- ✓ Data Processing
- ✓ Delivery/Messenger Service
- ✓ Equipment
- ✓ Fax Machine
- ✓ Federal ID Tax Number
- ✓ Graphic Design/Desktop Publishing/Typesetting
- ✓ Insurance
- ✓ Janitorial Service
- ✓ Leasing Space: Office/Retail/Warehouse
- ✓ Legal Services/Lawyers
- ✓ Licensing Requirements
- ✓ Loans/Start-up Capital
- ✓ Meeting Facilities/Conference Room
- ✓ Mission Statement
- ✓ Name (dba) Registration
- ✓ Office Furniture
- ✓ Office Machines/Typewriters, etc.
- ✓ Office Supplies/Business Forms
- ✓ Printing
- ✓ Secretarial Service/Word Processing
- ✓ Shipping & Mailing Supplies/Service
- ✓ Signage
- ✓ Space Planning & Design
- ✓ Telephone Equipment/Paging & Mobile Telephone
- ✓ Trademark/Service Mark Registration
- ✓ Transportation & Moving
- ✓ Trash Removal/Recycling Plan

## Business Incubators as Early Guardians

A business incubator shelters and protects a new enterprise just as the outer shell does a soon-to-be-born chick. Incubators customarily house somewhere between five and 30 new businesses under one roof, each with its own office or suite. Typically guidance on obtaining financing, management and marketing acumen—even such fringe benefits as secretarial services, conference rooms, faxes and copy machines—are part of the package. This setup sees to it start-ups don't operate in a vacuum. Usually there is great camaraderie and networking between incubator participants. They share the common bond of being new businesses. This approach is used to help launch fledgling enterprises; rarely does a firm stay in an incubator longer than two years.

Of course, the tiniest of towns don't offer this option. It takes about a 25,000 population base to support an incubator. To find out if one is planned for your area, check with the National Business Incubator Association, One President Street, Athens, OH 45701, 614-593-4331.

Another option is to establish a buddy business relationship with another new entrepreneur. Contact the chamber of commerce or economic development office to see who else is just opening up. You might be able to share costs of office supplies, bags or wrapping paper, direct mailers, etc. Such a strategy is really helpful when suppliers have minimum-order requirements. And you can also use each other as brainstorming partners and for mutual emotional support.

## Locating Reliable Suppliers

One disadvantage of living in remote areas is that you are sometimes a distance from needed suppliers. Additionally, distributors who service rural areas often maintain low stock levels. We've learned several ways of coping with these frustrating dilemmas. One is to plan ahead. Think through any project or your inventory level needs and make a materials list of what you will need. Then when you travel to a bigger town on a buying safari, you won't forget vital items.

If you're taking over a retail shop, consider approaching your vendors about replacing old stock with brand new merchandise. Our friend Rebecca, who purchased a bookstore, used this approach successfully to stock her store with all the latest best-sellers. It required no out-of-pocket expense for her as she simply rotated old inventory for new.

Another wise tactic if you're stocking a retail establishment the first time is to *visit wholesalers in person.* Get acquainted. Sell them on how successful you're going to be, and play one against the other for the best prices. This will also allow you to personally pick the most desirable merchandise, be aware of any close out specials, and negotiate a better discount for your large initial order. Of course, attending a trade show or exhibit in your field is another excellent way to find out what's hot and establish supplier relationships.

And consider taking items on consignment. When we added a little gift shop to our hotel in First Try, we carried a lovely assortment of fine Indian jewelry—all on consignment. The arrangement worked well for both parties. We had no money tied up in inventory and the lady who owned the jewelry had a new outlet to sell her wares. This also works beautifully with handcrafted items.

It makes sense to talk to locals about your needs. In rural areas people often don't advertise for business. People just know they're there . . . everybody except newcomers like you, that is. Ask around. You'll be surprised at the vast number of folks right in your own community who offer the very services you may need, or who carry items you require.

Consider shopping by mail. *The Catalog of Catalogs* can help you locate business suppliers as well as personal items. (See "Bibliography/Recommended Reading.") We buy the majority of our office supplies from Quill, 100 Schelter Road, Lincolnshire, IL 60069, 708-634-4800. Besides carrying name brand merchandise, they have their own label of less expensive items. And they'll place special orders.

Until you've established a business track record, you'll need good personal credit and must be willing to personally guarantee business accounts. Prepare a sheet detailing credit references and your bank account numbers so you appear businesslike. Another approach is to put up a deposit which you make purchases against. After six months or so of prompt payment, most companies will give you credit. Also consider asking your sales representatives for letters of recommendation once you've been in business for a few months. Get creative in proving you're a sound business risk.

If you plan on doing extensive building, repairs, or maintenance, it might make sense to set up a separate "dba" company. Ours is called Valley Service. We've established accounts with vendors all over Colorado and enjoy discounts of from 20 to 50 percent off retail prices. How so? We re-sell the items to one of our corporations. You'll also need a Federal ID number if you're re-selling items and want to avoid paying sales tax.

A wise lady once told us, "It's not how you *sell* things, it's how you *buy* them that spells the difference between success and failure." Sam Walton pinpoints buying strategies as one of the primary contributors to Wal-Mart's growth achievement.

One final note to help you save money when setting up. If you need office furniture or equipment—such as computers, typewriters, postage machine, photocopier, etc.—investigate getting them from the government. Overstocked items are auctioned off from several General Services Administration regional offices throughout the U.S. These used items are sometimes a steal. For information on dates, places, and offerings, contact the U.S. General Services Administration, 18th & F Streets NW, Washington, DC 20405, 202-557-7785.

## *Prospecting for Qualified Employees*

Most businesses grow out of the inspiration and perspiration of one person or couple. Successful ones, however, ultimately expand to the point where the founder(s) can't handle everything.

Taking the leap from doing it all yourself to hiring help is a big step. Frankly, finding good employees is one of the greatest challenges facing industry today. Ferreting out competent people with strong work ethics isn't easy. But there are some gems out there waiting for those willing to dig carefully.

Get the word out that you're looking. Now is the time to make The Gossip Monger work *for* you. Tell not only the president of the bank, but also the tellers. They're the ones who have day-to-day contact with area residents. Mention it when you get a haircut, at the grocery store, when filling up with gas. Tell your accountant, insurance agent, and attorney. Alert the chamber of commerce director. Talk about your opening at service club meetings, church, and other community gatherings. While the people you speak with may not be qualified or interested themselves, chances are one of them will have a daughter, cousin, or neighbor who might be ideal. This is how things often work in Small Town America.

When you run across someone who impresses you, plant a seed. We frequent a particular restaurant in town and got well acquainted with one of the waitresses. In the course of chatting with her, we learned she had taken a two-year secretarial course a couple of years before. She was working as a waitress because she made enormous tips in the summer. But then winter came. Her hours were cut and tips plummeted. We'd observed Susan was pleasant, efficient, and well-organized in the way she approached her job—traits that would follow her in any working situation. So one day Tom invited her to come and talk with us if she ever decided to make a change. A couple of months later we hired Susan.

Help wanted ads are another natural employee prospecting tool. And they're so cheap in little local papers. It may make sense to set your ad apart by putting a box around it and using larger type. This is called a classified display ad.

Let's suppose you've run an ad and received several intriguing resumés. What if you're just moving to the new town? You have no office in which to interview applicants. And using a restaurant or hotel is awkward. We solved this problem by asking for help from our real estate broker. She put us in touch with a local insurance agent who was kind enough to not only let us use her suite of offices one Saturday—she even had her secretary there to greet our prospective employees! How's that for small town hospitality? We found three new hires . . . and Kathy acquired another insurance client.

Because our business is rather specialized, we used to think we had to recruit from the larger cities of Denver and Colorado Springs for key positions. We spent hundreds of dollars on ads in their major newspapers to lure prospective employees to our small town. We got lost among the hundreds of other advertisements. Save your money. What do urban opt-outs do who want to move to a particular small town or area? They get ahold of the local paper! Your ad here will do double duty—not only alerting locals about the job opening, but also serving notice to those seeking to relocate. Over the years, we've hired people from Clearwater, Florida; Cincinnati, Ohio; plus Breckenridge, Colorado Springs, and Lamar, Colorado. They all saw our ads in the local paper. Or friends and loved ones alerted them to the openings.

If you must find a person with very specific expertise, try running an ad in a national trade journal or newspaper targeted to your industry. These specialized publications are a conduit between job hunters with experience in a given field and companies with professional openings. Be sure to highlight the fact that you offer an opportunity to pursue their chosen career while experiencing greater quality of life and a lower cost of living.

Don't overlook checking into federally funded placement programs such as the Job Training Partnership Act (JTPA). We found a delightful employee this way. While Hugh was a capable administrative assistant, he knew nothing about our particular business or word processing program. JTPA paid half of his salary for six months, plus footed the bill for him to go to school and learn WordPerfect. Our part of the bargain was to train him and provide an ongoing job. What a win-win situation! This help with payroll is also a real financial boon. Just be sure you aren't totally gobbled up in the training process.

If you employ certain types of people, such as dislocated workers or people who have lost their jobs because of competition, your business may qualify for a federal tax credit under the Targeted Jobs Tax Credit Program.

It can even be used in conjunction with JTPA. For more information, contact the Employment Training Administration, Office of Public Affairs, U.S. Department of Labor, Room S-2322, Washington, DC 20210, 202-535-0236.

Another way to supplement your own efforts is using interns and work study students from a local high school. Some internships provide free help in exchange for training; in others you pay the trainee a reduced salary. Check with the local school. Carol came to our facility two hours a day for a full semester. She learned about the real world of business and we had free clerical aid. Ginger is helping us in this capacity now. This is also a practical way to prospect locally for bright young people to add to your permanent staff.

And because grant money runs out before the need does, colleges also help students finance their educations by helping them find employment. Work/study programs can be found at virtually every school, from the small junior colleges to the ultra universities. Sometimes financial aid is available to the employer. At any, rate, you'll likely find exceptional help at reasonable rates.

Gallopade Publishing Group got discouraged trying to hire qualified people. Their innovative approach was to do just the opposite: get workers for free! They started an official apprenticeship program, ran ads in area newspapers, and were flooded with super candidates fighting each other for a chance to learn the publishing business firsthand.

Perhaps hiring subcontractors to assume responsibility for different aspects of the business is a workable solution for you. In this alternative you find other firms or individuals to whom you can spin off some tasks. Maybe an advertising/PR firm takes over your marketing, or a secretarial service does your letters, updates your database, and handles mailings. The primary advantage of subcontracting is that it's easier in many ways. You don't have personnel problems, payroll deductions to figure, nor such facility-related matters as rent or lease payments, insurance, or building upkeep.

Of course, you still have to find appropriate firms to work with. In a small town, you may already know someone suitable. If not, ask around. Here again, word-of-mouth recommendations—or cautions—are the best source of information. Failing that, try the Yellow Pages. Ask for references from those you're considering. And check them out. It's important you like and respect the person you choose. This individual will become an integral part of your team.

When you begin a new business relationship, be sure your expectations match theirs. To avoid later misunderstandings, be clear initially about such things as precisely what services they will render, deadlines to be met, plus how and when they will be compensated. Don't lock yourself into a long-range, subcontracting commitment until the relationship has proven itself.

By now you should feel confident about the details involved in beginning a business. So let's move on to that most fascinating of topics: marketing strategies! After all, it's the selling of your products or services—and the resulting livelihood—that holds special appeal for everyone.

# 17

# Creating Attention Getters and Revenue Reapers

Part of the exhilaration of having your own business is the initial creation process. There are many exciting decisions to be made in the beginning. One is the image you will project. What will you name your new baby? How you christen your venture can dramatically enhance its chances for success. Would a slogan help solidify your identification? What about logos, letterhead, and business cards? Does your enterprise need an eye-catching sign? We'll cover all these important topics.

## *Establishing Your Image*

If you are the only restaurant, gift shop, attorney, doctor, or repairperson in town, skip this part. (And realize you'll be living in a very tiny village!) But if there will be similar outlets or professionals operating in the area, the identity you project becomes of paramount importance. This is also true on a national scale if your client or customer base is located all over the country.

Sears is learning this lesson in spades. They flit—like a bewildered, frantic, moth—from one type of merchandise and style of operating to another. This retail giant no longer sends a clear signal. As a result, their quarterly reports look dismal and even their long-standing catalog is threatened. Meanwhile their arch competitor, Wal-Mart, is an enthusiastic collector with a huge butterfly net—capturing more and more of Sears' customer base. Why? People know what to expect when they walk into a Wal-Mart.

Have you ever noticed that in some hardware stores the employees are especially knowledgeable? Ace Hardware has parlayed this into a very successful TV ad campaign. Or maybe you've noticed the atmosphere of a certain clothing shop is unusually inviting. Perhaps you have auto repairs done by a favorite mechanic because he washes the exterior and vacuums the inside of your car—along with performing the required technical service. Maybe you patronize a certain chiropractor because he never keeps you waiting more than five minutes.

Each of these establishments has developed a certain image. The hardware store is known for its helpful workers. The clothing shop has created an appealing ambiance by decorating in a winsome way—playing classical guitar music—featuring a fragrant potpourri—and offering free herb teas and gourmet coffees to customers. Shopping there is *an experience*. The auto mechanic makes your life easier. The chiropractor values your time. What's the atmosphere in your store: friendly, avant garde, homey, funky, sophisticated?

Image revolves around how people perceive you. It's your firm's ability to satisfy expectations. And it sends a potent message about your capabilities and caring. Image-building should be PROactive, not reactive. This isn't the place for tippy-toe, soft-shoe stuff. Image involves visibility, charisma, respect, personal responsiveness.

And if you take image-building seriously, you'll romance your prospects in every way possible—cohesively, consistently. You'll woo them with carefully crafted collateral materials: business cards, stationery, brochures, fliers. Your signs will reflect the same image, as will your interior design and the very *feel* of your place.

Even the way you answer the phone projects your image. Is it friendly, unhurried, and professional? A favorable reaction gives you an important competitive edge. It contributes directly to why folks get their wrenches, sweaters, auto repairs, or back adjustments from you. Apply this knowledge to your own operation.

Developing an image applies to virtually every business. Let's say you find a mobile home park for sale below market value. While purchasing such a business is iffy because most park owners are struggling to maintain decent occupancy rates, such a venture can be turned into a gold mine by clever packaging. A major challenge is to replace the stigma of "trailer

## Trade Your Business Suit Blues for Blue Jean Dreams™

court" with something prestigious and fun. Let's do some brainstorming and see if we can create a different image.

What if we were to make this into a theme park? After all, everybody loves visiting Disneyland and other theme parks. How about a ranch motif? Here's what we would do to position this mobile home park as distinct and desirable. There are cottonwood trees on the property and a pond nearby, so let's call it Cottonwood Ranch.

To establish the mood, an old stagecoach greets visitors at the main entrance. Streets are renamed Rawhide Road, Buckboard Boulevard, Sagebrush Street, Lasso Lane, Chuck Wagon Court, and Desperado Drive. Rustic signposts mark each corner. Corral fencing—complete with wagon wheels and hitching posts—divides the lots. The clubhouse, dubbed "Wranglers' Roost," is redecorated with ranch-style furniture; branding irons, horse collars, and Indian rugs adorn the walls. The playground is called the "Kids' Korral" and includes blocks for building forts, a couple of sturdy old wagons, and wooden ranch critters—in addition to the normal swings and slide.

To further carry out the theme atmosphere, *homesteads* are rented rather than spaces. The staff wears western garb, and the manager—sporting a sheriff's badge—answers the phone "Howdy. Cottonwood Ranch." What about creating a spokesperson—maybe Bucky Bronco? He can appear in ads and on brochures, be featured on "Wanted" posters that detail the rules, even appear on tee shirts available for sale at the office and clubhouse.

If budget allows, and you want to carry the ambiance further, you might arrange to lease and stock the nearby pond for fishing. And offering free monthly hay rides or cookouts for park residents is almost guaranteed to build a waiting list. Of course, this idea would also work perfectly for positioning a campground. Be our guest. (And if you use it . . . write and share the results with us!)

For small town residents, quality of life is everything. Give it to them. Remembering that the more you give the more you get, go out of your way to satisfy people. Approach business with the attitude of being a good neighbor—always ready to please. Never be ordinary. Stand out from the crowd. Interestingly enough, bad comments travel faster than good so make sure they're good.

Whatever labor you provide or product you sell, please always remember outstanding service is your most important attribute. No matter what you sell, people can get it elsewhere. Folks like to trade at a certain place because of the way the proprietor or practitioner makes them *feel*. There should be no invisible customers. Every person deserves courtesy and

Creating Attention Getters and Revenue Reapers

respect, whether they drive a shiny Mercedes or a dilapidated pickup. Service is the rent we pay for the space we take on the planet Earth.

## *Deciding on a Seemly—or Sensational—Name*

Names, like fashions, go in cycles. Initials and acronyms are said to be passe. Trends in naming are moving away from letters and numbers because experts have found these symbols have minimal name recognition. If people don't think of your store or firm when they need your products or services, all is lost.

Today comfortable, environmental sounding names are in. So are approachable or friendly monikers that show you care about people. Apple computers was so successful, a British computer manufacturer has dubbed their company "Apricot." And in Japan there is a Tomato Bank and a Lettuce car. (Seriously!)

Your company name must both distinguish you from the competition and be appropriate to what you do. Be sure to check the competition. Choosing something too similar makes about as much sense as squatting on a land mine. It should be memorable, easy to pronounce, and fitting. It's also a good idea to invent a name that has your product or service *within it* to avoid confusion. Consider your customer or client base. Suitable names will vary widely depending on the age level of your prospects. Teenagers have different buttons than yuppies or retired folks. Don't settle for just one idea; list lots of possibilities. Then rank them. When you go to register your name, you may find it already taken. One large corporation ended up being christened with a meaningless group of letters because their first four choices were already in use.

To help you identify possibilities and stimulate your thinking, check the following Naming Notions list. Once you've come up with some ideas, get feedback from other people—especially those who are prospects. Something may be clear to you, yet as cloudy as a neglected aquarium to others. A name with a misleading connotation can be a real detriment.

*IB* (Independent Business) magazine recently ran a naming contest. Readers voted the winners to be: Juan In a Million, a restaurant in Lubbock, Texas; Twice Sold Tales, a used bookstore exchange in Pine Grove, California; Loch Ness Lure Company, a lure manufacturer in Crossville, Tennessee; and Bottoms Up Diaper Service of Clackamas, Oregon.

Sometimes the facility where your business is housed dictates the name. George Risolo located his florist shop in an empty bank building and renamed the company The Flower Bank. Furthermore the shop has a bank motif. Customers can order flowers from the drive-in windows and deliveries are made from an armored truck by men dressed like guards. So far everything is coming up roses. The Norwalk, Connecticut, florist took in $27,500 one Valentine's Day. Perhaps what you do lends itself to a clever naming twist. For instance, Deck the Walls specializes in expressive art and custom framing.

Those heavily dependent on Yellow Pages advertising—such as plumbers, mechanics, travel agents, florists, air conditioning repair shops, pet groomers, locksmiths, etc.—are wise to choose a name that falls early in the alphabet. This is also true of companies that do business nationwide. One of our firms, About Books, Inc., receives several inquiries each month from our listings in national directories. Certainly appearing at the head of the alphabetical list doesn't hurt.

Naming corporations is a multimillion dollar business. If you still feel inadequate to the task, there are consultants and computer programs to help you. One software program is "Namer by Salinon." This company also puts out a free booklet that contains helpful checklists. You can get it by writing them at: The Salinon Corporation, 7424 Greenville Avenue, Suite 115, Dallas, TX 75231, 214-692-9091.

Another excellent tool to stimulate creative thinking is IdeaFisher. This computer program contains a database of 61,000 cross-referenced idea words and phrases, plus over 700,000 idea associations. It's all arranged into 28 categories and 387 subcatagories. What all these numbers don't tell you is how much mental dynamite this program offers with its ability to associate and link ideas. In addition to being an outstanding brainstorming partner, it's also terrific for coming up with slogans and other marketing concepts. For further information, contact Fisher Idea Systems at 800-289-4332.

Before we leave this topic, let's also examine the pros and cons of using your own name for your business. One woman, who planned to work out of her home, elected to call her business Sara Steinman Productions. Upon learning zoning restrictions didn't allow her to post a company sign outside her house, she was pleased about this choice. You see, nothing stopped her from hanging a sign inscribed with her name! Thus business visitors could easily find her.

One advantage of using your full legal name and nothing else is you don't have to register it as a trade name. If, however, you tack on terms like Company or Son, in most states this puts you back in the trade name category. Of course, using your personal moniker has the disadvantage of not giving prospects any hint of what you do.

## NAMING NOTIONS

| | | |
|---|---|---|
| Agency | Exchange | Productions |
| Annex | Expeditions | Products |
| Arbor | Forum | Provider |
| Associates | Foundation | Rental |
| Association | Inn | Repair |
| Bazaar | Institute | Salon |
| Beat | Junction | Shelf |
| Browser | Gallery | Shop |
| Bureau | Group | Shoppe |
| Cache | Incorporated | Source |
| Call | Lodge | Society |
| Camp | Loft | Specialist |
| Carrier | Lounge | Stall |
| Cellar | Mall | Store |
| Center | Management | Supply |
| Channel | Market | Systems |
| Clinic | Mart | Trader |
| Communications | Maxi | Trading Post |
| Company | Mini | Training |
| Connection | Mobile | Tours |
| Consultant | Outlet | Vendor |
| Corner | Park | Villa |
| Corporation | Partnership | Village |
| Cottage | Peddler | Wagon |
| Deals | Place | Wares |
| Design | Plaza | Warehouse |
| Emporium | Plus | Works |
| Enterprise | Portable | |
| Equipment | Practitioner | |

## *Creating a Winning Slogan*

Is there a slogan in your future? Many businesses benefit from originating a saying connected to their product or service. Perhaps the most famous is "Where's the beef?" Wendy's soared to huge profits when this catchy phrase débuted a few years ago. The golden arches also saw a lot more business when "It's a good time for the great taste of McDonald's" captured the fancy of fast food fans beginning in 1983. Other national giants use similar marketing strategies. "Let Hertz put you in the driver's seat" helps them remain firmly seated in the number one car rental position. "You're in good hands with Allstate" reassures potential insurance buyers they'll get kid glove treatment. And the self-deprecating "With a name like Smucker's, it has to be good" pokes delicious fun at the company.

Such maxims aren't just for corporate giants though. A ski resort has as its motto *"Snow* ahead, make my day!" An ingenious florist plays on the beer commercial by saying "This bud's for you." And the previously mentioned business, the Lock Ness Lure Company, has as their tag line "We catch Monsters!" If you decide to coin a slogan, have the following handy: a thesaurus, rhyming dictionary, one of the mentioned computer software programs, a sense of humor, and lots of imagination.

## *Generating Logos, Letterhead, and Business Cards*

Once you know who you're going to be, have developed a slogan, and know your physical location, it's time to prepare stationery and cards. Many businesses hire a graphic artist to also design a logo. This is a symbol that helps identify you. We chose to name our public relations consulting firm Accelerated Business Images (ABI) partly because it has excellent visual potential. Then we worked with our artist to develop a logo that connotes movement, thus symbolizing the progress we achieve for our clients.

Keep in mind the image you want to portray. What's your "look?" Are you going for sophisticated elegance or popular glitz? A traditional or contemporary feel? Coordinate your letterhead, envelope, and business card. Choose a color other than white so your correspondence will stand out from the crowd. (It's also a good idea to order a ream of blank matching paper from the printer. Use it as second sheets for longer letters and to copy enclosures onto.) And be sure you include all pertinent information—such as your phone area code, zip code, and fax number if appropriate. When using a post office box, it's also a good idea to include a street address for in-person deliveries. Adding the street address also eliminates the fly-by-night image. Avoid tiny type. As the population ages, prospects' eyes appreciate larger print.

We contend business cards are *underrated* PR tools. They're like having a sales tool right in your hand. The business card dates back to the seventeenth century when different businesses began using what came to be known as trade cards to advertise their wares. What's a well thought out and creatively executed business card of today? A mini billboard! Just as freeway billboards tout certain items, so can your business card.

Our About Books, Inc. firm handles everything to do with books that isn't illegal or immoral. To aid people in getting a better handle on specifically how we can help them, we itemize these services on our card (manuscript critiquing, editing, ghostwriting, typesetting, design, printing, marketing, publicity, consulting, seminars). If you want to get even more mileage out of your card, consider using a double-sided, tent-style card. These have a fold along the top and print on both sides. We originated such a card for a boutique and used the inside for a listing of ladies sizes and favorite colors. Then each customer was encouraged to fill out a card for the man in her life. That simplified gift-giving for hundreds of husbands, boyfriends, and dads. Of course it also brought extra business into the boutique.

To be more unusual, design your card vertically instead of horizontally. One author created a card that resembles a book simply by drawing thin lines around the vertical edges. For some enterprises, using a florescent paper stock is a smart idea to attract attention. We know a plumber who had his card done on a rubberized magnetic material. It sticks to the refrigerator door and serves as a constant reminder of who to call in case of plumbing problems. Some people like to include a photograph, or even do the whole card as a color picture. To locate manufacturers of unusual cards, see Part III under "Selected Suppliers."

And consider whether you can do a cross-promotion with another business. We know of a fellow who got his business cards paid for by tying the location of his crafts gallery to that of a nearby hotel. On the back of his card, he drew a map which showed the location of his shop in relation to the hotel. The hotel then made his cards available to guests, who often visited the gallery.

## *Evaluating Signage Needs*

Virtually every business that isn't home-based requires a sign. This is not only excellent advertising, it helps prospects find you easily. Again, your sign should reflect the image you want to communicate. Integrate it with the other design aspects of your business. Clarity and simplicity are the bywords in sign design. Don't get cluttered. You want your company name and maybe the logo. Period. No slogan. No phone number. No distractions. And before you go too far, check on any regulations. There will no doubt be zoning ordinances you must obey.

Eye appeal leads to aye appeal. Colors should complement the surrounding buildings. Shy away from subtle shades; strong contrasts make for easier reading. Speaking of readability, be aware that to be seen about 100 feet away, letters should be four inches tall. If you have a sign on the highway, however, letters must be more like three *feet* high to be read at a distance when traveling fast.

Perhaps what you do lends itself to an unusually shaped sign. This gives additional visual clues. A music store might design its sign as the outline of a guitar or piano, a bowling alley in the image of a bowling ball or pin. For automobile-related businesses, how about the profile of a car? An optometrist's office sign might take the shape of eyeglasses, while an aquarium supplier could do well with a fish image.

Signs are made from a variety of materials: wood, plastic, metal, plexiglass, or neon. Neon has a distinct advantage as it sells 24-hours a day. So can florescent light or spotlights if you keep them on after dark. Other possible sign surfaces include vinyl awnings or banners, even exterior walls. This is not a place to skimp. A good-sized, professional sign will probably cost about $1,000. If you're in a retail venture, it could be one of your best investments.

Don't overlook other signage opportunities. Perhaps your business lends itself to advertising on vehicles. Commercials here can take the form of metallic signs, decals, or lettering on the actual auto body. A Taylors, South Carolina, man—who owns an electrical wiring company—transformed his truck into a roving billboard. He puts metallic signs across his side doors and along the back, then parks his truck in high visibility spots like country club parking lots and commercial construction sites. "I've gotten at least 100 jobs in a year from having the sign on the truck," reports owner Bobby Cox.

Now that we know our distinct image and have christened our enterprise, not to mention designed stationery and a sign, let's move on to developing a full-blown marketing campaign that leapfrogs the competition.

# 18

# Persuasive Marketing Strategies to Boost Your Bottom Line

Doing business without marketing is like winking at an attractive member of the opposite sex in the dark. *You* may know what you're doing—but nobody else does. Marketing is the vital cog in the wheel whether you own a retail store, offer a service, head a professional firm, make your living as a wholesaler, or manufacture a product. Here we'll show you how to get attention without weighing 300 pounds, throwing public tantrums, or disgracing the national anthem. You don't have to throw your weight around to get noticed. Just keep reading.

## *"Positioning" Yourself for Greater Profits*

Positioning is simply looking for a hole, then plugging it. It's doing something to set yourself apart from the crowd. Granted, in Small Town America the crowd is more sparse. But don't delude yourself into thinking that means you needn't differentiate yourself. If you want your market share (and a bit extra), seek ways to carve out a special niche. Try to identify and serve a segment all your own.

To better understand this concept, let's look at cookies. Some are chewy, others crunchy. There are ones like Grandma used to make for nostalgia buffs; nutritious ones for the health-conscious; gourmet cookies for the upscale crowd. And gigantic ones that are almost a meal in themselves contrast with dainty, bite-sized morsels. All of these manufacturers are going after their own sweet section of the market. They're avoiding cookie cutter approaches by positioning their product to appeal to certain consumers.

Will you become known as the place where a person can find almost anything in a given line of merchandise—or will your inventory be customized and selective? If you're in mental health care, will you cater to children, teens, adults, or perhaps retirees? As a physician, will you let people walk in without an appointment or might you make house calls? If real estate or appraising is your thing, do you plan to specialize in residential property, commercial holdings, or raw land?

Thinking of opening a restaurant? It might offer American, Italian, Chinese, Mexican, or other ethnic cuisine. And it could take the form of a deli, gourmet fare, homestyle cooking, fast food, family style, even a cafeteria. The ways you can segment the market go on and on. Do you deliver? What about catering parties and special events? Is the town large enough to support a non-smoking eatery? Can you play on a unique location? Maybe you will situate your restaurant in a charming church, railroad station, or historic landmark.

Suppose you want to start a maid service, but there are already a couple of them in town. Don't go head-to-head in the traditional way. Come from a different perspective. You could market a "luxury package" of special services to affluent households. Or maybe a monthly "quik 'n heavy clean" program for mature people who can't afford weekly service but need periodic help with difficult tasks.

Of course before you can sharpen your focus to set yourself apart, you must know the competition. Find out who your potential rivals are. Evaluate what they do well—and poorly. Now scrutinize your own operation. What could you do better, faster, and more innovatively? Go with your strengths.

Consider creating a mobile moneymaker. By offering free pickup and delivery you save customers time and endear yourself to them. What about Chinese fast food to go . . . or delivered? Setting up a mobile operation where you outfit a van or truck and take your enterprise on the road might make sense for certain occupations. Or do you want to do alterations, repair small appliances, or groom dogs? All three could fall under the "Have van will travel" category. How about being the Good Humor truck of the '90s where grownups run out to shop when they hear your bell? Such action just might guarantee you portable profits.

Look for ways to give your business an exotic or adventurous twist. A motel, shop, or restaurant might offer escapist entertainment by implementing a Polynesian, western, or futuristic theme, for instance. Appeal to our five senses in any way you can by adding sensory value: taste, smell, sound, light, color, texture. Make the experience "sensational."

For specific ideas, study the following 21 Ways to Separate Yourself from the Herd. Find your special niche; then really take care of your customers or clients. Proper positioning, teamed with genuine caring, makes the difference between doing business as usual . . . or doing business unusually well.

## *21 Ways to Separate Yourself from the Herd*

- **Price point:** Are you expensive, moderately priced, or cheap? Establish your image and let customers know it.
- **Size:** Small is beautiful; play on your personalized attention.
- **Atmosphere:** Are you laid back? Sophisticated? Hip? Continental?
- **Hours:** Do you stay open late (or early) to accommodate working people?
- **Days of operation:** Should you consider opening weekends? Holidays?
- **Location:** Are you convenient? Easy to find? Handy for walk-by traffic?
- **Portability:** Could you put your business "on the road?"
- **Ease of purchasing:** Do you offer credit cards? Lay away? Financing? Phone orders?
- **Convenience:** Can people get in easily, find what they want, and pay quickly?
- **Do you have a gimmick:** An environmental angle? A theme decor?
- **Delivery:** Do you offer pickup or delivery?
- **Guarantee:** Have you a unique money-back guarantee or service warranty policy?
- **Packaging:** Could you use innovative, reusable, or fun packaging?
- **Giveaways:** Do you offer free gifts to potential customers? To purchasers?
- **Piggybacking:** Can you combine two businesses to better serve people?
- **Samples:** Could you offer samples to entice prospects?
- **Seminars or demonstrations:** Should your product or service be showcased?
- **Contests:** Would some form of competition focus attention on you? People love contests . . . and winning.

- **Age/sex segmentation:** Should you slant towards women, men, teens, adults, retirees?
- **Service:** Do you offer extraordinary assistance to your customers/clients?
- **Technological edge:** Will a fax, modem, cellular phone, bigger computer, toll-free line, 900 number, etc. open new doors?

## Developing an Effective Marketing Plan

Once you've determined your distinctive difference, it's time to develop a marketing plan. Otherwise you'll be like the motorist whose method of driving his car from point A to point B is to enter the freeway, look for another driver who seems to know where he is going, and then follow him. While our motorist takes many interesting side trips, he never arrives at the destination he sets out for.

Neither will you unless you map out the goals you'll use to sell your product or service. This written blueprint will serve as the springboard for launching all the possible ways you plan to generate profits. Naturally it will vary, depending on the kind of business you're in—and whether your area of influence is local, regional, national, or global. To stay focused, refer to your mission statement.

Let's take a moment here to brainstorm potential markets. Not all of them will be limited to your local economy. Will you incorporate systems to bridge you to a regional or national market? What about exporting internationally? Don't flinch! These days state and local governments are more than willing to help connect you with outlets in other countries. They can furnish market studies or help you locate embassy officials willing to link you to foreign businesses interested in selling your wares. With the walls coming down in the global arena, international markets are on the rise. If these prospects interest you, contact your State Office of Economic Development in the state capitol.

An excellent new book is *Finding Your Niche . . . Marketing Your Professional Service*, a business volume by Bart Brodsky and Janet Geis. They cover everything from exploring career options to organizing your business. In addition they talk about client profiles, researching your market, promotion and marketing, even publicity and advertising in the mass media.

Marketing takes a different tack in rural America. If your business is dependent on the locals, make certain your neighbors know you. Go out of your way to make new friends. If you're asked to dinner, go and enjoy. Your new neighbors are also your new prospects. Find the longtime residents and make them your friends. Join the local chamber of commerce.

If you're a churchgoer, find a good one and become an active member. Making sure people know who you are and what you do is half the battle.

Some marketing plans are heavy on publicity and promotional events; others stress telemarketing or direct mail. Still others emphasize radio, specialty items, magazine, newspaper, or Yellow Page advertising. Another firm might rely on public relations (PR) and community involvement. One-on-one selling works wonders in some situations, window displays and prominent signage in others.

In most cases, however, there needs to be a good marketing *mix*. That means a balance of various sales and promotional approaches. Seldom will a venture be successful by using only one of the above strategies. If marketing strategies don't come easy to you, get professional help. The entire life of your business is dependent on getting off on the right foot. For that reason, we're often called upon by start-ups to assist them in developing a strong overall marketing philosophy and strategies to carry it out.

## *Budgeting: How to Be an Astute Spender*

First a few words of clarification. In discussing a marketing budget, we don't just mean costs of advertising. PR and promotional tactics need to be factored in too. They usually have a much greater payback than outright advertising.

The most typical methods for computing what to spend are 1) earmarking "all we can afford," 2) matching or outspending the competition, or 3) allotting a percentage of sales. Let's examine these. Number one is hopeless. You can *afford* nothing. It's all been gobbled up with the move, purchase of the property and inventory, etc., etc., etc. Right? Number two is also fraught with problems. When you enter a spending race, everyone loses because an unrealistic amount of profits is funneled off for advertising.

Number three, on the other hand, holds promise. This formula is used more often than any other method. For an existing business, it's simple and provides a sense of security. Of course if the previous year was weak, you run the risk of perpetuating a downslide by allocating a lessening amount for marketing. This is a dangerous trend, so take such situations into consideration before deciding what you will spend.

We recommend the SWAG approach: Scientific Wild Ass Guess. Now don't be deceived by this flippant formula. You'll notice the "wild ass guess" part is preceded by "scientific." First contact all trade associations that represent your kind of business. Locate them in the *Encyclopedia of Associations* at the library. Talk to the executive director or some other key person to determine what the *industry standard* is for a marketing budget in your field. This is information gleaned from much trial and error. Benefit from your peers' experience. Now contact owners of similar successful business ventures in other, non-competitive areas. Explain that you're just starting and need some advertising budget advice. Most people are happy to help.

The "wild ass guess" part treats advertising as an investment. Naturally in the beginning, expenditures will exceed income. You may allot as much as 10 or 20 percent of your first year's expenses to marketing. Wise new entrepreneurs plow all possible profits back into advertising, promotion, and sales activities in the beginning. But—hallelujah—not everything costs money. Be sure to tune in carefully to the tactics contained in this chapter. Many of them are shoestring ideas to greater profits.

## *Secrets for Capturing Free PR*

Tapping into no-cost public relations is one of the most FUNdamental aspects of marketing any business or professional practice. Yet many folks think you must be able to charm the lard off a hog to be effective in PR. 'Tain't so. What is important is being alert for every opportunity to focus attention on your venture and yourself.

The most common vehicle for doing this is the press release, which we prefer to call a *news* release in this electronic age. Do you realize over 75 percent of all news is "planted?" By that we mean it is supplied by publicists and people just like you—rather than being dug up by reporters, producers, or editors. News releases cover a multitude of issues. Well written ones are often used as is. Others are reworked to fit the style of the publication. Some are deemed worthy of greater attention; they result in full-blown stories done by a reporter, freelance writer, or editor.

We won't try to teach you how to write a powerful news release here. Kate Kelly's *The Publicity Manual* does a commendable job. *The Publicity Handbook*, by David Yale, shows how to develop a sophisticated publicity campaign that sends your message loud and clear. Here you'll find out how to get newspaper, broadcast, and magazine coverage worth thousands of dollars . . . at little or no cost. (See the "Bibliography/Recommended Reading" for both.) But we do want to sensitize you to the free exposure waiting on a local, regional, and national level via this instrument.

And don't think just because you have a *local* service you shouldn't publicize in the national press. Most people never get their names in print—so they're in awe by those who do. Piano teacher Mollie Wakeman was interviewed in *Entrepreneur* magazine. "I know I won't get any new students from this mention," she observes, "but if I put a copy of this article where my students' parents can see it, they'll be so impressed I can raise my rates!"

This brings us to a significant point about publicity: secondhand PR is often *more valuable* than firsthand PR. What does that mean? Let us tell you about a client we helped in The Woodlands, Texas. They were a consulting and training firm with annual receipts of more than $1 million a year. No slouches, these folks. But while they were brilliant in their field, they were naive in the ways of publicity. No less than the *Wall Street Journal* had run a piece about this firm and its founder. When the story broke, they celebrated their good fortune . . . then filed the article away in company archives. What a waste! We counseled them to print copies of any PR and use it *everywhere*!

Such pieces solidify your credibility. They provide an ideal, low-key reason to get in front of prospects and should be used as a mailing for anyone you're trying to woo. Also send copies to current clients or customers. Use them as enclosures in virtually everything you mail. And when soliciting additional publicity, include what has already been done. This helps establish your newsworthiness. Some firms even have prestigious articles matted and framed to hang in their offices.

## TOPICS FOR NEWS RELEASES

- ✓ The opening of your store, firm, plant, or office
- ✓ Announcement of new management
- ✓ An anniversary
- ✓ The hiring, or promotion, of a key staff member
- ✓ Being awarded a new contract
- ✓ Business expansion or remodeling
- ✓ Adding a new line of goods or service(s)
- ✓ The owner receiving an award, accreditation, or other honor
- ✓ Timely tie-ins with national holidays
- ✓ Demonstrations, plant tours, open houses
- ✓ Appointment or election to a board of directors
- ✓ Financial news
- ✓ Having an article or book published
- ✓ Special event or contest announcement
- ✓ Trend evaluations or reports
- ✓ Controversial rebuttals

Using the written word in other ways can assure you of more windfall visibility. How about Letters to the Editor? These are well read platforms for getting your message, and your name, into the public's consciousness.

Op-Ed pieces, which are run in larger newspapers opposite the editorial page, do the same. These are essays about area concerns or timely topics. Or you may want to develop a flier, quiz, or booklet of self-help information to be used as a giveaway. Professionals often find newsletters to be viable PR tools.

Besides print, don't forget radio and area TV stations. Media producers gladly book people who provide value to their listeners. Perhaps you can offer guidance for better health (by a doctor), hints on housekeeping (from a maid service), or effective parenting techniques (by a therapist). Then there could be tax guidance (from a CPA), Christmas gift ideas (from a gift shop owner or a craftsperson), and ways to keep your car in tiptop shape (compliments of a mechanic). The possibilities are endless. When you're interviewed by the media, you are perceived as *the expert* in the field.

Directory listings lead to good results for many companies. This is especially true for those not dependent on the immediate area for their well-being—such as consultants, speakers, writers, technological support people, and manufacturers. You'll find over 14,000 annotated listings in *Directories in Print*. The '92 edition lists business and industrial directories, professional and scientific rosters, entertainment, recreation, and cultural directories, directory databases, plus other lists and guides.

Scour it for appropriate directories, study the listings of your competitors, then craft an entry of your own that presents you in the best light. Fill out every possible line. The longer the listing, the more substantial you appear. If they allow up to 100 words for a description of your services, use all 100. Stress what you can do for prospective clients or customers: how you'll make their jobs easier, save them money, or expand their profits. Your aim here is to get them to contact you. Also notice if there is more than one section that applies to what you do.

A study by the Association of Industrial Advertisers found that when buyers look for sellers, 35 percent find them in business directories. This tops sales calls, direct mail, brochures, Yellow Pages, even word-of-mouth. Many consultants report that about a third of their business comes from various directories. And most of these entries are free! In the publishing industry, the primary directory is *Literary Market Place*. At last count our About Books, Inc., was listed under nine different categories. We get many inquiries from these listings.

In whatever you do, offer outstanding service. Ask not what your customer can do for you, but what you can do for your customer! According to the American Management Association, 65 percent of the average company's business comes from existing, satisfied customers. Happy repeat customers are your best source of free publicity.

## *Devising Dynamic Promotional Events*

Promotional events will enhance your image, plus put more fun and profits into your business. It's important you allow time for planning and consider appropriate timing to increase results.

Events use kooky angles to create synergy. A baby shop might do something around baby pictures; a pet store, sponsor an ugly pet contest. A camera or film shop could back a photography show. Merchants can have "roll back prices" days to boost sales during slow periods. Sports and recreation lend themselves beautifully: everything from golf to bowling, hunting to fishing. You can have people predict scores, guess attendance at activities, or estimate the biggest catch of the day.

Holidays are event bonanzas. How about a fashion show just before Mother's day or Valentine's day? Make it easy for the men in your town to shop for the ladies in their lives. (You might even have a pre-registration where the women list their sizes, favorite colors, etc.) Halloween brims with a caldron of possibilities: A market could have a pumpkin carving contest—or a craft store a pumpkin decorating contest. A bookstore might instigate a scary story contest.

And for Christmas, a music store could conduct a song contest. Anyone out there raising Christmas trees? Here's a TREEific idea: sponsor a contest where area churches and service organizations decorate trees (yours of course) for display at prominent local spots such as town hall, the park, the post office, etc.

You might even team up with others in the community to develop something purely for the enjoyment of area residents. Remember doing good is good for business. Volunteering your time or expertise often pays big dividends. You'll make strategic contacts, probably receive exposure in local newspapers and the organization's newsletter, and—best of all—feel good about what you're doing.

## *Advertising's Exciting Options*

Developing an effective advertising campaign makes perfect sense for some businesses . . . and very little for others. In the professions, for instance, word-of-mouth and publicity are typically much more productive. But if you have a retail outlet or service company, advertising may play a large role in your overall marketing scheme. You'll use it to bring in new customers and maintain old ones.

We're talking here primarily about advertising designed to generate an immediate response and bottom line results, not *institutional* ads—those created to establish a position and reinforce an image. Probably the most promising are ads in the local newspaper or a "shopper" (which is distributed free), Yellow Page advertising, direct mail, and radio commercials.

Ads come in two basic types: classified and display. Display ads cost more and consequently focus more attention on you. Some people go on a spree and blow their whole budget on one big ad. Don't. That's the wrong approach. Repetition is more valuable than size. Get in front of people and stay there: week after week, month after month. Every ad should include the store name and logo, address, phone, slogan, hours, and what's known as a "call to action" to motivate people to respond.

Here are various options to make your ad more outstanding: Use a reverse (meaning white ink on a black background). Include a screen (to do this, only 20 percent of the ink is used, creating a gray background). Use lots of white space so your ad looks open and inviting. Or surround it with a heavy or distinctive border.

Want some high-powered guidance for creating winning ads? *Which Ad Pulled Best?*, by Philip Ward Burton and Scott C. Purvis, shows 50 matched pairs of ads. Quiz yourself on why one works and the other doesn't—then find out what the experts say in the Answer Key. (To order this book see the "Bibliography/Recommended Reading" section.)

Classifieds can also be surprisingly effective. Especially in small towns, people really read the classifieds. We know businesses that keep a series of ads running constantly in the classified section. If you want to reach a broader audience, National Response Corporation has bulk ad buys where you get 25-word classifieds in 100 different newspapers in a particular geographic area for under $200. Reach them at 4524 McKinney Avenue, Suite 104, Dallas, TX 75205, 214-352-0612.

Of course, the where is only one part of a three-legged stool. Without the other two vital components, it won't stand upright. Advertising is only successful if it is the *right message* to the *right audience* at the *right time*. Your timing might be lousy. More likely, you could be targeting exactly the perfect place, but lack an ad that motivates people. Writing compelling advertising copy takes sensitivity and skill.

In our busy society, more and more people "let their fingers do the walking." Yet 55 percent of all Yellow Page users don't have a specific name in mind when they open the book. What an opportunity! These are pre-qualified prospects. They have a specific need to fill, whether it's finding a plumber, taxi, lawyer, appliance repairperson, beauty salon, air-conditioning and heating contractor, computer store, or whatever.

But since there's no place where you will be in more direct competition with rival companies, it's paramount you create an eye-catching ad. Layout, illustrations, type, headlines, body copy, border, and sometimes color, must work together to establish a dramatic whole. A key to remember is that you're not selling you or your business so much as you are selling *solutions to people's problems*. Tell readers about the benefits of doing business with you rather than the competition. Your aim is to be believable, to convey trust. Citing family management, size, years in the industry, and association affiliations help to confirm your reliability. Mottos, slogans, and catchy phrases are also appropriate.

Ads are placed in a given section according to their size. Half-pagers precede the quarter-page sized, and so on. If you determine this vehicle will contribute greatly to your success, purchase the largest ad you can afford. Yellow Page advertising requires long-term planning and a sizeable financial commitment. You will be billed each month for a year. What you create today must be just as appropriate 12 months from now. Be sure you select the right listing or heading. Maybe even get a cross-reference listing. It often pays to work with a professional consultant who understands the quirks of this advertising medium.

The same is true if you go into direct mail in a big way. For some, this is an immensely profitable endeavor; for others, an expensive and painful lesson. When entering into this area, be as careful as a nudist crossing a barbed wire fence. A successful national direct mail campaign must be orchestrated by someone who knows what he or she is doing. An excellent book on the subject is Bob Stone's *Successful Direct Marketing Methods*. (See the "Bibliography/Recommended Reading.")

But if you're just concocting a flier or postcard to circulate in the neighborhood, you can probably do it yourself. This medium works well to announce grand openings to those who live nearby, champion special sales, tell about a new line or service, or plug special events. Many direct mail promotions include discount coupons to increase traffic.

In fact, several merchants can go together on a Discount Coupon Book. This goodwill builder is a real winner in tourist spots, charming area visitors and prospering local businesses. It could include two-for-one dinners, a percentage off lodging accommodations, or free items with the purchase of another. Other ideas are complimentary wine or dessert with dinner, free souvenirs with purchase of a recreational activity, plus assorted 10 to 25 percent discount coupons for a variety of merchandise. Such books can be given away at the chamber of commerce or made available at participating merchants.

Broadcast media can be very effective in stimulating traffic. In larger towns where there are several radio stations, you can target those who like classical, country, rock, or easy-listening. If you want to sell to teens, the rock station holds potential, while upscale merchandise will move better when advertised on the classical station.

Because the radio tends to be background listening for most people, incorporate attention getters into your commercials. Special effect sounds, silence, unusual speech patterns, and good voice inflection help grab listeners by the scruff of the neck and shout, "pay attention to me!" Commercials usually run as 15-, 30-, or 60-second spots. Be sure to repeat your name and phone number two or three times. One other clue: refer people to the telephone *White* Pages rather than the Yellow Pages—where they'll also be exposed to all your competition.

Commercials can be purchased as *ROS* (run of station), which means they will be aired any time the station is on the air, or *prime time*, the busy driving hours when people are usually traveling to and from work. In rural areas it doesn't pay to spend the extra money to get prime time.

Another option is segment purchasing. This is when a business regularly endorses a certain show, such as a Gardening Tips by Lane Landscaping or Stock Market News brought to you by Dunkirk Brokerage. Buying a program regularly builds listener awareness because of the repetition. In a small town you can get some excellent buys: 26 30-second spots, for instance, for only $169. Consider staging a "remote," which is a live radio broadcast done outside the studio. It might be broadcast from the shopping mall, a sporting event, or a festival.

Often the production of your commercial is free, as long as you're willing to settle for the station's staff. They have facilities for producing a taped commercial and often disc jockeys who will lend their voice to your cause. While you have less control over the results, live ads sometimes do double duty . . . especially if they feature a popular DJ. Listeners assume he or she is endorsing your product or service.

## *More Innovative Sales Techniques*

Seek out ways to expand your horizons. You can do this by exploring methods to get businesses or individuals to use more of what you supply. Suppose you're a window cleaner. Why not encourage local merchants to paint their windows for Halloween, Easter, and Christmas? Then you'll have extra business, the merchants will attract fresh attention to their establishments, and community beautification results.

Along this same line, diversify to multiply. Seek ways to create more to sell. Let's say you own a beauty school. How about starting refresher courses for those who haven't worked in a while? Or business courses for operators who plan to open their own shops? Or why not sell cosmetics, jewelry, or beauty books to generate more revenue?

Look for opportunities to gain strength in numbers. Five bed and breakfast inns in the Eugene, Oregon, area have banded together to create a phone loop to be sure they don't miss phone calls. Each B&B has two phone numbers—its own and the group's. Using call-waiting and call-forwarding the group number rings at the first inn, then at the others in turn if no one answers. By working together these entrepreneurs boost their occupancy rate and better serve their clientele. When one inn is full it also refers guests to others in the group.

Testimonials and referrals are like money in the bank—especially for professional practices and service businesses. Cultivate them. It's harder to sell *intangibles* like consulting, repairs, maintenance, or health services, for instance. There is no garment, appliance, or gift for consumers to see. So when you get verbal accolades, ask the person to put it in writing. And respond to a written compliment with a prompt, sincere thank you. Then request permission to use it. (See the following Permission Form.) Weave these kudos into future ads, brochures, and sales letters. Frame and hang them in your office or store. They help establish your credibility.

---

## PERMISSION FORM

I hereby give my consent for About Books, Inc. or their assignees to use the comments in my letter dated _____ in any manner of form, or for any medium, without restriction or limit for the purposes of nationwide publicity, advertising, or display. I understand I will receive no payment or compensation for this permission.

Signed _____ Date _____

---

Word-of-mouth praise can't be bought at any price. Yet it's an invaluable sales tool. A recent Whirlpool Corporation study proved Americans are six times more likely to base a buying decision on the judgement of others than on advertising. Such praise can be yours for the asking! A discreet sign in an attorney's office that says, "We Appreciate Your Referrals" might do the trick. A financial planner, insurance agent, or real estate salesperson might make a friendly follow-up phone call to check on a client's satisfaction . . . and tactfully inquire about other individuals this person knows who could use some help.

It really behooves physicians to keep their patients happy. A recent *USA Today* piece that looks at statistics shaping our nation found 50 percent of people choose their doctors based on recommendations from friends and relatives!

Especially if you depend on tourism, give your employees hospitality training. Be sure each person who interfaces with the public *exceeds* their expectations. Repeat visitors become next year's valued customers. A courteous, informed, motivated staff creates ripples of customer satisfaction.

So does structuring win-win arrangements. Here in Buena Vista, Game Trail—which is a real estate development selling mountain properties—has devised an intriguing coupon program. They have $25 gift certificates tucked into their brochures, which are then displayed by various local merchants. When prospects visit this real estate development, they receive a certificate redeemable at the merchant where they picked up the brochure. This clever approach encourages local businesses to display Game Trail's literature because it literally results in money in the merchants' pockets.

Are you practicing suggestive selling? It's done all the time in better clothing stores and by conscientious waitresses. Remember the last time you succumbed to a recommendation about the delicious, freshly baked pie for dessert? A carpet cleaning firm, for instance, might suggest customers also hire it to clean the drapes or wax wood floors. A phone order department could significantly impact sales on incoming calls simply by using telemarketing techniques to suggest related add-on items. And assertive consultants often convince their clients to hire them for additional services.

There are many ingenious ways to draw prospective customers into your establishment. Some restaurants post taste-tempting menus outside to lure hungry patrons inside. Others post signs offering free ice to attract travelers. A clever screen printing shop owner uses his hobby to entice people. He has a showroom where he displays his Montana breweriana collection. Many who come to browse buy screen printed T-shirts. (He also parlayed his unusual hobby and business combination into an article published in *Screenprinting* as well as area newspapers.)

Of course store display windows offer retailers opportunities limited only by their imagination. A map store owner decided to make what could be boring, one-dimensional displays into something exciting. In the coldest winter month she used a dummy exhibiting a map of the Caribbean. At Thanksgiving she created turkeys . . . made from maps of Turkey. And she always capitalizes on current events to display maps of places in the news.

A bookstore owner ties into holidays, or any other excuse she can find, to enliven her windows. At Easter a giant rabbit is the centerpiece for an array of children's books. Her February windows are alive with hearts, cupids, and gift books. Around graduation there are symbolic decorations, plus books about job hunting and careers. Summertime is greeted with beach towels, sunglasses, and stacks of novels for lazy day reading.

During slow times, offer financial incentives to boost business. While restaurants pioneered two-for-one dinners years ago, this can also be used by recreational facilities and others. A dentist or massage therapist might give a family discount. Another spin on this idea is used by one of our California clients. We helped this heating and air conditioning company develop a special Service Insurance Policy. It protects homeowners from expensive repairs—and generates up-front cash for our client.

The local paper might be your road to fame and fortune. Probe it for leads. We know of a diaper service that watches birth announcements, and a woman who owns an event-planning/bridal-service firm and garners leads by reading about engagements. One man who operates a small advertising/PR firm immediately contacts area people when they announce their candidacy for political office. He has picked up several clients this way.

Remember the 80/20 rule. This is a universal principle that applies to every business. Simply stated, 80 percent of your business will come from 20 percent of your customers or clients. Do you know who those 20 percent are? Find out! Get better acquainted. Focus attention on them instead of frittering away valuable time and resources on marginal accounts—or searching for new prospects.

How many times have you called or written for information about something you were considering buying . . . and never received anything in return? It amazes us how lazy some companies are about responding to a lead. Cherish every one. You never know which may be the pivotal point in your business—that one person who opens up a whole new window of opportunity. Furthermore you never get a second chance to make a first impression. Handling leads promptly, effectively, and courteously is not only good manners—it's good business. Why bother to arouse interest, then ignore the prospect? Sourcing your inquiries is also crucial. This means finding out how or where prospects heard about you. Knowing what's working—and what isn't—is invaluable feedback.

Allowing consumers to put purchases on credit cards like VISA and MasterCard dramatically increases the profits of most businesses. But for certain kinds of enterprises, achieving this merchant status happens about as fast as getting your teeth straightened. Bankers are especially leery of mail order, telemarketing, and home-based merchants. The reason is risk.

The bank assumes the financial obligation of returning customers' money if problems arise and the merchant has gone out of business.

While our big city colleagues often bemoan the fact they can't get merchant status, we had absolutely no problem when we approached our small town banker. Even if they're unwilling at first, chances are this will change. After you get known in the community, establish a solid reputation, and become acquainted with the bank officers, it's amazing how much easier it is to leap over such stumbling blocks.

If you make and sell a product, your quest for sales outlets is continuous. Since you can only reach so many people by yourself, it makes sense to consider getting sales representation. Rather than hiring your own sales force, why not consider using independent reps? These people function as independent contractors who sell products for several different manufacturers and make a commission on what they sell. Some even have a permanent showroom in a merchandise mart. For your convenience, we've listed contact information for the major rep organizations in Part III.

Ever consider bartering? Trading goods or services can be a realistic solution for mutual gain. It doesn't require out-of-pocket expense, yet it meets the needs of both parties. And it's as natural to country ways as congestion is to freeways. Maybe you're a printer with scant ability to do your own taxes. How about exchanging printing services with the CPA down the street who has oodles of tax expertise—and also needs new letterhead? Or you may find someone with a milk cow who hankers for your handmade pottery. Bingo! Everybody benefits.

Speaking of benefiting, if you want more ideas on how to publicize, advertise, and maximize your small business or professional practice, we've devoted a whole book to this vital subject. Get a copy of our *Big Marketing Ideas for Small Service Businesses.* It overflows with 229 practical, innovative strategies to make you more profitable. Send $29.95 plus $3 shipping to Communication Creativity, Box 909-CB, Buena Vista, CO 81211, or call credit card orders to 800-331-8355. As an additional brainstorming partner, see The Ross Marketing Idea Generator.

Have you ever noticed you have to give to get? Tune into the Universal Law that says "what goes around comes around." Be generous. Be helpful. Be thoughtful. Let your light really shine. The person who reaches out to fill the needs of others automatically finds his or her own cup running over. Go out of your way to share your business contacts. Write thank you letters to worthy suppliers. Praise deserving employees. Show loyal customers you appreciate their patronage.

## THE ROSS MARKETING IDEA GENERATOR

- Try to find an angle that makes your product or service controversial.
- Pursue newspaper features about your subject.
- Write Op-Ed (opposite editorial) pieces addressing your topic.
- Submit Letters to the Editor targeting related articles or stories.
- Join the chamber of commerce and local service clubs.
- Volunteer your time and expertise for worthy causes.
- Provide gratis articles to area newspapers or magazines.
- Conduct a survey or poll and announce the results.
- Offer exceptional service—always.
- Request testimonials from leaders in the industry.
- Ask your satisfied clients/customers for referrals.
- Prepare a "Here's What People Are Saying" flier of comments.
- Do mailings to your Christmas card list, address book, Rolodex entries.
- Develop a PR mailing list of key contacts and major players.
- Practice overcoming typical objections about your products or services.
- Send local celebrities notes of congratulations on their accomplishments.
- Establish rapport with area legislators.
- Always carry business cards—everywhere.
- Create an "event" centered around your outlet, product, or service.
- Establish a local, regional, or national award.
- Publish a newsletter.
- Launch a contest.
- Hold an open house.
- Tie in with a special national day/week/month.
- Create an internal bulletin board with photos of patients/clients.
- Found a regional or national association.
- Pursue radio and TV interviews.
- Clip and mail "FYI" articles and information to contacts.
- Give public speeches or mini-seminars at every opportunity.
- Look for ways to provide in-store demonstrations.
- Do co-op mailings with other compatible firms.
- Sponsor a team, group, or individual.
- Cultivate personal listings in who's who publications.
- Get your company listed in appropriate directories.
- Use creative signage to promote special sales or activities.
- Consider posters, balloons, even a blimp to promote your endeavor.
- Be alert to piggybacking with current news events and local hot issues.
- Seek out catalogs that sell related merchandise.
- Write a book to establish yourself as "the expert" in your field.
- Enter all contests for which you qualify.

- Have free drawings to generate an in-house mailing list.
- Team up with other merchants for special promotions.
- Send news releases to highlight your awards, accomplishments, etc.
- Become professionally certified or registered if applicable.
- Donate your products or time to community fund-raising auctions.
- Honor some deserving individual in your community or industry.
- Handle complaints quickly, quietly, and graciously.
- Follow up, *follow up*, FOLLOW UP.

Now that you have some sure-footed marketing moves that work well even in a slippery economy, let's explore how to keep yourself professionally stimulated.

# 19

# Tactics for *Staying* Prosperous and Happy

It's one thing to get caught up in the excitement of moving and launching a new business. But what then? Will you continue to be satisfied—or will the bloom fade from the rose? That depends on you! This isn't lifestyles of the rich and aimless. In this chapter we'll chat about ways to cultivate personal contentment and keep a sense of exhilaration in your life. We'll also share some small town strategies for developing and keeping your business at a peak.

## *Community Involvement: Reaching Out—Getting In*

Community is back. Civic pride, social consciousness, grassroots activism: these are the lifeblood of towns, large and small. This widespread yearning for community is showing up in our popular culture. It's why nostalgic movies and TV programs about small towns have become a national pastime.

If your company can successfully position itself as a leader in community issues, you'll have tapped into one of the best ways to generate mass appeal . . . and made yourself feel better. Fortunately, in rural America it doesn't take mammoth movements. It can be as simple as sponsoring a charity, using recycled paper or biodegradable chemicals, offering a senior-citizen discount, donating a small percentage of your sales to a worthy cause. Then make sure what you do is *publicized*.

A word processing firm donates one cent of every dollar it makes to buy computers for a local school. A clothing store gives its outdated, hard-to-move merchandise to a clearinghouse for the needy. A restaurant donates its leftovers and old-dated dairy products to a church that feeds out-of-work families. An attorney does *pro bono* work one day a month.

Doing good is good for business. In deciding where to invest your time and expertise, choose activities that showcase your competence. For instance, if your business is in the financial area, engage in fund-raising or being the treasurer of a prominent organization. This demonstrates to people that you're proficient with money. If you're an artist, perhaps you should be the person to make the eye-catching posters to announce the chamber of commerce's raffle or membership drive. Is promotional writing your *forte*? See that you spearhead the writing of the new brochure to publicize the local museum. Sharing your talents strengthens the community and helps you become known.

Consider participation in area government. With only 25 percent of the population, rural areas have 75 percent of the local government units in the United States. This enhanced opportunity for citizen involvement also implies an increased role for community leadership. Make your voice heard in local politics.

High on this agenda might be preserving your paradise. Encourage efforts to intelligently control development and the environment so you and your neighbors don't lose the very enticements that attracted you. There's a feeling of personal impact when you participate in shaping the destiny of a small town. From being a helpless observer, you progress to being an active contributor. It's a visible, tangible contribution that can put new meaning in your life.

# *Mingle Management: The Art of Networking*

Networking is nothing more than effective interaction with other people. Polished networking skills equal added professional power. Whether you're at an official networking function, attending a conference, or mingling at a large party—knowing how to "work a room" gives you a business edge and makes the event more fun. This means the ability to circulate, meet, converse, and extricate yourself.

Being prepared is half the secret of successful networking. If you can get a list of attendees beforehand, do so. Decide who you particularly want to chat with. Formulate a short, pithy self-introduction. Saying you are John Jones with the Weaverly Company doesn't cut it. But if you introduce yourself as John Jones and continue by explaining, "We help people analyze their financial goals, then guide them to the most practical and lucrative investment," you've given the other person something to go on. Your attitude needs to be bright and on straight. If it's sulky and askew, people will avoid you.

Please have something to say. Listen to the news, read the daily paper, scan news magazines and general interest periodicals. Taking the initiative and asking the other parties how long they have been in the business, what they do, or where they're from originally is fine. But eventually it's going to be your turn to contribute to the conversation. When schmoozing, find new *angles* that take a fresh look at a topic. *Bridges* that connect the current subject to a related one. Or *catapults* that jump to a new, unrelated issue. Don't monopolize the discussion, however. A good networker has two ears and one mouth . . . and uses them proportionately.

Always take a hefty stack of business cards. Don't worry about brochures or other promotional materials. You only want to exchange cards (preferably by asking for theirs first). You'll mail other materials as a follow-up procedure. Eat before you go. It's impossible to greet people and converse with a drink in one hand and *hors d'oeuvres* in the other—and in your mouth.

If you're especially shy, consider volunteering to serve on the welcoming committee. Then you have a "role," a purpose for being friendly. Another hint is to arrive early and get acquainted with a few people. Then when the room fills up you won't feel alienated by the crowd. One woman we know considers herself an unofficial hostess at every function she attends. Instead of hanging back and feeling self-conscious, she is proactive and treats people as if they were guests in her home.

What if you want to meet and greet people who are already engaged in a discussion? It's not easy to break uninvited into a group. One way is to move physically into their space. Once they notice you, move back slightly. Another approach is to ask permission. You might say, "Excuse me. I'm interested in what you're talking about. May I introduce myself?" Repeat each name as it's said and shake hands firmly.

We've all been in the situation where somebody has captured us and doesn't want to let go. One way to handle this is to say, "Well, it's been great talking to you. I see someone across the room I need to connect with." Then leave. Pronto.

When you want a person's card, simply ask. Jot a few notes on the back so you can recall his or her needs and pertinent details later. Be sure to follow up promptly with a call or mailing of materials. When you promise something, do it. By keeping your commitments you prove your reliability and begin to establish rapport.

Suppose you're attending a meeting, workshop, or conference. Where you sit will determine your networking success. Don't plop down next to an associate or friend. You already know that person. Choose an empty chair between two strangers. If you're really serious about networking, change seats at the break to meet more new people.

Actual network clubs flourish in larger cities. The purpose of these organizations is to swap leads. They are also starting to sprout in Small Town USA. In Kalispell, Montana (population 11,000) about 30 local businesspeople meet every week and generate business for each other. Such a club can prosper you in several ways: Other club members become customers. Links are forged and members' friends and clients become your clients too. Contact spheres or networking teams also evolve. These are noncompetitive businesses that are looking for the same kind of leads you are.

As in life, so in networking, givers get. If you want to manage your mingling successfully, remember this principle.

## *Growing Your Business to Its Zenith*

Ask yourself, "What business am I really in?" Sure you offer goods or services. But that isn't the business you're in. Sound crazy? Read on. The publishers of this book, for example, aren't in the publishing business—they're in the information business. That's one of the reasons they have decided to add a newsletter, so people can continue to get cutting-edge information about relocating successfully.

A neighborhood food store may well be in the convenience business. They might decide to make it easier for customers to shop for items besides food: videos to rent or inexpensive gift items. The store might even consider a delivery service. Get the idea?

If you buy an established store, be sure to make any changes gradually. One of the primary reasons for purchasing an existing business is that you inherit a proven customer base. If you change everything right away, these people's loyalty will probably falter. Tom and Carole Reamer left suburban New Jersey for Spencertown, a hamlet outside a small town in Columbia County. The pastoral setting appeals to weekend escapees from Manhattan. The Reamers bought an old-fashioned country store. Their challenge was to maintain a delicate balance of keeping the locals happy while pleasing the weekenders.

To increase profits, they got rid of the gas pumps. They were a lot of trouble and the insurance was expensive. Next they stopped selling fresh meat; they couldn't compete with a nearby supermarket. While they now stock limited groceries and produce, you can find a variety of other items at their store. If you need anything from a toothbrush to a toilet plunger, this is the place. To satisfy the broader taste of their citified clientele, they added goat cheese, bottled spring water, imported beer, blended coffees, and other gourmet items. To keep locals happy there's still a pour-your-own coffee counter and deli.

Perhaps the most lucrative innovation was adding their own home-baked goods. They produce their own breads, cakes, pies, and cookies. This went over so well, they began making prepared entrees—lasagna, chicken divan, curried beef, chicken pies—which appeal both to vacationers and the townsfolk. The Reamers make a comfortable living. Carole comments, "We don't need as much money here, and we certainly enjoy ourselves more. Besides, you can't put a money value on lifestyle."

Some people forget why they moved to the country and get all caught up in beating the opposition. Do you know the dirty 11-letter word? It's "competition." When you focus on the competition it actually detracts from your optimum performance. It places the emphasis on aspects outside of your control. We recommend you compete with *yourself*, rather than others. This challenges you to excel: to be more energetic, more innovative—more service oriented. It focuses your attention on the customer instead of the competitor.

Think of you and your customers or clients as being a privileged partnership. In return for their trust and patronage, they are entitled to the best you can give. According to the U.S. Office of Consumer Affairs, between 37 and 45 percent of people are unhappy with the *service* they receive. They don't complain—they simply go elsewhere. Ouch!

Different people want to be served in different ways. Age plays a major role in how they look at service. Mature folks care more about courtesy, security, and how well a professional (such as a doctor, dentist, or attorney) knows them. Middle-aged people want reliability, competence, and access. They look for convenient hours and easy accessibility both physically and by phone. While retirees can take their time shopping, wage earners seek convenience. They buy in a hurry. Young folks look for cheaper prices and in-vogue items.

If you run a retail establishment, it will be feast or famine. During those feast times—when there's an abundance of *them* and too little of *you*—handle it with tact. By acknowledging them in the first couple of minutes, people are usually willing to wait. They see how busy you are. Greet each person with something like: "Good to see you. I'll help you find just what you're looking for (or take your order) as soon as I'm finished with this customer. Thanks for your patience."

Capture names, addresses, and phone numbers of customers. Get an attractive guest book and encourage each to sign it for advance notice of special sales, products, announcements, or new courses being offered. Or jot down the information off their checks. On credit card orders, simply ask for the details.

> Marilyn: *When I worked in women's ready-to-wear, I made this part of the sales receipt procedure. Then during slow times, I'd write them a personalized postcard saying something about the item they bought and thanking them for their business. I got lots of positive feedback. Hardly anybody does this. And it makes people feel valued.*
>
> *I also set up a file card system by name, size, and personal preference. When we'd get in a shipment with something that "looked like them," I'd pick up the phone and alert customers about the new item. This really helped build sales.*

Developing your own mailing list is an astute business procedure. You might cull only the most promising customers for a personalized mailing, or go to the whole list to announce something special. You can use mailings to build store traffic, generate goodwill, introduce new lines or products, or ask for referrals.

"When it comes to playing hard to get, you just can't beat profits," jokes one businessman. Yet profits are waiting for those who nurture their patrons and buy properly. One secret is to keep your inventory lean. Record what you have in stock, then rank items by how fast they move. Get rid of the losers. Check with your trade association to see how many times a year your inventory should turn over. Be sure you don't lag behind the norm. Cut better deals on your purchases by keeping an eye out for discounts. And if you have a lot of merchandise shipped in, consider making your own freight-hauling arrangements and pocketing the volume discount, rather than relying on your suppliers for shipping. When sales slump, remember what worldwide acclaimed minister Dr. Robert Schuller says: "Tough times never last, tough people do."

## *Outsmarting the Isolation Factor*

You're only as isolated as you want to be. There are always activities going on, you just have to find them. True, they will be different forms of entertainment than you were used to in the city. But wasn't escaping sophisticated suburbia one of the reasons you moved?

Before writing this chapter, we polled our employees—most of whom have come here from other places—for ideas. Their advice was that being friendly and outgoing opens all doors. Have pleasant conversations with everyone you meet: the service station attendant, bank teller, grocery store cashier. Check out local organizations and clubs that relate to something you like to do. A new face and willing hands are always welcome. Most rural areas have a shortage of people amenable to helping. Join up and jump in! Get on a committee or volunteer for an office right away. Being just a member never gives you as much of an opportunity to get acquainted as does working in small groups. And anything you do socially will also help your business to get known and moving.

Scour the local newspaper for activities. Look not only at the articles, but also at the regular ads, the classifieds, and the notices section. Read posters and bulletin boards around town to keep up with the happenings. Attend chamber mixers, potlucks sponsored by service groups, school performances. If you have children, get involved in the PTA and acquainted with playmates' parents.

For many families, a spiritual connection is the perfect antidote for feelings of isolation. Check the Yellow Pages for churches and synagogues. Visit some and decide which group you feel most comfortable with. Sports is another ideal icebreaker. Is there a softball team, snowmobile club, or hiking group you might join?

And don't forget the folks back home. Sending and receiving letters keeps you feeling connected. Or you may want to telephone or record an audio cassette tape. Keep pictures of loved ones and friends where you can see them. Spend a few minutes each week in silent, *heartwarming* communion with each of these people. Further keep them in your life by clipping articles and cartoons you see that you know would appeal to them. Drop these items in the mail as a spontaneous "thinking of you" gesture. They may even start reciprocating.

Loneliness is an attitude. It's a negative force that weakens your motivation, stifles your productivity, and squelches your joy. It is combated by positive expectations and specific acts. Having an upbeat outlook and taking action to help you get acquainted provides the cure. Loyal friendships don't happen overnight. It takes time and nurturing to develop these relationships. Give yourself permission to take the time needed to pursue this camaraderie. As the saying goes, "To make a friend you must first be one."

There's a plethora of things to do and ways not to be bored. Find out what your neighbors do for fun, then choose your new favorite pastimes from this list.

## *Remaining Mentally Stimulated*

To help you stay sharp, consider getting a brainstorming buddy. Asking for another opinion from a planning partner—especially someone with a different or broader perspective—can prove very rewarding. Approach someone in church or in the community whom you like and respect. Suggest you get together a couple of times a month to share ideas.

Teaching is another method for staying sharp. Whenever we've taught, we've also learned. As you develop lesson plans or seminar outlines, you automatically hone your own skills. And the questions students sometimes pose—wow! They push you to the outer limits of your own experience and expertise. Opportunities exist in the country for teaching at community colleges as well as setting up informal classes in your home or a public building. And don't overlook *taking* courses yourself. While the offerings won't be as diversified as they were in the city, there's probably something to interest you. This is another excellent way to meet potential friends.

Practice the three R's (readin', writin', and roamin') yourself.

Subscribe to—and *read*—at least one industry trade journal. This will help you keep up with what is going on in your field. You may want to read the *Wall Street Journal*. If you can't spend the money for a subscription, peruse it at your local library. Use the library in other ways: to take in the latest bestsellers, read general interest magazines, or join a book discussion group.

Even if you're not an accomplished writer, you can contribute to the Letters to the Editor section of your local newspaper. Getting fired up about local issues, organizing your thought in a rational flow, and presenting your opinion in convincing language will definitely get your adrenalin flowing.

Mental stimulation can go in other directions too. Find out about this new land you've claimed as your own. Roam around the back country. Explore! Discover ghost towns, trails, and nature sanctuaries. Seek historical spots. Visit neighboring towns. If you've never been camping, find friends who have and go with them. Buy a birdfeeder and learn the names of new birds. Enjoy the gift of nature that surrounds you.

Perhaps you have an interest you think others would share, but there is no existing group for these people. Start one! Ideas run the gamut from a Great Books Discussion Group to a Toastmasters Club, from a race walking group to a TOPS Club. Put a classified ad in the paper, ask the editor to run a short story introducing your idea, and create fliers to place at strategic places interested people might frequent.

## *Staying Abreast of Your Industry*

Remaining knowledgeable about your industry is difficult when you live in the country. Eleanor Perry-Harrington tells the story of how she had a small gift shop in a town of 2,000 in Kansas. "I loved it and was settling in nicely. Fortunately, I was invited to go to the gift show in Dallas after awhile," she relates. "There was another world out there. I realized I had gotten into a rut and stagnated. I was jarred back to reality. After that, I made it a point to get out every six months to see what was going on in the big cities."

A hairstylist here in Buena Vista told us of going into Denver each quarter to attend a networking club where salon owners bring their problems. As a first time businessman, he learned about hiring, taxes, motivating employees, and marketing. He also regularly attends hair shows and educational events sponsored by hair care product manufacturers. When in the city, he also stops in and gets acquainted with hairstylists to swap tips and keep in the know about current trends.

Bernard Kamoroff lives in Laytonville, California. This off-the-beaten-path place spawned a publishing company that produces one of the most successful entrepreneurial books around: *Small Time Operator.* Kamoroff keeps tabs on his industry by attending the American Booksellers Association convention each year. "I hang out for 2½ days with all the people in the book world and hobnob and shoot the breeze," he says.

> Tom: *To keep informed about the publishing industry, and give something back, I currently serve on the board of directors of COSMEP, the International Association of Independent Publishers. We have an annual convention where experts speak and much networking occurs. There are also board meetings where I can discuss things with my peers. And frequent correspondence from the executive director keeps me informed about issues in the publishing community.*

James Kennedy publishes two highly respected newsletters, *Consultants News* and *Executive Recruiter News,* from rural New Hampshire. He stays abreast of his field by spending his work days talking to sources on the telephone and reading dozens of business publications.

We'd be remiss if we didn't again point to computers and modems as wonderful tools for keeping up-to-date. Once you learn how to use your modem and databases, there's instant gratification. Computer cliques exist for every interest. There's no reason you can't harness top-notch brainpower in your field with a little investment in time and money.

Now that you know how to stay prosperous and happy in the country, it's time to move on. Let's look at large corporations that have decided small towns are the *pièce de résistance*.

# 20

# Big Business Bolts: Large Companies Find Small Towns

Corporate America is in transition. First small branch offices, R&D labs, and management training centers left their old traditional urban clusters for simpler, more pastoral surroundings. As big cities and suffocating suburbs lost their luster, regional offices followed. Now corporate headquarters are escaping to the booming backwaters.

Some big city sophisticates no longer look down their soot-smudged noses at small towns. In fact, many crinkle their noses at $50 a square foot office space and $11 an hour maintenance people. They're tired of trying to be cool when they're in hot water, of trying to compete in a global economy when only 65 percent of their potential work force has even graduated from high school. All this bodes well for the new corporate frontier.

Says financial guru Louis Rukeyser in his nationally syndicated column, "A hot new trend in American business is turning your back on the metropolises and heading happily back to the boonies." He credits improved telecommunications and mounting urban ills as being the incentives for corporations to choose a greener lifestyle. "With the latest advances in telecommunications, a CEO can run his company from the moon—or Minnesota," adds *Fortune's* Alan Farnham.

According to the September 16, 1991, issue of *Forbes*, corporate America now is entering stage three of its revolutionary wandering through the national landscape. The aim of this stage is clear: Companies want to escape from large cities and their suburban rings and find new homes for their headquarters in smaller metropolitan areas. Says author James Cook, "Moving to smaller towns is the equivalent of giving many executives big raises and a better standard of living."

Indeed, technology not available a decade ago makes the hinterlands entirely more habitable. Distance has been redefined by personal computers, faxes, modems, electronic pagers, cellular phones, and fiber optics. New telephone features and overnight delivery services further facilitate doing business in the boonies. Video conferencing now makes it possible to conduct business meetings, training sessions, or motivation rallies over long distances.

And as we detailed in a previous chapter, more than three million employees telecommute. They perform tasks from their homes, only going into "the office" occasionally. American Express, J.C. Penney, AT&T, and Blue Cross/Blue Shield are just a sampling of the companies taking advantage of this technological opportunity.

Geography is becoming increasingly irrelevant. Except for utility companies and place-specific media like newspapers and television stations, virtually all companies are potentially footloose.

## *Household Name Companies with Country Addresses*

"Success in the Sticks" might be the theme song for some corporations you'd never guess had rural addresses. J.M. Smucker Company dominates the jam and jelly business . . . from little Orrville, Ohio (population 7,712). Phillips Petroleum is headquartered in Bartlesville, Oklahoma (34,256)—while the Kellogg company hails from Battle Creek, Michigan—population 53,540. Gerber products have been babying infants for decades. They're also largely responsible for the paychecks that get spent in tiny Fremont, Michigan (3,875). Newton, Iowa, (14,789) is home base for Maytag, which manufacturers household appliances.

And what about Corning Glass Works? They're located in no less than Corning, New York, which sports a population of 11,938. Sears is no longer the major tenant of Chicago's Sears Tower. The retail giant opted to move the 6,000 employees of their merchandising group to Hoffman

Estates, Illinois (population 44,761). Adidas USA Inc. relocated a portion of its operational headquarters, plus some office and support functions, from Warren, New Jersey to Spartanburg, South Carolina. Adidas chose this small city of 43,000 because it has "a good solid labor force, transportation system, and infrastructure, and living costs are low."

Big industry has also discovered penturbia. General Motors put over $3 billion into its Saturn plant in little-known Maury County, Tennessee. And the Big Three moved many of their strategic functions to such pastoral places as Troy, Warren, and Auburn Hills, Michigan. Even purchasing less expensive property and wooing competent workers hasn't fortified them against foreign competition.

The legendary mail-order giant L.L. Bean runs a $600 million empire that includes catalogs of country clothing, hunting and fishing gear, plus other outdoorsy products. The hub for all this activity is Freeport, Maine, where the population hovers near the 7,000 mark. That is, except when tourists come to visit their 24-hour-a-day, 365-day-a-year retail outlet. Upwards of 2 million people stroll through the store each year. What kind of telephone traffic does a company of this size need to be prepared to handle? They can receive over 12,000 orders in a single day. Whoever said you have to take off your business suit to realize blue jean dreams?

Of course, Sam Walton's Wal-Mart Stores are the premier blue jean dream success story. Benton, Arkansas—with 11,257 residents—is headquarters for this colossal retail organization. Not only does he work out of a rural environment, his whole focus is to serve small town America. Walton had a vision to bring a discount store concept to southern towns of under 25,000 that other retailers felt weren't worth the effort. His foresight—and "efforts"—have made him one of the richest men in the world.

## *What Prompts Urban Flight?*

Sleepy backwoods areas are becoming fashionable for major corporate relocations. But it isn't chic that's drawing firms like Sears, Roebuck & Company and Adidas to countrified settings. Style has nothing to do with it. The reasons are much more basic: significant cost savings, pools of eager employees, executives who want job stimulation coupled with a simpler lifestyle. Stressed-out CEOs seek more time with their families and some *leisure* to enjoy. (It's ironic that we're the only country in the world with a mountain called "Rushmore.") Yet they also want a serious business environment. While they won't find it in some parts of rural America, they will in others.

Thousands of astute small towns, counties, and economic development entities are courting this corporate culture. "The most favored frontier towns are often linked to a major university, a state capital, a research park, or a similar institution that tends to provide the diversity and cultural spark sought by young professionals," says David A. Heenan. He is the author of a recently released book, *The New Corporate Frontier: The Big Move to Small Town USA*. While many of these towns are somewhat isolated, they're not hickish and clannish, Heenan points out.

The greatest attraction is saving money. A survey by Runzheimer International revealed that over 27 percent of companies moved because they wanted a lower-cost operating environment. Yet metropolitian areas are synonymous with high office and commercial property rents, escalating labor costs, and the burden of municipal and state taxes. These can range from 20 to 50 percent more in cities or suburbs.

Tom Houghton, president of H.S. Precision, Inc. needed to expand his manufacturing operation to keep up with customer demand. But industrial property in Arizona where his company was located was very expensive. "About $125,000 an acre," explains Houghton. And the tax structure for running a business was high. The company also required bank financing, almost impossible to get in Arizona. After much study, H.S. Precision moved up and out: clear out to Rapid City, South Dakota.

Rapid City put together a deal he couldn't refuse. It allowed him to move with minimal financial risk to the company. "They built us a building, loaned us some money at 3 percent for some new equipment, and put together the operating line at the bank." says Houghton. How long did all this take? Only seven days from the time the city got his final application until he had a letter of commitment! Such near miracles can happen when a company seeking relocation goes into partnership with an assertive town looking to enhance the local economy.

In his book, Heenan tells of Coral Gables—once a sleepy bedroom community in southern Florida. Today it has become "the Gateway City to Latin America" with more than 75 multinational corporations calling it home for their regional offices. Why did these companies hopscotch over larger and more prestigious Miami? Because Coral Gables, though it had only 41,000 people, went after their business. It drew them like bears to a honey pot.

# *An Abundant Resource of Conscientious Employees*

Ask executives and entrepreneurs to name their top three challenges in business, and you'll hear "finding good employees" virtually every time. And the problem will worsen as we head into the new millennium. Especially for manufacturing operations, a pivotal point is the availability of a labor pool. Rural areas can provide a positive alternative.

Jetson Direct Mail Services originally headquartered its entire operation in Hauppage, a community on Long Island, New York. This region suffers from a work force shortage—thus the head of Jetson, Vincent Carosella, was constantly frustrated. "A worker comes in at 8:45, you tell her she's fifteen minutes late, she walks across the street and is employed by somebody else by 9:00 A.M. That's the scenario on Long Island," he complained in an article in the *Wall Street Journal*.

Carosella now has practically no employee turnover. Why? Because he moved his printing and mailing division, and the 500 jobs it represents, to St. Clair, Pennsylvania. With an unemployment rate of 11 percent, the depressed coal-mining town of 4,000 welcomed him with open arms. He pays workers the same wages as he pays on Long Island and everybody's happy.

Philadelphia's Hal Rosenbluth had a similar experience. President of Rosenbluth Travel Inc., his move of 20 temporary data-entry jobs to tiny Linton, North Dakota, was prompted primarily by a desire to help Midwest drought victims. When 80 people applied for these positions, he decided to hire 40 of them. What happened next shocked him.

"There was virtually no absenteeism or turnover," reports Rosenbluth. "The quality of the work was extremely high." This doesn't surprise area economic development personnel. North Dakota boasts a high school dropout rate of less than 2 percent and a higher education rate of more than 70 percent. Because of the positive results, Rosenbluth made the jobs permanent, and kept hiring.

The locals work in a former John Deere implement dealership refurbished into modern offices. Called "associates," they dress smartly in business outfits to help dispel the preconceived notions about rural North Dakota. Rosenbluth anticipates having 200 Linton residents on his payroll eventually. "It's almost become a crusade of our company to blend rural and corporate America," he says.

Charles Gleason has the best of two worlds. His life-insurance firm is in dual markets: urban Michigan and a Florida wildlife refuge. Consequently, it has two work pools to draw from. In fact, he often conducts business from his summer home on Sanibel Island, Florida. Modern technology switches 800 calls from location to location. Service inquiries are routed to his administrative assistant's office in her home near Pontiac, Michigan. "Business in Detroit has been a disaster for the past two years," Gleason recently told the *Wall Street Journal*. "But Florida is booming."

The nation's largest relocation firm, PHH Fantus, reports that 11 percent of companies they surveyed in the Boston-Washington corridor said they were forced to relocate operations to meet their labor needs. The same was true for firms on the West Coast.

Anderson-Barrows Metal Corporation is a manufacturer of brass fittings for the plumbing industry. They recently built a large facility in Palmdale, California, on the edge of the Mojave Desert. (Many of their employees had already moved there to dodge the high living costs in greater Los Angeles.) When the company opened its doors, there were 10 positions available; 1,300 people applied!

Not only do smaller towns provide an abundance of potential employees, the dedication of these people is usually superior. "Loyalty is still in style in frontierland," says Heenan. "Not only is productivity higher, but turnover is lower." Trust and commitment combine to forge a strong bond between company and work force.

Are you tired of escalating operating costs and declining worker allegiance? Ready to consider a rural relocation for your company? Below is a Checklist for CEOs. Use it to help gauge how adaptable you are.

## A CHECKLIST FOR CEOs

*THE NEW CORPORATE FRONTIER: THE BIG MOVE TO SMALL TOWN USA by David A. Heenan. Copyright © 1991 by McGraw-Hill, Inc. Reproduced with permission of McGraw-Hill, Inc.*

Despite the benefits, penturban living is not for every company. What's your firm's small-town index? Here are 10 questions CEOs should consider if they are contemplating a move to the new corporate frontier.

1) Will relocating to a small town enhance your firm's survival, growth, and profitability? What is the likely impact to the bottom line?

2) Can you distance yourself from the rest of your industry and not be penalized? Will your key customers react favorably to your new address?

3) Can telecommunications adequately replace face-to-face contact in your business? If so, are your prepared to make a major investment in state-of-the-art technology?

4) Are you willing to spend possibly large amounts of time traveling to and from your small-town headquarters? Are your customers, suppliers, bankers, and other resource people willing to entertain a similar increase in travel? Are you willing to purchase corporate aircraft?

5) How much pruning can be done at corporate, regional, and divisional headquarters? Do you really have your heart in a mini-headquarters, or do you need strength in numbers at your side?

6) Are you prepared to adopt a decentralized philosophy that a smallish head office in penturbia requires? Do the corporate culture and your own management style encourage delegation and discourage hands-on involvement in day-to-day operations? How talented are your operating company personnel? Are they up to the task of managing with limited guidance?

7) Are you willing to trade off the anonymity of urban living for the fishbowl environment of a small town? Does your management team share this view?

8) Can future generations of top-notch talent in your industry be attracted to a frontier locale?

9) Would your small-town destination accommodate the two-career couples among your management? Are you prepared to assist with spousal employment? How will women, Blacks, Hispanics, and other groups be received?

10) Most important, do you and your top executives really want to live and work in the penturbs? Are these values shared by all their family members?

If you answered "yes" to these questions, penturban living may be for you. If not, stay put!

## *More Corporate Success Stories*

Some of the most interesting feats are being accomplished in the most unusual places. Replacements, Ltd., a firm that sells discontinued china and crystal, has plunked its facility in the middle of agricultural fields in McLeansville, North Carolina. But that doesn't mean they're small potatoes. Replacements, Ltd. did $15.2 million worth of business in 1991. It carries over 40,000 patterns and has an inventory of 1.4 million individual pieces of crystal and china. Founder and president Bob Page was just named Entrepreneur of the Year by the state of North Carolina.

*Trade Your Business Suit Blues for Blue Jean Dreams™*

The Bacova Guild, Ltd. is headquartered in Bacova, Virginia . . . population 50. Their annual receipts? Would you believe 16.6 million! Nestled deep in a remote valley in the Allegheny Mountains, this privately held company is a national leader in the silkscreening industry. They produce decorative mats, rugs, and mailboxes. *Inc.* magazine recognized them as one of the 500 fastest growing small companies in America in '87 and '88.

While Bacova normally employs about 200 people, their payroll swells to 300 during the peak Christmas season. When asked her opinion of the local work force, a company spokesperson observed, "They're great, down-to-earth people. They take pride in their work and give 110 percent." She personally enjoys the "calm" atmosphere of her work environment. Bath County, where the plant is located, not only benefits from paychecks and property taxes, but also from having a non-polluting industry that doesn't deplete the area's natural resources.

EMRG—which stands for Electronic Marketing Resource Group—provides software, consulting, and data-processing services for college financial aid offices. They control 40 percent of the national market. Where does all this activity take place? In Kearney, Nebraska. With 23,000 residents, it seems like a quiet farm community.

But inside an old house on 25th Street, Dave Waldron and his staff sometimes got so busy they overran the capacity of the local phone system! Fortunately, that technological obstacle has been overcome by creating a direct link between Kearney and the Grand Island switches. Says Waldron, "People don't care where you are if you get your job done."

Spartanburg, South Carolina, is the home of Executive Quality Management (EQM). Starting out of rented desk space in 1986, founding partners Joe Black and George W. "Pudge" Tate have developed EQM into a consulting firm with an international reputation and clientele. Their custom-designed quality processes train employees to implement the aspect of quality in *everything* they do. This leads to enhanced customer satisfaction, greater employee fulfillment, and improved bottom lines. Their philosophy? Quality is a total organizational issue.

"*Care ratio* is my decision to make your problem my problem," explains Black. "It's a major strategy in showing your commitment to quality improvement." EQM is unique in the industry as they stay with their client companies for an average of 24 months. One would expect such high-touch savvy to emanate from a large city on one of the coasts, not from a town of less than 45,000.

Jokes and half-truths have plagued small towns ever since the industrial revolution began. Today the laugh is often on blighted big cities. Although a small town may be off the beaten path, it isn't necessarily out of the mainstream. With bold new breakthroughs in technology pointing the way, major companies are getting geographically adventuresome. There is a new celebration of community. Bucolic has once again become beautiful.

# Afterword

Thanks for sharing this journey with us. We hope our efforts will make your trip easier, safer, and happier. Writing this book has been sometimes frustrating, usually exhilarating, always probing for us. We've laid our souls bare, sharing what works (easy)—and what doesn't (not so easy).

We're always interested in hearing from our readers. What did you like best about *County Bound!*? How can we improve the next edition? Tell us about your needs, expectations, and experiences.

We'd also really appreciate your help in another way. Many more people need to be exposed to this life-enriching message. Do you have contacts on major radio or TV shows? Have a friend, relative, or colleague who writes for a national magazine or daily newspaper? Tell them about *Country Bound!* Also consider recommending it to your employer if you work for a large corporation that is moving part of its personnel to a smaller city location—or has employees who could telecommute.

We are also professional speakers and consultants who love to share our vision of countrypreneuring with corporations, associations, and government agencies. And naturally, we hope you'll want another copy or two as gifts for friends, associates, or loved ones who want to escape the rat race.

Meanwhile . . we wish you an easy move, a stress-free transition, and a life changed from endurance to empowerment as you switch from the fast track to a country lane!

Contact the Rosses at:
P.O. Box 922-CB
Buena Vista, Colorado 81211-0922

# Part III
Resources

# State Tourism Offices and Chambers of Commerce

To aid you in your quest for information, below are the state tourism offices and the chambers of commerce for each state. If no statewide chamber exists, the group serving the state's largest city is listed.

**ALABAMA**
State Tourism Office
532 S. Perry Street
Montgomery, AL 36130
800-252-2262

Business Council of Alabama
468 S. Perry Street
Montgomery, AL 36104-4236
205-834-6000

**ALASKA**
State Tourism Office
P.O. Box E
Juneau, AK 99811
907-465-2010

State Chamber of Commerce
217 2nd Street, Suite 201
Juneau, AK 99801-1267
907-586-2323

**ARIZONA**
State Tourism Office
1480 E. Bethany Home Road,
Suite 180
Phoenix, AZ 85014
602-542-8687

Chamber of Commerce
1221 E. Osborn Road
Phoenix, AZ 85014-5539
602-248-9172

*Trade Your Business Suit Blues for Blue Jean Dreams™*

**ARKANSAS**
State Tourism Office
1 Capitol Mall
Little Rock, AR 72201
800-643-8383

State Chamber of Commerce
410 S. Cross Street
Little Rock, AR 72201-3014
501-374-9225

**CALIFORNIA**
State Tourism Office
1121 L Street, Suite 103
Sacramento, CA 95814
800-862-2543

Chamber of Commerce
1201 K Street, 12th Floor
Sacramento, CA 95814-3918
916-444-6670

**COLORADO**
State Tourism Office
1625 Broadway, Suite 1700
Denver, CO 80202
800-433-2656

Association of Commerce & Industry
1776 Lincoln Street, Suite 1200
Denver, CO 80203-1029
303-831-7411

**CONNECTICUT**
State Tourism Office
210 Washington Street
Hartford, CT 06106
203-258-4290

Business & Industry Association
370 Asylum Street, 5th Floor
Hartford, CT 06103-2025
203-547-1661

**DELAWARE**
State Tourism Office
99 Kings Highway, P.O. Box 1401
Dover, DE 19901
800-441-8846

State Chamber of Commerce
1 Commerce Street, Suite 200
Wilmington, DE 19801-5401
302-655-7221

**FLORIDA**
State Tourism Office
107 W. Gaines Street, Suite 410D
Tallahassee, FL 32301
904-488-4141

State Chamber of Commerce
136 S. Bronough Street
Tallahassee, FL 32301-7706
904-222-2831

**GEORGIA**
State Tourism Office
230 Peachtree Street, Suite 605
Atlanta, GA 30303
800-847-4842

Business Council of Georgia
233 Peachtree Street, Suite 200
Atlanta, GA 30303
404-223-2264

**HAWAII**
State Tourism Office
3440 Wilshire Blvd., Suite 502
Los Angeles, CA 90010
213-385-5301

Chamber of Commerce
735 Bishop Street, Suite 220
Honolulu, HI 96813-4897
808-522-8800

**IDAHO**
State Tourism Office
State Capitol, Room 108
Boise, ID 83720
800-635-7820

Boise Area Chamber of Commerce
300 N. 6th Street
Boise, ID 83702-5956
208-344-5515

State Tourism Offices and Chambers of Commerce

## ILLINOIS
State Tourism Office
100 W. Randolph Street, Suite 3-400
Chicago, IL 60601
800-223-0121

State Chamber of Commerce
20 N. Wacker Drive
Chicago, IL 60606-3084
312-372-7373

## INDIANA
State Tourism Office
1 N. Capitol, Suite 700
Indianapolis, IN 46204
800-289-6646

State Chamber of Commerce
1 N. Capitol Avenue, Suite 200
Indianapolis, IN 46204-2248
317-634-6407

## IOWA
State Tourism Office
600 E. Court Avenue, Suite A
Des Moines, IA 50309
800-345-4692

Department of Economic Development
200 E. Grand Avenue
Des Moines, IA 50309-1834
515-281-3251

## KANSAS
State Tourism Office
400 W. 8th Street, 5th Floor
Topeka, KS 66603
913-296-3966

Chamber of Commerce & Industry
500 Bank IV Tower
Topeka, KS 66603-3406
913-357-6321

## KENTUCKY
State Tourism Office
Capitol Plaza Tower, 22nd Floor
Frankfort, KY 40601
800-225-8747

Chamber of Commerce
452 Versailles Road
Frankfort, KY 40601-3832
502-695-4700

## LOUISIANA
State Tourism Office
P.O. Box 94291
Baton Rouge, LA 70804-9291
504-342-8119

Association of Business & Industry
3113 Valley Creek Drive
Baton Rouge, LA 70808-3147
504-928-5388

## MAINE
State Tourism Office
97 Winthrop Street
Hallowell, ME 04347
207-289-2423

Chamber of Commerce & Industry
126 Sewall Street
Augusta, ME 04330-6822
207-623-4568

## MARYLAND
State Tourism Office
45 Calvert Street
Annapolis, MD 21401
800-543-1036

Chamber of Commerce
275 West Street, Suite 400
Annapolis, MD 21401-3400
410-269-0642

## MASSACHUSETTS
State Tourism Office
100 Cambridge Street
Boston, MA 02202
800-447-6277

Office of Business Development
100 Cambridge Street, 13th Floor
Boston, MA 02202-0001
617-727-3206

## MICHIGAN
State Tourism Office
Box 30226
Lansing, MI 48909
517-373-1700

State Chamber of Commerce
600 S. Walnut Street
Lansing, MI 48933-2262
517-371-2100

## MINNESOTA
State Tourism Office
240 Bremer Bldg., 419 N. Robert St.
St. Paul, MN 55101
612-296-5029

Chamber of Commerce
480 Cedar Street, Suite 500
Saint Paul, MN 55101-2240
612-292-4650

## MISSISSIPPI
State Tourism Office
P.O. Box 849
Jackson, MS 39205
800-647-2290

Economic Council
P.O. Box 23276
Jackson, MS 39225-3276
601-969-0022

## MISSOURI
State Tourism Office
P.O. Box 1055
Jefferson, MO 65102
314-751-4133

State Chamber of Commerce
428 E. Capitol Avenue
Jefferson City, MO 65101-3069
314-634-3511

## MONTANA
State Tourism Office
1424 9th Avenue
Helena, MT 59620
800-541-1447

Chamber of Commerce
2030 11th Avenue
Helena, MT 59601
406-442-2405

## NEBRASKA
State Tourism Office
P.O. Box 94666
Lincoln, NE 68509
800-742-7595

Chamber of Commerce & Industry
1320 Lincoln Mall
Lincoln, NE 68508
402-474-4422

## NEVADA
State Tourism Office
Capitol Complex
Carson City, NV 89710
800-638-2328

State Chamber of Commerce
P.O. Box 3499
Reno, NV 89505-3499
702-786-3030

## NEW HAMPSHIRE
State Tourism Office
P.O. Box 856
Concord, NH 03301
603-271-2343

Business & Industry Association
122 N. Main Street, 3rd Floor
Concord, NH 03301-4917
603-224-5388

## NEW JERSEY
State Tourism Office
1 W. State Street
Trenton, NJ 08625
800-JERSEY-7

State Chamber of Commerce
5 Commerce Street
Newark, NJ 07102-3906
201-623-7070

## NEW MEXICO
State Tourism Office
Bataan Memorial Bldg.
Santa Fe, NM 87503
800-545-2040

Assn. of Commerce & Industry of NM
2309 Renard Place SE, Suite 402
Albuquerque, NM 87106-4259
505-842-0644

## NEW YORK
State Tourism Office
1 Commerce Plaza
Albany, NY 12245
800-225-5697

Chamber of Commerce & Industry
200 Madison Avenue, 3rd Floor
New York, NY 10016-3901
212-493-7400

## NORTH CAROLINA
State Tourism Office
430 N. Salisbury Street
Raleigh, NC 27611
800-847-4862

Citizens for Business & Industry
225 Hillsborough Street, Suite 460
Raleigh, NC 27603-1767
919-828-0758

## NORTH DAKOTA
State Tourism Office
State Capitol Grounds
Bismarck, ND 58505
800-437-2077

Greater North Dakota Association
808 3rd Avenue S
Fargo, ND 58103-1865
701-237-9461

## OHIO
State Tourism Office
P.O. Box 1001
Columbus, OH 43216
800-282-5393

State Chamber of Commerce
35 E. Gay Street
Columbus, OH 43215-3138
614-228-4201

## OKLAHOMA
State Tourism Office
500 Will Rogers Bldg.
Oklahoma City, OK 73105
800-652-6552

State Chamber of Commerce & Industry
4020 N. Lincoln Blvd.
Oklahoma City, OK 73105-5219
405-424-4003

## OREGON
State Tourism Office
595 Cottage Street NE
Salem, OR 97310
800-547-7842

Portland Metro. Chamber of Commerce
221 NW 2nd Avenue
Portland, OR 97209-3999
503-228-9411

## PENNSYLVANIA
State Tourism Office
416 Forum Bldg.
Harrisburg, PA 17120
800-847-4872

Chamber of Business & Industry
222 N. 3rd Street
Harrisburg, PA 17101-1502
717-255-3252

## RHODE ISLAND
State Tourism Office
7 Jackson Walkway
Providence, RI 02903
401-277-2601

Greater Providence Chamber of Commerce
30 Exchange Terrace
Providence, RI 02903-1748
401-521-5000

## SOUTH CAROLINA
State Tourism Office
P.O. Box 71
Columbia, SC 29202
803-734-0101

Chamber of Commerce
1201 Main Street, Suite 1810
Columbia, SC 29201-3229
803-799-4601

## SOUTH DAKOTA
State Tourism Office
P.O. Box 6000
Pierre, SD 57501
800-843-1930

Industry & Commerce Assoc. of SD
108 N. Euclid Avenue
Pierre, SD 57501
605-224-6161

## TENNESSEE
State Tourism Office
P.O. Box 23170
Nashville, TN 37202
800-847-4886

Nashville Area Chamber of Commerce
161 4th Avenue N
Nashville, TN 37219-2411
615-259-4755

## TEXAS
State Tourism Office
Box 12008, Capitol Station
Austin, TX 78711
800-888-8839

State Chamber of Commerce
900 Congress Avenue, Suite 501
Austin, TX 78701-2447
512-472-1594

## UTAH
State Tourism Office
Council Hall, Capitol Hill
Salt Lake City, UT 84114
801-538-1030

Provo/Orem Chamber of Commerce
777 S. State Street
Orem, UT 84058-6307
801-224-3636

## VERMONT
State Tourism Office
134 State Street
Montpelier, VT 05602
802-828-3236

Chamber of Commerce
P.O. Box 37
Montpelier, VT 05601
802-223-3443

## VIRGINIA
State Tourism Office
202 N. 9th Street, Suite 500
Richmond, VA 23219
800-847-4882

Chamber of Commerce
9 S. 5th Street
Richmond, VA 23219-3823
804-644-1607

## WASHINGTON
State Tourism Office
101 General, Administration Bldg.
Olympia, WA 98504
800-544-1800

Greater Seattle Chamber of Commerce
600 University Street, Suite 1200
Seattle, WA 98101-1129
206-389-7200

## WASHINGTON, DC
State Tourism Office
P.O. Box 27489
Washington, DC 20038-7489
800-422-8644

Chamber of Commerce
1411 K Street, NW, Suite 500
Washington, DC 20005-3404
202-347-7201

**WEST VIRGINIA**
State Tourism Office
1900 Washington Street E.,
Bldg. 6, Room B-564
Charleston, WV 25305
800-225-5982

Chamber of Commerce
300 Capitol Street, Suite 1000
Charleston, WV 25301-1794
304-342-1115

**WISCONSIN**
State Tourism Office
P.O. Box 7606
Madison, WI 53707
608-266-2147

Manufacturers & Commerce
501 E. Washington Avenue
Madison, WI 53703-2944
608-258-3400

**WYOMING**
State Tourism Office
Frank Norris, Jr. Travel Center
Cheyenne, WY 82002
800-225-5996

Greater Cheyenne Chamber of Commerce
301 W. 16th Street
Cheyenne, WY 82001-4437
307-638-3388

# Government Sources

## *Business and Commerce*

To aid you in finding the answers to questions–or discovering questions you didn't even know you had–we've put together this meaty resource section on business and commerce. It contains references to many government agencies and helpful details about the small business administration.

**Department of Commerce**
14th & Constitution Ave. NW
Washington, DC 20230
202-377-4901
202-377-2000

**Patent & Trademark Office**
Washington, DC 20231
703-557-5168

**Bureau of Economic Analysis**
1401 K Street NW
Tower Bldg., Room 705
Washington, DC 20230
202-523-0693

**International Trade Administration**
14th St. & Constitution Ave. NW,
Room 3414
Washington, DC 20230
202-377-3808

Dallas Regional Office
1100 Commerce Street
Suite 7B-23
Dallas, TX 75242
214-767-8001

New York Regional Office
26 Federal Plaza
Room 3720
New York, NY 10278
212 264 3262

San Francisco Regional Office
221 Main Street
Suite 1280
San Francisco, CA 94105
415-744-3001

Washington Regional Office
14th St. & Constitution Ave NW
Room 6723
Washington, DC 20230
202-377-8275

**Office of Business Liaison**
14th St. & Constitution Ave. NW,
Room 5898
Washington, DC 20230
202-377-3942

**Business Advice: Roadmap Program**
U.S. Department of Commerce
14th & Constitution Avenue NW
Washington, DC 20230
202-377-3176

**Library**
U.S. Department of Commerce
14th & Constitution Avenue NW
Washington, DC 20230
202-377-5511

**Bureau of the Census**
Washington, DC 20233
   Public Information Office
   301-763-4040
   Data User Services Division
   301-763-4100

**Minority Business Development Centers**
14th St. & Constitution Ave. NW,
Room 5055
Washington, DC 20230
202-523-0030

   Atlanta Regional Office
   401 Peachtree Street NE
   Suite 1930
   Atlanta, GA 30308
   404-347-4091

   Chicago Regional Office
   55 East Monroe Street
   Suite 1440
   Chicago, IL 60603
   312-353-0182

   Dallas Regional Office
   1100 Commerce Street
   Suite 7B-23
   Dallas, TX 75242
   214-767-8001

New York Regional Office
26 Federal Plaza
Room 3720
New York, NY 10278

San Francisco Regional Office
221 Main Street
Suite 1280
San Francisco, CA 94105
415-744-3001

Washington Regional Office
14th Street &
Constitution Ave. NW
Room 6723
Washington, DC 20230
202-377-8275

**Department of Labor**
200 Constitution Ave. NW, Room S-1032
Washington, DC 20210
202-523-7316, 202-523-4000

**Bureau of Labor Statistics**
441 G Street NW
Washington, DC 20212-0001
202-523-1913

**Occupational Safety & Health Administration (OSHA)**
200 Constitution Ave. NW,
Room N3647
Washington, DC 20210
202-523-8148

**Government Contracts for Small Business**
Office of Small & Disadvantaged
Business Utilization
Department of Labor
200 Constitution Avenue NW,
Room S1004
Washington, DC 20210
202-523-9148

*Trade Your Business Suit Blues for Blue Jean Dreams™*

## Other Government Agencies

**Chamber of Commerce of the United States**
1615 H Street NW
Washington, DC 20062
202-659-6000

**Library of Congress**
101 Independence Avenue SE
Washington, DC 20540
202-707-2905

**U.S. Copyright Office**
Library of Congress
Washington, DC 20559
202-479-0700

**Internal Revenue Service (IRS)**
800-424-3676

**Federal Information Center**
U.S. General Services Administration
18th & F Streets NW
Washington, DC 20405
202-566-1937

**Small Business EPA-Help Hotline**
Environmental Protection Agency
401 M Street SW
Washington, DC 20460
800-368-5888

**Bruce Phillips:**
**Director of Database Branch**
Office of Advocacy
U.S. Small Business Administration
1441 L Street NW
Washington, DC 20146
202-634-7600

**Telecommunications & Information Administration National**
Department of Commerce
14th & Constitution Avene NW
Room 4898
Washington, DC 20230
202-377-1551

**Senate Committee on Small Business**
Suite SR-428A
Russell Senate Office Building
Washington, DC 20510
202-224-5175

**House Committee on Small Business**
2361 Rayburn House Office Building
Washington, DC 20515
202-225-5821

**Federal Communications Commission (FCC)**
1919 M Street NW
Washington, DC 20554
202-632-7000

**Federal Trade Commission (FTC)**
Pennsylvania Ave & 6th Street NW
Washington, DC 20580
202-326-2000

**Interstate Commerce Commission**
12th Street & Constitution Ave. NW
Washington, DC 20423
202-927-7119

## Small Business Administation (SBA)

The U.S. Small Business Administration is the primary source of federal government assistance to small businesses. It provides financial help through loans and loan guarantee programs, distributes publications, holds workshops and offers management assistance and counseling through it's various entities. For the local SBA office, see the blue government pages of your phone book or call (800) UASK-SBA.

U.S. Small Business Administration
409 Third Street SW, Washington, DC 20416
202-205-6600

**Answer Desk Hotline**, 800-UASK-SBA (827-7522) offers contact details for additional resources and recorded information on a myriad of topics. One hint: to escape from the menu of recorded messages and talk with a real person, touch "3" on your touch-tone phone.

**Small Business Development Centers (SBDCs)** are organized in all 50 states and typically operate on a college campus. About 700 locations dispense small business counseling in the areas of finance, marketing, technical, and other advice. SBDCs are aimed primarily at start-ups. To find one, contact your local SBA office.

**Small Business Institutes (SBIs)** are organized on some 500 university and college campuses. They're staffed by senior business administration and marketing students who are led by faculty advisors. They offer free guidance to small firms. Get information about them from a district office.

**SCORE** stands for the Service Corps of Retired Executives. It's a network of 13,000 retired business executives and professionals who volunteer to help small businesspeople with virtually any problem. Advice is offered on a spot basis or continuing indefinitely. SCORE also sponsors low-cost business management seminars. To locate the office nearest you, call 202-653-6279.

The SBA also maintains a **library**, which is open to the public for reference.
1441 L Street NW, Room 218
Washington, DC 20416
202-653-6914

## Regional Offices (SBA)

The SBA has field offices comprised of regional offices, district offices, branch offices, post-of-duty offices, and disaster area offices. Whew! The country has been divided into 10 regions. Here are the SBA regional offices. Contact the one nearest you for guidance on how to reach the district office. This is the ideal contact point for loan information and management assistance.

**Region I**
155 Federal Street, 9th Floor
Boston, MA 02110
617-451-2030

**Region II**
26 Federal Plaza, Room 31-08
New York, NY 10278
212-264-7772

**Region III**
Allendale Square, Suite 201
475 Allendale Road
King of Prussia, PA 19406
215-962-3806

**Region IV**
1375 Peachtree Street NE, 5th Floor
Atlanta, GA 30367-8102
404-347-2797

**Region V**
300 S. Riverside Plaza, Suite 1975
Chicago, IL 60606-6611
312-353-0359

**Region VI**
8625 King George Drive, Bldg. C
Dallas, TX 75235-3391
214-767-7643

**Region VII**
911 Walnut Street, 13th Floor
Kansas City, MO 64106
816-426-2989

**Region VIII**
999 18th Street
North Tower, Suite 701
Denver, CO 80202
303-294-7001

Trade Your Business Suit Blues for Blue Jean Dreams™

**Region IX**
71 Stevenson Street
San Francisco, CA 94105-2939
415-744-6402

**Region X**
2615 Fourth Avenue, Room 440
Seattle, WA 98121
206-442-5676

# Money Lending and Real Estate Property Sources

There are numerous sources for obtaining funds and bargain real estate through the U.S. Government. Here is seldom seen information to help you in this quest.

## Federal Deposit Insurance Corporation (FDIC)

Division of Liquidation Offices
Regional and Consolidated Offices

**Chicago Regional Office**
Federal Deposit Insurance Corporation
30 South Wacker Drive, 32nd Floor
Chicago, IL 60606
312-207-0200
   States covered: AR, IL, IA, KS, LA, MN, MO, NE, ND, SD, WI

**Dallas Regional Office**
Federal Deposit Insurance Corporation
1910 Pacific Avenue, Suite 1700
Dallas, TX 75201
214-754-0098
   States covered: OK, TX

**New York Regional Office**
Federal Deposit Insurance Corporation
452 5th Avenue, 21st Floor
New York, NY 10018
212-704-1200
   States covered: AL, CT, DE, DC, FL, GA, IN, KY, ME, MD, MA, MI, MS, NH, NJ, NY, NC, OH, PA, RI, SC, TN, VT, VA, WV, Puerto Rico, Virgin Islands

**San Francisco Regional Office**
Federal Deposit Insurance Corporation
25 Ecker Street, Suite 1900
San Francisco, CA 94105
415-546-1810
   States covered: AK, AZ, CA, CO, HI, ID, MT, NV, NM, OR, UT, WA, WY, Guam

## Resolution Trust Corporation (RTC)

Office of Corporate Communications
Washington, DC 20434

**Houses From Failed Saving & Loans Companies Resolution Trust Corp.**
Washington, DC 20429
800-431-0600

**National Sales Center**
1133 21st Street NW
Washington, DC 20036
202-416-4200

**Eastern Regional Sales Center**
Marquis One Tower, Suite 1100
245 Peachtree Center Avenue NE
Atlanta, GA 30303
800-234-3342

**Central Regional Sales Center**
Board of Trade Building II
4900 Main Street
Kansas City, MO 64112
800-365-3342

**Southwestern Regional Sales Center**
300 North Ervay, 24th Floor
Dallas, TX 75201
800-933-4782

**Western Regional Sales Center**
1225 17th Street, Suite 3200
Denver, CO 80202
303-291-5700

## More Real Estate Possibilities

**Country Homes: USDA**
Farmers Home Administration,
Single Family Housing Division
14th & Independence Avenue SW
Washington, DC 20250
202-382-1474

**Veterans Administration**
**Foreclosed Property**
Listing Remote Bulletin Board
Veterans Administration
Washington, DC 20420

**Veterans Foreclosed Homes**
Department of Veterans Affairs
810 Vermont Avenue NW
Washington, DC 20420
202-233-4000

## Federal Grants and Loans

**Economic Development Administration**
Washington, DC
202-377-4671
Small business loans for people who live in an economically depressed area.

**Office of Disaster Operations**
Small Business Administration
Washington, DC 20416
202-653-6376

Inquire here about "displaced business loans." Sometimes the SBA provides direct and guaranteed insured funds up to $900,000 to help small companies stay in business—or to assist individuals in purchasing a business, or establishing a new venture in the case of economic injury.

**Office of Financing**
Small Business Administration
Washington, DC 20416
202-653-6570

This is a source for "economic opportunity loans." Here the SBA provides direct and guaranteed insured funds for loans to small businesses owned by low-income or socially or economically disadvantaged people. They go as high as $315,000.

**Director of Business Loans**
Small Business Administration
Washington, DC 20416
202-653-6570

This program is designed to assist in the start-up or operation of a business owned by a handicapped person. It provides direct and guaranteed insured funds ranging from $500 to $350,000.

**Rural Communities Financial Assistance**
Farmers Home Administration (FmHA)
U.S. Department of Agriculture
Washington, DC 20250
202-447-4323

## *Miscellaneous Information*

You'll find data here from agriculture to energy, geography to climate, health to human services. There's even a catch-all section of various sources that defy categorization. And at the end, is a list of Federal Information Center toll-free phone numbers to help you get answers to any questions we haven't clarified.

## Agriculture

**Department of Agriculture**
14th St. & Independence Ave. SW
Washington, DC 20250
202-720-2791

   **National Agricultural Statistics Service**
   State Statistical Division
   14th St. & Independence Ave. SW
   South Bldg., Room 4143
   Washington, DC 20250
   202-720-2791

**Office of Economics**
USDA Administration Bldg.
Room 227E
Washington, DC 20250
202-720-8732

**Rural Information Center (RIC)**
National Agricultural
Library-Room 304
Beltsville, MD 20705
800-633-7701

**Appropriate Technology Transfer For Rural Areas (ATTRA)**
P.O. Box 3657
Fayetteville, AR 72702
800-346-9140 or 501-442-9824

   ATTRA falls under the umbrella of the Department of the Interior. It specializes in informing farmers, those interested in getting into farming, and agriculture professionals about sustainable agriculture for a cleaner environment and improved profits. Specializing in rural areas, they have resources on a large variety of topics and can search electronic databases or refer you to experts. Free help for everything from truck farming, to raising earthworms, to animal husbandry.

## Energy

**Department of Energy**
1000 Independence Ave. SW
Washington, DC 20585
202-586-6827

**National Energy Information Center**
1000 Independence Ave. SW,
Room 1F-048
Washington, DC 20585-0001
202-586-8800

## Geography and Climate

**Department of the Interior**
1849 C Street NW
Washington, DC 20240
202-343-3171

**Bureau of Land Management**
1849 C Street NW, Room 5600
Washington, DC 20240
202-208-3801

**Bureau of Mines**
2401 E Street NW, MS-1040
Washington, DC 20241
202-634-1001

**Geological Survey**
1849 C Street NW, MS-2646
Washington, DC 20240
202-208-3888

**National Park Service**
1849 C Street NW, Room 3424
Washington, DC 20240
202-208-7394

**National Earthquake Information Center**
Box 25046, MS 967
Denver Federal Center
Denver, CO 80225
800-525-7848

**National Flood Insurance Program**
P.O. Box 159
Lanham, MD 20706
800-638-6620

**USGS-National Water Information Clearinghouse**
423 National Center
Reston, VA 22092
800-H20-9000

**USGS-Geologic Inquiries Group**
907 National Center
Reston, VA 22092
703-648-4383

**Coastal Engineering Research Center**
U.S. Army Corps of Engineers
3909 Halls Ferry Road
Vicksburg, MS 39180-6199
601-634-2000

**Landslide Information Center**
1711 Illinois Street, MS 966
Golden, CO 80401
303-236-1599

**National Climatic Data Center**
Federal Building
Asheville, NC 28801
704-259-0682

**Natural Resources Center**
Department of Environmental Protection
165 Capitol Avenue
State Office Building, Room 533
Hartford, CT 06106
203-566-3540

**Environmental Protection Agency (EPA)**
401 M Street SW
Washington, DC 20460-0001
202-260-2090

**Consumer Publications**
Public Information Center
Environmental Protection Agency
401 M Street SW, PM-211 B
Washington, DC 20460
202-475-7751

**NCAR Outreach Program**
National Center for Atmospheric Research
P.O. Box 3000
Boulder, CO 80307
303-497-1174 or 303-497-8600

**Forest Service**
U.S. Department of Agriculture
P.O. Box 96090
Washington, DC 20090
202-447-3760

**Hydrologic Information Unit**
U.S. Geological Survey
419 National Center
Reston, VA 22092

## Health and Human Services

**Department of Health & Human Services**
200 Independence Ave. SW
Washington, DC 20201
202-619-0257

**National Center for Health Statistics**
6525 Belcrest Road, Room 1100
Hyattsville, MD 20782-2003
301-436-8500

**Health Care Financing Administration**
6325 Security Blvd. Rm. 700
Baltimore, MD 21207-5161
301-966-3000

## Various Helps

**Information on Demand**
General Reading Rooms Division
Library of Congress, LJ 144
Washington, DC 20540
202-707-5543

**Last Resort Interlibrary Loan**
Loan Division
Library of Congress
Washington, DC 20540
202-707-5444

**Uniform Crime Reports**
Superintendent of Documents
Government Printing Office
Washington, DC 20402
202-783-3238

**Shopping By Mail**
Federal Trade Commission
Marketing Practices
6th & Pennsylvania Avenue NW
Washington, DC 20580
202-326-3128

**Moving**
Office of the Secretary
Interstate Commerce Commission
12th Street & Constitution Avenue NW
Washington, DC 20423
202-275-7833

**Government Printing Office**
North Capitol & H Streets NW
Washington, DC 20401
202-275-3204

**Stamps By Mail**
U.S. Postal Service
P.O. Box 533
Clarion, IA 50526
800-782-6724

## Federal Information Centers

| | | | |
|---|---|---|---|
| Akron | 800-347-1997 | Minneapolis | 800-366-2998 |
| Albany | 800-347-1997 | Missouri | 800-735-8004 |
| Albuquerque | 800-359-3997 | Mobile | 800-366-2998 |
| Anchorage | 800-729-8003 | Nashville | 800-366-2998 |
| Atlanta | 800-347-1997 | Nebraska | 800-735-8004 |
| Austin | 800-366-2998 | New Haven | 800-347-1997 |
| Baltimore | 800-347-1997 | New Orleans | 800-366-2998 |
| Birmingham | 800-366-2998 | New York | 800-347-1997 |
| Boston | 800-347-1997 | Newark | 800-347-1997 |
| Buffalo | 800-347-1997 | Norfolk | 800-347-1997 |
| Charlotte | 800-347-1997 | Oklahoma City | 800-366-2998 |
| Chattanooga | 800-347-1997 | Omaha | 800-366-2998 |
| Chicago | 800-366-2998 | Orlando | 800-347-1997 |
| Cincinnati | 800-347-1997 | Philadelphia | 800-347-1997 |
| Cleveland | 800-347-1997 | Phoenix | 800-359-3997 |
| Colorado Springs | 800-359-3997 | Pittsburgh | 800-347-1997 |
| Columbus | 800-347-1997 | Portland | 800-726-4995 |
| Dallas | 800-366-2998 | Providence | 800-347-1997 |
| Dayton | 800-347-1997 | Pueblo | 800-359-3997 |
| Denver | 800-359-3997 | Richmond | 800-347-1997 |
| Detroit | 800-347-1997 | Roanoke | 800-347-1997 |
| Fort Lauderdale | 800-347-1997 | Rochester | 800-347-1997 |
| Fort Worth | 800-366-2998 | Sacramento | 916-973-1695 |
| Gary | 800-366-2998 | Saint Louis | 800-366-2998 |
| Grand Rapids | 800-347-1997 | Saint Petersburg | 800-347-1997 |
| Hartford | 800-347-1997 | Salt Lake City | 800-359-3997 |
| Honolulu | 800-733-5996 | San Antonio | 800-366-2998 |
| Houston | 800-366-2998 | San Diego | 800-726-4995 |
| Indianapolis | 800-347-1997 | San Francisco | 800-726-4995 |
| Iowa | 800-753-8004 | Santa Ana | 800-726-4995 |
| Jacksonville | 800-347-1997 | Seattle | 800-726-4995 |
| Kansas | 800-735-8004 | Syracuse | 800-347-1997 |
| Little Rock | 800-366-2998 | Tacoma | 800-726-4995 |
| Los Angeles | 800-726-4995 | Tampa | 800-347-1997 |
| Louisville | 800-347-1997 | Toledo | 800-347-1997 |
| Memphis | 800-366-2998 | Trenton | 800-347-1997 |
| Miami | 800-347-1997 | Tulsa | 800-366-2998 |
| Milwaukee | 800-366-2998 | West Palm Beach | 800-347-1997 |

# Private Sector Help

## *Home-Based Businesses (HBB)*

For the work-from-home crowd, here are resources to make your heart race. With these associations, contacts, and newsletters, you need never feel isolated again.

### AT&T Home Office Network

This is a dynamite *free* deal! Until October of 1992 they are offering charter memberships at no charge to people who work out of their homes and use AT&T service. And the free charter opportunity may be extended further. You can get discounts on such products as office supplies, Egghead software, Panasonic home office copiers, AT&T equipment, and other items. Discounted services run a wide gamut: rental cars, legal advice, tax services, etc. To request information, call 800-446-6311, extension 1000, or fax them at 800-446-6399.

**NATIONAL ASSOCIATION OF HOME BASED BUSINESSES**
*Home Based Business Newspaper*
P.O. Box 30220
Baltimore, MD 21270
301-363-3698

**NATIONAL HOME BUSINESS REPORT**
Barbara Brabec
P.O. Box 2137
Naperville, IL 60567

**HOME OFFICE COMPUTING MAGAZINE**
P.O. Box 51344
Boulder, CO 80321-1344
212-505-3000

**NATIONAL ASSOCIATION FOR THE COTTAGE INDUSTRY**
Newsletter: *The Cottage Connection*
P.O. Box 14850
Chicago, IL 60614
312-472-8116

**AMERICAN HOME BUSINESS ASSOCIATION**
397 Post Road
Darion, CT 06820
203-655-4380

## *Telecommuting*

These sources may be of interest if you want further information on the field of telecommuting.

**MANAGEMENT AND SYNERGY PLANNING**
E.M. and Linda T. Risse
12501 North Lake Court,
Suite 100
Fairfax, VA 22033
703-968-4300 or 703-968-4302

**GLOBAL TELEMATICS**
John S. Niles, President
322 NW 74th Street
Seattle, WA 98117-4931
206-781-9493

**THE GORDON REPORT**
Gil Gordon
Telespan Publishing
50 A West Palm Street
Altadena, CA 91001
908-329-2266

**THE KERN REPORT**
Coralee Smith Kern
P.O. Box 14850
Chicago, IL 60614
312-472-8116

## *Education*

If you seek schooling options for your children, the three sources listed below may be of interest.

**NATIONAL HOMESCHOOL ASSOCIATION**
P.O. Box 290
Hartland, MI 48353
313-632-5208

**ALTERNATIVE VS. TRADITIONAL SCHOOLS**
ERIC Clearinghouse on Educational Mgmt.
University of Oregon
1787 Agate Street
Eugene, OR 97403-5207
503-346-5043

**RURAL EDUCATION & SMALL SCHOOLS CLEARINGHOUSE**
ERIC Clearinghouse on Rural Education
& Small Schools Appalachia
Educational Laboratory, Inc.
P.O. Box 1348
Charleston, WV 25325-1348
304-347-0400

*Trade Your Business Suit Blues for Blue Jean Dreams™*

# Telephone Information

Here are toll-free 800 phone number options. Prices on such services have dropped significantly over the last few years. For information call:

| | |
|---|---|
| AT&T | 800-222-0400 |
| US Sprint | 800-877-4000 |
| MCI Telecommunications | 800-888-0800 |

## Where to Ring the Baby Bells

**AMERITECH AUDIOTEX SERVICES**
Herb Zureich, President
600 S. Federal, Suite 122
Chicago, IL 60605
312-906-3130

**AMERITECH SERVICES**
Karen Rausch
Manager of Information
Industry Development
2000 W. Ameritech Center Dr.
Location 4B41C
Hoffman Estates, IL 60196
708-248-4485

**BELL ATLANTIC CORP.**
Thomas Gorman, Asst. VP of
Information Services
1310 North Courthouse Road
Arlington, VA 22201
703-974-3000

**BELLSOUTH ADVANCED NETWORKS**
Linda Coyner
Director of Gateway Marketing
1100 Johnson Ferry Road
Suite 900
Atlanta, GA 30342
404-847-2900

**NYNEX CORP.**
1113 Westchester Ave.
White Plains, NY 10604
914-644-6400

**NYNEX INFORMATION RESOURCES**
Neil Connors
Manager, Public Affairs
35 Village Road
Middleton, MA 01949-1202
508-762-1000

**PACIFIC BELL INFORMATION SERVICES**
Jean Graham
Manager of New Business Development
3401 Crow Canyon Road, Room 2500P
San Ramon, CA 94583
510-867-5087

**SOUTHWESTERN BELL CORP.**
Russ Lindenlaub
Director of Corporate Planning
1 Bell Center, Room 40C1
St. Louis, MO 63101
314-235-5070

**US WEST COMMUNICATIONS**
Ron Dulle, Manager
1801 California Street, Room 1650
Denver, CO 80202

# Lending Sources

Finding money isn't easy. To simplify this task, we've listed here firms willing to consider financing franchises and some other enterprises.

**ALLIED LENDING CORP.**
(subsidiary of Allied Capital Corp.)
1666 K Street NW, Suite 901
Washington, DC 20006
202-331-1112

**AT&T COMMERCIAL FINANCE CORP.**
5613 DTC Parkway, Suite 450
Englewood, CO 80111
303-741-4144

**BUSINESS LOAN CENTER, INC.**
704 Broadway, 2nd Floor
New York, NY 10003
212-979-6688

**CAPITAL FUNDING SERVICES**
P.O. Box 424
Waco, TX 76703
817-753-3114

**CAPTEC FINANCIAL GROUP, INC.**
315 E. Eisenhower Parkway, Suite 315
Ann Arbor, MI 48108
313-994-5505

**CHRYSLER FIRST BUSINESS CREDIT CORP.**
24 Olivia Drive
Yardley, PA 19067
215-321-3305

**DIAMOND CAPITAL CORP.**
805 Third Avenue, Suite 1100
New York, NY 10022
212-838-1255

**FIRST WESTERN SBLC, INC.**
1380 Miami Gardens Drive, Suite 225
North Miami, FL 33179
305-891-0823

**FRANCHISE CAPITAL CORP.**
1935 Camino Vida Roble
Carlsbad, CA 92008-6599
619-431-9100
800-421-7188

**GULF AMERICAN SBL, INC.**
P.O. Box 191
Panama City, FL 32405
904-769-3200
800-228-9868

**INDEPENDENCE MORTGAGE, INC.**
3010 LBJ Freeway, Suite 920
Dallas, TX 75234
214-247-1776

**ITT SMALL BUSINESS FINANCE CORP.**
2055 Craigshire Road, Suite 400
St. Louis, MO 63146
314-576-0872
800-447-2025

**KANALY TRUST COMPANY**
4550 Post Oak Place, Suite 139
Houston, TX 77027
713-626-9483

**LOANSOURCE FINANCIAL SERVICES**
3840 North 32nd Street, Suite 1
Phoenix, AZ 85018-4929
602-954-0062

**MAJOR LEASING, INC. / MAJOR CAPITAL CORP.**
3220 Peachtree Road NE
Atlanta, GA 30305
404-233-3300
800-476-9700

**MONEY STORE INVESTMENT CORP., THE**
17530 Ventura Boulevard
Encino, CA 91316
818-906-2999
800-877-1722

**NATIONAL COOPERATIVE BANK**
1630 Connecticut Avenue NW
Washington, DC 20009
202-745-4691

**NATIONAL WESTMINSTER BANK USA**
592 Fifth Avenue
New York, NY 10036
212-602-2842

**PACIFIC FUNDING GROUP**
17534 Von Karman Avenue
Irvine, CA 92714
714-474-1788

**SANWA BUSINESS CREDIT CORP.**
One S. Wacker Drive, Suite 3900
Chicago, IL 60606
800-331-5247

**SOUTHWESTERN COMMERCIAL CAPITAL, INC.**
1336 E. Court Street
Sequin, TX 78155
512-379-0380

**STEPHENS FRANCHISE FINANCE**
1400 Worthen Bank Building
Little Rock, AR 72201
501-374-6036
800-234-2271

*Trade Your Business Suit Blues for Blue Jean Dreams™*

**COMDISCO INC.**
6111 North River Road
Rosemont, IL 60018
708-698-3000

**DOMINION VENTURES INC.**
44 Montgomery Street, #4200
San Francisco, CA 94104
415-362-4890

This Lending Sources List is reprinted from the *Franchise Opportunities Guide*, published by the International Franchise Association.

## Associations

There are hundreds of associations that are helpful to entrepreneurs. It's impossible to list all of them here. Instead we've selected a few unusual ones you may find worthwhile.

**AMERICAN SOCIETY OF ASSOCIATION EXECUTIVES**
Information Central
1575 Eye Street NW
Washington, DC 20005
202-626-2723

**NATIONAL ASSOCIATION OF MANUFACTURERS**
1331 Pennsylvania Avenue NW,
Suite 1500 North
Washington, DC 20004-1703
202-637-3000

**NATIONAL COALITION FOR ADVANCED MANUFACTURING**
1331 Pennsylvania Avenue NW,
Suite 1500 North
Washington, DC 20004
202-347-0090

**NATIONAL BUSINESS INCUBATION ASSOCIATION**
Dinah Adkins, Executive Director
1 President Street
Athens, OH 45701
614-593-4331

**INTERNATIONAL FRANCHISE ASSOCIATION**
1350 New York Avenue NW, Suite 900
Washington, DC 20005
202-628-8000

**DIRECT MARKETING ASSOCIATION**
6 East 43rd Street
New York, NY 10017
212-768-7277

## Selected Suppliers

Here are sources for unusual business cards: distinctive designs and shapes, full-color cards, and Rolodex versions. You'll also find some useful miscellaneous vendors—everything from home swapping organizations to backwoods power sources, computer bulletin boards to a PR firm that specializes in helping small rural businesses.

### Business Card Printers

**HIRSCHHORN COMPANY, THE**
P.O. Box 8848
New Haven, CT 06532-0848
203-562-5830

**LABELS UNLIMITED**
P.O. Drawer 709
New Albany, IN 47150
812-945-2617

**RAYOD HOUSE**
P.O. Box 520
North Arlington, NJ 07032
800-238-2862

**DESIGN GRAPHICS**
5073 Dorchester Road
Charleston, SC 29418
803-552-9000

**DIRECT PROMOTIONS**
23935 Ventura Blvd.
Calabasas, CA 91302

**GENTILE BROTHERS SCREEN PRINTING**
116A High Street
P.O. Box 429
Edinburg, VA 22824
800-368-5270

## Miscellaneous Vendors and Resources

**HARRISON PUBLISHING CO.**
624 Patton Avenue
Asheville, NC 28806
704-254-4420
(Clever greeting cards for business purposes.)

**ORNAAL GLOSSIES, INC.**
24 West 25th Street
New York, NY 10010
800-826-6312
(Inexpensive quantity photo supplier.)

**U.S. TOY COMPANY, INC.**
1227 East 119th Street
Grandview, MO 64030
800-255-6124
(Source for novelty items and PR gimmicks)

**MONTCLAIR CRAFT GUILD**
P.O. Box 111
Emerson, NJ 07630
201-261-0071
(They offer a unique insurance package for craftspeople. Call their Craft Insurance Hotline for details.)

**ACCELERATED BUSINESS IMAGES**
P.O. Box 1500
425 Cedar Street
Buena Vista, CO 81211
719-395-2459; FAX 719-395-8374
(Public relations firm that specializes in marketing campaigns and promotional literature for small rural businesses)

---

Want an inexpensive way to check out a locale? These organizations specialize in matching home swapping. Perhaps you can trade your home for that of someone else for a few weeks.

**BETTER HOMES AND TRAVEL**
30 E. 33rd Street
New York, NY 10016
212-689-6608

**INTERVAC U.S.**
San Francisco, CA
415-435-3497

**VACATION EXCHANGE CLUB**
Youngtown, AZ 85363
602-972-2186

Bulletin Board Services (BBSs) are subscription services that allow you to access electronic bulletin boards on your computer. Here are just two of many fine ones.

**COMPUSERVE INC.**
5000 Arlington Centre Blvd
Columbus, OH 43220
800-336-3366 or 800-848-8199

**GENIE**
401 N. Washington Street
Rockville, MD 20850
800-638-9636

For ways to power an an independent lifestyle, see the next page for a couple of vendors who can get you started.

*Trade Your Business Suit Blues for Blue Jean Dreams™*

PHOTOCOMM, INC.
930 Idaho Maryland Road
Grass Valley, CA 95945
800-544-6466

BACKWOODS SOLAR
ELECTRIC SYSTEMS
Steve Willey
8530 Rapid Lightning Creek Road
Sandpoint, ID 83864
208-263-4290

## *Manufacturers' Representative Associations*

Here's a helpful listing of product- or market-specific associations that have reps who may be interested in carrying what you manufacture. The salespeople who belong to these various groups sell everything from books to safety equipment, sporting goods to home furnishings.

**AGRICULTURAL & INDUSTRIAL MANUFACTURERS REPRESENTATIVES ASSOCIATION**
Frank Bistrom, Executive Director
5818 Reeds Road
Mission, KS 66202
913-262-4510

**AIRCRAFT ELECTRONICS ASSN**
Monte Mitchell, Executive Director
P.O. Box 1981
Independence, MO 64055
816-373-6565

**AMERICAN BEAUTY ASSOCIATION**
Paul Dykstra, Executive Director
401 North Michigan Avenue
Chicago, IL 60611
312-644-6610, ext. 3285

**AMERICAN FISHING TACKLE MANUFACTURERS ASSOCIATION**
Dee McIntyre, Executive Director
1250 Grove Avenue, Suite 300
Barrington, IL 60010
708-381-9490

**AMERICAN LIGHTING ASSOCIATION**
Bob Toani, Administrative Director
c/o Bostrom Corporation
435 North Michigan Avenue
Chicago, IL 60611
312-644-0828

**ARMED FORCES MARKETING COUNCIL MANUFACTURERS REPRESENTATIVES**
Rip Rowan, Executive Director
1750 New York Avenue NW
Washington, DC 20006
202-783-8228

**ASSOCIATION OF INDUSTRY MANUFACTURERS REPRESENTATIVES**
Inga Calderon, Executive Director
222 Merchandise Mart Plaza, #1360
Chicago, IL 60654
312-464-0092

**ASSOCIATION OF VISUAL MERCHANDISE REPRESENTATIVES**
Paul Bolinger, President
17610 Midway Road, Suite 133-340
Dallas, TX 75252
214-248-2452

**AUTOMOTIVE AFFILIATED REPRESENTATIVES (ASIA Division)**
David R. Roland, President
222 North Michigan Avenue
Chicago, IL 60611
312-836-1300

**AUTOMOTIVE BOOSTER CLUBS INTERNATIONAL**
Donn Proven, Vice President/CEO
1545 Waukegan Road
Glenview, IL 60025
708-729-2227

**AUTOMOTIVE SERVICE
INDUSTRY ASSOCIATION**
James F. Goodhew, Executive Dir.
The Ridge Company
1535 South Main Street
South Bend, IN 46680
219-234-3143

**BROKER MANAGEMENT COUNCIL**
William Bess, Executive Director
P.O. Box 150229, 1903 Turf Club Dr.
Arlington, TX 76015
817-465-5511

**COSTUME JEWELRY
SALESMAN'S ASSOCIATION**
Michael Gail, President
303 Fifth Avenue
New York, NY 10016
212-532-7595

**ELECTRICAL EQUIPMENT
REPRESENTATIVES ASSOCIATION**
John S. McDermott, Executive Director
406 West 34th Street, Suite 728
Kansas City, MO 64111-2736
816-221-0918

**ELECTRONICS
REPRESENTATIVES ASSOCIATION**
Raymond J. Hall, Executive VP/CEO
20 East Huron Street
Chicago, IL 60611
312-649-1333

**FOODSERVICE GROUP, INC., THE**
Kenneth W. Reynolds, Exec Director
P.O. Box 76533
Atlanta, GA 30358
404-977-1476

**HEALTH INDUSTRY
REPRESENTATIVES ASSOCIATION**
Frank Bistrom, Executive Director
5818 Reeds Road
Mission, KS 66202
913-262-4510

**INCENTIVE MANUFACTURERS
REPRESENTATIVES ASSOCIATION**
Karen Renk, Executive Director
1555 Naperville/Wheaton Road
Naperville, IL 60563
708-369-3466

**INFANT'S FURNITURE
REPRESENTATIVES ASSOCIATION**
Steve Bruder, President
Tinton Falls Business Center
1 Executive Drive
Tinton Falls, NJ 07701
908-747-8048

**INTERNATIONAL HOME
FURNISHINGS REPRESENTATIVES
ASSOCIATION**
William A. Harper, Executive VP
P.O. Box 670
High Point, NC 27261
919-889-3920

**MANUFACTURERS' AGENTS
ASSOCIATION
OF NORTH AMERICA**
Gordon Rogers
15 Toronto Street, Suite 200
Toronto, Ontario, CANADA M5C 2R1

**MANUFACTURERS AGENTS
NATIONAL ASSOCIATION**
James T. Gibbons, President
P.O. Box 3467
Laguna Hills, CA 92654

**MANUFACTURERS
REPRESENTATIVES OF AMERICA**
(Specific products include:
paper, plastic sanitary
supply products)
William Bess, Executive Director
P.O. Box 150229, 1903 Turf Club Rd.
Arlington, TX 76015
817-465-5511

**MARKETING AGENTS FOR
FOOD SERVICE INDUSTRY**
Brad Parcells, Executive Director
Smith, Bucklin & Associates, Inc.
401 North Michigan Avenue
Chicago, IL 60611
312-644-6610, ext. 3311

**MECHANICAL EQUIPMENT MANU-
FACTURERS REPRESENTATIVES**
Clark Franke, President
c/o Engineering Center
11 West Mt. Vernon Place
Baltimore, MD 21201
301-574-2727

*Trade Your Business Suit Blues for Blue Jean Dreams™*

**NATIONAL ASSOCIATION GENERAL MERCHANDISE REPRESENTATIVES**
Jack Springer, Executive Director
Smith, Bucklin & Associates, Inc.
401 North Michigan Avenue
Chicago, IL 60611
312-644-6610

**NATIONAL ASSOCIATION OF INDUSTRIAL AGENTS**
Frank Bistrom, Executive Director
5818 Reeds Road
Mission, KS 66202
913-262-4510

**NATIONAL ASSOCIATION OF LIGHTING REPRESENTATIVES**
Paul Saunders, Executive Director
P.O. Box 214
Sea Girt, NJ 08750
201-974-1900

**NATIONAL ASSOCIATION OF PUBLISHERS REPRESENTATIVES**
Thomas J. Kenny, Executive Director
200 East 15th Street, Suite A
New York, NY 10003
212-643-9600

**NATIONAL ELECTRICAL MANUFACTURERS REPRESENTATIVES ASSOCIATION**
Henry P. Bergson, Executive VP
222 Westchester Avenue
White Plains, NY 10604
914-428-1307

**NATIONAL FOOD BROKERS ASSOCIATION**
Robert Schwarze, President
NFBA Building
1010 Massachusetts Avenue NW
Washington, DC 20001
202-789-2844

**NATIONAL INGREDIENTS MARKETING SPECIALISTS, INC.**
Kenneth W. Reynolds, Executive Dir.
P.O. Box 76422
Atlanta, GA 30358
404-977-1476

**NATIONAL OFFICE PRODUCTS ASSOCIATION**
Jim Herman,
Director of Sales/Marketing
301 North Fairfax Street
Alexandria, VA 22314
703-549-9040

**NATIONAL ORNAMENT & ELECTRIC LIGHTS CHRISTMAS ASSOCIATION**
Phyllis Southard, Executive Secretary
230 Fifth Avenue
New York, NY 10001
212-889-8343

**NATIONAL SHOE TRAVELER'S ASSOCIATION**
Norman Weaver, President
11701 Borman Drive, #324
St. Louis, MO 63146-4100
314-993-3141

**OFFICE PRODUCTS REPRESENTATIVES ASSOCIATION**
Barbara Boden, Executive Director
600 South Federal Street, Suite 400
Chicago, IL 60605
312-992-6222

**POWER TRANSMISSION REPRESENTATIVES ASSOCIATION**
Frank Bistrom, Executive Director
5818 Reeds Road
Mission, KS 66202
913-262-4510

**SAFETY EQUIPMENT MANUFACTURERS AGENTS ASSOCIATION**
George Hayward, Executive Secretary
7200 Paddison Road
Cincinnati, OH 45230
513-231-4266

**SALES ASSOCIATES OF THE CHEMICAL INDUSTRY**
Paul B. Slawter, Jr.,
Administrative Assistant
287 Lakawanna Avenue, Suite A7
West Paterson, NJ 07424-2985
201-254-5547

**SPECIALTY ADVERTISING MANUFACTURERS REPRESENTATIVES ASSOCIATION**
Arnold Silberman, President
3467 Daniel Crescent
Baldwin, NY 11510
516-378-0155

**SPORTING GOODS AGENTS ASSOCIATION**
Lois E. Halinton, Executive Director
P.O. Box 998
Morton Grove, IL 60053
708-296-3670

**STATIONERY REPRESENTATIVES ASSOCIATION**
M.S. Kellner, Managing Director
230 Park Avenue
New York, NY 10069
212-687-2484

**TACKLE/SHOOTING SPORTS ASSN**
Bob Kavanagh, Executive Director
1250 Grove Avenue, Suite 300
Barrington, IL 60010
708-381-3032

**TEXTILE SALESMAN'S ASSOCIATION**
Karen Stone
295 Fifth Avenue
Textile Building, Suite 621
New York, NY 10016-7201
212-685-0530

**SOCIETY OF MANUFACTURERS REPRESENTATIVES, INC.**
Carol Scheid, Managing Director
29200 Vassar, Suite 520
Livonia, MI 48152

**UNITED ASSOCIATION OF MANUFACTURERS REPRESENTATIVES**
H. Keith Kittrel
P.O. Drawer 6266
Kansas City, KS 66106

List provided by:
**MANUFACTURERS' REPRESENTATIVES EDUCATIONAL RESEARCH FOUNDATION (MRERF)**
Dr. Marilyn Stephens, Executive Dir.
P.O. Box 247
Geneva, IL 60134
708-208-1466

# Maps, Tables, Charts

## Maps

Topographic maps, specialized maps, even aerial photography overviews can be obtained to help you make wise decisions. If you were considering investing in a large piece of land, for instance, certain maps can help you judge the terrain, etc. Here are some sources for obtaining these tools:

### U.S. Geological Survey

**Eastern Distribution Branch**
1200 South Eads Street
Arlington, VA 22202
  (For maps of areas located *east*
  of the Mississippi River,
  plus Minnesota.)

Eastern Mapping Center (NCIC-e)
536 National Center
12201 Sunrise Valley Drive
Reston, VA 22092

**USGS-Topographic mapping and aerial photography**
507 National Center
Reston, VA 22092
800-USA-MAPS

**National Atlas Updates**
**Distribution Branch**
Building 810
Denver Federal Center, Box 25286
Denver, CO 80225
800-USA-MAPS

**Western Distribution Branch**
Box 25286, Federal Center
Denver, CO 80225
  (For maps of areas located west
  of the Mississippi River,
  including Alaska and Hawaii.)

**Federal Emergency Management Agency**
Flood Insurance Rate Maps
Flood Map Distribution Center
6930 (A-F) San Tomas Road
Baltimore, MD 21227-6227
800-638-6620 continental U.S.
800-492-6605 Maryland only

**DeLorme Mapping**
P.O. Box 298-6565
Freeport, ME 04032
800-227-1656

Also the Library of Congress at (202)707-6277 has a cartographic collection that houses some 4 million maps, over 50,000 atlases, plus globes and related reference books. Information derived from satellites can also be obtained.

**Geography and Map Division**
Library of Congress
Washington, DC 20540
202-707-6277

*Note: For specific maps showing much useful information, refer back to the visuals in chapter 2 of Country Bound!*™

# *Tables and Charts*

The following tables and charts explain population counts, sources of financing, and capital investment levels.

## Percent Distribution of Resident Population by Race and Origin, for the U.S., Regions, and States: 1990.

| U.S./ Region/ State | White | Black | American Indian, Eskimo, or Aleut | Asian or Pacific Islander | Other Race | Hispanic Origin* |
|---|---|---|---|---|---|---|
| **U.S.** | **80.3%** | **12.1%** | **0.8%** | **2.9%** | **3.9%** | **9.0%** |
| **NORTHEAST** | **82.8%** | **11.0%** | **0.2%** | **2.6%** | **3.3%** | **7.4%** |
| CT | 87.0% | 8.3% | 0.2% | 1.5% | 2.9% | 6.5% |
| ME | 98.4% | 0.4% | 0.5% | 0.5% | 0.1% | 0.6% |
| MA | 89.8% | 5.0% | 0.2% | 2.4% | 2.6% | 4.8% |
| NH | 98.0% | 0.6% | 0.2% | 0.8% | 0.3% | 1.0% |
| NJ | 79.3% | 13.4% | 0.2% | 3.5% | 3.6% | 9.6% |
| NY | 74.4% | 15.9% | 0.3% | 3.9% | 5.5% | 12.3% |
| PA | 88.5% | 9.2% | 0.1% | 1.2% | 1.0% | 2.0% |
| RI | 91.4% | 3.9% | 0.4% | 1.8% | 2.5% | 4.6% |
| VT | 98.6% | 0.3% | 0.3% | 0.6% | 0.1% | 0.7% |
| **MIDWEST** | **87.2%** | **9.6%** | **0.6%** | **1.3%** | **1.4%** | **2.9%** |
| IL | 78.3% | 14.8% | 0.2% | 2.5% | 4.2% | 7.9% |
| IN | 90.6% | 7.8% | 0.2% | 0.7% | 0.7% | 1.8% |
| IA | 96.6% | 1.7% | 0.3% | 0.9% | 0.5% | 1.2% |
| KS | 90.1% | 5.8% | 0.9% | 1.3% | 2.0% | 3.8% |
| MI | 83.4% | 13.9% | 0.6% | 1.1% | 0.9% | 2.2% |
| MN | 94.4% | 2.2% | 1.1% | 1.8% | 0.5% | 1.2% |
| MO | 87.7% | 10.7% | 0.4% | 0.8% | 0.4% | 1.2% |
| NE | 93.8% | 3.6% | 0.8% | 0.8% | 1.0% | 2.3% |
| ND | 94.6% | 0.6% | 4.1% | 0.5% | 0.3% | 0.7% |
| OH | 87.8% | 10.6% | 0.2% | 0.8% | 0.5% | 1.3% |
| SD | 91.6% | 0.5% | 7.3% | 0.4% | 0.2% | 0.8% |
| WI | 92.2% | 5.0% | 0.8% | 1.1% | 0.9% | 1.9% |
| **SOUTH** | **76.8%** | **18.5%** | **0.7%** | **1.3%** | **2.8%** | **7.9%** |
| AL | 73.6% | 25.3% | 0.4% | 0.5% | 0.1% | 0.6% |
| AR | 82.7% | 15.9% | 0.5% | 0.5% | 0.3% | 0.8% |

| | | | | | | |
|---|---|---|---|---|---|---|
| DC | 29.6% | 65.8% | 0.2% | 1.8% | 2.5% | 5.4% |
| DE | 80.3% | 16.9% | 0.3% | 1.4% | 1.1% | 2.4% |
| FL | 83.1% | 13.6% | 0.3% | 1.2% | 1.8% | 12.2% |
| GA | 71.0% | 27.0% | 0.2% | 1.2% | 0.7% | 1.7% |
| KY | 92.0% | 7.1% | 0.2% | 0.5% | 0.2% | 0.6% |
| LA | 67.3% | 30.8% | 0.4% | 1.0% | 0.5% | 2.2% |
| MD | 71.0% | 24.9% | 0.3% | 2.9% | 0.9% | 2.6% |
| MS | 63.5% | 35.6% | 0.3% | 0.5% | 0.1% | 0.6% |
| NC | 75.6% | 22.0% | 1.2% | 0.8% | 0.5% | 1.2% |
| OK | 82.1% | 7.4% | 8.0% | 1.1% | 1.3% | 2.7% |
| SC | 69.0% | 29.8% | 0.2% | 0.6% | 0.3% | 0.9% |
| TN | 83.0% | 16.0% | 0.2% | 0.7% | 0.2% | 0.7% |
| TX | 75.2% | 11.9% | 0.4% | 1.9% | 10.6% | 25.5% |
| VA | 77.4% | 18.8% | 0.2% | 2.6% | 0.9% | 2.6% |
| WV | 96.2% | 3.1% | 0.1% | 0.4% | 0.1% | 0.5% |
| **WEST** | **75.8%** | **5.4%** | **1.8%** | **7.7%** | **9.4%** | **19.1%** |
| AK | 75.5% | 4.1% | 15.6% | 3.6% | 1.2% | 3.2% |
| AZ | 80.8% | 3.0% | 5.6% | 1.5% | 9.1% | 18.8% |
| CA | 69.0% | 7.4% | 0.8% | 9.6% | 13.2% | 25.8% |
| CO | 88.2% | 4.0% | 0.8% | 1.8% | 5.1% | 12.9% |
| HI | 33.4% | 2.5% | 0.5% | 61.8% | 1.9% | 7.3% |
| ID | 94.4% | 0.3% | 1.4% | 0.9% | 3.0% | 5.3% |
| MT | 92.7% | 0.3% | 6.0% | 0.5% | 0.5% | 1.5% |
| NV | 84.3% | 6.6% | 1.6% | 3.2% | 4.4% | 10.4% |
| NM | 75.6% | 2.0% | 8.9% | 0.9% | 12.6% | 38.2% |
| OR | 92.8% | 1.6% | 1.4% | 2.4% | 1.8% | 4.0% |
| UT | 93.8% | 0.7% | 1.4% | 1.9% | 2.2% | 4.9% |
| WA | 88.5% | 3.1% | 1.7% | 4.3% | 2.4% | 4.4% |
| WY | 94.2% | 0.8% | 2.1% | 0.6% | 2.3% | 5.7% |

\* Persons of Hispanic origin can be of any race. Source: *Bureau of the Census, 1991*

# Population Changes by State: 1980-1990

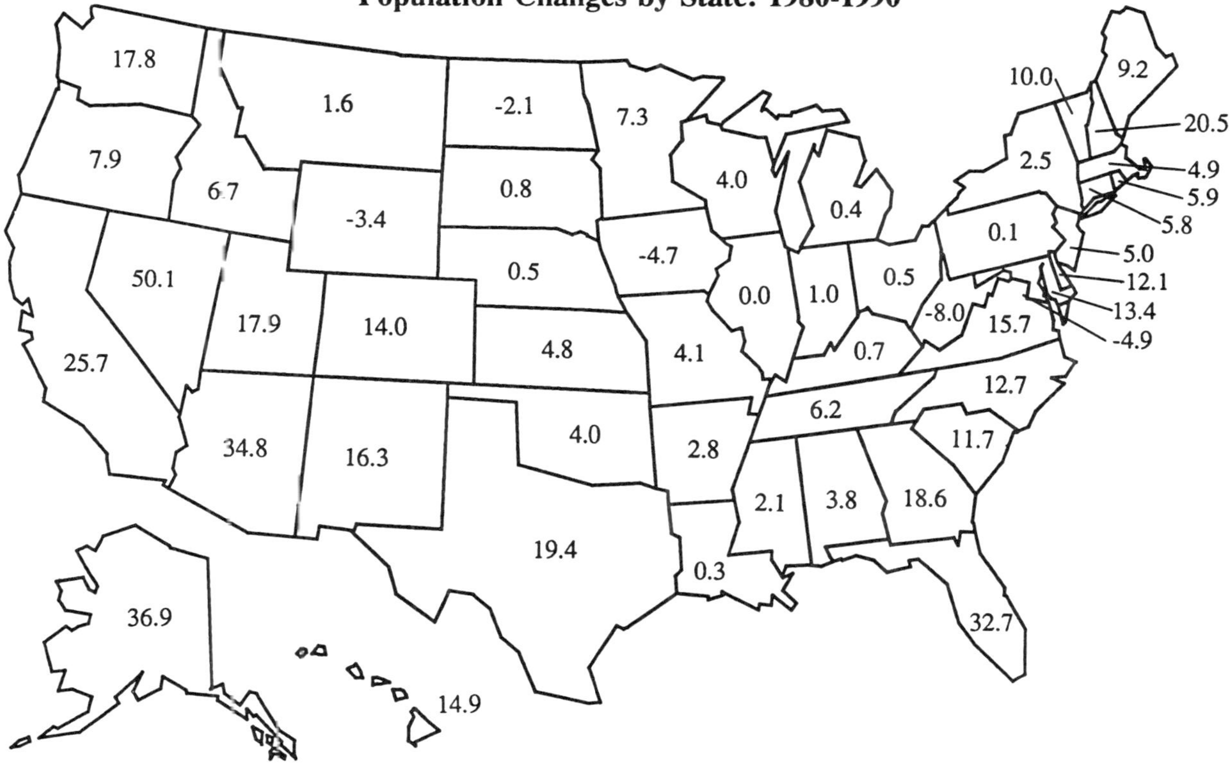

Source: *U.S. Department of Commerce, Bureau of the Census.*

**Capital Investment Prior to First Sale**

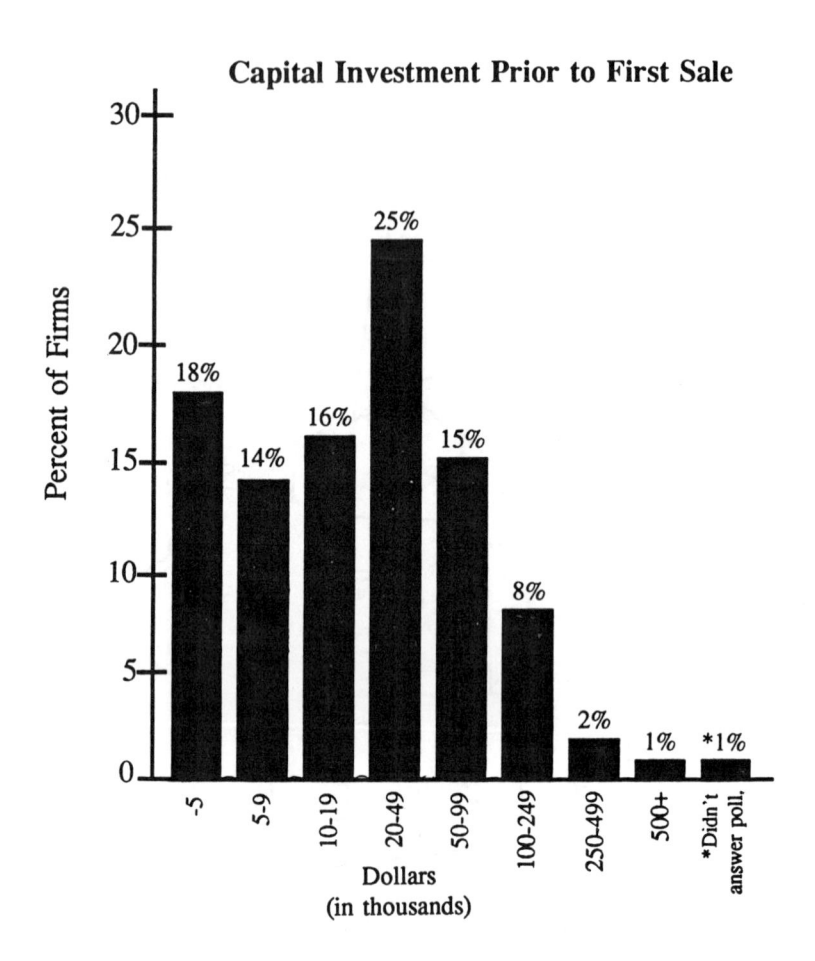

| Dollars (in thousands) | Percent of Firms |
|---|---|
| -5 | 18% |
| 5-9 | 14% |
| 10-19 | 16% |
| 20-49 | 25% |
| 50-99 | 15% |
| 100-249 | 8% |
| 250-499 | 2% |
| 500+ | 1% |
| *Didn't answer poll. | *1% |

Source: The NFIB Foundation

*Trade Your Business Suit Blues for Blue Jean Dreams™*

## Sources of Business Ideas

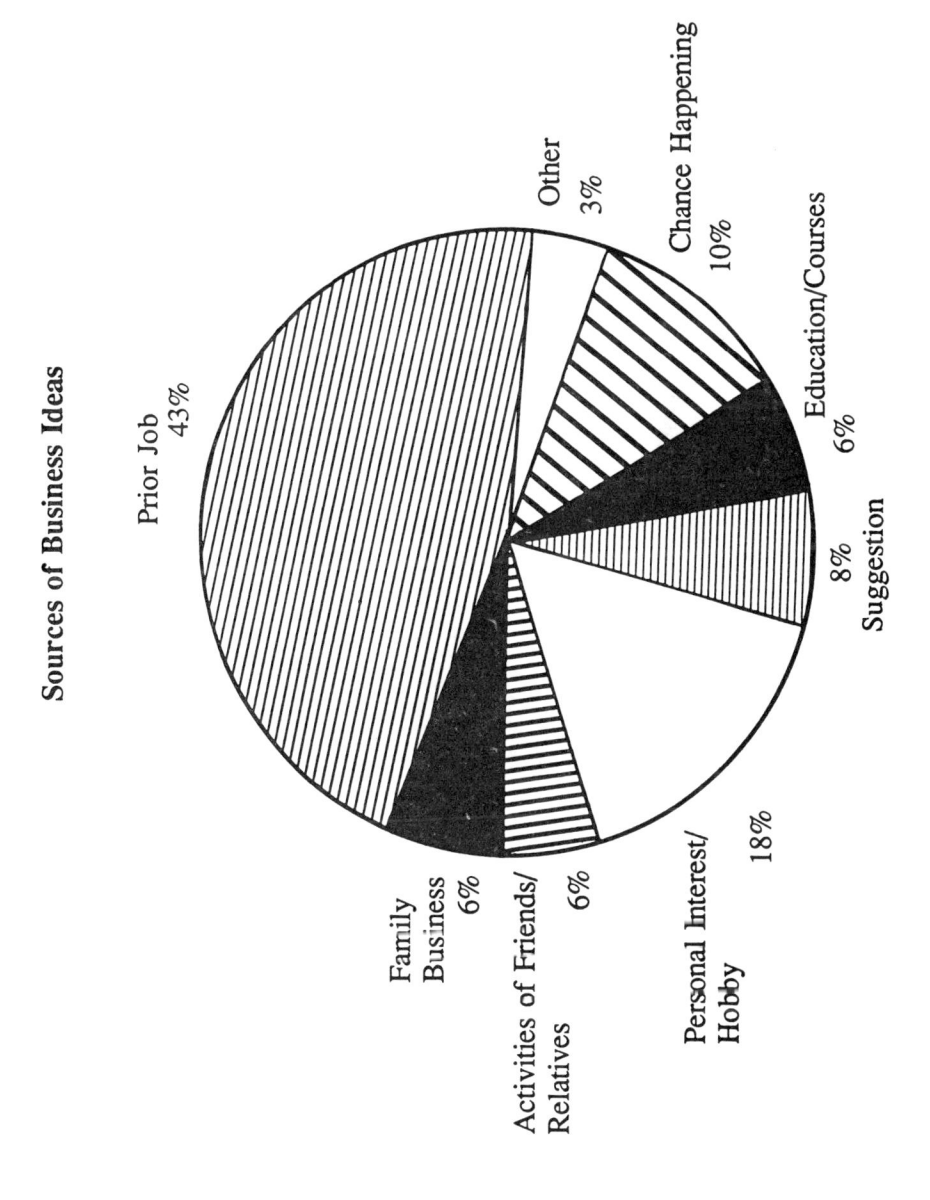

- Prior Job 43%
- Other 3%
- Chance Happening 10%
- Education/Courses 6%
- Suggestion 8%
- Personal Interest/Hobby 18%
- Activities of Friends/Relatives 6%
- Family Business 6%

## Sources of Financing to Purchase a Business

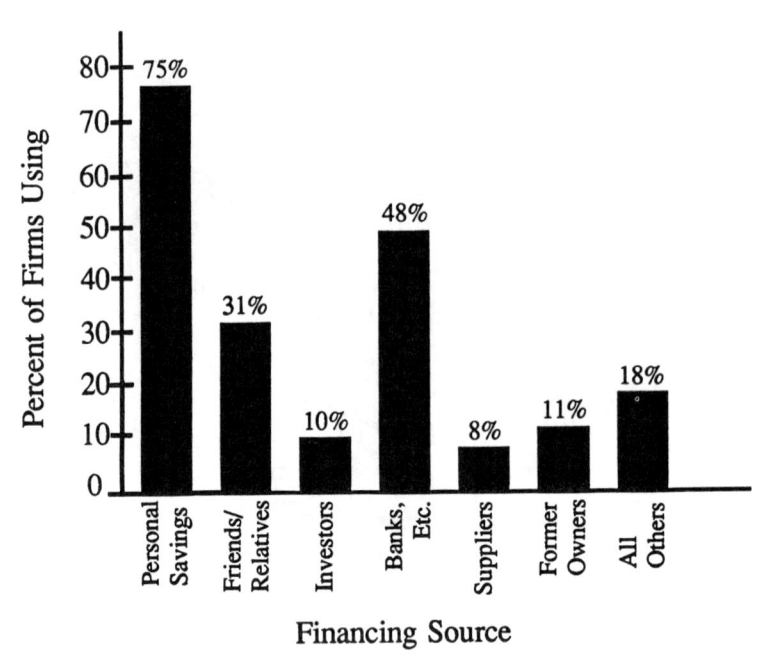

| Financing Source | Percent of Firms Using |
|---|---|
| Personal Savings | 75% |
| Friends/Relatives | 31% |
| Investors | 10% |
| Banks, Etc. | 48% |
| Suppliers | 8% |
| Former Owners | 11% |
| All Others | 18% |

Source: The NFIB Foundation

# Bibliography
# Recommended Reading

Did you enjoy this book, but have a taste for more? Let us help in your search for the simple life. **All the books in bold are available from us by mail order.** (Look for the others at your local bookstore or library.) Perfect for anyone with a countrypreneurial spirit, these tools will guide you toward comfortable, profitable living in the country. And there's no risk. If you're not satisfied with any book, it may be returned for a refund—for up to a full year! What an easy, one-stop shopping opportunity. All you have to do is complete and return the order form on the page following this Bibliography, or call our toll-free phone number (1-800-331-8355, ext. CB) and use your VISA or MasterCard.

## BOOKS
## to make your relocation easier and more rewarding

*ALTERNATIVE ENERGY SOURCEBOOK 1991: A Comprehensive Collection of the Finest Energy-Sensible Technologies*, edited by John Schaeffer, Real Goods Trading Corporation.

*AMERICAN RURAL COMMUNITIES*, Edited by A. E. Luloff and Louis E. Swanson, Westview Press, Inc.

**BEST HOME BUSINESSES FOR THE '90s, by Paul and Sarah Edwards, Jeremy P. Tarcher, Inc. Here is the inside information you need to know to select a home-based business that's right for you. These self-employment experts profile 70 top businesses. They reveal how each works, what you can earn, start-up costs, where to get customers, plus how much to charge. Dynamite stuff if you're not sure which way to go, $10.95.**

*BIG MARKETING IDEAS FOR SMALL SERVICE BUSINESSES,* by Marilyn and Tom Ross, Business One Irwin. Details 229 innovative strategies ideal for any businessperson or professional. Jay Conrad Levinson, author of *Guerrilla Marketing Attacks,* declares: "jammed with useful, practical, helpful, and profitable ideas for any right-thinking entrepreneur . . . I recommend it without a moment's hesitation." A terrific business start-up tool or refresher course for those who seek cost-effective business builders, $29.95.

*CASH COPY: How to Offer Your Products and Services So Your Prospects Buy Them . . . Now!!!,* by Dr. Jeffrey Lant, JLA Publications. When writing promotional copy, you'll want to refer to this book time and time again to reinforce the often overlooked point that one's job is to *sell,* not just create pretty prose. This 480-page handbook addresses it all, as only Jeffrey Lant can, $24.95.

*THE CATALOG OF CATALOGS: The Complete Mail-Order Directory,* by Edward L. Palder, Woodbine House. The ultimate catalog resource. This indispensable reference lists more than 5,000 catalogs. Both the ordinary and unusual are covered in 850 categories ranging from automobiles to water skiing. Fun to browse through, it makes ordering virtually *anything* easy. (And what an extraordinary place to prospect for sales outlets if you have a product to sell!) $14.95.

*COMPANY RELOCATION HANDBOOK: Making the Right Move,* by William Gary Ward and Sharon Kaye Ward, PSI Research/The Oasis Press. Designed for executives planning to relocate a company or plant, this is a unique and in-depth guide. It contains rating scales to compare prospective locations, plus dozens of useful forms and checklists for intelligent site selection. Well documented lists of relocation consultants, state-by-state summaries of economic development support agencies, and help with handling employee transitions make it a must for any established company planning a move, $19.95.

*THE COMPLETE GUIDE TO SELF-PUBLISHING: Everything You Need to Know to Write, Publish, Promote, and Sell Your Own Book,* by Tom and Marilyn Ross, Writer's Digest Books. Planning to write and publish books or booklets to sell by direct mail from your country paradise? Then you need this book! Full of practical and innovative advice, it's considered the "Bible" on this subject. 420 information-packed pages tell you everything about successfully creating, selling, and profiting from books, $16.95.

*THE COMPLETE WORK•AT•HOME COMPANION: Everything You Need to Know to Prosper As a Home-Based Entrepreneur or Employee,* by Herman Holtz, Prima Publishing & Communications.

*THE CONSULTANTS KIT,* by Dr. Jeffrey Lant, JLA Publications. Lant doles out a healthy portion of proven advice for establishing and operating a successful consulting business. Recommended by the Small Business Administration, it's a must for anyone just entering this field. An excellent self-training program for those living in remote areas, $35.00.

*THE COUNTRY CONSULTANT: A Comprehensive Guide to Getting Established in the Expanding Field of Rural Business Consulting,* by Brian R. Smith.

*COUNTRY DREAMS: Your Guide to Saving Time and Money, While Still Getting What You Want and Need in Country Property*, by Alan Schabilion, Misty Mountain Press, Inc.

*COUNTRY LIVING: A Source Book of Projects and Friendly Advice*, by Lewis and Nancy Hill, Rodale.

*CREATIVE CASH: How to Sell Your Crafts, Needlework, Designs and Know-How*, by Barbara Brabec, Barbara Brabec Productions. One of the most popular craft marketing books in print, it is directed to craft-needlework beginners in business. This is a step-by-step guide to success that includes 24 ways to profit from your creative skills, $14.95.

*DIRECTORY OF RELOCATION AND REAL ESTATE SERVICES, 1991*, Relocation Information Service, Inc.

*DOING WHAT YOU LOVE, LOVING WHAT YOU DO*, by Dr. Robert Anthony, The Berkley Publishing Group.

*THE EDEN SEEKER'S GUIDE*, edited by William L. Seavey, Loompanics Unlimited.

*EDITING YOUR NEWSLETTER*, by Mark Beach, Coast to Coast. Shows you how to design and produce an effective publication—on schedule and within budget—using traditional tools and computers. This excellent third edition helps you manage production-planning through distribution. If you intend to publish a newsletter from the boonies, get this book! $18.50.

*THE ENTREPRENEUR'S ROAD MAP TO BUSINESS SUCCESS*, by Lyle R. Maul and Dianne Craig Mayfield, Saxtons River Publications, Inc.

*FINDING THE GOOD LIFE IN RURAL AMERICA: A City Slicker's Guide to Buying Real Estate in the Sticks Without Losing Your Shirt!*, by Bob Bone, United National Real Estate. With rural relocation on the grow, how do you find a good piece of property? By buying this book! Bob Bone not only addresses real estate as an investment, he also talks about pitfalls to avoid, making the offer, financing your dream, even selling your home in the city, $10.95.

*FINDING YOUR IDEAL JOB*, by Richard N. Diggs, Progressive Publications.

*FINDING YOUR NICHE... MARKETING YOUR PROFESSIONAL SERVICE*, by Brad Brodsky and Janet Geis, Community Resource Institute Press. The authors cover everything from exploring career options to organizing your business, client profiles to researching your market, promotion and marketing to publicity and advertising in the mass media. A terrific value for the money, $15.95.

*FOLLOW YOUR BLISS: Let the Power of What You Love Guide You to Personal Fulfillment in Your Work and Relationships*, by Hal Zina Bennett, Ph.D., and Susan J. Sparrow, Avon Books.

*FRANCHISE OPPORTUNITIES GUIDE*, The International Franchise Association.

*GOODBYE CITY, HELLO COUNTRY*, by Julie Hayward and Ken Spooner, Highland Books.

***GOVERNMENT GIVEAWAYS FOR ENTREPRENEURS*** by Matthew Lesko, Information USA, Inc. A practical, comprehensive road map for those who want to start or expand a business. Perfect for anyone who lives in a remote area, Lesko does Uncle Sam's job and shows taxpayers where to tap into 9,000 sources of free help, information, and money. Be one of the over 150,000 businesses that will get money from the government to begin operation! $33.95.

***GREEN INDEX, 1991-1992: A State–By–State Guide to The Nation's Environmental Health***, by Bob Hall and Mary Lee Kerr, Island Press. This is a remarkable compendium of information drawn from dozens of government and private sources. It assesses environmental conditions in each region and state. The best tool available to find your most healthy spot in our toxic world, $18.95.

***GREENER PASTURES RELOCATION GUIDE:*** *Finding the Best State in the United States for You*, by Alfred Shattuck, Prentice-Hall.

***HOMEMADE MONEY:*** *The Definitive Guide to Success in a Homebased Business*, by Barbara Brabec, Betterway Publications, Inc. Recommended by SBA and SCORE specialists across the country, this is a wonderful nuts and bolts book. It includes an A-to-Z legal financial section and a 500-listing resource chapter of free and low-cost sources of information. The author is a leader in the home-based business field and offers many savvy marketing tips as well, $18.95.

*HOW TO BUY LAND CHEAP*, by Edward Preston, Loompanics Unlimited.

***HOW TO FIND AND BUY YOUR BUSINESS IN THE COUNTRY***, by Frank Kirkpatrick, Storey Communications, Inc. This is a highly readable guide packed with realistic advice from a gentleman who was previously a vice-president at the Young and Rubicom advertising agency in Manhattan. He's now a country consultant and tells you how to get the feel of a place, learn how well the business has been doing, get a bank loan, and go for it, $11.95.

***HOW TO MAKE AT LEAST $100,000 EVERY YEAR AS A SUCCESSFUL CONSULTANT IN YOUR FIELD***, by Dr. Jeffrey Lant, JLA Publications. Though the title smacks of hyperbole, the contents are exceptional. This is the last word on succeeding in the advice business. Lant shows consultants sophisticated ways to profit from providing problem-solving information. Like all the others in his series, it's stuffed with practical, precise ideas that help you turn your expertise into cash, $35.00.

*HOW TO PROFITABLY BUY AND SELL LAND*, by Rene A. Henry, Jr., John Wiley and Son.

*HOW TO QUIT THE RAT RACE–SUCCESSFULLY*, by John F. Edwards, New Era Press.

***HOW TO SET YOUR FEES AND GET THEM***, by Kate Kelly, Visibility Enterprises. So you've decided to become a consultant. Do you know what to charge? How much will your chosen market bear? What are you really worth? Seldom-seen information on how to set appropriate rates for your consulting services awaits you in this book, $17.50.

*HOW TO UNCOVER AND CREATE BUSINESS OPPORTUNITIES*, by Dr. Dale Rusnell and Bill Gibson, Newport Marketing and Communications.

*HOW YOU CAN LEAVE THE CITY FOREVER!: Secrets of Earning a Living in The Country*, by Charles A. Peterson, Peterson Publications, Ltd.

*JOB CREATION IN AMERICA*, by David Birch, The Free Press.

**LESKO'S INFO-POWER, by Matthew Lesko**, Information USA, Inc. Here you'll find over 30,000 sources of free and low-cost information that will help you on your way to success in the country. A sampling of chapters includes: agriculture and farming, energy, your community, weather and maps, careers and workplace, selling to the government, even international trade, $33.95.

*LIFE AFTER THE CITY: A Harrowsmith Guide To Rural Living*, by Charles Long, Camden House Publishing.

**THE *LIFESTYLE ODYSSEY: 2,001 Ways Americans' Lives Are Changing*, by Eric Miller** and the editors of Research Alert, Sourcebooks, Inc. This forward-thinking company has compiled research that shows the trends that will shape our lives in the years to come. Prospecting here is an excellent place to get new business ideas to meet the needs of tomorrow's consumers, $15.95.

*THE LOST CONTINENT: Travels in Small-Town America*, by Bill Bryson, Harper & Row Publishers.

***MAKING IT ON YOUR OWN: Surviving and Thriving on the Ups and Downs of Being Your Own Boss*, by Sarah and Paul Edwards**, Jeremy P. Tarcher, Inc. Being your own boss can be the greatest ... or the pits. This books helps you master the psychological side. Oodles of tips to take the stress out of your path to success, $10.95.

***MONEY MAKING MARKETING*, by Dr. Jeffrey Lant**, JLA Publications. Gives detailed instructions on how to find the people who need what you're selling—and make sure they buy it. Both informational and inspirational, it contains Jeffrey's usual practical advice, $35.00.

*NEW BUSINESS IN AMERICA: THE FIRMS AND THEIR OWNERS*, by Arnold C. Cooper, William C. Dunkelberg, Carolyn Y. Woo, and William J. Dennis, The NFIB Foundation.

*THE NEW CORPORATE FRONTIER: The Big Move to Small Town USA*, by David A. Heenan, McGraw-Hill, Inc.

***THE NEW TOOLS OF TECHNOLOGY: A User Friendly Guide to the Latest Technology*, by Daniel Burrus and Patti Thomsen**, Burrus Research Associates, Inc. A terrific product idea-generator and futuristic problem-solver, this book has been called the businessperson's guide to the next century. It pinpoints 20 key technologies entrepreneurs and managers need to know about for short- and long-term planning, $24.95.

*OFFBEAT CAREERS: The Directory of Unusual Work*, by Al Sacharov, Ten Speed Press.

*THE ONE-MINUTE COMMUTER: How to Keep Your Job and Stay at Home Telecommuting*, by Lis Fleming, Acacia Books.

*PENTURBIA: Where Real Estate Will Boom After the Crash of Suburbia*, by Jack Lessinger, Ph.D., Socio Economics. This book gives carefully plotted strategies for finding the new real estate boom areas and coping with the crash of suburbia. Thoughtful and precise predictions found nowhere else. Written by a noted expert in the field, it can lead you to the ideal place to invest in property, $22.95.

*PLACES RATED ALMANAC: Your Guide to Finding the Best Places to Live in America*, by Richard Boyer and David Savageau, Prentice Hall. Anyone who anticipates moving and doesn't get a personal copy of this book is doing it the hard way. The facts and figures compiled here are astonishing. Yet it is all presented in easy-to-read charts and lists to give you a complete picture of your options. Use this remarkable tool to break the decision process into easily digested chunks, $16.95.

*THE POPCORN REPORT: Faith Popcorn on the Future of Your Company, Your World, Your Life*, by Faith Popcorn, Doubleday Publishers.

*THE POWER OF 900: A Guidebook of Caller-Paid Services*, by Rick Parkhill, InfoText Publishing, Inc. If you want encyclopedic knowledge of the 900 industry–where it is today and where it's headed tomorrow–this is the book. It cuts to the chase and shows specifics found nowhere else on how to make money in this lucrative field. Expensive? Yes. Worth it? Definitely! $95.00.

*POWER UP YOUR PROFITS REPORT*, by Ronald L. Hanus, 900 Enterprises, Inc. This report contains information on setting up your own 900 number system. You'll find out how to operate and promote this innovative approach to the best advantage for your company, $20.00.

*THE PUBLICITY HANDBOOK: How to Maximize Publicity for Products, Services, & Organizations*, by David Yale. N.T.C. Business Books. This sophisticated manual shows how to develop publicity campaigns that send your message loud and clear. You'll find out ways to get newspaper, broadcast, and magazine coverage worth thousands of dollars–at little or no cost, $29.95.

*THE PUBLICITY MANUAL*, by Kate Kelly, Visibility Enterprises. Written by a practicing PR pro, this book tells how to develop good publicity relationships and write compelling news releases. All the hows and whys are covered here, $29.95.

*THE RATING GUIDE TO LIFE IN AMERICA'S SMALL CITIES*, by G. Scott Thomas, Prometheus Books. If you're seriously considering moving, you'll do yourself a big favor by getting this book. It's a compendium of lifestyle factors in 219 "micropolitan areas"–towns with 15,000 to 50,000 residents. Each community is graded in terms of performance in eight primary categories. Save yourself tons of worry and work with this unusual reference, $18.95.

*REAL ESTATE TAX SALE MANUAL: How to Research, Bid and Profit at County Tax Sales,* by Thomas Hendricks, Tax Property Investor, Inc.

*RETIREMENT PLACES RATED: All You Need to Plan Your Retirement or Select Your Second Home,* by David Savageau, Prentice Hall Press. This gem makes planning your retirement or selecting your second home so easy. It lists 151 top retirement areas, then ranks and compares them based on cost of living, housing, climate, personal safety, services, work opportunities, and leisure living, $18.00.

*SMALL TIME OPERATOR: How To Start Your Own Small Business, Keep Your Books, Pay Your Taxes, & Stay Out of Trouble!,* by Bernard Kamoroff, CPA, Bell Springs Publishing. Want to stay clear of the I.R.S.? Seek help setting up your books? Need to know the bottom line on the new tax laws? This excellent business book—written and revised annually by a CPA—tells all. It's a great start-up tool, and also offers many useful tips for established business barons, $14.95.

*THE SOURCEBOOK OF ZIP CODE DEMOGRAPHICS: Census Edition: Volume One,* CACI Marketing Systems.

*SUCCESSFUL DIRECT MARKETING METHODS,* by Bob Stone, NTC Business Books. A classic 575-page book on marketing. This new edition is *the* definitive book on direct mail selling. If this is how you plan to market your products or services, you need Stone's professional advice to keep you in the forefront of the direct marketing revolution. This all-inclusive reference answers questions you never thought to ask, $34.95.

*TAKE YOUR LIFE OFF HOLD,* by Ted Dreier, Fulcrum, Inc.

*THE TELECOMMUTER'S HANDBOOK,* by Brad Schepp, Pharos Books.

*THE TRAUMA OF MOVING: Psychological Issues for Women,* by Audrey T. McCollum, Sage Publications. Any woman who has followed her partner from one community to another will relate to this book. It looks at psychological issues for women with great sensitivity and unusual candor. Case histories describe what challenges are involved, help remove the "aloneness," and offer ways of successfully coping, $19.95.

*TUNE IN TO SUCCESS: Strategies for Achieving Your Greatest Potential,* by Robert M. Unger and John H. Kupillas, Jr., Wynwood Press.

*UNABASHED SELF-PROMOTER'S GUIDE, THE,* by Dr. Jeffrey Lant, JLA Publications. We can unabashedly say this is one great book. It reveals what every person or organization needs to know about getting ahead by exploiting the media. Seldom-told tips and imaginative ways to focus attention on yourself, your product, and your company, $35.00.

*UPCOUNTRY: Reflections From a Rural Life,* by Robert Kimber, News from Lyons & Burford.

*THE VACATION HOME EXCHANGE AND HOSPITALITY GUIDE,* by John Kimbrough, Kimco Communications.

*WHAT COLOR IS YOUR PARACHUTE? THE 1992: A Practical Manual for Job-Hunters & Career-Changers,* by Richard Nelson Bolles, Ten Speed Press.

*WHERE TO FIND BUSINESS INFORMATION: A Worldwide Guide for Everyone Who Needs the Answers To Business Questions,* by David M. Brownstone and Gorton Carruth, A Hudson Group Book.

*WHICH AD PULLED BEST?* by Philip Ward Burton and Scott C. Purvis, NTC Books. Want some high-powered guidance for creating winning ads? This unique book shows 50 matched pairs of ads. Quiz yourself on why one works and another doesn't. Then find out what the experts say in the Answer Key. A wonderful training ground for learning how to write convincing ad copy, $18.45.

*WORKING FROM HOME: Everything you Need to Know About Living and Working Under the Same Roof,* by Paul and Sarah Edwards, Jeremy P. Tarcher, Inc. The Edwards again team up here to offer their perceptive business advice. You'll learn about solving zoning problems–juggling family, friends, children, and work–managing self-discipline–and combatting the isolation factor. Loaded with useful nuts and bolts tips, $14.95.

*YOU CAN'T PLANT TOMATOES IN CENTRAL PARK: The Urban Dropouts Guide to Rural Relocation,* by Frank Ruegg and Paul Bianchina, New Horizon Press.

## NEWSLETTERS AND MAGAZINES
### of interest to rural relocators

*BACKWOODS HOME MAGAZINE,* Word Publishing, P. O. Box 2630, Ventura, CA 93002.

*BUSINESS OPPORTUNITIES JOURNAL,* Box 60762, San Diego, CA 92106.

*THE COUNTRY BOUND!™ CONNECTION,* edited by Marilyn Ross. Complete, up-to-the-minute information to help you make the best relocation decision possible. This newsletter is chock-full of the latest facts and figures, new career ideas, entrepreneurial marketing strategies, country trends, real estate tips for finding distressed and bargain properties, and much more. If you contemplate moving to a country paradise in the future, you need the Rosses' continuing advice! *The Country Bound!™ Connection* picks up where the book you're reading leaves off, $89 per year—includes two indispensable reports.

*COUNTRY JOURNAL,* P. O. Box 8200, Harrisburg, PA 17105.

*COUNTRYSIDE,* subscription information: 800-444-8783.

***GREENER PASTURES GAZETTE,*** Greener Pastures Institute, edited by William Seavey. This newsletter is dedicated to the search for countryside edens where the good life still exists. It's a potpourri of information helpful to prospective migrants. Reviews of books, articles on moving, self-employment ideas, commentary on relocation trends, useful statistics, and more fill each issue, $22 per year.

*HARROWSMITH COUNTRY LIFE,* Camden House Publishing, Inc., Ferry Road, Charlotte, VT 05445.

*HOME POWER MAGAZINE,* Box 130, Hornbrook, CA 96044-0130.

*JOHN NAISBETT'S TREND LETTER,* Newsletter Services, Inc., 1545 New York Avenue, N.E., Washington, DC 20077-0576.

***THE KERN REPORT,*** edited by Coralee Smith Kern. This is a sophisticated newsletter about telecommuting and electronic cottages. It tracks trends and issues to keep readers informed about up-to-the-minute changes in these fascinating areas. Brimming with facts on which to base decisions that affect both the private and public sector, $89 per year.

*MOTHER EARTH NEWS,* New American Magazines, 80 5th Avenue, New York, NY 10011.

***NATIONAL HOME BUSINESS REPORT,*** edited by Barbara Brabec. Written in a breezy, informal way, this report contains a smorgasbord of information for home-based businesspeople. There's plenty of experienced advice from the editor, plus articles from accomplished contributors in the field. Imaginative, low-cost marketing strategies–money-saving tips–hard-learned success secrets–it's all here, $24 per year.

*RURAL PROPERTY BULLETIN, The National Marketplace for Rural Property,* P. O. Box 4331, Prescott, AZ 86302.

*SLOW LANE JOURNAL,* McClelland & McClelland, P. O. Box 876, Sacramento, CA 95812-0876.

*SMALL FARMER'S JOURNAL,* P. O. Box 2805, Eugene, OR 97402-0318.

***SMALL TOWN OBSERVER,*** edited by Tom Evons. This is a meaty quarterly magazine that helps urban escapees discover America's heartlands. It profiles inviting individual small towns and includes personal stories of why people moved there. With special emphasis on the northwest, it also includes relocation hints, real estate advertisements, listings of special events, etc., $24 per year.

*WORKAMPER NEWS,* 201 Hiram Road, HCR 34 Box 125, Heber Springs, AR 72543.

See the Order Form on the next page to purchase *bold* titles only

COUNTRY BOUND!™

## Bibliography/Recommended Reading Order Form

**Yes!** I want to become a more savvy, productive, and profitable countrypreneur. Please send the items listed below. I understand if I'm not satisfied with any item, it may be returned for a refund—up to a full year! Ship to: (please print)

Name _____

Company _____

Address _____

City/State/Zip _____

Phone (___) _____ Signature _____
☐ Check or money order payable to Communication Creativity
☐ Charge my credit card: ☐ VISA ☐ MasterCard
Card # _____ Expires _____

| Qty | Title | Price |
|---|---|---|
| ____ | _____ | $_____ |
| ____ | _____ | $_____ |
| ____ | _____ | $_____ |
| ____ | _____ | $_____ |
| ____ | _____ | $_____ |
| ____ | _____ | $_____ |
| ____ | _____ | $_____ |

Shipping and Handling: ($3 per item) $_____
Sales Tax: (Colorado residents please add 7%) $_____
**TOTAL (Thanks for your order!)** $_____

If a price has been raised by the publisher, please:
☐ Send the book or newsletter, bill me the difference. ☐ Cancel my order.
**U.S. currency only.** Prices and availability subject to change and slightly higher in Canada. Allow 4-5 weeks for delivery. For special handling please call us at:

### Credit Card Orders: 1-800-331-8355, ext. CB
8 A.M. - 5 P.M. Mountain Time
(Please have your VISA or MasterCard handy)

You may fax credit card orders to 719-395-8374
**Or mail to:** CB-MOB Order Department, P.O. Box 909, Buena Vista, CO 81211

# Index

## A

AARP  174
About Books, Inc.  206, 324, 333
Aburdene, Patricia  8, 217, 282
Accelerated Business Images (ABI)  323, 388
Acid rain  75
*Ad Weekly*  218
Ades, Andy  254
Adidas USA Inc.  356
Adjustment  154
Advertising  334-37; *See also* Marketing strategies
    as a percentage of sales  330
    business cards  346
    classified ads  335
    display ads  335
    industry standards  331
    institutional ads  334
    message, audience, timing  335
    options to make yours outstanding  335
    repetition  335
    "shopper"  335
    word-of-mouth  334
*Advertising Age*  218
Advice business; *See* Consulting
*Advocate* newsletter  98
Affirmations  204, 270
Agri-Jobs  265
Agriculture  9, 379
Albin, Phil  199
Allergies  71
*Alternative Careers for Teachers*  264
*Alternative Energy Sourcebook*  131
American Academy of Allergy & Immunology  71
American Association for Public Opinion Research  228
American Chamber of Commerce Researchers Association (ACCRA)  36
*American Demographics*  7, 8, 97, 218
American dream  2, 7, 9, 15, 18, 24-25, 97, 154-55

American Management Association 185, 333
*American Renaissance* 9
American Society of Association Executives 215-16
*An Aging Market* 186
Anderson, Patrick 24
Anderson-Barrows Metal Corporation 359
Andrade, Christian and Lea 20-21
Animal terms 158
Animals 136-37, 156-57, 258
Anonymity, loss of 153-54
Appropriate Technology Transfer For Rural Areas (ATTRA) 379
Area economy 187
Artisans 199-200
Arts, the 18-19, 77-79, 114-15, 166, 173-74
Association of Industrial Advertisers 333
Associations 216, 387, 389
AT&T Home Office Network 383
Atmosphere 318
Attitude 150-52, 350; *See also* Viewpoint, small town
Auctions, government 313
Auto club 103
Avocational pastimes into regular paydays 198-200

# B

Backtracking 224
*Backwoods Home Magazine* 131
Backwoods Solar Electric Systems 131
Bacova Guild, Ltd. 361
Bainbridge, William 88
Bakery 26-27
Banks, rural 289
Barkett, Terry 156
Barr, Dr. Deland 66-67
Bartering 26, 341
Basket Source Reports 194

Bastress, Frances 264
Be somebody 157-58
Beard, Marna L. 264
Bed and Breakfast (B&B) 9, 20-21, 186, 192, 251, 337
Best Western hotels and motels 106
Better Business Bureau 273
Big businesses, bolting 355-62
 success stories 355-60
Big fish 157-58
*Big Marketing Ideas for Small Service Businesses* 198, 340
Birch, David 1, 183
Black, Joe 361
Bolles, Richard Nelson 224, 266
Bond, Brian 242
Bone, Bob 121, 127
Booms 152
Bootstrapping 297
Boss, be your own (BYOB) 178-228, 247
*Boston Globe* 285
Boyer, Richard 49, 100
Brabec, Barbara 200, 209, 251, 255, 383
BrainReserve 2
brainstorming 165, 178, 188-89, 224, 258, 311, 319-21, 329-30, 341-43, 351-52
Brainstorming Guidelines 188-89
Brodsky, Bart 329
Broker, real estate 120-21
BTA Economic Research Institute 36
Budgeting 330-31
Buena Vista 10-11, 19, 26-27, 79, 81-82, 86, 158, 197, 199, 225, 239, 298, 338, 340, 351, 362, 388
*Builders of the Dawn: Community Lifestyles in a Changing World* 100
Bulletin Board Services (BBSs) 388

Bulletin boards 166, 258, 341, 378, 388
Burrows, Irene 199
Burrus, Daniel 203, 218
Burton, Philip Ward 335
*Burwell's Directory of Fee-Based Information Services* 228
Bush, George 282
Business
   cards 323-24, 346-47, 387
   classifications of 300-02
   entertainment-oriented 193
   family run 233
   idea first/location second 215
   incubators 311
   plan, development of 295
   recreation-oriented 193
   seasonal lulls 235
Business Considerations 116-17
Business Development Office of the Small Business Administration 242
Business Ideas, Source of 399
*Business Opportunities Journal* 231
Buy or sell first? 120
Buying existing business/professional practice 229-36, 347
   appraisal for 295
   cash reserves 236
   down payment 236
   "grandfathering" 234
   inventory 235
   living quarters with 232-33
   manipulated figures 234
   owner financing 235, 297
   owner involvement 236
   owners eager to sell 231-32
   purchase agreement 233
   UCC search 233-34
   warnings 234-35

## C

Calling 201
Capital; *See* Generating capital
Capital Investment 400
Career choices, hot 217-18, 270
Career counselor 201
Career poll 1
Career volunteer 171
Careers, Reading Your Way to the Hot 217
*Caretaker Gazette* 105, 265
Carjacking 51
Carosella, Vincent 358
Case histories; *See* Success stories
Cash flow 291
Cash reserves 236
Cashing Out 2, 93
*Catalog of Catalogs, The* 156, 312
Celente, Gerald 218
Cetron, Marvin 9
Chaffee County 156, 199, 224-25
Chamber of commerce 79, 101, 108-10, 214, 302, **366-372**, 375
   Questions To Ask 109-10
Change 150-51, 203
*Changing Times* 7, 22
Checklist for CEOs 359-60
Checklists 11-12, 108, 112, 127, 146, 309-10, 321, 359
*Chicago Tribune* 205
Child care 154-56
Children 5, 20, 74, 98, 138, 144, 256, 258, 277, 282, 350
   care for 155-56
   fun for 107
   involvement in move 132
   schooling of 87-89
   with country perspective 27-28, 84
Choices 14, 156
Church 18, 22, 26, 66, 88, 102, 120, 135, 155, 173, 211,

Index   413

272, 298, 313, 327, 345, 351
Churchill, Winston  200
*City and County Data Book*  101
City Lot Versus Country Acreage  125
City slicker  130, 231
Classified ads  101-02, 313, 335
Climate  54-63, 113, 379-80
   Comparative Data  61
   Mildest and Wildest Metro Areas  64
Climatic Data  56-59
*Climatography of the United States, Series 20*  63
Clustering  189
Cognetics, Inc.  1, 183
Coldwell Banker  92-94, 102
Cole, Ann  7
College town  19
Colorado  10-11, 18, 27, 96, 126, 142, 199-200, 224, 226, 254, 263, 265-66, 276, 282, 298, 312, 314, 363, 367, 382
Communities, intentional  99-100
Community involvement  15-16, 112-13, 344-53; *See also* Social life
   for business growth  347-49
   isolation, coping with  349-51
   listening  346
   mingling  345-47
   needs in  239
   reaching out  344-45
   shyness, remedies for  346
Commuting, alternatives to  276
Companionship  171
*Company Relocation Handbook*  306
*Comparative Climatic Data for the United States*  60
Competition  224, 348
   check the  220, 232, 320, 333
   visit the  215

*Compleat Guide to Finding Jobs in Government, The*  262
*Complete Guide to Self-Publishing, The*  16, 197
*Complete Out-of-Doors Job, Business and Professional Guide*  264
Computers  4, 88, 166, 174, 190, 198, 203, 206, 225, 242, 249, 253-55, 258-60, 262, 275-76, 280, 309-10, 320-21, 352-53, 387-88
Conant, Dr. James  160
Conference Board, The  74
Confidences, keeping  158
*Consultants News*  352
Consulting  190-92, 309, 334, 338
Consulting Areas  191
Contemplating a Country Move  14-33
Continuity  152
Control  180, 248
Cook, James  355
Coolidge, Calvin  269
Cooperative Extension Service; *See* County extension agent
Corning Glass Works  355
Corporate America, in transition  354-62
Cost of living  21-22, 29, 35-49, 114
Cost savings  356
*Country*  101-02, 131
Country Bound!™ T-shirts  211
*Country Bound!™ Connection, The*  77, 211
Country Bounty  81
*Country Consultant, The*  192
Country inn; *See* Bed and Breakfast
*Country Journal*  131
Countrypreneuring  21, 85, 184, 237, 252, 363
*Countryside*  9, 131
*County Business Patterns* 1989  224-25

County extension agent  111, 173, 219
*Creative Cash*  200
Creativity  189-90
Credit card, merchant status  111, 340-41
Credit, personal  312
Crime  16-17, **49-53**, 116, 381
   figures for  53
   gangs  51
   property, against  51, 53
   reports  381
   violent  49
*Crime in the United States*  53
*Crockery Cookery*  217
Culture; *See* Arts, the
Customer satisfaction  333, 338, 348-49

## D

Daniel Yankelovich Group, Inc.  15
Databases  100, 226-27, 258, 321, 352-53
Davis, Owen  9
Day, Margaret  199
Day Care; *See* Child care
Daydreams  31
dba (doing business as)  302, 312
Decision-making  29-31
Dedication  359
*Denver Post*  254
Dependency  187
Destiny shaping  345
Dial-a-doctor  206
*Dictionary of Holland Occupational Codes*  224
*Dictionary of Occupational Titles (DOT)*  224
Diggs, Richard N.  268
*Directories in Print*  216, 333
*Directory of Centers for Older Learners*  174
*Directory of Experts, Authorities & Spokespersons*  221

*Directory of Franchising Organizations*  243
*Directory of Intentional Communities*  100
*Directory of Venture Capital Clubs*  288
Disadvantages
   of home-based businesses  256-58
   of rural business  24, 233, 311
   of rural living  2, 22, 29, 89-90, 115-16, 127
   of telecommuting  278-79
   of wrong business location  220
   undesireable conditions  115-16
Diversification  210, 337-38
Diversity, ethnic  98, 225, 394
Doctor shortage  192
Doing good  345
Dorio, Mark and Lindsay  157
Downsizing  4, 185, 190, 237, 261, 264, 286
Drucker, Peter  4
Dun and Bradstreet (D&B)  274
Dwyer, Don  292
Dwyer Group  292

## E

Earthquakes  60, 62
ECHO (East Coast Hang Out)  167
Echo technique  117
Economic development, rural  105-06, 111, 118, 219, 272, 357, 378
   solutions for  6-7
   telecommuting to bolster  282-83
Education  28, 87-89, 112, 174, 264, 383; *See also* Home schooling
Edwards, Mark and Gina  291-92
Edwards, Paul and Sarah  8, 185, 251
80/20 rule  340

Ekin, Noel  263
Electric, revenue per kilowatt hour  47
Electronic bulletin boards  167
Electronic Marketing Resource Group (EMRG)  361
Emerson, Ralph Waldo  183
Employees, prospecting for  313-16; *See also* Start-up considerations
   apprentices  315
   classified ads  314
   conscientious  358-59
   interns  315
   Job Training Partnership Act (JTPA)  270, 314
   resumés  201, 267-68, 314
   talk about openings  313
   tax credits for  314
*Encyclopedia of Associations*  216, 232, 330
Energy  378
Enterprise zones  294-95
Entertainment  79-80, 115, 165-67; *See also* Social life
*Entrepreneur* magazine  218, 331
Entrepreneurs  **178-213**
   buying existing business/professional practice  184, 229-36, 347
   characteristics of  179-80
   combining  190
   couples working together  186-87
   filling a need  182-84
   franchising  221, 237-46
   looking at angles  189
   mail order  197
   manufacturing  194
   minimizing/maximizing  190
   multi-function  213
   personal services  197
   planning  284
   publishing  197
   questions for  181-82
   related services clustered  213
   restaurant  230
   selling relationships  187
   sideline businesses  211
   variations  190
Environment  **73-77**, 114, 184, 217, 223, 234, 240, 265, 281-82, 320, 328, 375, 379-80; *See also* Health
   acid rain  76
   Clean Air Act  75
   longevity ramifications  17-18
   nuclear power reactors  79
   odor  75
   pollution  5-6, 74, 194, 282
   traffic congestions  21
   20th century tampering  73-74
   water contamination  76
Environmental Concerns  73-74
Environmental Illness (EI)  71
Environmental Protection Agency (EPA)  74, 76, 223, 234, 380
Ergonomics  254
Ethnic diversity  97-98, 225, 395
Evons, Tom  91-92
Executive Quality Management (EQM)  361
*Executive Recruiter News*  352
Expenses, analyzing  35-36
Expertise, tapping your  190-92

# F

F.Q. (Fun Quotient) Quiz  160-65
Family issues  167-68, 256
Family unity catalyst  248-49
Fantasize  175, 263
Farmers' market  166
Farming  32-33, 124, 194-96, 211
Farnham, Alan  354-55
Fate shaper  169-70
Fears  30
*Federal Career Opportunities*  262
Federal Deposit Insurance Corporation (FDIC)  102, 116, 298-99, 377

Federal Express 252
Federal ID number 312
Federal Information Centers 382
*Federal Jobs Digest* 262
Feeling at home 152
Fiber optics 280
Financial independence 250
Financing, by owner 235
Financing, Government 292
Financing, Sources of 398
Financing Structure Worksheet 289-90
*Findex, the Directory of Market Research Reports, Studies and Surveys* 228
*Finding Private Venture Capital for Your Firm* 287
*Finding the Good Life in Rural America* 121
*Finding Your Ideal Job* 268
*Finding Your Niche . . . Marketing Your Professional Service* 329
*First Time Review* 293
First Try 10, 16, 70, 81, 108, 151, 154, 168, 211, 230, 312
Flexibility 151, 250
Flextime 277
Focus, shifting 266
Foote, Cone & Belding 8
*Forbes* 355
*Fortune* 354-55
*Franchise Annual, The* 243
Franchise Evaluation Exam 245-46
*Franchise Opportunities Guide* 242
Franchising 221, **237-46**
　accessibility 241
　definitions 237
　disclosure laws, by state 221, 222-23
　easy-entry opportunity 237
　evaluating franchisors 243-46
　examining records 244
　extended family aspect 244-45
　financing 291-92
　helps 242
　home-based opportunities in 240-41
　initial investment 238
　insider information about 244
　International Franchise Assn. (IFA) 238, 242, 387
　licensing of rights 237
　matchmaking 241
　recent expansion 238-39
　royalty fees 238
　success stories 291-92
　support networks 239
　training program 244
Freedom 14, 180, 250
Freewriting 189
Friendships; *See also* Social life
　be responsive to 168-69
　distractions from 256
　in clubs and classes 169, 351-52
　input from 202
　making new 28, 168-71, 173, 175
Frontier territory 96-99
Fulghum, Robert 170
Fuller, Ron 199
Fun Quotient Quiz 160-65
Funding ideas, creative 296-99
Future work force 276
*Futurist, The* 5, 21, 218

# G

*Gale's Directory of Publications* 101
Gallup Poll 1, 15
Game Trail 338-39
Gangs 51
Gardening 173, 194
Gaston, Robert 287
Geis, Janet 329
General Motors 356
Generating Capital 284-89
　angels as source 287-88
　annuities 285

balloons 291
bank officers 286
bootstrapping 297
business plan development 295-96
cash flow 291
chattel mortgages 289
community development funds 295
conventional finanacing 288-91
credit cards, using 285
deferred payments 289-91
double payments 291
dual strategy 289
enterprise zones 294-95
family and friends 287
Financing Structure Worksheet 289-90
franchise financing 291-92
funding ideas 296-99
golden parachute 208, 286
government funding 292-94, 378-79
incentives 294
inheritance 285
installment sales 297-98
investors 288
life insurance 286
needed to start business 208
negotiating 298
other assets 285
other people's money (OPM) 285
owner financing 297
pawn shop 286
personal credit history 285-86
personal resources 285-87
purchase orders, financing using 296
retirement fund/pension plan 286
SBA loans 293, 376-77
seed grants 293
Small Business Investment Companies (SBICs) 293, 376
state funds 293
unemployment insurance 287
venture capitalists 287-88
Geography 379-80
Gerber products 355
Getting away 1
Gibson, Bill 203
*Gift Basket Review* 194
Gift baskets 193-94
Gil Gordon Associates 281
Givers get 150, 343, 347
Gleason, Charles 358-59
Global Telematics 282
Globalization 217
Good Faith Fund, The 297
Goodwill 235, 336
Gordon, Gil 281
Gossip 154, 158, 313
*Governing* magazine 7
Government agencies 375; *See also* Economic development, rural
*Government Giveaways for Entrepreneurs* 294
Government Printing Office 381
Government sources 373-82
  business and commerce 373-74
  climate 379
  crime reports 381
  energy 379
  Federal Information Centers 382
  geography 379
  health 381
  information on demand 381
  interlibrary loan 381
  money lending 377
  real estate 377
"Grandfathering" 234
Grants and loans, federal 378-79
*Green Index* 73-74
*Greener Pastures Gazette* 91-92

Greener Pastures Institute 91-92
Groups 351
*Growing A Business* 209
*Growing Without Schooling* 89
Growth 99

# H

H.S. Precision, Inc. 357
Habits 151
Hall, Bob 74
Hanus, Ron 207
Happiness 344-353
Harmon, Donna 200
*Harrowsmith Country Life* 131
Hawken, Paul 209
Health 6, 17-18, **63-73**, 115; *See also* Environment
   creative solutions for 66-67
   doctors, rural 66-67
   Environmental Illness (EI) 70-71
   evaluating care 63-66
   government help 67-70
   insurance for 71, 209-10
   Multiple Chemical Sensitivities 70-71
   physician's assistants 70
   Physicians per 1,000 Residents by State 69
   professionals 192
   rural 23-24
   state rankings 72-73
   Urban and Rural Community Hospitals Comparison 68
Heenan, David A. 357, 359
Hemingway, Tom and Sarah 158
Herbers, John 96
Heuser, Dr. Gunnar 70
High-tech wizardry 253
Hoffman, Mable 217
Home Affordability Index 36-44
*Home Education Magazine* 89
*Home Office Computing* 7, 247, 249, 383
Home Office Message Echo 258

*Home Power Magazine* 131
Home prices, comparable 93-94
Home schooling 88-89, 248, 384; *See also* Education
Home site 126
Home swapping 388
Home-based businesses (HBBs) 4, 383-84, **247-60**
   amateurism, alleviation of 251
   attitude 251, 258-59
   crime insurance for 251
   deadlines 252
   distractions 256-58
   employee limitations 259
   equipment as staff 253-54
   family issues 248-49, 256
   home 247
   isolation in 258
   lifestyle patterns 257
   melding business and personal 256
   network selling 250
   office atmosphere 255
   office design 252, 254-56
   organization 256
   participant profile 247
   privacy 257
   professionalism 252
   reasons for 247, 250
   routine, importance of 252
   subdivisions, catering to 260
   telephone usage 254
   Top 10 249
   zoning restrictions 259-60
Home-equity 96
*Homemade Money* 251
Homesteading 32-33, 97, 130-31
Honor system 27
Hotel/Restaurant, owned by Rosses 10, 86, 211, 230-31, 312
Houghton, Tom 357
Housing costs 36-44
*How to Find and Buy Your Business in the Country* 236

*How to Set Your Fees and Get Them* 191
*How to Uncover and Create Business Opportunities* 203
Humidity 55-59

# I

*IB (Independent Business)* magazine 320
IdeaFisher 321
IFA's *Publications and Products Catalog* 242
Image, establishing yours 317-20, 323
*Inc.* magazine 1, 220, 361
Incorporation 301
Incubators for business 387
Industrial Home Work Act of 1943 260
Information management 8-9
Infrastructure 84-90, 113, 152, 355
   education 88
   planning approaches 85-87
   transportation 90
Innkeeping; *See* Bed and Breakfast
Insurance, crime 251
Intellectual properties 209
Interest Analysis 163-65
Internal Revenue Service (IRS) 250-51
International Franchise Association (IFA) 238, 242, 387
*International Yearbook* 100-01
Inventions 196
Inventory 349
   investment 235
Isolation factor 23, 51, 77, 131, 255, 258, 278, 283, 349-51, 357, 383
   spiritual connection 174, 351
*It Was on Fire When I Lay Down on It* 170

# J

J.M. Smucker Company 355
JALA Associates 280
Jan's Restaurant 81-82
Janal, Dan 253
Janos, Debra 292
Jetson Direct Mail Services 358
*Job Creation in America* 183
Job hunting **261-74**
   caretaking 264-65
   choosing a company 273-74
   employee benefits 268-69
   fantasize 263
   generic occupations, ideal 263
   government jobs 262
   health insurance 269
   homemaker skills, applying 266
   hot spots 270
   impact of local economy 262
   job titles 269
   mirror interviewer's style 267
   negotiating salary 268
   occupations outdoors 264-65
   overall recommendations 261-63
   overqualified 267
   part-time 262
   persistence 269
   personal contacts 219, 269
   planning 267-70
   proactive, being 269
   rapport development 274
   recruitment 279
   referrals 269
   regional job markets 262
   results 267
   resumé 267-68
   stewardship 264
   success stories 263
   supporting materials 268
   teaching 263-64
   transferable skills 263
   23 Tips for 271-73
   volunteering 271

Job stimulation  356
Job Training Partnership Act (JTPA)  270, 314
*John Naisbitt's Trend Letter*  88, 218, 264
Joseph, James  7, 264
Joy List  30
Juicy Lucy  292

## K

Kamoroff, Bernard, CPA  303, 352
Kates, Henry E.  280
Kellogg Company  355
Kelly, Kate  191, 331
Kennedy, James  17, 352
Kennedy, John F.  269
Kerr, Mary Lee  73-74
Kimbrough, John  106
*Kiplinger's Personal Finance Magazine*  192
Kirkpatrick, Frank  236

## L

L.L. Bean  356
Labor pool  24, 356, 358-59
Lacey, Dan  185
Land, living off the  130-31; *See also* Homesteading
Large companies, moving  354-62
Lauber, Daniel  262
Layoffs; *See* Downsizing
Le Shan, Dr. Lawrence  263
Leisure  77-84, 356; *See also* Social Life
  arts, the  77
  library  80
  national parks and recreation areas  83
  sports  80
Lending sources  385-87
Lesko, Matthew  102, 223, 294
*Lesko's Info-Power*  102, 221
Lessinger, Jack, Ph.D.  3
Letters to the Editor  332-33, 351

Library  23, 49, 80, 88, 100, 103, 109, 115, 155, 193, 216, 220, 224, 226-27, 232, 254, 262, 274, 330, 351, 374-76, 379, 381, 394
*Lifestyle Odyssey, The*  2, 3, 218
Likes, inventory of  201
Link Resources  247, 282
Link Resources National Work at Home Survey  281
LinkThink  213
*Literary Market Place*  333
Local business license  303
Location
  downtown  305
  foot traffic  305
  importance in business  304-307
  site history  306
  strip mall  305
  traffic flow  306
Logos  323
Loneliness; *See* Isolation
Loyalty  359

## M

Mail order  197, 350
Mailbox economy  186
*Making It on Your Own*  8, 185
Map reconnaissance  103
Maps, Tables, Charts  393-400
  population  395
  Population Changes by State  397
Marketing Plan  321, 329-30, 387
Marketing strategies  183, 326 43, 335; *See also* Advertising; Public relations
  advertising as a percentage of sales  330
  bartering  341
  budgeting  330-31
  classified ads  102, 314, 335
  commercials  337

competition, studying the  220, 224, 232, 320, 333, 348
consultants  333
credit card merchant status  112, 340
customer satisfaction  333, 338, 348-49
direct mail  336
directory listings  334
discount coupon book  336
display ads  335
display windows  339-40
diversification needed  337-38
doing good  334
80/20 rule  340
financial incentives  340
give to get  150, 343, 347
global  329
holidays, playing to  334, 340
lead handling  340-41
Letters to the Editor  332-33, 351
listings  334
mailing lists  349
marketing plan development  321, 329-30, 387
multi-level marketing (MLM)  250
national publicity  332
neighbors as prospects  329-30
news releases  331-32
niche  217
Op-Ed pieces  333
permission form  338
Permission Letter  339
positioning  326-28
promotional events  334
radio  336-37
recycled publicity  332
referrals/testimonials  338
repetition  335
ROS (run of station)  337
Ross Marketing Idea Generator  341-43
sales techniques  183, 337-43
segmentation  327

shoestring ideas  331
solutions to problems  336
suggestive selling  339
topics for news releases  332
trade associations  330-31
21 Ways to Separate Yourself  328-29
white pages  337
word-of-mouth  334, 338
Maslow, Abraham  25
Mature people  138, 174, 181, 198, 262, 347; *See also* Retirees
 as entrepreneurs  4, 181, 262-63
 financing available to  286
 marketing to  185-86, 240
 medical considerations  63-66
 mental stimulations for  174
 parental households  99
 retirees moving  5, 116
 tax advantages for  49
Maytag  355
McCollum, Audrey T.  150
McGahey, Michael J.  264
Measurement criteria  34-90
 cost of living  35
 crime  49
 environmental concerns  74
 health  63
 infrastructure  84
 leisure  77
 weather  54
Meer, David  15
*Megatrends 2000*  8, 218
Mental stimulation  351-52
Merchants' Association  305
Merritt Hawkins & Associates  66-67
Merry Maids  292
Meyer, Chris  203
"*Micro*politan"  7, 100
*Middle Markets*  274
Migration  15
Military  106-07, 123
Miller, Eric  2
Miller, Phil  67

Miller, Tom  282
Milton, Tom  218
Mingling  117-18, 232, 267, 313, 345-47, 350; *See also* Social life
Minority Business Development Center  374
Mission statement  307
Mobile homes  119, 318-19
Mobile operations  327
Money, for start-ups  208-10
Money lending  377-79
Moonlighting  184
*Mother Earth News*  131
Moving  **132-48**
　at the new destination  144
　attitude  132-33
　Calendar For  145-48
　children, with  144
　doing it yourself  133-34
　evaluating  91-107
　family/couple time  144
　files  134-35
　garage sale  138-39
　large corporations  354-62
　List of Lists  146-48
　lists  138-40
　moving day  141-42
　packing hints  138-41
　patterns  96-99
　place to place  92-93
　planning for  134-35
　saying goodbye  137-38
　school transfers  135-36
　traveling  143
　with animals  136-37
Moving companies  133-34, 141
Moving work to people  275
Moyer, Peter  16
Multi-level marketing  250
Music  174
Mutual Benefit Life  280

# N

Naisbitt, John  8, 217-18, 238, 264, 282
Namer by Salinon  321
Naming Notions List  320, 322
Naming your business  320-22
*National Ad Search, The*  265
National Association of Female Executives  265-66
National Association of Realtors  45, 121
National Association of Towns and Townships  7
National Business Association  293
*National Business Employment Weekly*  265
National Business Incubator Association  311
National Center for Education Information  264
National Congress of Community Economic Development  295
National Council of State Legislatures  294
National Federation of Independent Business  181, 185, 284
National Health Service Corps  192
*National Home Business Report*  210, 251
National Parks and Recreation Areas  83
National Response Corporation  335
Natural gas prices  46
Negative feelings, towards outsiders  98-99, 153
　combatting  151-52
Negotiating  298
Neighborhoods, personalities of  123
Nelson, Bob  263-64
Networking
　financing options  288

in the job market  265, 269-73, 345-47
personal, via computer  166
through business incubators  311
Networking, clubs  347, 352
*New Corporate Frontier, The: The Big Move to Small Town USA*  357
*New England Journal of Medicine, The*  51
*New Tools of Technology, The*  203, 218
*New York Times, The*  96, 185
Newcomer functions  169
News releases  331
Newspaper  161
Niles, Jack  275
Niles, John  282
Novaco, Raymond, Ph.D.  21
Nuclear power  77-78

# O

Oasis, custom-made  119-31
Occupational Satisfaction Scale  204
Odor pollution  75; *See also* Environment
*Offbeat Careers—The Directory of Unusual Work*  185
Older people; *See* Mature people
*On Achieving Excellence* newsletter  281
On-line electronic information systems (OEIS)  226-27
Organize  256
OSHA requirements  234-35
Ostroff, Jeff  186
Outdoor occupations  264-65
*Outside* magazine  81
Owner financing  121, 297

# P

Pak Mail  292
Parental households  99
Parkhill, Rick  208
Partnership
 general  301-02
 limited  301
 privileged  348-49
Passion, what's yours?  200-05
Pelli, Roger  66
Pennsylvania's Ben Franklin Partnership Program  293
*Penturbia*  3
Penturbia  356
Perception  317-20
Permission letter  340
Perry-Harrington, Eleanor  352
Personal Balance Sheet  202
Personal Inventory  29-30
Personal stories  10, 71, 81, 85, 120, 130-31, 142, 151, 154, 169, 179, 183-84, 194-96, 212, 230-31, 253, 257, 298, 349, 352
Peters, Tom  281
PHH Fantus  359
Phillips Petroleum  355
*Places Rated Almanac*  49, 64, 65, 100, 214
Planning  91, 106, 284, 311, 345
Pollution, *See* Environment
Popcorn, Faith  2, 140, 167, 213, 217, 254
*Popcorn Report, The*  2, 213, 217
Population by Race  395-96
Population Changes by State  397
Population Trends  85-87
Portable profits  327
Positioning  319, 325-328
Possibilities, finding suitable  229-32
Power costs, other expenses  45
*Power of 900, The*  208
*Power Up Your Profits Report*  207

*Powershift* 218
PreLOCATION 215
Preparation; *See* Planning
Press release; *See* News releases
Pricing 200
Primary research 215
Priorities 25, 30, 100, 112, 151, 214, 241, 242
Private Sector Help Resources 383-92
 associations 387
 AT&T Home Office Network 383
 education 384
 home-based businesses (HBB) 383
 lending sources 385-87
 selected suppliers 387
 telecommuting 384
 telephone information 385
 vendors and other resources 388
Promotional events 334
Property, recreational 5
Property considerations 99-100
Property Tax Rankings 48
Prospector, The 81
Prosperity 344-53
*Psychology Today* magazine 63
*Public Opinion* magazine 16, 49
Public relations (PR) 317-25; *See also* Marketing strategies
 business cards 323-24
 cross-promotion 325
 free PR, obtaining 331-33
 image 317-20
 letterhead/envelopes 323
 logos 323
 mobile home park example 318-19
 Naming Notions List 322
 naming your business 320-22
 national PR 331-32
 news releases 331-32
 outstanding customer service 319, 333
 recycled PR 332
 romancing prospects 318
 signage needs 324-25
 slogans 322-23
 telephone, as a PR tool 318
 unusual design 324
Publicity; *See* Public relations
*Publicity Handbook, The* 331
*Publicity Manual, The* 331
*Publishers Weekly* 218
Purchasing land; *See* Real estate
Purvis, Scott C. 335

# Q

Quality of life 2-3, 17-20, 34, 91, 99, 192, 209, 276, 314, 319
Quill 312

# R

Race; *See* Ethnic diversity
*Rating Guide to Life in America's Small Cities, The* 7, 100
Real estate 8, 22, 92-96, 101-02, 105-06, 118-20, 131, 285, 298, 377-78
 auctions 299
 bargains 121
 broker 120-21
 City Lot Versus Country Acreage 125
 conditions, covenants, and restrictions (CC&R) 259-60
 easements and encumbrances 126
 home inspection 123
 home site 126
 mineral rights 126
 natural hazards, avoiding 127
 owner financing 121
 Quickie Rural Home/Store Evaluation Sheet 122
 Rural Checklist 127-30
 septic system 126

soil 126
tax sales 297
water 124, 126
Reality check 131, 202, 220
Reamer, Tom and Carole 347-48
Recreation ideas 81-84, 165-67
Referrals/testimonials 338
Relatives 167-68, 350
Relaxation; *See* Social life
Relocation Assessment 37
Relocation of major corporations 354-62
Relocation research; *See* Research
Replacements, Ltd. 360
Research 100-105, 214-28, 293-95, *See also* Competition, checking the; Map reconaissance
  annual reports 274
  appraisals 295
  areas 100-05, 108, 118
  business 110, 232-35, 273-74
  cost of living 36-49
  county courthouse 223
  databases 101, 225-26
  doctoral dissertations 221
  environmental 73-77
  examining records 244
  Form Letter for 103-04
  franchising options 244-46
  government funding options 293-95
  insider information 244
  interviewing others 218-20
  job opportunities 214-28, 273-74
  library 103, 105, 111, 216, 220, 226, 262
  newspapers 100-01, 111, 219
  on-line electronic information systems (OEIS) 226
  primary 215
  proprietary information 223
  secondary 215, 228
  see company in operation 273-74

site history 306
state corporation office 224
study the competition 220
tax returns 234
think tanks 228
trade associations 331
trade journals 220
visiting 106
Research Alert 2, 218
Resolution Trust Corporation (RTC) 102, 116, 298-99, 377-78
Restaurant business 193, 230-31
Resumé 201, 267-68, 314
Retirees 5, 22, 91, 106, 119, 215, 232, 262, 289, 327, 329, 348; *See also* Mature people
*Retirement Places Rated* 49, 100, 209
Right Choice, Inc. 36
Risk 184, 229
Risolo, George 320-21
Rochester Institute of Technology 217
Rock picking 195
*Rocky Mountain Employment Newsletter, The* 265
Roots 8, 15-16, 84, 154-55, 248
Rosenbluth, Hal 358
Rosenbluth Travel Inc. 358
Ross Marketing Idea Generator 341-43
Ross Relocation Checklist 112-17
Ross, Teri 249
Roth, Joann 198
Rukeyser, Louis 354-55
Runzheimer International 35, 357
Rural Home/Store Evaluation Sheet 122
Rural Network 98
*Rural Property Bulletin* 121
Rural Real Estate Checklist 127-30
Rusnell, Dr. Dale 203

## S

Sacharov, Al  185
Salida  79, 81, 225, 263
San Diego  7, 10, 23, 44-45, 71, 74, 120, 142, 151, 169, 231, 382
Savageau, David  49, 100, 209, 214
Saying goodbye  137-38
Schaeffer, John  131
Scheibal, Tom  251
Schepp, Brad  279
Schmoozing  218-19, 346
School; *See* Education
School transfers  135-36
SchoolMatch  88
Schools, private  88
Schuller, Dr. Robert  349
*Screenprinting*  339
Sears  355
Seavey, William  91, 168, 187, 262
Second home  5
Securities and Exchange Commission (SEC)  274
Security  16-17
Self-image  170
Self-Employment potential  179
Self-sufficiency  24, 32-33, 130-31
Selling price, establishing  235-36
Senior citizens; *See* Mature people; Retirees
Sensory signals  152
Separate Yourself from the Herd, 21 Ways to  328-29
SERVAS  174
Service, outstanding  187, 319, 333
Service Corps of Retired Executives (SCORE)  296, 376
Settling in  152
Shealy, Norman  17
Sheehan, Carol  9
Shepherd, Jackieanne  199

Shopping  23, 29, 45, 51, 112, 116, 130, 156, 198, 202, 208, 213, 249, 292, 312, 318, 337, 348, 381
Shrinkage  210
Signage needs  324-25
Simpler lifestyle  130-31, 356
Single people  98, 166-67
Sky Field  282
Slogans  322-23
Small Business Administration (SBA)  196, 242, 288, 293, 309, 373, 375-77
  SBA Regional Offices  376
Small Business Development Centers (SBDCs)  296, 309, 376
Small Business Institutes (SBIs)  309, 376
Small Business Investment Companies (SBICs)  293
*Small Farmer's Journal*  196
*Small Time Operator*  303, 352
*Small Town Observer*  91-92
Smith, Brian  192
Smith, Dan  292
Social life  18-20, 137-38, 159-75, 349-51; *See also* Community involvement; Entertainment; Friendships, developing; Leisure; Mingling
  analyzing yours  29-30
  friendships  160
  Fun Quotient Quiz  160-65
  involvement in  165-66
  patterns  164
  spiritual connections  350
  via computer  166-77
  when moving  157-58
Social Security benefits  262-63
Sole proprietorship  301
*Sourcebook of ZIP Code Demographics, The*  225
*Southern Living*  101-02
Spirituality  18, 173, 350

Sports 80-81, 166
Staff 253-54
Stamps By Mail 381
Standard Industrial Classifications (SIC) 224
Start-Up considerations 300-16; *See also* Employees, prospecting for; Telephones
  buddy business relationship 311
  business plan 307
  cash flow 307-08
  checking account 308
  consignment 312
  consultants, using 309
  drive-in service 307
  fax machines 304
  federal employer ID number (FEIN) 302, 312
  government auctions 313
  incubators 311
  leasing facts 306-07
  licensing/regulatory procedures 302-03
  mission statement 307
  name registration requirements 302
  planning 311
  pricing 308
  suppliers 311-13
  tax resale number 303
  trademarks 303
  wholesalers 311-12
  window displays 305-06
  zoning restrictions 308
Start-up Stimulator Checklist 309-10
State Agencies Administering Franchise Disclosure Laws 221-23
State and Local Tax Burden 50
State chambers of commerce 101, 366-72
State Office of Economic Development 329
State Publicly-Accessible Databases 226
State tourism offices 101, 366-72
*Statistical Abstract of the United States* 101
Status symbols 25
Staying current 352-53
Stewardship 264
Stone, Bob 336
Storms 60-61
Stress 14, 20-21, 28, 63, 96, 131, 134, 137-38, 186, 263, 277, 330, 333, 363-64
Strout Realty 231
Subchapter S Corporation 301
Subdivisions 119
*Success* magazine 8
Success stories 16, 17, 20-21, 28, 66-67, 87-88, 157, 198-200, 210, 239, 253, 263, 291-92, 320-21, 331-32, 347-48, 355-62
*Successful Direct Marketing Methods* 336
*Sunset* 101-02
Suppliers 209, 311-13, 387-89; *See also* Vendors
SWAG (Scientific Wild Ass Guess) 307, 330-31
Synergy 210, 335

# T

Talk of the Town Cafe 81
Targeted jobs tax credit program 314
Tate, George W. "Pudge" 361
Taxes 45, 48-50, 113
*Teachers in New Careers* 264
Teaching 263-64, 352
Teaching Company, The 174
*Teaching Home, The* 89
Technology 8, 19, 70, 110, 196, 203, 206-08, 216-218, 275-76, 279-80, 282, 293, 297, 355, 359, 362, 379

Technology, lack of  86, 130-31
Tele-Lawyer  206
*Telecommuter's Handbook, The*  279
Telecommuting  4-5, 31, **275-83**, 354-55, 384; *See also* Home-based businesses
   administrative hassles  278
   answers personal needs  276-79
   community benefit  281-83
   corporate perspective  279-81
   criteria for  281
   definition of  275-76
   disadvantages of  278-79
   electronic cottages  253
   employee retention, better  279-80
   family issues  277
   isolation in  278
   large companies doing  277
   lowers overhead  280
   off-site management  278
   practicality  280
   productivity, increased  279
   recruitment  279
   reduces absenteeism  278
   Sampling of Ideal Jobs  277
   Telluride, Colorado as a model  282
   training for  281
Telephones  254, 385
   absentee owner suggestions  207
   800 toll-free numbers  304
   image-maker, as an  317
   900 numbers  32, 205-08
   opportunity lifeline, as a  303-04
   pay-per-call numbers  205-08
   Personalized Ring  304
Testimonials/referrals  338
Thomas, G. Scott  7, 100, 385, 391
Thomas Edison Seed Development Fund  293-94
Thomsen, Patti  218
*Time*  7

Time  19, 25, 151-52
Tips to Enhance Your Chances  271
Toffler, Alvin  218
*Touring with Towser*  137
Tourism offices  101, 366-72
Trade-offs  154-55, 156-57
Trademarks  303
Traditions  168
Traffic congestion  21
Traffic flow  306
Transportation  23, 87-90, 114
*Trauma of Moving, The*  150
Traveling  143
*Trend Tracking*  218
Trends  2-3, 6-8, 77, 85, 88, 91, 185, 192-93, **216-18**, 220, 240, 264, 282, 320, 330, 332, 354
2500 AD Software  157

# U

*U.S. Census of Retail Trade*  216
*U.S. Industrial Outlook*  216
*U.S. Real Property Sales List*  102
*U.S. Statistical Abstract*  216
Ulrich, Dr. Roger  82
Undercapitalization  209
Uniform Franchise Offering Circular (UFOC)  243-44
United National Real Estate  101, 111, 121, 127, 231
United Parcel Service  252
United States Department of Agriculture (USDA)  111, 294
University Microfilms International  221
Urban equity  92-96
Urban flight  356-57
*USA Today*  3, 97, 100, 218, 231, 338
*USA Weekend*  7

Index  429

## V

Vacation home  5
*Vacation Home Exchange and Hospitality Guide, The*  106
Vacations  105-06, 165-68
Valley Service  312
Values  15, 25, 151-52, 277
VenCap Data Quest  288
Vendors  203, 219, 296; *See also* Suppliers
Ventures, evaluating prospective  232-34
VetFran (Veterans Transition Franchise Initiative)  243
Viewpoint, small town  26-27, 97-99, 149-58; *See also* Attitude
  anonymity  153-54
  big fish/small pond  157-58
  child care  155-56
  negativity, combatting  150-51
  negativity, towards outsiders  153
  settling in  152
  trade-offs  154-57
  values  151-52
Visiting potential towns  105-07
Visualization  204, 270
Volcanoes  60
Volunteering  23, 45, 66, 87, 117, 120, 165, **171-72**, 201, 203, 220, 271, 334, 342, 346, 350, 376
Volunteer Self-Evaluation  172

## W

Wakeman, Mollie  331-32
Wal-Mart  312, 318, 356
*Wall Street Journal, The*  1-2, 218, 231, 265, 332, 351, 358, 359, 333
Walton, Sam  312, 356
Ward, William Gary and Sharon Kaye  306

Warner, Stephen  9
*Wary Canary, The*  70
*Washingtonian, The*  24
Water  76-77, 121, 124, 129
Weather  54-63, 107, 118, 151, 173
  cantankerous considerations  60
  Climatic Regions of the United States  65
  Earthquake Hazard Zones  62
  Tornado and Hurricane Risk Areas  61
  Weather Watch Questionnaire  54-55
WELL (The Whole Earth 'Lectric Link)  167
Wellness  63
Welty, Curt and Cheri  200
*What Color is Your Parachute?*  224, 266
*Which Ad Pulled Best?*  335
White Supremacist Groups  52
Wholesalers; *See* Suppliers; Vendors
Williams, Jane  248
Work alternatives  31-32
*Working From Home*  8, 251
Working-from-Home Forum  258
*Workplace Trends*  185
*World Almanac and Book of Facts, The*  100
Wunderlich, Judith  248-49

## Y

Yale, David  331
*Yankee*  101-02
Yellow Pages  102-03, 194, 201, 215, 231, 272, 303, 315, 321, 330, 333, 335-37, 350

## Z

Ziglar, Zig  150-51
Zoning  124-26, 127, 259-60, 308

# Give the Gift of Country Freedom to Your Friends and Loved Ones!

## ORDER FORM

☐ **YES**, I want ___ copies of *Country Bound!*™ *Trade Your Business Suit Blues For Blue Jean Dreams*™ at $19.95 each, plus $3 shipping per book. (Colorado residents please include $1.40 state sales tax.) Canadian orders must be accompanied by a postal money order in U.S. funds. Allow 30 days for delivery.

☐ **YES**, I want ongoing, up-to-the-minute information to help me make the best relocation decision possible. Start my subscription to *The Country Bound!*™ *Connection* newsletter immediately. I understand for $89 a year I'll receive this quarterly newsletter chock-full of new country trends, career ideas, entrepreneurial marketing strategies, real estate bargain tips, and more. Sign me up now!

☐ **YES**, I want *Country Bound!*™ T-shirts for myself or as gifts. (They're a blaze of color, cost $14.95 each, and resemble the book cover.) Sizes M, L, or XL. Specify size and quantity below!

☐ **YES**, I'd like information about your Colorado Country Bound!™ "EduTaining" weekend retreats and relocation seminars. It sounds like a fun way to get personalized help.

_____ Check/money order enclosed • Charge my _____ VISA _____ MasterCard

Name _____ Phone ( ___ ) _____

Organization (if applicable) _____

Address _____

City/State/Zip _____

Card # _____ Exp. _____ Signature _____

T-shirt sizes and quantities wanted:   M _____   L _____   XL _____

**Check your leading bookstore or call credit card orders to:**
## 1-800-331-8355

Call 8 A.M. to 5 P.M. Mountain Time—or
fax your order to: 719-395-8374
Please make your check payable and return to:
**Communication Creativity**
**P.O. Box 909, Dept. CB**
**Buena Vista, CO 81211**